Autodesk AutoCAD 2021
Learn CAD With Ease
(For Beginners)

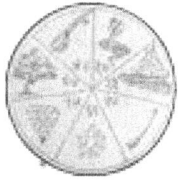

Madhumita Kshirsagar

Copyright © 2020 Madhumita Kshirsagar
All rights reserved. No part of this book may be reproduced or modified in any form, including photocopying, recording or by any information storage and retrieval system, without permission in writing from the publisher.
ISBN: 979-8-7118-7061-6

Preface

This book is all original and specifically designed to get you working with AutoCAD 2D and Productivity tools as knowledgeable as possible. This book is comprehensive and aims to give you a deeper understanding and a better learning experience. This book is designed for students related to different engineering fields according to their needs. This content helps students to understand drafting in AutoCAD.

This book is useful for students who want to learn AutoCAD on any version like 2013, 2014, 2015, 2016, 2017, 2018, 2019, 2020, 2021.

This book is based on AutoCAD 2021, with its new features. This book contains all the commands with their relative diagrams and their dialog boxes.

No previous knowledge of software required to learn AutoCAD by this book. After completing this book, you will be able to create your own projects on AutoCAD with all detailed drawings.

I am always committed to giving students the best and advance.

Madhumita Kshirsagar
Madhumita Kshirsagar
Design Head (Arch.)
CadEasy.

CONTENTS

2 DIMENSIONS..1-219

CHAPTER 1: INTRODUCTION OF AUTOCAD............1-9

1.1 Parts of AutoCAD according to working criteria
1.2 Launching of AutoCAD
    How to start a "new" drawing file in AutoCAD
    How to open an existing drawing file
1.3 Workspaces of AutoCAD
1.4 How to save drawings

CHAPTER 2: BASIC DRAW COMMANDS.................. 10-33

2.1 Line
2.1.2 Point Fixing Methods
  i. Cartesian Co-ordinate System
    Absolute Co-ordinate System
    Relative Rectangular Co-ordinate System
    Relative Polar Co-ordinate System
    Entering co-ordinates using AutoCAD drawing aid tools.
  ii. Pick Point Method.
2.2 Circle
  a. Center Radius
  b. Center Diameter
  c. 3 Point
  d. 2 Point
  e. Tan, Tan, Radius
  f. Tan, Tan, Tan
2.3 Arc
    3 Point
    Start, Center, End
    Start, Center, Angle
    Start, Center, Length
    Start, End, Angle
    Start, End, Direction
    Start, End, Radius

          Center, Start, End
          Center, Start, Angle
          Center, Start, Length
          Continue
2.4   Polygon
          Inscribed in Circle
          Circumscribed about Circle
          Edge
2.5   Ellipse
          Axis, End
          Center
          Elliptical Arc
          Rotation
2.6   Donut
2.7   Construction Line
2.8   Ray
2.9   Revision Cloud.

CHAPTER 3: DIFFERENT SELECTION METHODS.......34-39

    a)   Window Selection
    b)   Crossing Window Selection
    c)   Implied Window Selection
    d)   The Undo Option
    e)   Selecting All Objects
    f)   Fence Selection
    g)   Window Polygon Selection
    h)   Crossing Polygon Selection
    i)   Previous Selection
    j)   Selecting the Last Object
    k)   Adding & Removing Objects.

CHAPTER 4: DRAFTING SETTINGS........................35-50

    1)   Ortho mode
    2)   Object Snap
    3)   Object Snap Tracking
    4)   Polar Tracking

5) Dynamic Input
6) Grid & Snap
   How to Draw Isometric View
7) Selection Cycling
8) Quick Properties

CHAPTER 5: MODIFY COMMANDS..........................51-77

5.1 Offset
5.2 Trim
5.3 Extend
5.4 Move
5.5 Copy
5.6 Mirror
5.7 Rotate
5.8 Stretch
5.9 Scale
5.10 Break
5.11 Join
5.12 Array

CHAPTER 6: UTILITIES & PROPERTIES....................78-94

6.1 Measure
6.1.2 Distance
6.1.3 Radius
6.1.4 Angle
6.1.5 Area
6.2 Id Point
6.3 Point
6.4 Point Style
6.5 Color
6.6 List
6.7 Line Type
6.8 Line Type Scale
6.9 Line Weight
6.10 Properties
6.11 Match Properties

6.12   Quick Calculator

CHAPTER 7: POLYLINES & HATCH.........................95-111

7.1   Polyline
7.1.1   Polyline Edit
7.2   Rectangle
7.3   Region
7.4   Explode
7.5   Hatch
7.6   Hatch Edit

CHAPTER 8: DRAWING SETUP..............................112-117

8.1   Units
8.2   Limits

CHAPTER 9: FILLET & CHAMFER............................118-123

9.1   Fillet
9.2   Chamfer
9.3   Blend

CHAPTER 10: ANNOTATION................................124-204

10.1   Single Line Text
10.2   Text Style
10.3   Multiline Text
10.4   Text Edit
10.5   Mirror Text
10.6   Scale Text
10.7   Linear Dimension
10.8   Aligned Dimension
10.9   Angular Dimension
10.10   Arc Length
10.11   Radius
10.12   Diameter
10.13   Ordinate

10.14 Jogged Dimension
10.15 Baseline Dimension
10.16 Continue Dimension
10.17 Break Dimension
10.18 Center Mark
10.19 Inspect
10.20 Adjust Space
10.21 Quick Dimension
10.22 Tolerance
10.23 Dimension Style
10.24 Dimension Update
10.25 Dimension Edit
10.26 Dimension Text Edit
10.27 Dimension Override
10.28 Multileader
10.29 Add leader
10.30 Remove Leader
10.31 Align Leader
10.32 Multileader Style
10.33 Multileader Collect
10.34 Table & Table Style

CHAPTER 11: LAYERS... 205-219

11.1 Layer
    a. Layer off
    b. Layer on
    c. Layer Freeze
    d. Layer Thaw
    e. Layer Lock
    f. Layer Unlock
    g. Layer Isolate
    h. Layer Unisolate
    i. Match Layer
    j. Change to current Layer
    k. Copy Object's to new layer
    l. Layer Walk
    m. Layer Merge

  n. Layer Delete
  o. Layer Previous
  p. Make Current

PRODUCTIVITY TOOLS............................220-322

CHAPTER 1: ADVANCE SELECTION METHODS.........221-225

 1.1 Quick Select
 1.2 Filter
 1.3 Selection Cycling

CHAPTER 2: BLOCKS & ATTRIBUTE.......................226-256

 2.1 Design Center
 2.2 Tool Palettes
 2.3 Create Block
 2.4 Insert Block
 2.5 Block Editor
 2.5.1 Dynamic Block
 2.6 Divide
 2.7 Measure
 2.8 Attribute
   Define Attribute
 2.9 Editing of Attributes
   Edit Attribute
 2.10 Attribute Display
 2.11 Block Attribute Manager

CHAPTER 3: GROUP & EDITING COMMANDS..........257-264

 3.1 Group
   Creating a Group
   Managing Groups
   Group Bounding Box
   Manipulating Group Objects
   Group Selection ON/OFF
   Edit Group

Group Manager
3.2 About Using Clipboard
Cut, Copy, Copy with base point, Paste, Paste as Block
Paste to Original co-ordinates.

CHAPTER 4: LINKINGS & REFERENCES................... 265-285

4.1 Hyperlink
4.2 Data Extraction
4.3 Data Link
4.4 OLE Object
4.5 External References Or Attach
4.6 Xclip Or Clip
4.7 Adjust
4.8 Etransmit

CHAPTER 5: PARAMETERIC CONSTRAINTS.............286-300

5.1 Geometric Constraints
5.1.1 Coincide
5.1.2 Horizontal Constraint
5.1.3 Perpendicular Constraint
5.1.4 Vertical Constraint
5.1.5 Concentric Constraint
5.1.6 Fixed Constraint
5.1.7 Collinear Constraint
5.1.8 Parallel Constraint
5.1.9 Tangent Constraint
5.1.10 Smooth Constraint
5.1.11 Symmetric Constraint
5.1.12 Equal
5.1.13 Auto Constrain
5.1.14 Show/ Hide Geometric Constraint
5.1.15 Hide All
5.1.16 Show All Geometric Constraints
5.2 Dimensional Constraints
5.2.1 Linear Constraint
5.2.2 Vertical Constraint

5.2.3   Aligned Constraint
5.2.4   Radius Constraint
5.2.5   Diameter Constraint
5.2.6   Angular Constraint
5.2.7   Convert
5.2.8   Show/ Hide Dimensional Constraint
5.2.9   Show all Dimensional Constraints
5.2.10 Hide All Dimensional Constraints
5.3   Parameters Manager

CHAPTER 6: PRINTING..301-316

6.1   Direct Printing
6.2   Print by Layout
6.3   Sheet Set Manager

SHORTCUT KEYS USED IN AUTOCAD.......................317-322

Autodesk AutoCAD 2021
Learn CAD With Ease.

CHAPTER 1
INTRODUCTION OF AUTOCAD

AutoCAD is a software application for **Computer-Aided Drafting (CAD)**. The software supports both **2D** and **3D** formats. The software is developed and sold by **Autodesk, Inc.**

The company was founded by **John Walker** in 1982. He was also a co-author of **AutoCAD**. This software was first released in **December 1982**.

AutoCAD is derived from the program **"Interact CAD"** which began in 1977 and released in 1979.

AutoCAD is Autodesk's flagship product and by March 1986 had become the most ubiquitous **microcomputer** design program in the world, utilizing functions such as **"polylines"** and **"curve fitting"**.

AutoCAD is used in different industries by the wide range of Architects, Civil Engineers, Mechanical Engineers, Graphic designers, and many other working professionals.

Parametric functionality and **mesh modeling** was firstly introduced in **AutoCAD 2010**.

The modern AutoCAD includes a full set of **3D tools** to model perfect **3D**.

The latest version of AutoCAD (AutoCAD 2021) was released on 25th March 2020.

1.1 Parts of AutoCAD according to working criteria:

AutoCAD is divided into three sections according to working criteria.

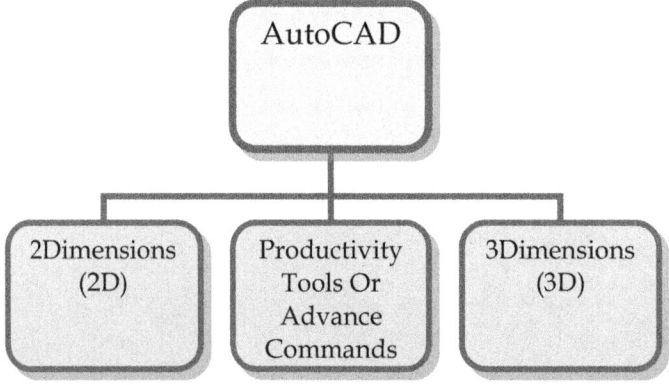

Autodesk AutoCAD 2021
Learn CAD With Ease.

2 Dimensions: In this section, you will get knowledge about, how to draw 2D drawings in AutoCAD.

2D means two-dimensional objects. In 2D we show only two dimensions of an object like:

L X B=Plan, Top View, Bottom View

BXH=Elevations/sections   LXH=Elevations/sections.

Elevation Views are; Front View, Back View, Side Views of an object.

In 2D there are only 2 co-ordinates x and y due to these co-ordinates we show only 2 dimensions of an object.

2D UCS

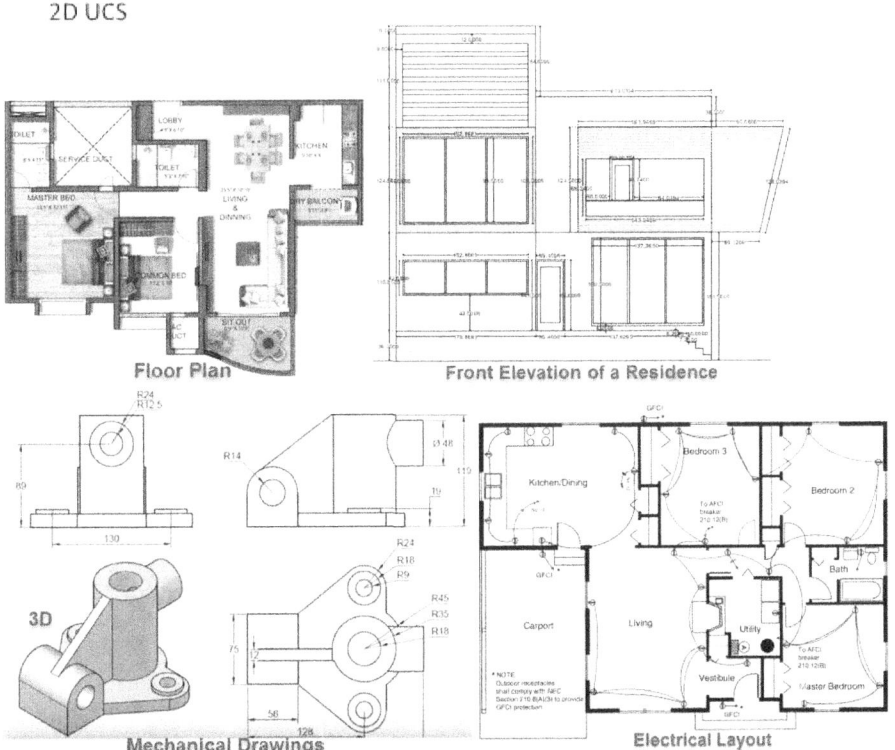

Advance Commands (Productivity Tools): By using these commands you will create better designs faster. In this section, you will learn how to create your own objects library in AutoCAD, Linking different software files with AutoCAD, plotting of your drawings on different scales.

By Madhumita Kshirsagar

Autodesk AutoCAD 2021
Learn CAD With Ease.

In this section, you will also get the knowledge to add parameters to a simple drawing to create parametric drawings. You can use these tools with both 2D & 3D sections of AutoCAD.

3D (3 Dimensions): 3D means **THREE-DIMENSIONAL**, i.e. something that has **LENGTH, WIDTH, HEIGHT,** or **DEPTH**. Our physical environment is three-dimensional and we move around in 3D every day. There are three axes in 3D – **X, Y,** and **Z.**

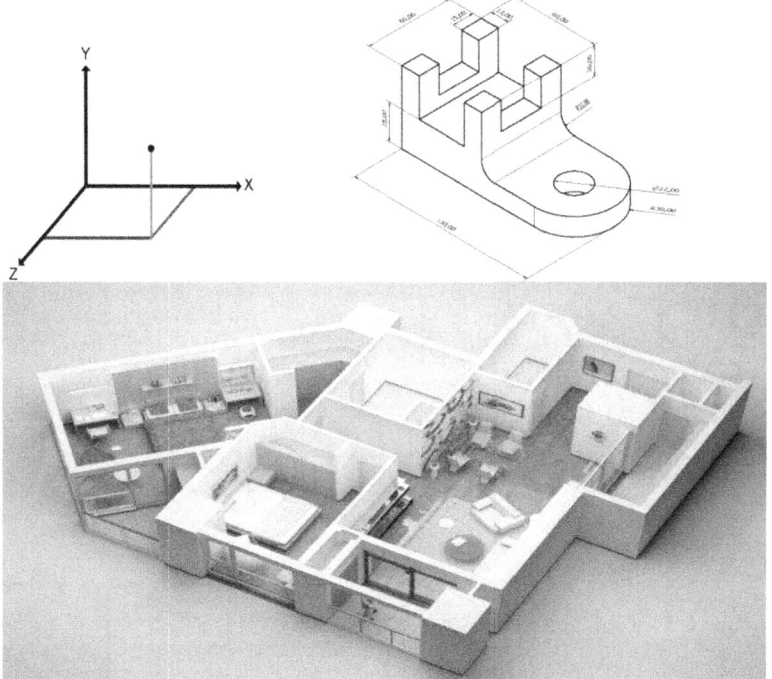

1.2 Launching of AutoCAD:

To launch AutoCAD double click on the software's icon **A**, existing on desktop.

You can also launch it by **"Start Menu"**

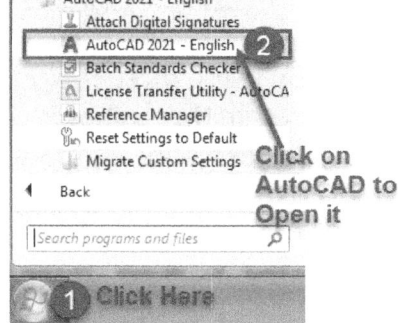

Autodesk AutoCAD 2021
Learn CAD With Ease.

How to start a "New" drawing file in AutoCAD?

After open this software you will get a startup screen, now click on **"Start Drawing"** in the **"Get Started"** section to start a new drawing.

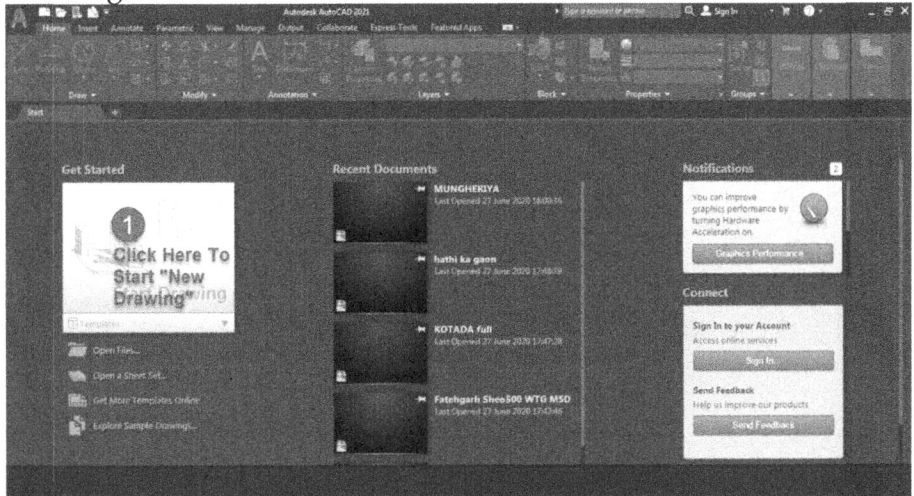

Note: You can also start a new drawing by select any template from the **Template pull-down menu** available at the bottom of **"Start Drawing"**. Generally, we select **"acad.dwt"** template.

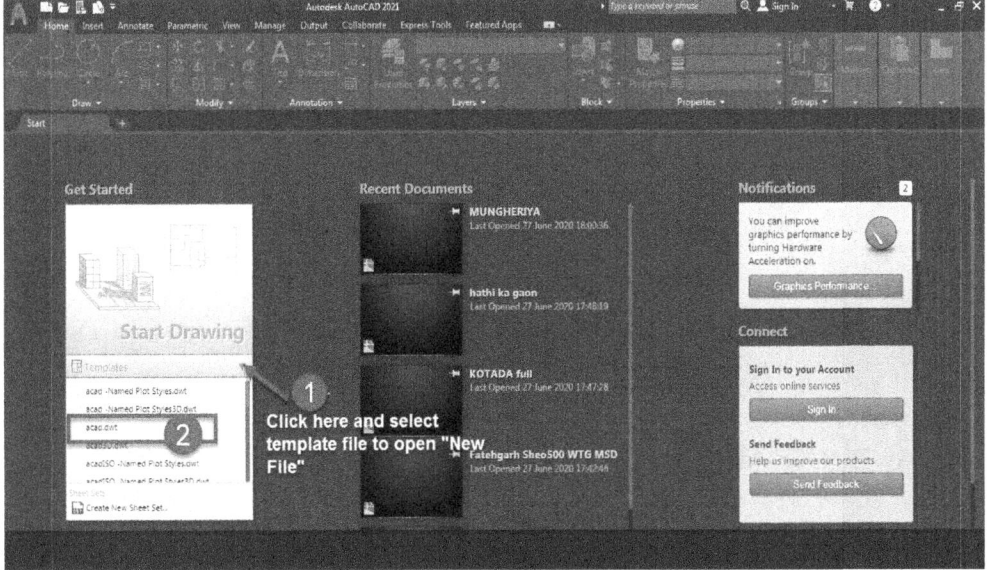

By Madhumita Kshirsagar

Autodesk AutoCAD 2021
Learn CAD With Ease.

How to open an existing drawing file in AutoCAD?
Click on **"Open Files"** and select any AutoCAD file (.dwg file) and click on **"Open"** to open it.

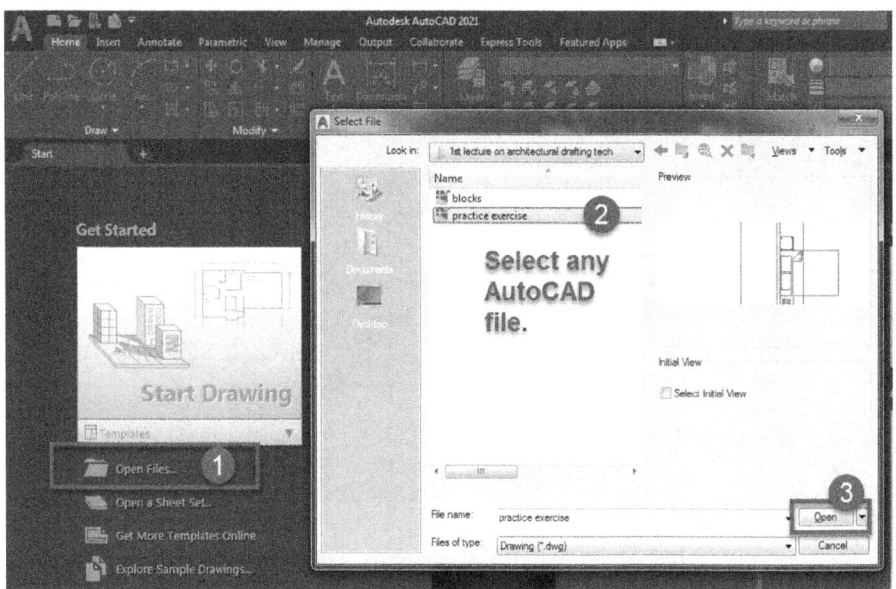

Note: You can also open an existing drawing file in which you worked recently, by selecting it from the **"Recent Documents"** section available in the start-up screen.

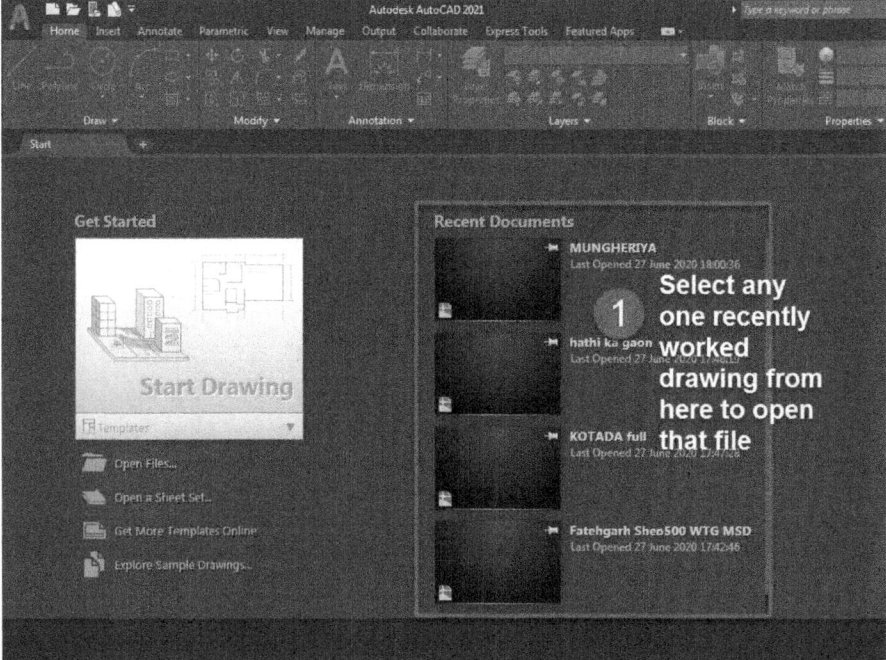

Autodesk AutoCAD 2021
Learn CAD With Ease.

1.3 Workspaces of AutoCAD:
There are three workspaces available in AutoCAD 2021.
   a) Drafting & Annotation
   b) 3D Basics
   c) 3D Modeling

Drafting & Annotation:

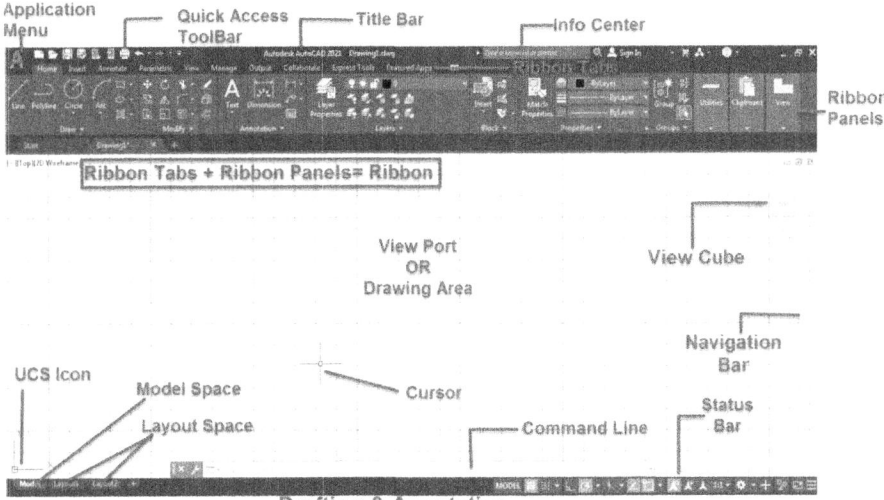

Application Menu: From Application Menu you can access tools related to the application like; New, Open, Save, Save As, Export and Print, etc.

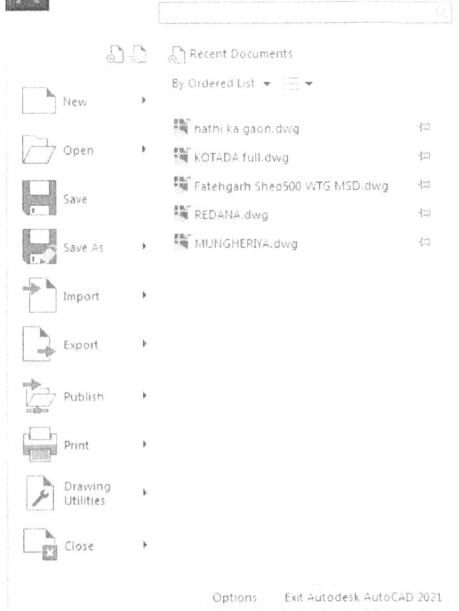

Autodesk AutoCAD 2021
Learn CAD With Ease.

Quick Access Toolbar: This toolbar contains frequently used tools or commands. You can add more tools in this toolbar by drop-down menu available at the right side of **"Quick Access Toolbar"**.

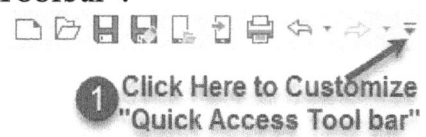

Title Bar: This bar shows the software version name and current drawing name.

Autodesk AutoCAD 2021 Drawing1.dwg

Info Center: This toolbar is used to get information about tools or commands by online help or offline help.

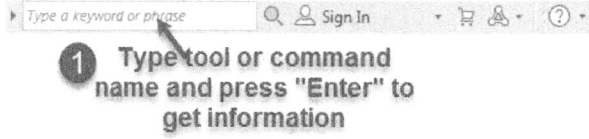

Ribbon: You can access AutoCAD tools and settings from here. AutoCAD has several "Tabs" which are known as "Ribbon Tabs". These tabs include several "Panels", these panels are known as "Ribbon Panels" and these tabs and panels are jointly known as "Ribbon".

Ribbon Tabs

Autodesk AutoCAD 2021
Learn CAD With Ease.

Ribbon Panels

Command Line: We can activate different tools or commands by typing them here. The command line also provides information about what you should do next to complete the task by activated command.

UCS Icon: This icon shows x-axis and y-axis direction.

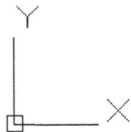

Status Bar: **Status Bar** contains tools that affect your drawing environment. You can easily control the drafting settings of AutoCAD by tools available in the status bar.
It also displays cursor location.

Note 1: You can also access additional settings of some tools by click on their drop- down arrow.

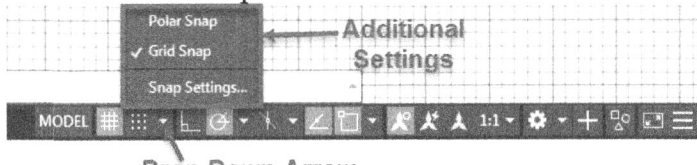

Note 2: You can also customize the status bar by adding or removing tools by **"Customization Menu"**.

By Madhumita Kshirsagar

Autodesk AutoCAD 2021
Learn CAD With Ease.

Viewport or Drawing Area: You will draw objects or drawings here.

Model Space: We should always draw drawings in **"Model Space"**.

Layout Space or Paper Space: We use it to set drawings for print on different scales.

1.4 How to save drawings?
Command: Save
Alias : Ctrl+S
Application Menu →Save
Quick Access Bar→ Save

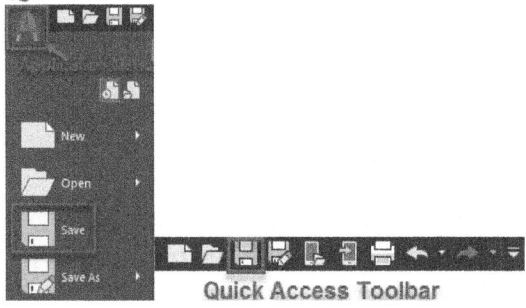

To save AutoCAD drawing firstly draw an object in the drawing area & go to **"Application Menu"** & select **"Save"** then write the name by which you want to save your file in **"file name"** & click on **save** button. If you want to save an existing file by another name then you select **"Save As"** option.

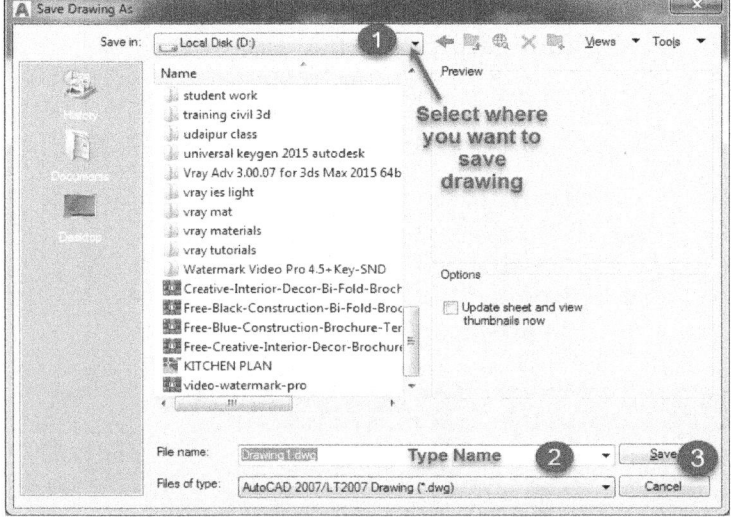

Autodesk AutoCAD 2021
Learn CAD With Ease.

CHAPTER 2
BASIC DRAW COMMANDS

In this chapter, you will get knowledge about difi
commands available in AutoCAD.

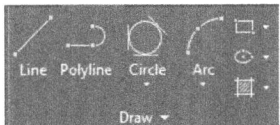

2.1 Command: **Line**
    Alias   : **L**
    Home Tab → Draw Panel → **Line**

Use: This command is used to draw a line segment by specifying two points.

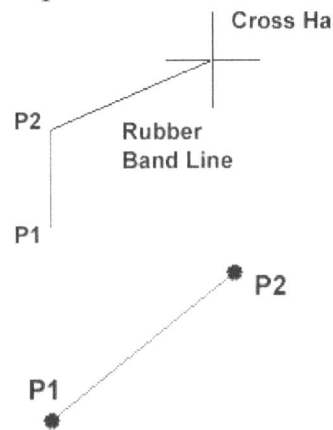

With the Line command, you can draw a simple line from one point to another. When you pick the first point and move the cross-hair to the location of the second point you will see a rubber band line which shows you where the line will be drawn when the second point is picked.

You can continue picking points and AutoCAD will draw a straight line in between every two points. To end this command, just hit the "Enter" or "Esc" key on the keyboard.

2.1.2 Point Fixing Methods:
There are some points fixing methods available in AutoCAD to fix points. You can use these methods to fix points in different commands of AutoCAD.
  i. Cartesian Coordinate System
  ii. Pick Pont Method

i. Cartesian Coordinate System: "Cartesian Coordinate System" is used to specify the position of each point in a plane through two co-ordinates **x** and **y**.

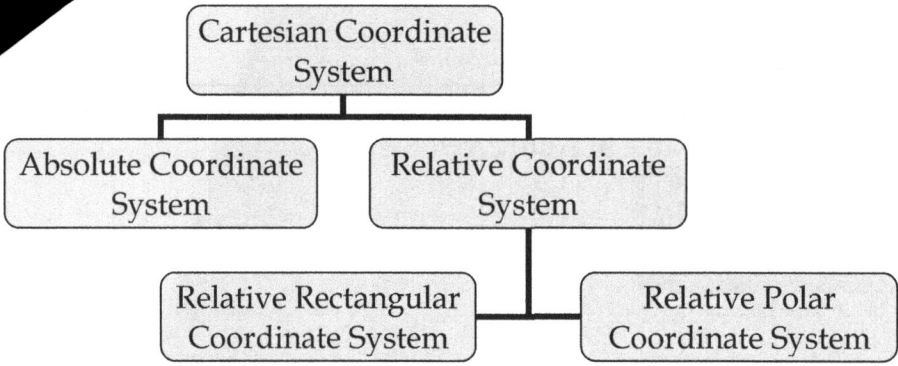

Absolute Coordinate System: In this coordinate system we enter real **x** and **y** coordinates of a point.

Let's draw a 4 X 2 rectangle by using the **"Absolute Coordinate System"** in the **"Line"** command.

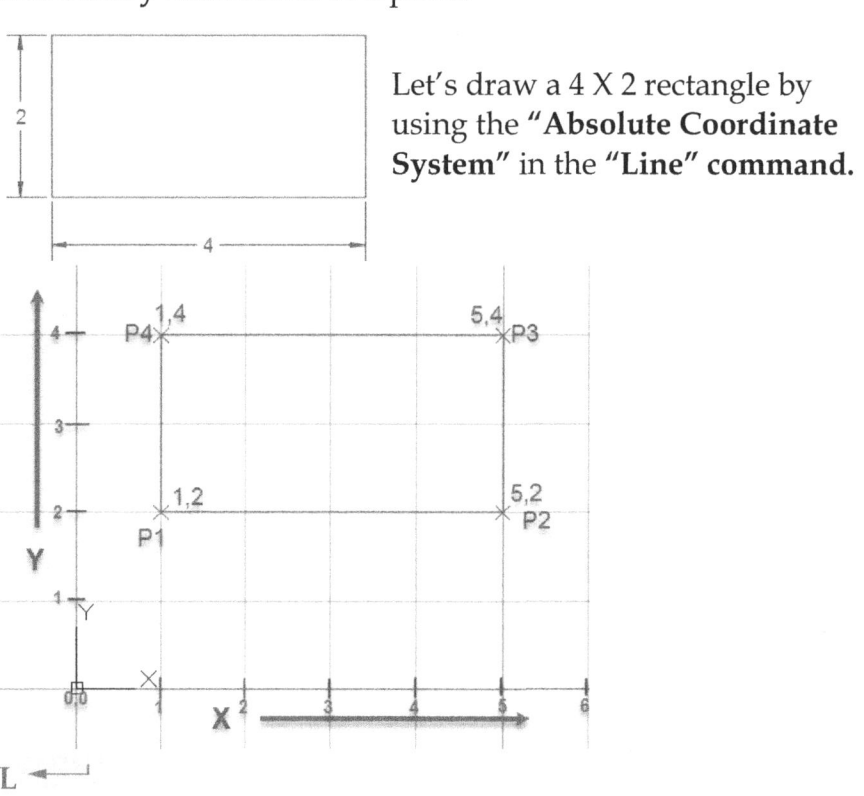

Specify first point: 1,2 ↵
Specify next point(Undo): 5,2 ↵
Specify next point(Undo): 5,4 ↵
Specify next point(Close/Undo): 1,4 ↵
Specify next point(Close/Undo): 1,2 ↵
Specify next point(Close/Undo): ↵ (press "Enter" to finish Command)

Autodesk AutoCAD 2021
Learn CAD With Ease.

Note: You can also type C↵ to close figure instead of specifying the last point coordinates 1,2↵,this will automatically finish the command.

Relative Rectangular Co-ordinate System: In this coordinate system, the location of a point specified by giving their distance from a reference point.

In this system, you will specify coordinates of a point in a particular format "@x distance, y distance".

Let's draw 4 X 2 size rectangle by fixing point by using the **"Relative Rectangular Co-Ordinate System"** in the **"Line"** command.

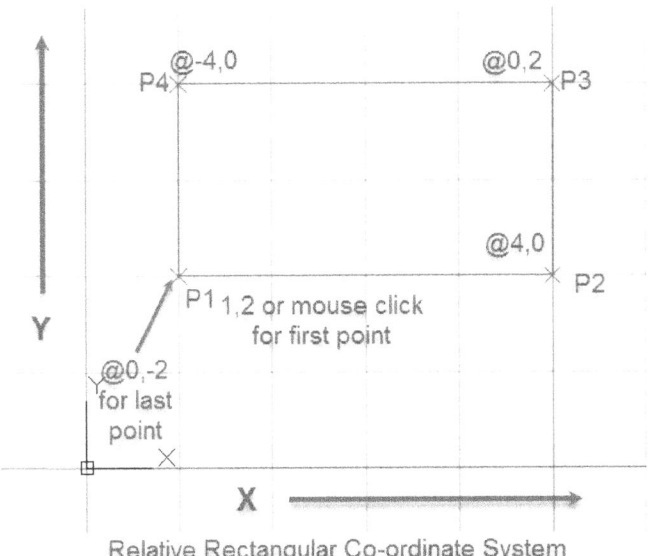

Relative Rectangular Co-ordinate System

Specify first point: 1,2 ↵ or mouse click.
Specify next point(Undo): @4,0 ↵
Specify next point(Undo): @0,2 ↵
Specify next point(Close/Undo): @-4,0 ↵
Specify next point(Close/Undo): @0,-2 ↵ or C ↵

Note: If you specify the last point by entering coordinates

Autodesk AutoCAD 2021
Learn CAD With Ease.

(@0,-2 ↵), then press **"Esc"** or **"Enter"** to finish the command. If you type **C**↵ to close figure instead of specifying the last point coordinates 1,2↵, this will automatically finish the command.

Relative Polar Coordinate System: This coordinate system is used to specify the point at a particular angle.
This co-ordinate system is mostly used to draw angular lines, move and copy objects at a particular angle, etc.
In this system, you will specify coordinates of a point in a particular format "@ Distance < Angle".

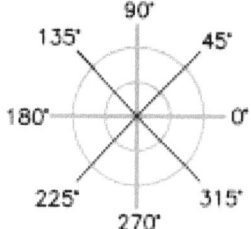

Let's draw the same diagram by using **"Relative Polar Coordinate System"**.

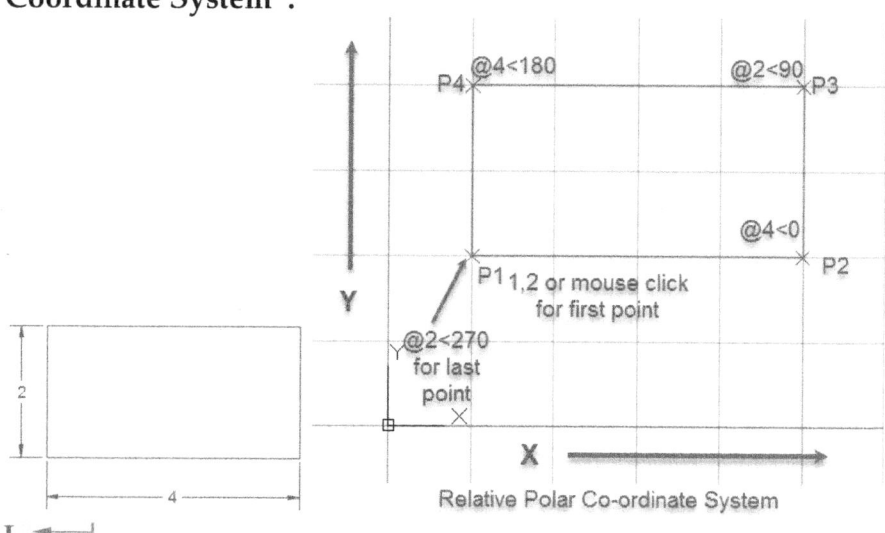

Specify first point: 1,2 ↵ or mouse click.
Specify next point(Undo): @4< 0 ↵
Specify next point(Undo): @2<90 ↵
Specify next point(Close/Undo): @4<180 ↵
Specify next point(Close/Undo): @2<270 ↵ or C ↵

Autodesk AutoCAD 2021
Learn CAD With Ease.

Let's draw an equilateral triangle by **Polar Coordinate System** entries.

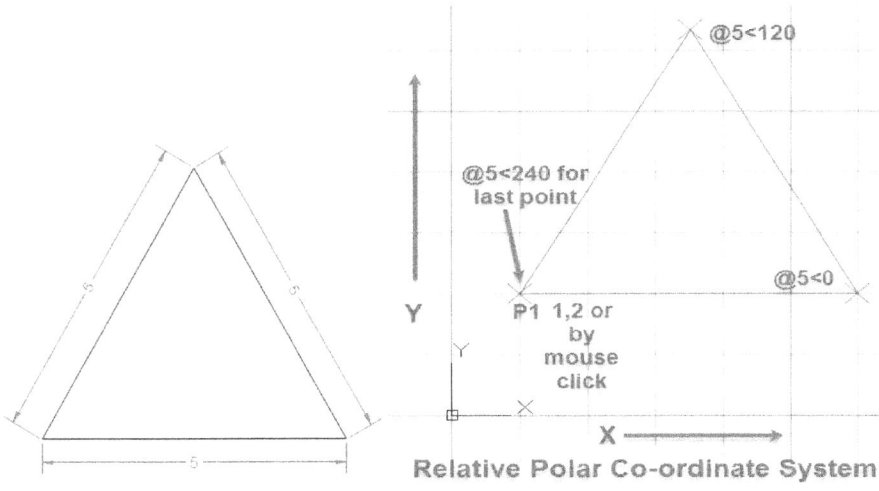

Specify first point: 1,2 ↵ or mc.
Specify next point(Undo): @5< 0 ↵
Specify next point(Undo):@5<120 ↵
Specify next point(Close/Undo): @5<240 ↵ or C ↵

Entering coordinates by using AutoCAD drawing aid tools:
You can also give co-ordinates by turn on **Dynamic Input** or **Dynamic Entries**. "**Dynamic Input**" mode is available in "**Status Bar**", if you don't see **dynamic input** icon, you can add it in the status bar by - click on "**Customization Menu**" and then select "**Dynamic Input**" (as specified in chapter 1, topic 1.3 Workspaces of AutoCAD/ Drafting & Annotation/ Status Bar).
Now turn on "**Dynamic Input**" by click on icon or by pressing function Key **F12** in the keyboard.
  a. Angle is locked but Distance is dynamic.
  b. Distance and Angle both specified on screen dynamically.
a. Angle is locked but Distance is dynamic:
Firstly turn on "**Dynamic Input**".
Activate the "**Line**" command.
Then specify the first point by mouse click.
After that type "**<45**" and press "**Enter**". That will lock angle at 45 degrees.

Autodesk AutoCAD 2021
Learn CAD With Ease.

Now you can manage distance by cursor or type it and press **"Enter"**.

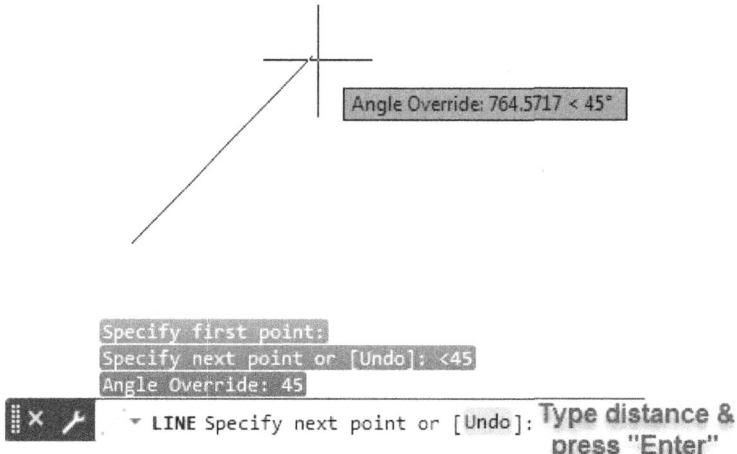

b. Distance and Angle both specified on screen dynamically.
Firstly turn on **"Dynamic Input"**.
Activate the **"Line"** command.
Then specify the first point by mouse click.
Now you can specify both distance and angle by a cursor.

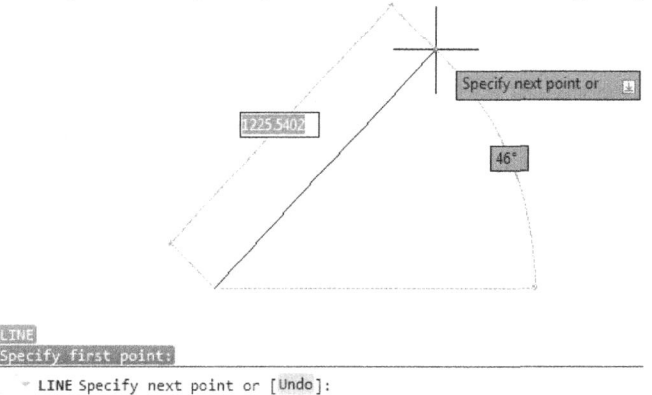

Note: When the dynamic input mode is on, you can give and see all entries on a screen instead of the command line.

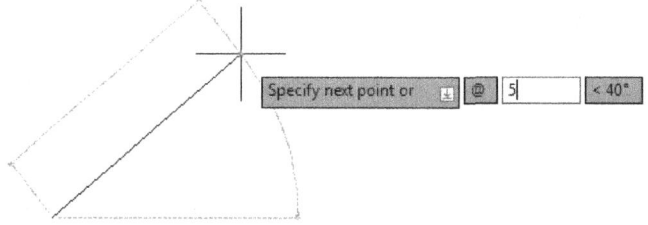

Autodesk AutoCAD 2021
Learn CAD With Ease.

You can turn on/off "**Dynamic Input**" by pressing the **F12** function key or by clicking on the "**Dynamic Input**" icon available in **Status Bar**.

ii. Pick Point Method:
In this method, you will specify the first point by cursor then press **F8** (functional key) to turn on **"Ortho mode"** to get points straight at four directions **x, y, -x,** and **–y,** then specify the direction by moving a cursor, type distance and press **"Enter"**.

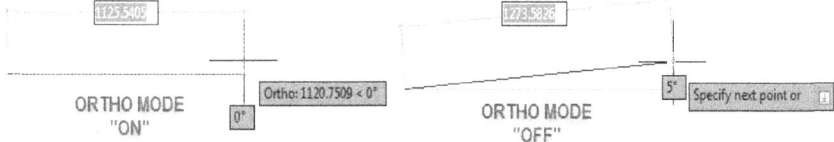

You can turn on/off "**ortho mode**" by pressing **F8** function key or by clicking on the "**Orthomode**" icon available in **Status Bar**.

Note 1: You can specify points in any command by using these point fixing methods.

2. You can **turn on/off grids** of the drawing area or view port by pressing **F7** function key in the keyboard.

Autodesk AutoCAD 2021
Learn CAD With Ease.

Exercise 1: Draw the given diagrams by fixing points by "Absolute Coordinate System, Relative Rectangular Coordinate System, Relative Polar Coordinate System, and Pick Point Method" in the **line** command.

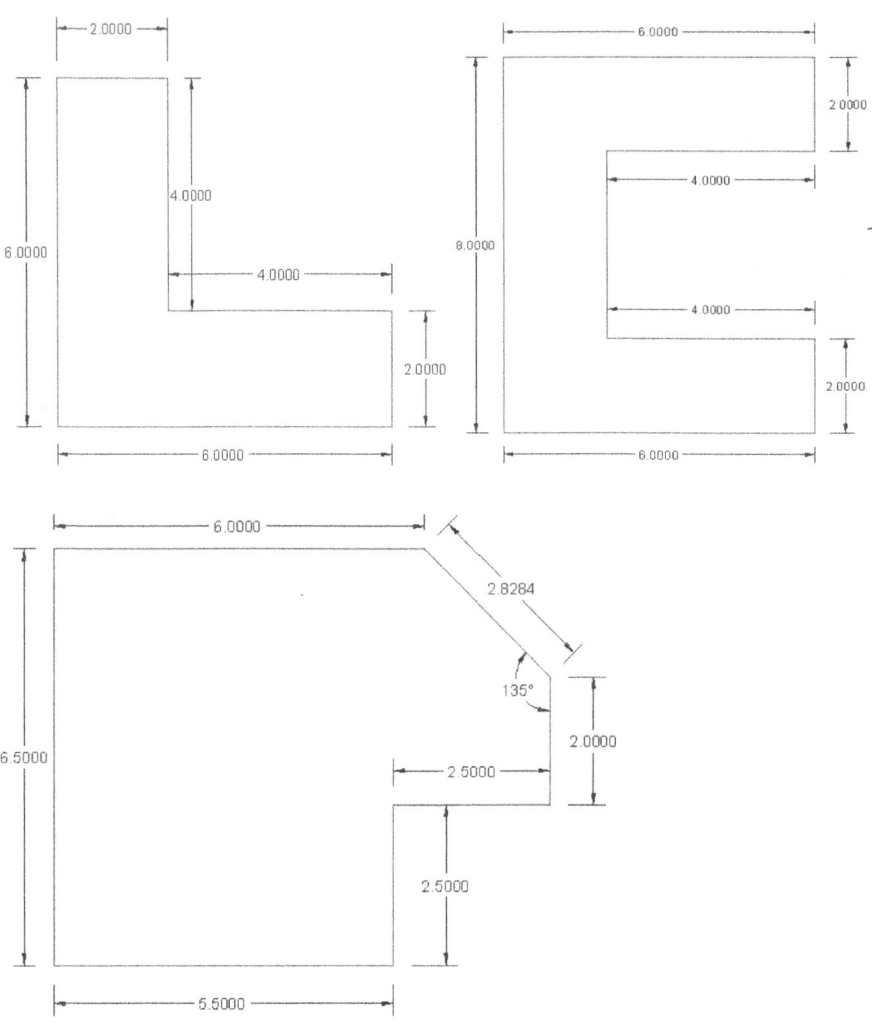

Autodesk AutoCAD 2021
Learn CAD With Ease.

2.2 Command: Circle
Alias: C

Home tab → Draw Panel → Circle

Use: To draw circle.

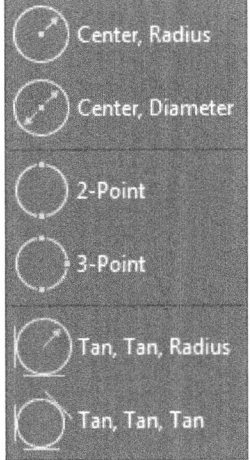

Different options available under the circle submenu are:-
a) Center Radius:
b) Center diameter:
c) 3 Point:
d) 2 Point:
e) Ttr (Tangent, tangent, radius):
f) Ttt (tan, tan,tan):

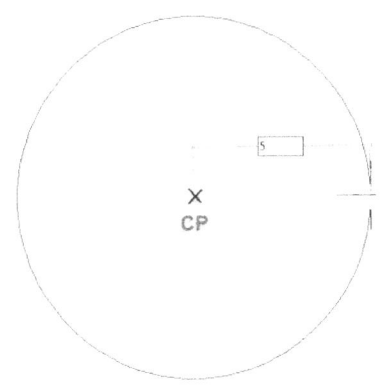

a) Center Radius:
This option or method is used to draw a circle based on a center point and a radius.
C ↵
Specify center point for circle or (3P/2P/Ttr): by mouse click or by any point fixing method
Specify radius of circle (Diameter):5 ↵

b) Center Diameter:
This option is used to draw a circle based on a center point and a diameter.
C ↵
Specify center point for circle or (3P/2P/Ttr): by mouse click or by any point fixing method
Specify radius of circle (Diameter): D ↵
Specify diameter of circle: 15 ↵

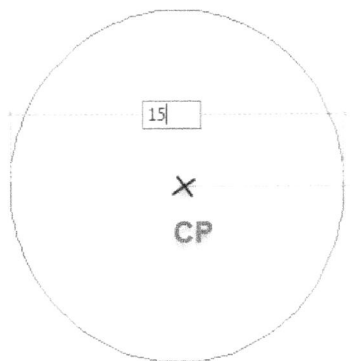

By Madhumita Kshirsagar

Autodesk AutoCAD 2021
Learn CAD With Ease.

c) 3 Point:
This option is used to draw a circle based on three points on the circumference.

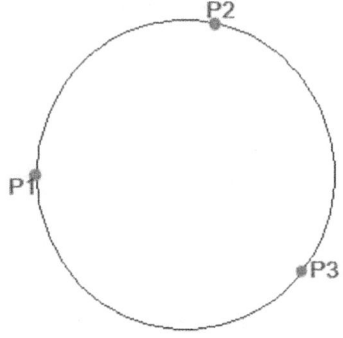

C ⤶
Specify center point for circle or (3P/2P/Ttr): 3P ⤶
Specify first point on circle: by mouse click or by any point fixing method
Specify second point on circle: by mouse click or by any point fixing method
Specify third point on circle: by mouse click or by any point fixing method

d) 2 Point:
This option is used to draw a circle based on two endpoints of the diameter.

C ⤶
Specify center point for circle or (3P/2P/Ttr): 2P ⤶
Specify first end point on circle's diameter: by mouse click
Specify second end point on circle's diameter: by mouse click

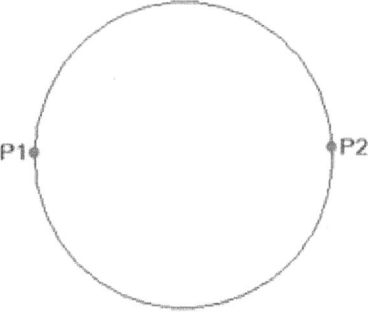

e) Ttr (Tangent, Tangent, Radius):
This option is use to draw a circle with a specified radius which touches two objects as tangents.

C ⤶
Specify center point for circle or (3P/2P/Ttr): T ⤶
Specify point on object for first tangent of circle: by mouse click
Specify point on object for second tangent of circle: by mouse-click
Specify radius of circle <1>: 3 ⤶

Autodesk AutoCAD 2021
Learn CAD With Ease.

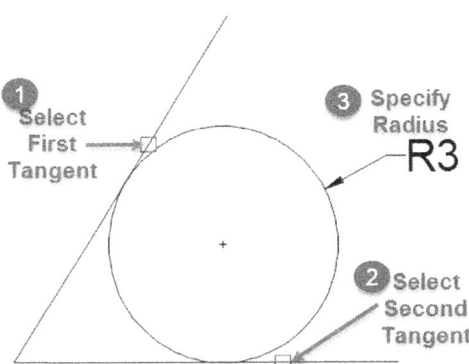

g) **TTT (Tan, Tan, Tan):**
This option is used to draw a circle by selecting three objects as tangents.
This method of creating a circle is not available by activating the **circle command** by **command line** you have to activate it by selecting "**Tan, Tan, Tan**" option directly from the **"Home Tab/ Draw Panel/ Circle"**.
After that, select all three tangents one by one and you will get a circle that touches all three tangents.

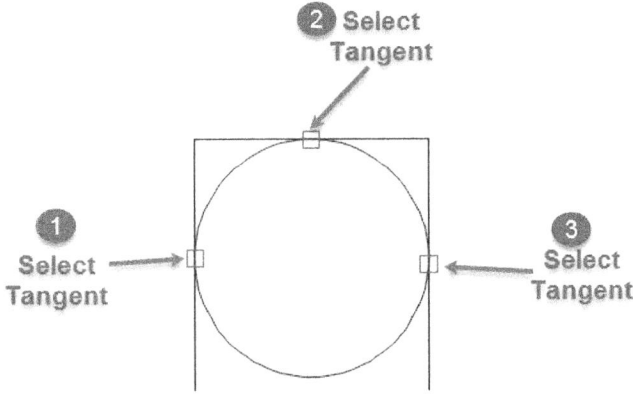

Tan, Tan, Tan

Note: You can directly activate all options of the circle command by selecting them from the **Home Tab/ Draw Panel/Circle** .

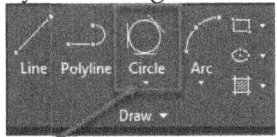

click here to get other options

20

By Madhumita Kshirsagar

Autodesk AutoCAD 2021
Learn CAD With Ease.

Exercise 2: Draw the given diagrams by using line and circle commands.

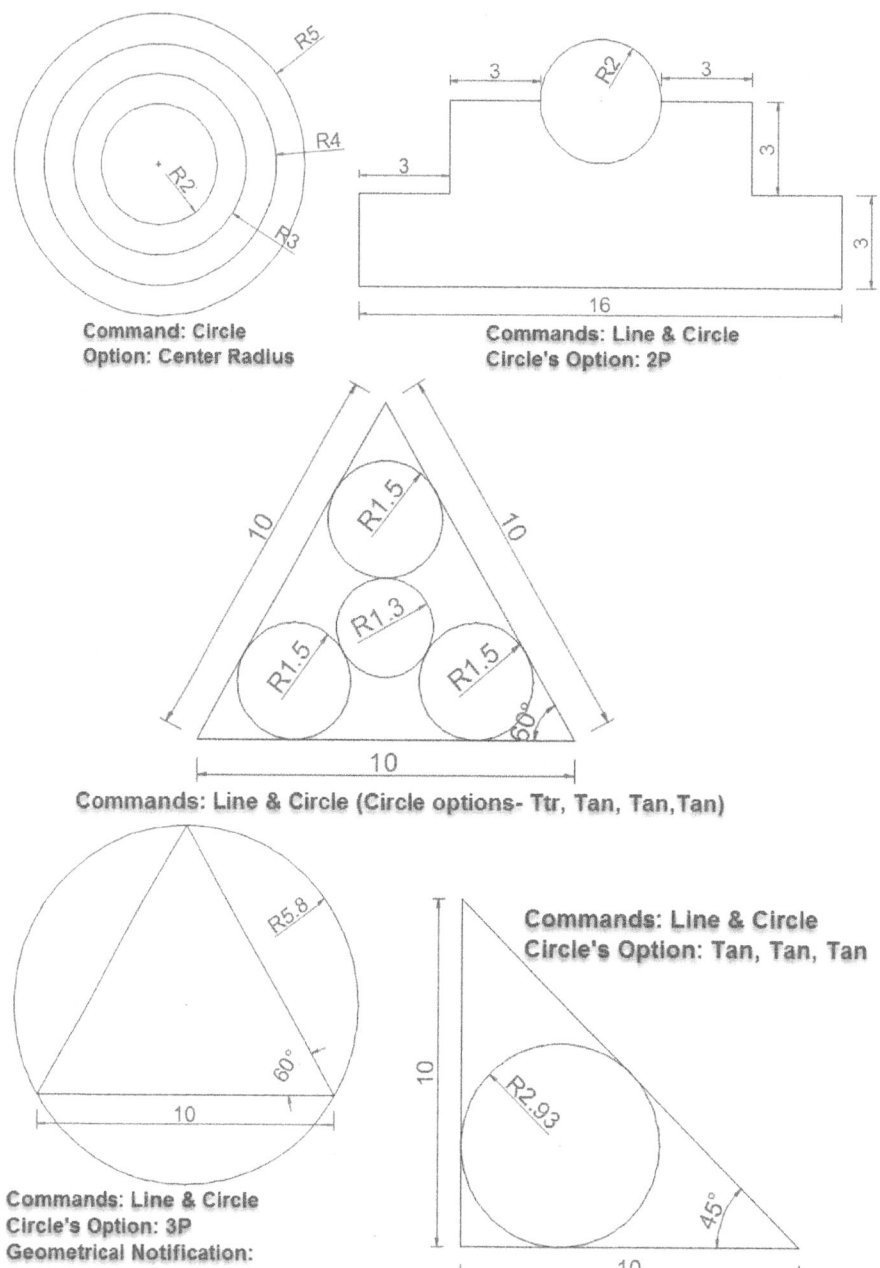

Autodesk AutoCAD 2021
Learn CAD With Ease.

2.3 Command: Arc
   Alias   : A

   Home Tab →Draw Panel →Arc

Use: To draw arcs.

There are many methods or options are available in AutoCAD to create arcs.

These methods of creating an arc, is a combination of the center point, endpoint, start point, radius, angle, chord length, and direction values.

Methods of creating an arc:

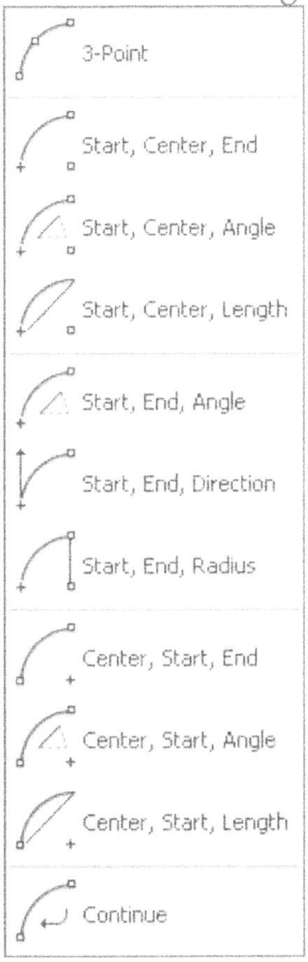

a) 3-Point: In this method, you will give three points by mouse to create an arc.

A ←┘

Specify start point of arc or [Center]: mouse click (P1)
Specify second point of arc or [Center/End]: mouse click (P2)
Specify end point of arc: mouse click (P3)

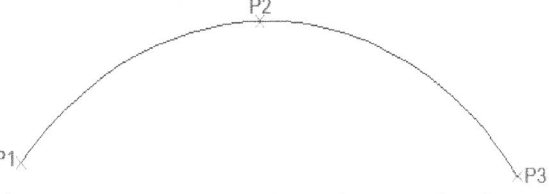

b) Start, Center, End: In this method, you will specify the start point, center point, and end point to draw an arc.

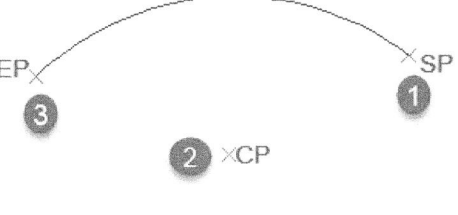

A ←┘
Specify start point of arc or [Center]: mouse click (SP)
Specify second point of arc or [Center/End]: C ←┘
Specify center point of arc: mouse click (CP)
Specify end point of arc or [Angle/chord Length]: mouse click (EP)

22

By Madhumita Kshirsagar

Autodesk AutoCAD 2021
Learn CAD With Ease.

c) **Start, Center, Angle:** In this method, you will specify the center point, start point, and angle of the arc to create it.

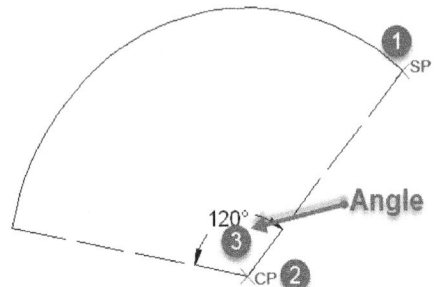

A ←⏎
Specify start point of arc or [Center]: mouse click (SP)
Specify second point of arc or [Center/End]: C ←⏎
Specify center point of arc: mouse click (CP)

Specify end point of arc or [Angle/chord Length]: A ←⏎
Specify included angle: 120 ←⏎

d) **Start, Center, Length:** In this method, you will draw an arc by specifying its start point, center point, and the chord length.

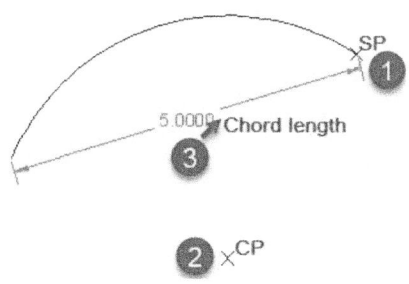

A ←⏎
Specify start point of arc or [Center]: mouse click (SP)
Specify second point of arc or [Center/End]: C ←⏎
Specify center point of arc: mouse click (CP)
Specify end point of arc or [Angle/chord Length]: L ←⏎
Specify length of chord: 5 ←⏎

e) **Start, End, Angle:** In this method, you will specify the start point, end point, and angle of the arc to draw it.
A ←⏎
Specify start point of arc or [Center]: mouse click (SP)
Specify second point of arc or [Center/End]: E ←⏎
Specify end point of arc: mouse click (EP)
Specify center point of arc or [Angle/Direction/Radius]: A ←⏎
Specify included angle: 45 ←⏎

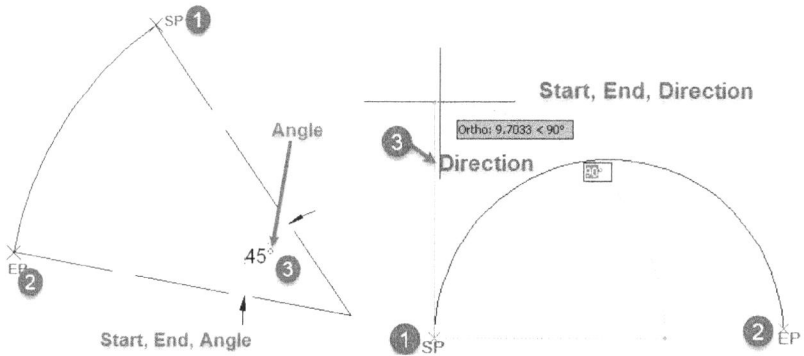

f) Start, End, Direction: In this method, you will draw an arc by specifying its start point, end point, and its direction.

A ←

Specify start point of arc or [Center]: mouse click (SP)
Specify second point of arc or [Center/End]: E ←
Specify end point of arc: mouse click (EP)
Specify center point of arc or [Angle/Direction/Radius]: D ←
Specify tangent direction for the start point of arc: 90 ←

Note: You can also give a direction of an arc by using a cursor.

g) Start, End, Radius: In this method, you will draw an arc by specifying its start point, end point, and radius.

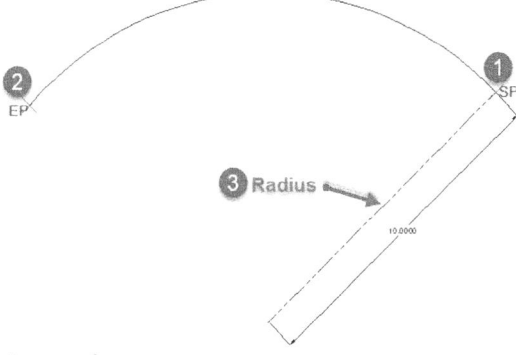

A ←

Specify start point of arc or [Center]: mouse click (SP)
Specify second point of arc or [Center/End]: E ←
Specify end point of arc: mouse click (EP)
Specify center point of arc or [Angle/Direction/Radius]: R ←
Specify radius of arc: 10 ←

Autodesk AutoCAD 2021
Learn CAD With Ease.

h) Center, Start, End: In this method, you will draw an arc by specifying its center point, start point, and end point.

A ⏎
Specify start point of arc or [Center]: C ⏎
Specify center point of arc:
        mouse click (CP)
Specify start point of arc:
        mouse click (SP)
Specify end point of arc or [Angle/chord Length]:
        mouse click (EP)

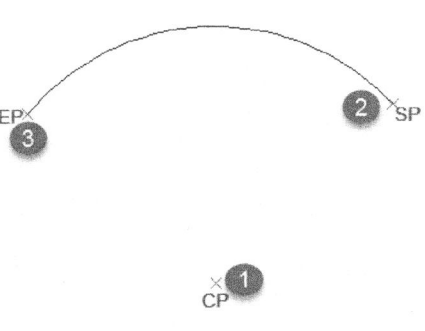

i) Center, Start, Angle: In this method, you will draw an arc by specifying its center point, start point, and included angle.

A ⏎
Specify start point of arc or [Center]: C ⏎
Specify center point of arc: mouse click (CP)
Specify start point of arc: mouse click (SP)
Specify end point of arc or [Angle/chord Length]: A ⏎
Specify included angle: 60 ⏎

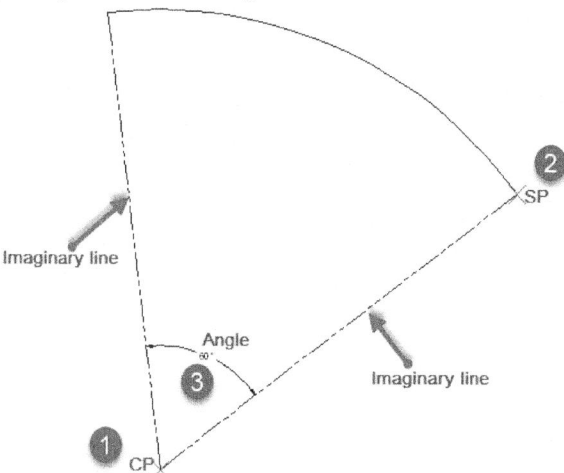

j) Center, Start, Length: In this method, you will draw an arc by specifying its center point, start point, and the chord length.

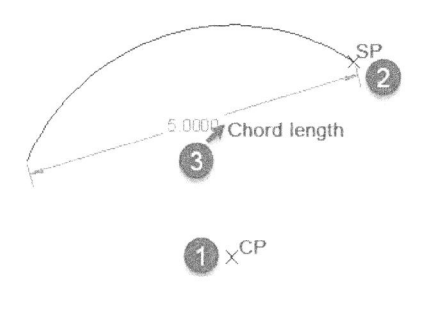

Autodesk AutoCAD 2021
Learn CAD With Ease.

A ←┘
Specify start point of arc or [Center]: C ←┘
Specify center point of arc: mouse click (CP)
Specify start point of arc: mouse click (SP)
Specify end point of arc or [Angle/chord Length]: l ←┘
Specify length of chord: 15 ←┘

k) **Contniue:** This method is used to create continous arcs.

Note: You can activate different methods and options of creating arcs by directly selected them from the **Home tab/ Draw Panel/ Arc (drop down arrow).**

2.4 Command: Polygon
    Alias   : Pol
    Home tab→ Draw Panel →Polygon

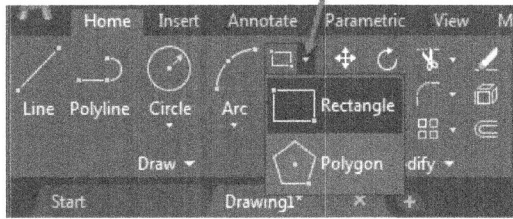

Use: The Polygon command is used to draw any regular polygon.
Minimum and Maximum number of sides:
Minimum= 3 Sides
Maximum= 1024 Sides

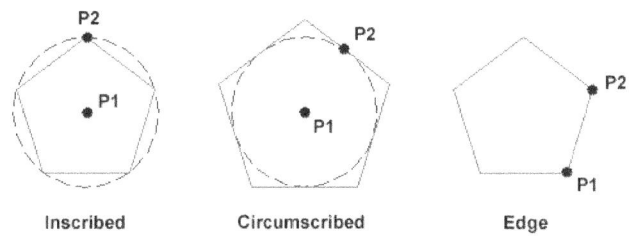

Inscribed   Circumscribed   Edge

Firstly draw a circle of 6 unit radius. Then activate polygon command.

Autodesk AutoCAD 2021
Learn CAD With Ease.

Pol ←
Enter number of sides <4>: 5 ←
Specify center of polygon or [Edge]: pick P1 by mouse click
Enter an option [Inscribed in circle/Circumscribed about circle] <I>: ←to accept the inscribed default or (type C ← for circum.)
Specify radius of circle: 6 ←

Inscribed in circle: To draw a polygon, inside the circumference of a circle.

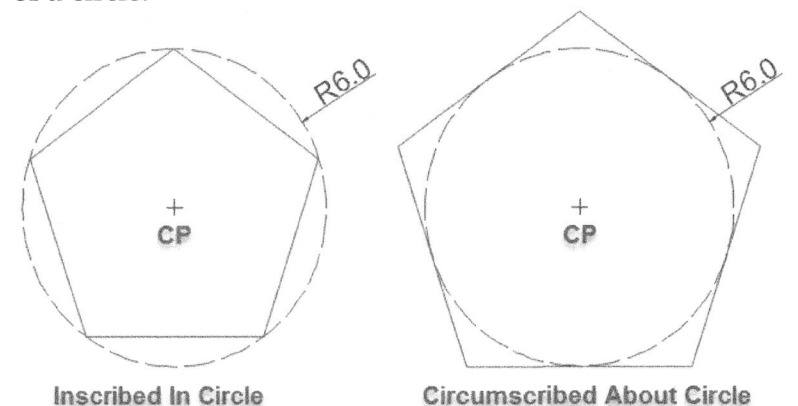

Inscribed In Circle   **Circumscribed About Circle**

Circumscribed about circle: To draw a polygon, outside the circumference of a circle.

Edge: This command also allows you to define the polygon by entering the length of a side using the **Edge** option.

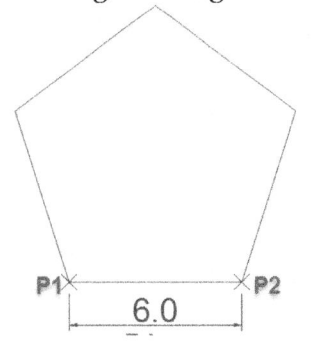

Pol ←
Enter number of sides <4>: 5 ←
Specify center of polygon or [Edge]: E ←
Specify first endpoint of edge: (pick P1 by mouse click)
Specify second end point of edge: (pick P2 by mouse click Or 6 ←)

2.5 Command: Ellipse
   Alia   : EL
   Home Tab → Draw Panel → Ellipse 
Use: To draw an ellipse.

Autodesk AutoCAD 2021
Learn CAD With Ease.

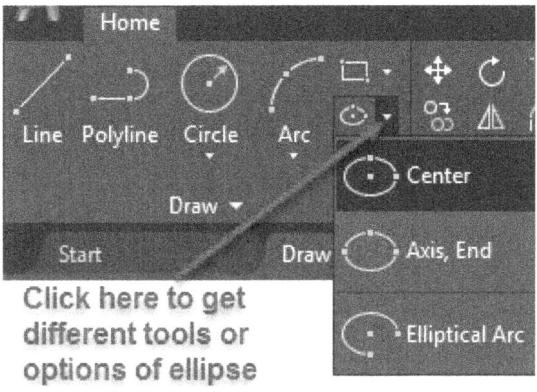

Click here to get different tools or options of ellipse

Options & Methods to draw ellipse:
a) Axis, End
b) Center
c) Elliptical Arc

a) Axis, End:
EL ←┘
Specify axis endpoint of ellipse or [Arc/Center]: mouse click (P1)
Specify other endpoint of axis: 10 ←┘ or mouse click (P2)
Specify distance to other axis or [Rotation]: 3 ←┘ or mouse click (P2)

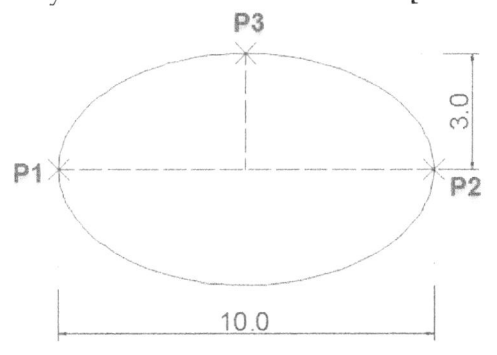

Note: The first two points of the ellipse determine the location and the length of the first axis. The third point determines the distance between the center of the ellipse and the end point of the second axis.

b) Center:
EL ←┘
Specify axis endpoint of ellipse or [Arc/Center]: C ←┘
Specify center of ellipse: mouse click (P1)
Specify endpoint of axis: 5 ←┘ or mouse click (P2)
Specify distance to other axis or [Rotation]: 3 ←┘ or mouse click (P3)

Autodesk AutoCAD 2021
Learn CAD With Ease.

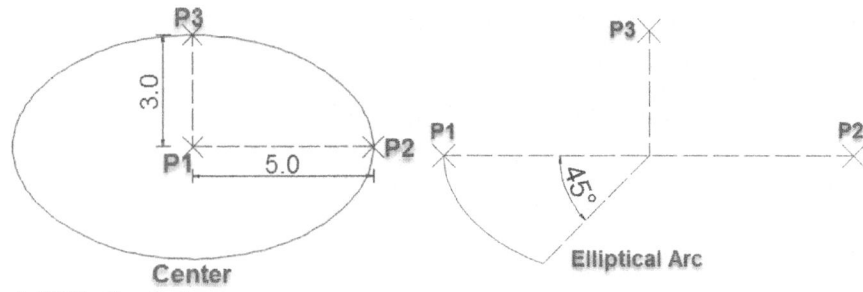

c) Elliptical Arc:

EL ↵

Specify axis endpoint of ellipse or [Arc/Center]: A ↵
Specify axis endpoint of elliptical arc or [Center]: mouse click (P1)
Specify other endpoint of axis: 10 or mouse click (P2)
Specify distance to other axis or [Rotation]: 3 ↵ or mouse click (P2)
Specify start angle or [Parameter]: 0 ↵
Specify end angle or [Parameter/Included angle]: 45 ↵

Note: Remember that, angles are measured in an anti-clockwise direction, and starting at the first point of the arc.

d) Rotation: It creates the ellipse by appearing to rotate a circle about the first axis.

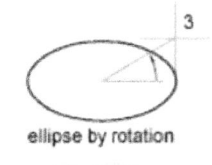

EL ↵

Specify axis endpoint of ellipse or [Arc/Center]: A ↵
Specify axis endpoint of elliptical arc or [Center]: mouse click (P1)
Specify other endpoint of axis: 10 or mouse click (P2)
Specify distance to other axis or [Rotation]: R ↵
Specify rotation around major axis: 45 ↵

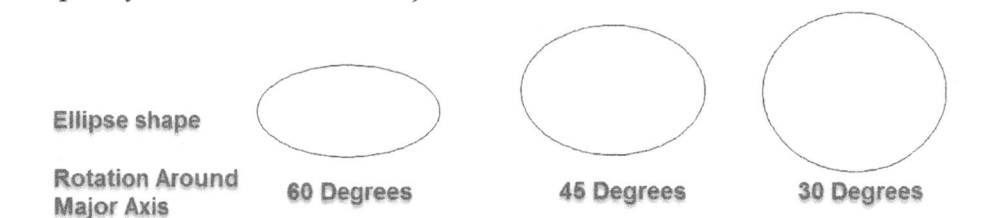

Ellipse shape			
Rotation Around Major Axis	60 Degrees	45 Degrees	30 Degrees

Autodesk AutoCAD 2021
Learn CAD With Ease.

Note: The value of "Rotation around major axis" affects the eccentricity of the ellipse.
Higher value makes an ellipse more eccentric and lower value makes an ellipse more circular.

2.6 Command: Donut
   Alias   : Do

   Home tab→ Draw Panel →Donut.

Use: To create Donut.

Do ←
Specify inside diameter of donut <0.5000>: .5 ←
Specify outside diameter of donut <1.0000>:1 ←
Specify center of donut or <exit>: mouse click

2.7 Command: Construction Line
   Alias   : XL

   Home tab→ Draw Panel→ Construction Line

Use: This command is used to create a line of infinite length.

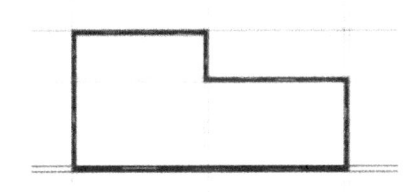

XL ←
Specify a point or [Hor/Ver/Ang/Bisect/Offset]: mouse click
Specify through point: mouse click
Specify through point: ← to end the command

Horizontal: To create horizontal xline.
XL ←
Specify a point or [Hor/Ver/Ang/Bisect/Offset]: H ←
Specify through point: mouse click
Specify through point: ←

By Madhumita Kshirsagar

Autodesk AutoCAD 2021
Learn CAD With Ease.

Vertical: To create vertical xline.
XL ↵
Specify a point or [Hor/Ver/Ang/Bisect/Offset]: V ↵
Specify through point: mouse click
Specify through point: ↵

through point

Vertical

through point

Angle

Ang: To create xline on some angle which you enter.
XL ↵
Specify a point or [Hor/Ver/Ang/Bisect/Offset]: A ↵
Enter angle of xline (0) or [Reference]: 45 ↵
Specify through point: mouse click
Specify through point: mouse click
Specify through point: ↵

Bisect: Creates an xline that passes through the selected angle vertex and bisects the angle between the first and second line.

Offset: To create an xline parallel to another xline just like offset command.

2.8 Command: Ray
   Alias   : RAY

   Home tab → Draw Panel → Ray

Use: This command is used to create a line that starts at a point and continues to infinity.
RAY ↵
Specify start point: mouse click
Specify through point: mouse click
Specify through point: ↵ to end the command

Note: You can use both xline and ray command to draw projection lines when you create front view (elevation) of object from its top view (Plan).

2.9 Command: Revision Cloud
   Alias   : REVCLOUD
   Home tab → Draw Panel → Revision Cloud

Use: A revcloud is used to highlight problems or errors in a drawing.

You might also want to create a Revcloud to highlight a question you have with your own work.

There are three options available in revision cloud:

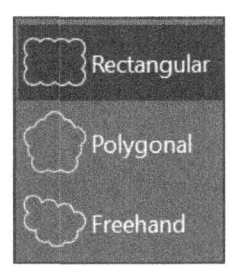

To create a revcloud, start the command. Then set the arc length to about 12 for an architectural drawing, or test out different arc lengths.

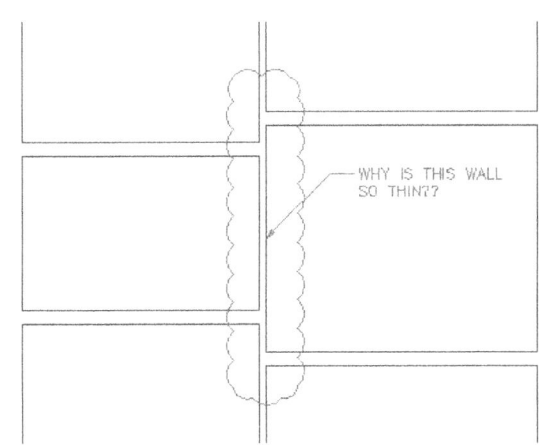

Rectangular: This option is used to draw rectangular revision cloud.
Polygonal: This option is used to draw polygonal revision cloud.
Freehand: This option is used to draw free hand revision cloud.

Autodesk AutoCAD 2021
Learn CAD With Ease.

REVCLOUD ⏎
Minimum arc length: 1'-4 9/16"   Maximum arc length: 2'-9 1/8"
Style: Normal   Type: Rectangular
Specify first corner point or [Arc length/Object/Rectangular/Polygonal/Freehand/Style/Modify] <Object>: F ⏎
Minimum arc length: 1'-4 9/16"   Maximum arc length: 2'-9 1/8"
Style: Normal   Type: Freehand
Specify first point or [Arc length/Object/Rectangular/Polygonal/Freehand/Style/Modify] <Object>: A ⏎
Specify approximate length of arc <2'-0 13/16">: 10 ⏎
Specify first point or [Arc length/Object/Rectangular/Polygonal/Freehand/Style/Modify] <Object>: mouse click
Guide crosshairs along cloud path...

Note: Try "Rectangular and Polygonal" option yourself.

Autodesk AutoCAD 2021
Learn CAD With Ease.

CHAPTER 3
DIFFERENT SELECTION METHODS

There are some selection methods available in AutoCAD to select objects. These are:

a) Window Selection
b) Crossing Window Selection
c) Implied Window Selection
d) The Undo Option
e) Selecting All Objects
f) Fence Selection
g) Window Polygon Selection
h) Crossing Polygon Selection
i) Previous Selection
j) Selecting the Last Object
k) Adding and Removing objects.

Let's get knowledge about different selection methods:
For that, firstly activate any modify command, here I activate the **"Erase"** command.

E ←

Select objects: now you can use any selection method & press ←

a) **Window Selection:** The **Window Selection** method is invoked by typing **"W"** ←, when AutoCAD asked to "Select objects" during "modify" command. In **"window selection method"** you will select objects by defining a rectangle picking two points and its select objects that lie entirely in the selection window or rectangle.

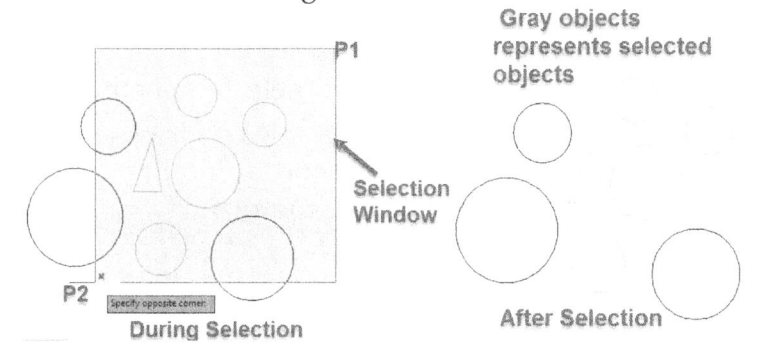

Gray objects represents selected objects

During Selection   After Selection

Autodesk AutoCAD 2021
Learn CAD With Ease.

E ⏎
Select objects: W ⏎
Specify first corner: mouse click P1
Specify opposite corner: mouse click P2
Select objects: press ⏎ (to erase object)

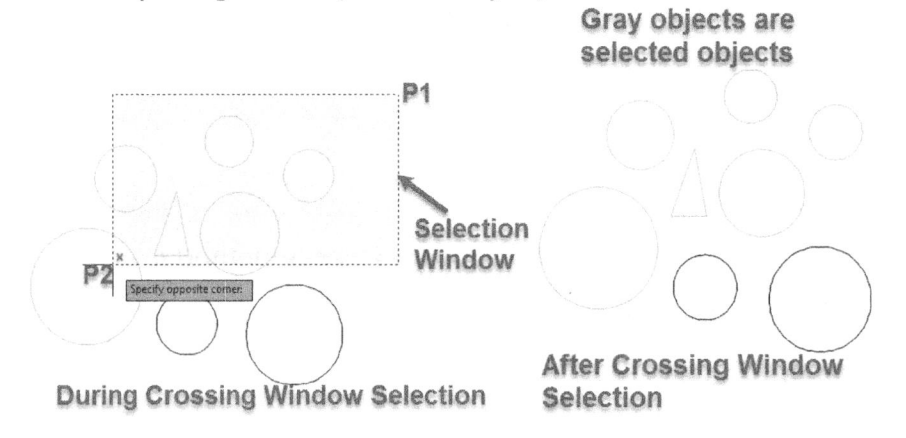

b) **Crossing Window Selection:** The Crossing Window Selection method is invoked by typing "**C ⏎**" when AutoCAD asked to "Select objects" in the command line during "modify" command.

In the **"crossing window selection"** we select objects by defining a rectangular window. It selects objects that even touched by the selection window.

E ⏎
Select objects: C ⏎
Specify first corner: mouse click P1
Specify opposite corner: mouse click P2
Select objects: press ⏎ (to erase object)

Gray objects are selected objects

During Crossing Window Selection

After Crossing Window Selection

c) **Implied Window Selection:** This is most commonly used selection method in AutoCAD.

This method is a combination of the window selection method and the crossing window selection method.

In this method you don't have to type "W" and "C" in the command line while applying any "modify command".

Autodesk AutoCAD 2021
Learn CAD With Ease.

You only have to draw rectangular window by specifying first point at upper right corner and then specify second point or opposite corner at lower left corner, to make crossing window selection.

For Window selection, specify first point at upper left corner and opposite corner at lower right corner.

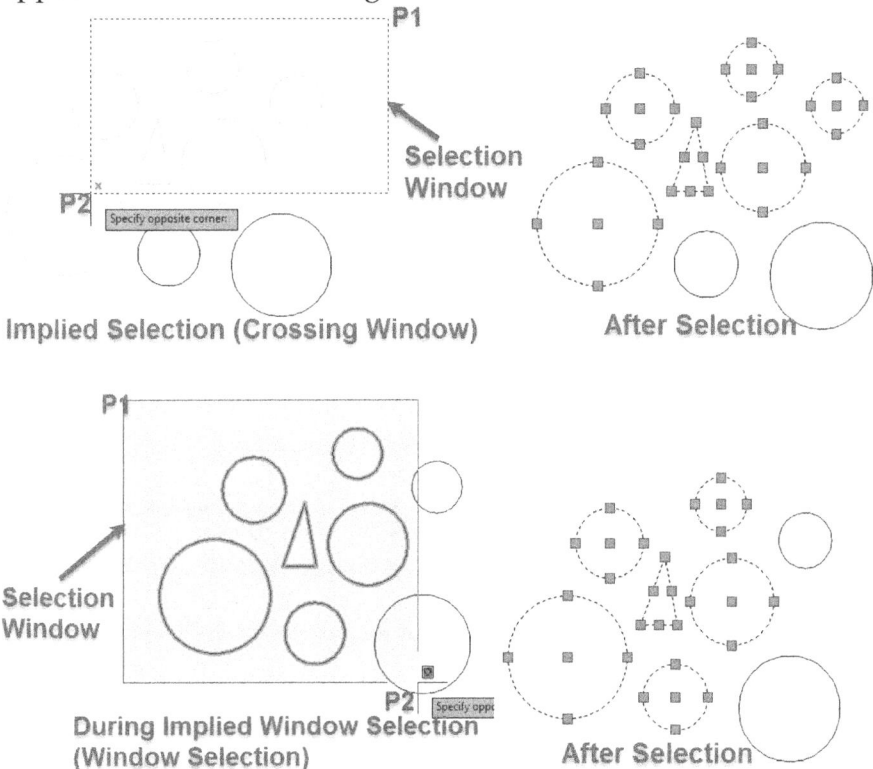

Implied Selection (Crossing Window)　　After Selection

During Implied Window Selection
(Window Selection)　　After Selection

You can directly select object by the "Implied Window Selection" without activating any command.

d) The Undo Option: AutoCAD allows you to undo the last selection made during the compilation of a selection set. All you need to do is enter "U" when AutoCAD asked to "Select objects" during applying any modify command, to remove the last selected object from the selection set.

E

Select objects: select ojects one by one, by mouse.
Select objects: U ↵ (to remove last selection)

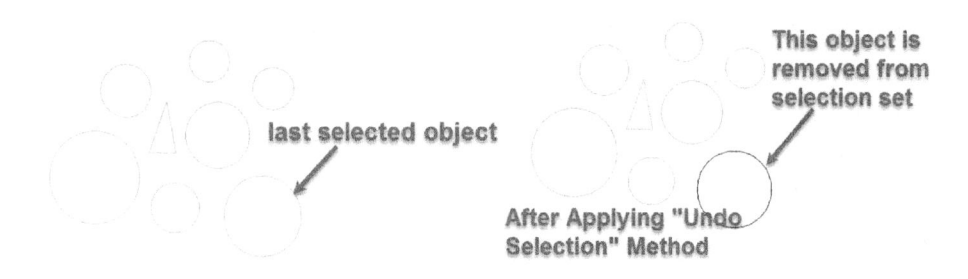

Autodesk AutoCAD 2021
Learn CAD With Ease.

e) Selecting All Objects: This selection method is used to select all the objects available in the drawing area, when AutoCAD asked to **"select objects"** during "modify command" like erase, move, and etc.

To apply this selection method type **"ALL"** and press ↵ in "select objects" prompt.

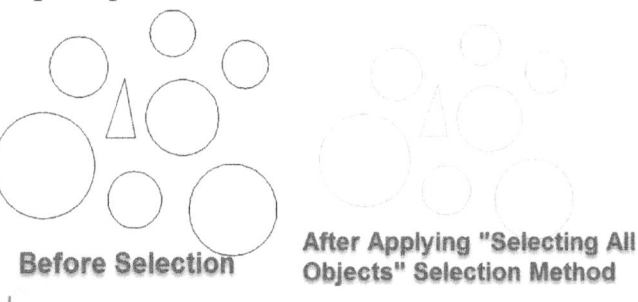

E ↵
Select objects: all ↵
Select objects: press ↵ (to erase objects)

f) Fence Selection: The Fence option allows you to draw a multi-segment line, like a Polyline. All objects which crossed by the fence line will be selected. The Fence option is invoked by typing **"F"** and press ↵ in the **"Select objects"** prompt during command.

E ↵
Select objects: f ↵
Specify first fence point or pick/drag cursor: mouse click
Specify next fence point or [Undo]: mc
Specify next fence point or [Undo]: mc
Specify next fence point or [Undo]: mc
Specify next fence point or [Undo]: mc
Specify next fence point or [Undo]: ↵

g) **Window Polygon Selection:** In this selection method, you will select objects by drawing irregular polygon. It selects objects which lie entirely in the selection window. To activate this selection method, you have to type **"WP"** and press ↵, when AutoCAD asked to select object during command.

E ←

Select objects: WP ↵
First polygon point: pick first point by mouse
Specify endpoint of line or [Undo]: pick second point by mouse
Specify endpoint of line or [Undo]: pick third point by mouse
Specify endpoint of line or [Undo]: pick another point by mouse
Specify endpoint of line or [Undo]: pick another point by mouse
Specify endpoint of line or [Undo]: pick another point by mouse
Specify endpoint of line or [Undo]: pick another point by mouse
Select objects: ↵ to complete the selection set.

Window Polygon Selection **After Selection**

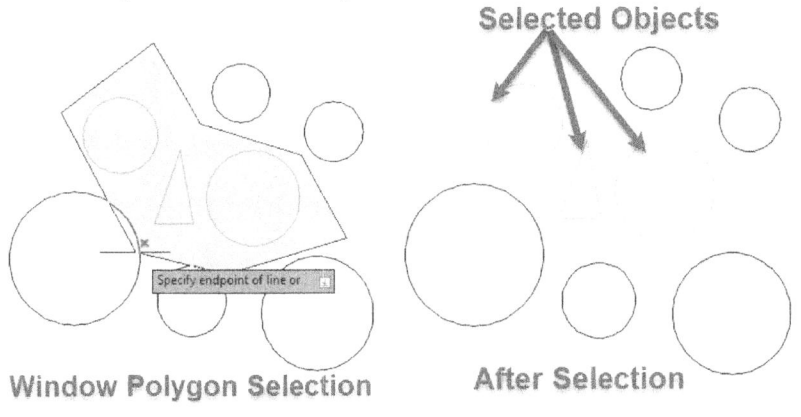

Note: A polygon is formed by picking at least three points.

---

h) **Crossing Polygon Selection:** The Crossing Polygon option can be used in exactly the same way as the Window Polygon option but it has the same selection criteria as the Crossing Window option, i.e. objects will be selected if they fall entirely within or touch the polygon boundary. This option is invoked by typing "**CP**" ↵ at the "Select objects", during command.

Autodesk AutoCAD 2021
Learn CAD With Ease.

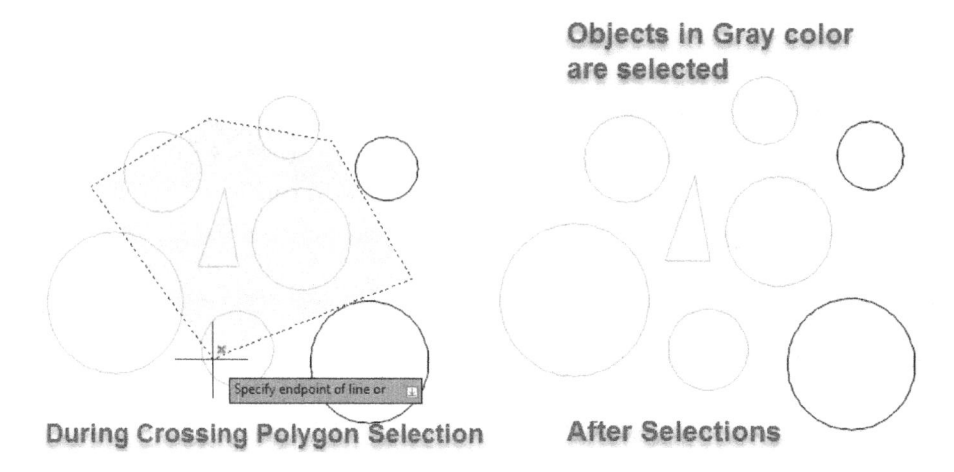

Objects in Gray color are selected

During Crossing Polygon Selection   **After Selections**

i) **Previous Selection:** AutoCAD always remembers the last selection set you defined. This is very useful because you may need to make a number of changes using different commands to the same group of objects. In order to re-select the last selection set you can use the **"Previous"** option. This selection method is invoked by typing **"P"** ↵ at the "Select objects" prompt.

j) **Selecting the Last Object:** By this method you can select last created object of a drawing.
This selection method is invoked by typing **"l"** ↵ at the "Select objects" prompt.
E ↵
Select objects: L ↵

k) **Removing Objects From Selection Set:** Select objects with **"Shift"** key on the keyboard to remove objects from selection set.

Autodesk AutoCAD 2021
Learn CAD With Ease.

CHAPTER 4
DRAFTING SETTINGS

AutoCAD has some drawing aids or drafting settings that can help you to draw different drawings. These drafting settings are placed in the status bar. These tools help you to:
a) Draw horizontal and vertical lines.
b) Show different object snap points like center point, endpoint, midpoint, tangents and etc.
c) Turn on/off grids on viewport.
d) Draw Isometric View.
e) Track different angles.
f) On/ Off Dynamic Inputs
g) Select objects according to their properties.
h) Advance selection by Selection Cycling.

Drafting Setting Tools:

1) **Ortho Mode**: This tool is used to draw horizontal and vertical lines or to pick points in x, y,-x and -y directions during any command. You can turn on/off ortho mode by clicking on ortho mode icon or by pressing **F8** functional key available on keyboard.
   When ortho mode is turned on, you can draw straight lines in horizontal and vertical directions or pick points in x, y, -x and –y directions.

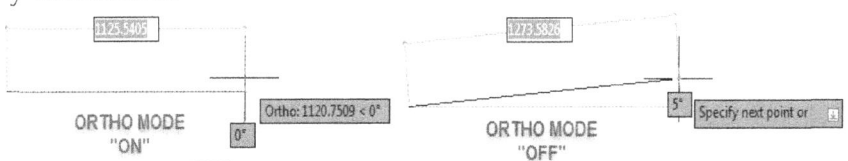

2) **Object Snap**: This tool is used to get different object snap points like: end point, center point, mid point and etc, on the object during command when AutoCAD asked to "specify point". **F3** is a fuctional fey to turn on and off Object Snap Mode. You can also turn it on/off by clicking on icon.

40

By Madhumita Kshirsagar

Autodesk AutoCAD 2021
Learn CAD With Ease.

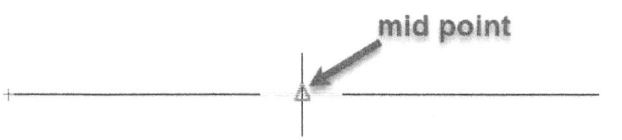

mid point

Note: Object snap is only working when AutoCAD is asking you for a point.

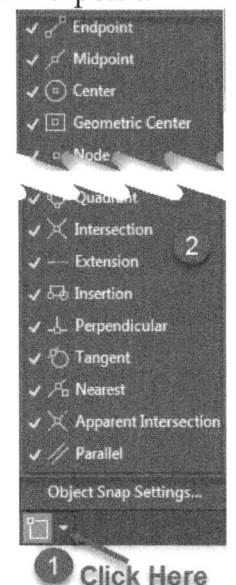

Object Snap Settings: By this option you can turn on or off different object snaps. Activating all the object snaps is not a wise decision, it will create problem during drafting complex drawings. You have to turn on object snaps according to your need to draw drawings properly.

Click on dropdown menu available in front of **object snap icon** to turn on and off different object snaps.

Note: Click on **"Object Snap Settings"** to get object snap settings in **"Drafting Settings"** dialog box.

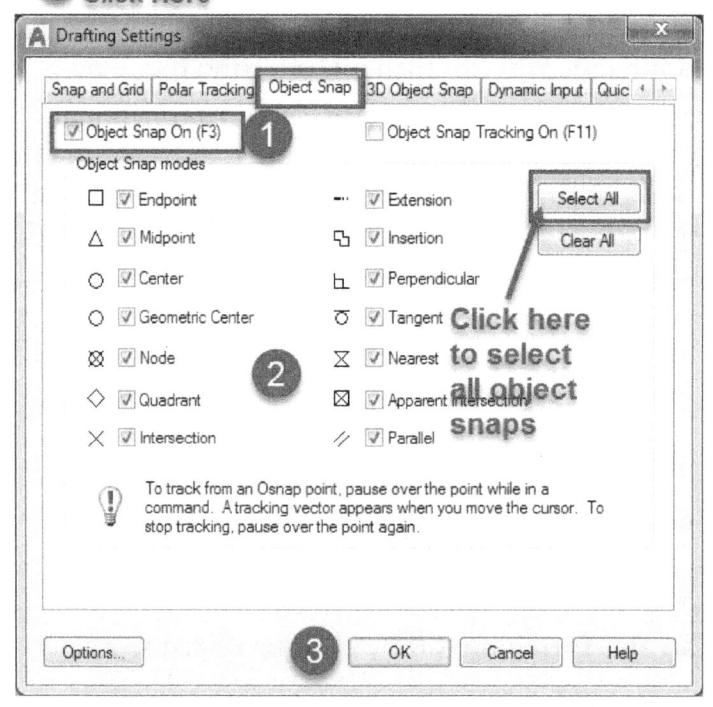

Autodesk AutoCAD 2021
Learn CAD With Ease.

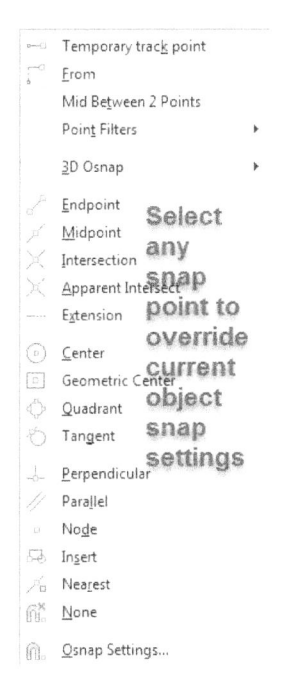

Overriding Object Snap Mode: Overriding object snap mode is very useful during working on a drawing. Suppose you turned on many object snap points when you start working on a drawing but now you want to get only one snap point for that hold the **shift** key then **right click** your mouse and select any **object snap point**. This will ignore your object snap settings temporarily and show only the snap mode you choose.

Select any snap point to override current object snap settings

3) **Object Snap Tracking**: Object snap tracking works with object snap. If you turn object snap off, then this tool will not work. This tool will help you to define a point from another point in an object.

In this example, I want to define circle center 5 units to the right of a rectangle corner. So I activate circle tool, place my pointer above the corner point. Wait for a while until AutoCAD recognize the point, and move your pointer to the right. The dynamic input should say 'extension:…'. Type the distance and press [enter].

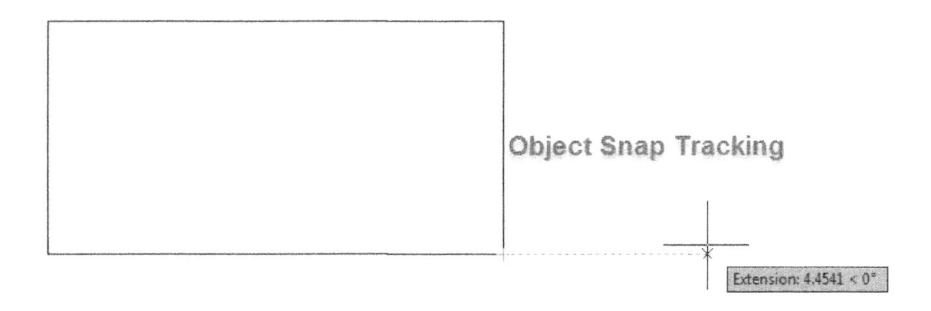

Autodesk AutoCAD 2021
Learn CAD With Ease.

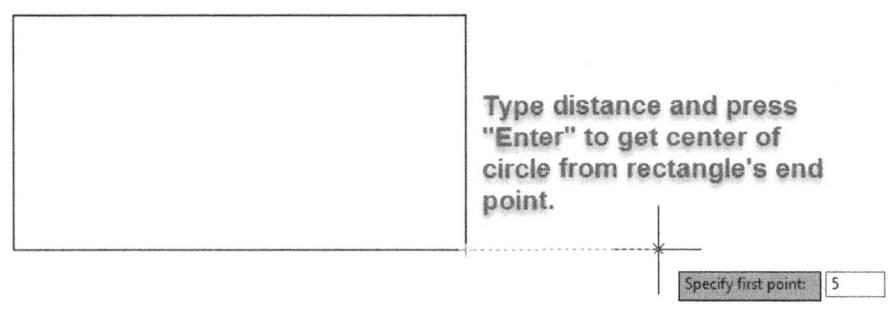

Type distance and press "Enter" to get center of circle from rectangle's end point.

You can use more than one point as reference. In this example, I use object snap tracking to find a rectangle center.

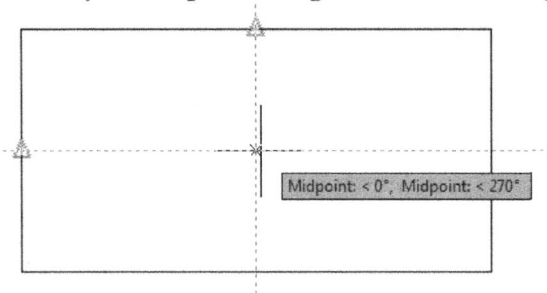

You can also get extended intersection of two lines.

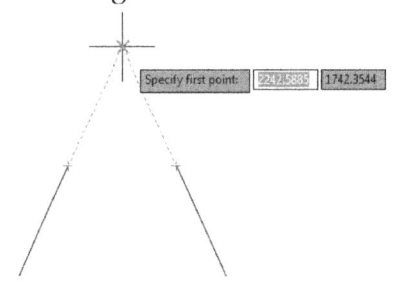

Now you have enough knowledge to start drawing with AutoCAD precisely.

Notes: Object snap tracking only works during commands.
F11 is a functional key to turn on and off object snap tracking.

4) Polar Tracking: This tool is used to get polar tracking of different angles in a drawing.

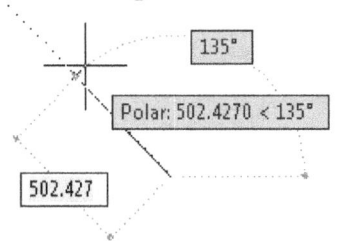

Usually it shows angles in multiplication of 90 degrees.
You can type the relative distance without typing the angle.
Simply move your pointer, snapped to the axis and type the desired distance.
By default, it will track your pointer

Autodesk AutoCAD 2021
Learn CAD With Ease.

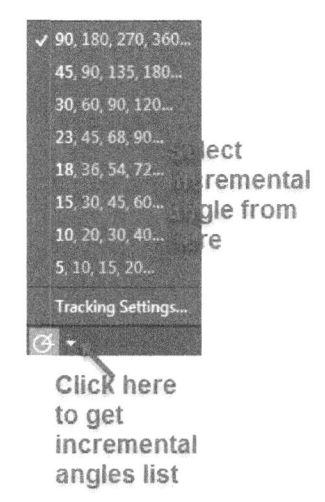

when it's at 90 deg, 180 deg, 270 deg, and 360 deg.
You can select incremental angles from list by click on drop down menu available in front of polar tracking icon.

F10 is a functional key used to turn on and off polar tracking.

You can also add additional angle by click on tracking settings.

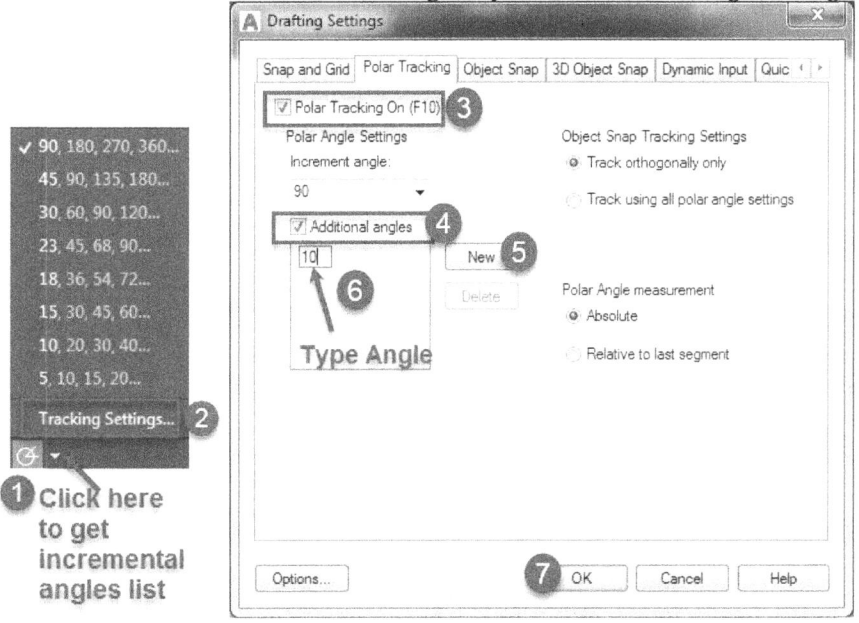

Now it will show 10 degrees angle with other angles.

5) **Dynamic Input**: The information shown in dynamic display is similar to that shown in the command-line, and the intent of this feature is to keep your eyes on the screen as much as possible. The specific information displayed depends, as it does on the command line, on what you're doing at the time.

Autodesk AutoCAD 2021
Learn CAD With Ease.

It's controlled by several settings that you access by right clicking the Dynamic Input button on the status bar and selecting **Settings** from the context menu. This opens the Drafting Settings dialog box with the **Dynamic Input** tab activated.

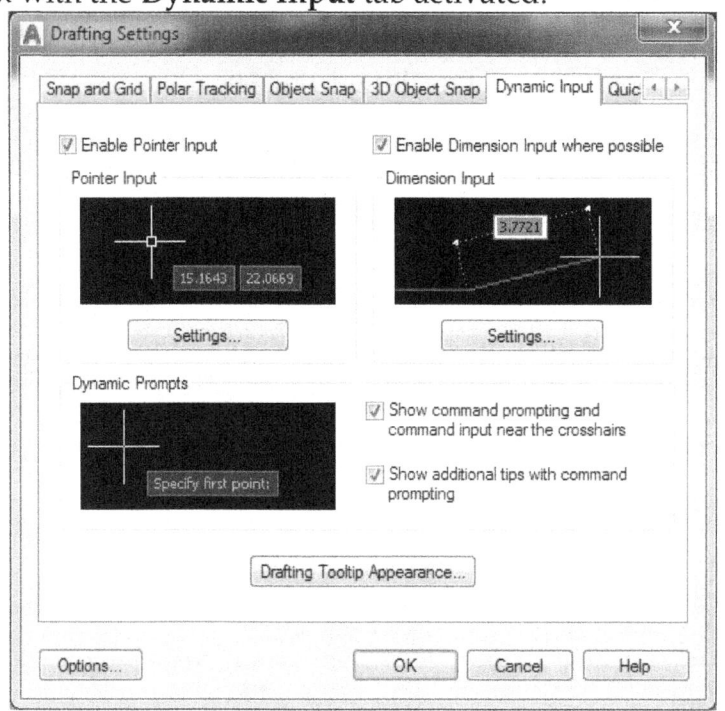

This tab has four check boxes (two at the top, and two near the middle on the right) and three buttons to open three feature-specific Settings dialog boxes.

F12 is a functional key to turn on and off **Dynamic Input.**

You can also turn on and off dynamic input by click on icon.

6) Grid & Snap :

F7 is a functional key used to turn on and off grids on viewport or drawing area.

You can also turn it on and off by click on grid icon available in status bar.

You can also manage distance between each grid from snap settings option. You can get this option by click on drop down menu available in front of grid and snap icon .

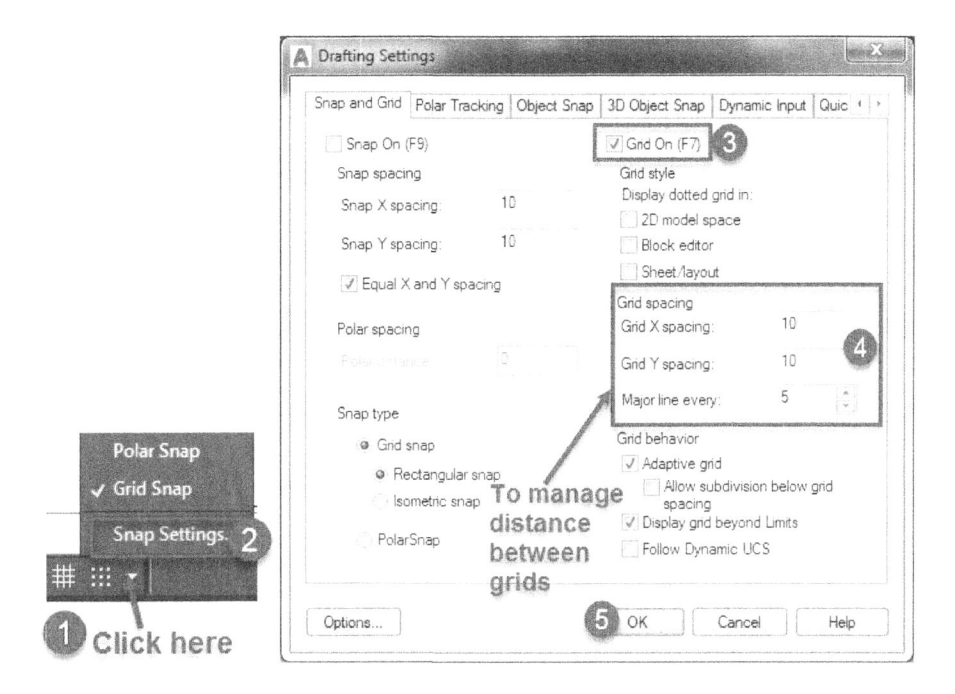

Autodesk AutoCAD 2021
Learn CAD With Ease.

Snap Mode:
You can also see **"snap on"** option in above dialog box.
F9 is a functional key used to turn on and off snap mode.
Snap mode restricts the movement of cursor on regular intervals. You can manage these intervals by specifying x and y spacing from **"snap spacing"** option available in a dialog box.
Snap mode is useful for specifying precise points with the cursor.

At bottom left corner of the dialog box you can see **"Snap Type"** option.
There are two snap types available here.
   a) Grid Snap
   b) Polar Snap

Grid snap has two options: Rectangular and Isometric.
Grid snap works along a grid system where the axes are either orthogonal (90 degrees) or isometric (combinations of 30 and 60 degrees).

46

By Madhumita Kshirsagar

Autodesk AutoCAD 2021
Learn CAD With Ease.

Isometric Snap is used to draw isometric views in a AutoCAD. The third snap type, Polar, creates snap intervals along whatever polar tracking angles you select.

i. Firstly set incremental angle in polar tracking as given in topic **"Polar Tracking"** of this chapter. Here I am setting 30 degrees as increment angle.

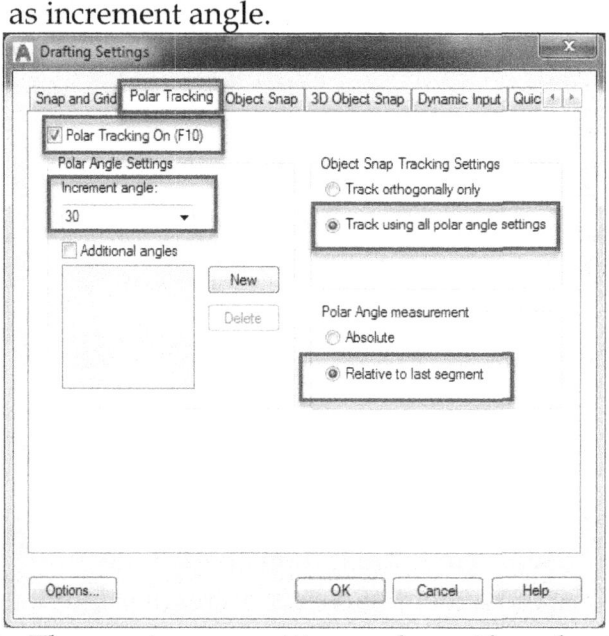

ii. Then go to snap setting and specify **polar distance** as shown in given figure and then select **Polar Snap** in **Snap Type**.

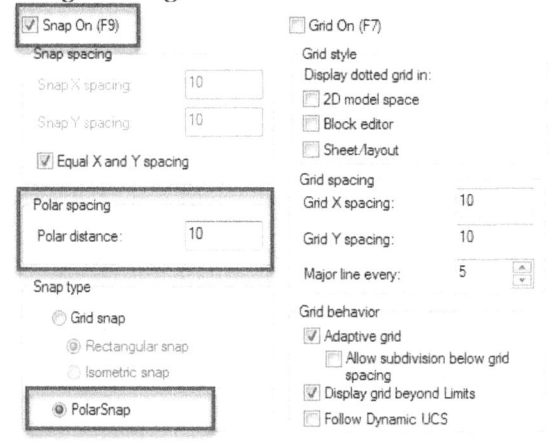

iii. Now activate line command, specify first point then move cursor you can see that your cursor restrict on 10 units in 30 degrees.

Autodesk AutoCAD 2021
Learn CAD With Ease.

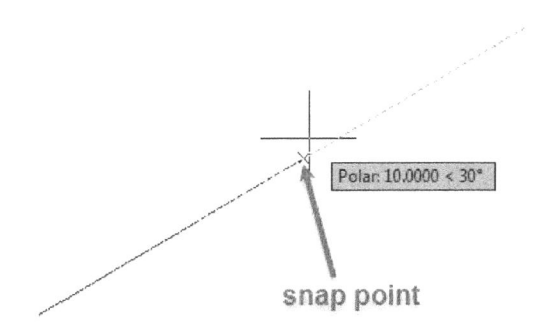

How to create Isometric View in AutoCAD?
Firstly go to snap setting and select **Isometric Snap** in the snap type, keep snap mode **off**.
Then press **Ok**.
Now you can draw isometric view.
Note: You can also turn on/ off isometric snap by clicking on "**Isodraft**" icon.
You can also change isoplane or working plane by **F5** functional key.
Draw cube with circles, for that activate line command and draw cube moving cursor to desire side then specify distance and press enter. You can change isoplane by F5 to draw other face of a cube.

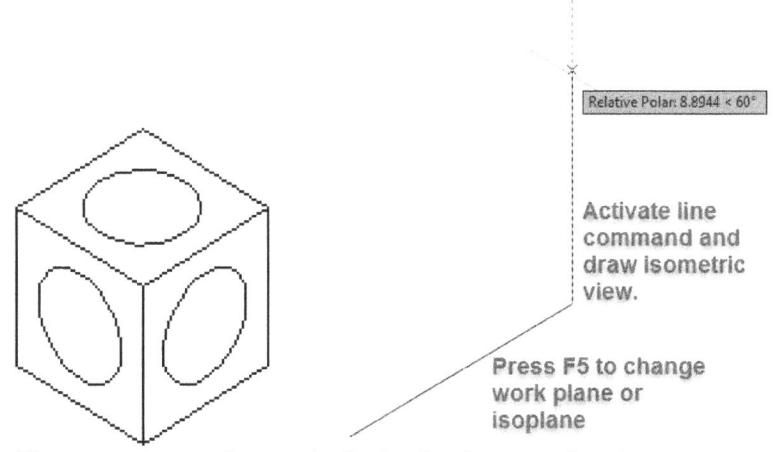

If you want to draw circle in the isometric view, you can draw it by isocircle option of ellipse.

EL ↵
Specify axis endpoint of ellipse or [Arc/Center/Isocircle]: I ↵

Autodesk AutoCAD 2021
Learn CAD With Ease.

Specify center of isocircle: by mouse click
Specify radius of isocircle or [Diameter]: 3 ↵ (Press F5 to set
Circle's orientation)

7) Selection Cycling : In complicated drawings, it is difficult to select particular object because it is either very close to or overlies another object. You can turn on **"selection cycling"** by clicking on icon available in status bar to avoid this problem.

If you turn on **selection cycling** and select an object which is overlapped to other objects, it will open a list of objects to be selected, then you can pick name of object from list which you want to select.

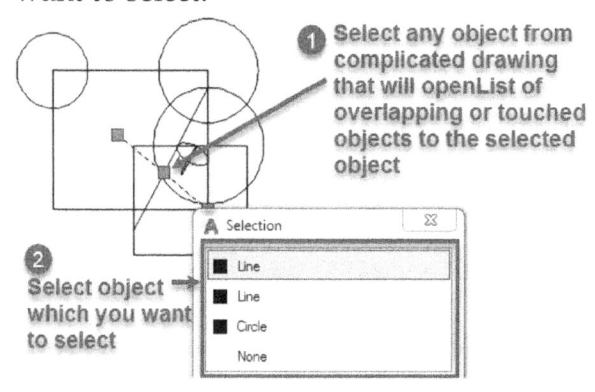

8) Quick Properties : This tool is used to get some basic properties of selected object.

This tool is turn on/off by clicking on **Quick Properties** icon available in the status bar.

"Ctrl+Shift+P" is a short cut key to turn on and off **Quick Properties mode.**

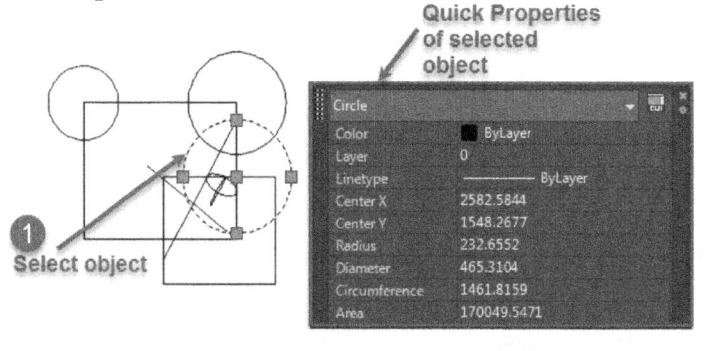

Autodesk AutoCAD 2021
Learn CAD With Ease.

Note: You can open **Quick Properties settings** by right click on Quick Properties icon and select **Quick Properties settings** option.

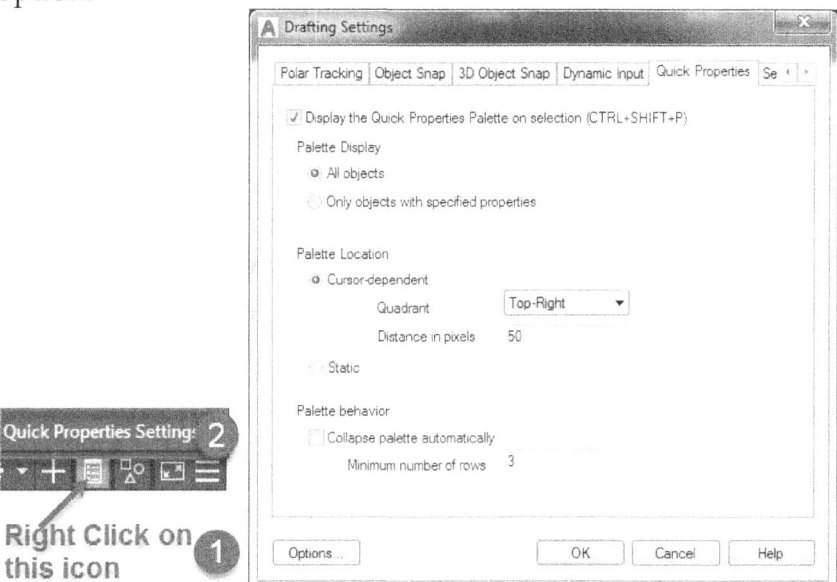

50

By Madhumita Kshirsagar

Autodesk AutoCAD 2021
Learn CAD With Ease.

CHAPTER 5
MODIFY COMMANDS

In this chapter you will get knowledge about some modify commands to do modifications in the drawings. AutoCAD drawings are rarely completed simply by drawing lines, circles etc. Most likely you will need to modify these basic drawings in some way in order to create the image you need.

AutoCAD provides a whole range of modify tools such as Move, Copy, Rotate and Mirror. With the help of these commands you are able to get best drawings without wasting time.

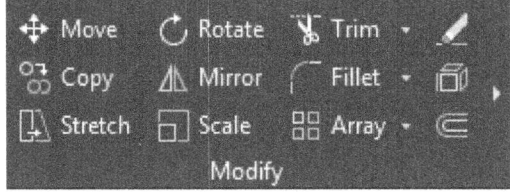

Let's start modify commands.

5.1 Command: Offset
    Alias   : O

Home tab → Modify Panel →Offset

Use: To create concentric circles, arcs, parallel lines &parallel curves.

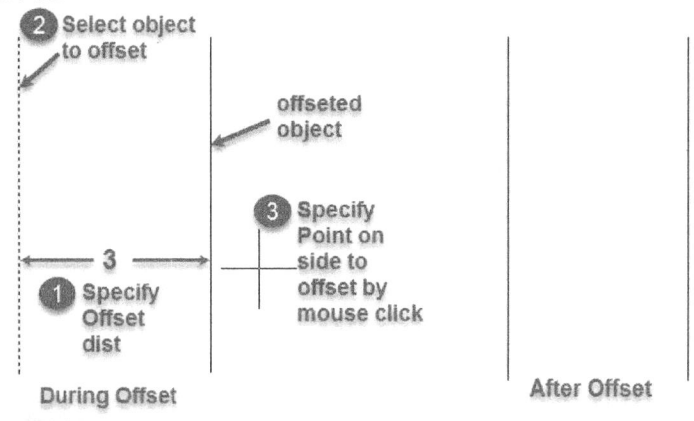

During Offset — After Offset

O ↵
Specify offset distance or [Through/ Erase/Layer] <Through>:
                                                         3 ↵

Select object to offset or [Exit/Undo] <Exit>: by mouse.
Specify point on side to offset or [Exit/ Multiple/Undo] <Exit>:
                                                        by mouse click

Select object to offset or [Exit/Undo] <Exit>: by mouse.
Specify point on side to offset or[Exit/ Multiple/Undo] <Exit>: by mouse click
Select object to offset or [Exit/Undo] <Exit>: ↵ or Esc to finish

Through: This option is used to get offset passing through a specified point.

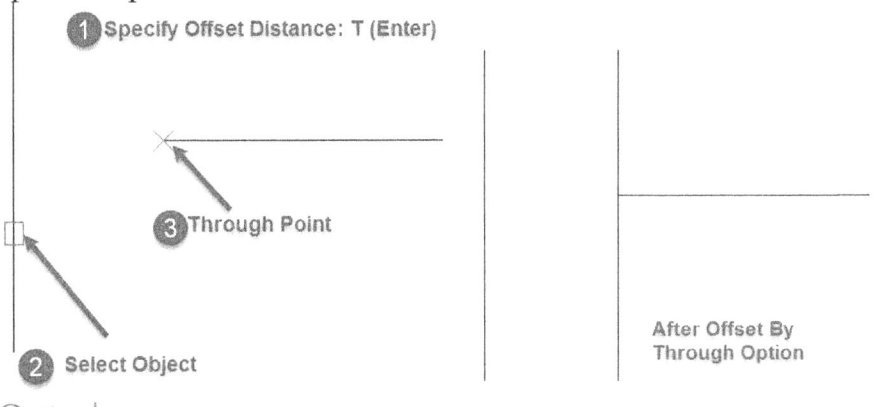

O ↵
Specify offset distance or [Through/Erase/Layer] <Through>: T ↵
Select object to offset or [Exit/Undo] <Exit>: (by any selection method)
Specify through point or [Exit/Multiple/Undo] <Exit>: by mouse click
Select object to offset or [Exit/Undo] <Exit>:(by any selection method)
Specify through point or [Exit/Multiple/Undo] <Exit>: by mouse click.

Multiple: This option is used to get multiple offsets using current offset settings.

O ↵
Specify offset distance or [Through/Erase/Layer] <Through>: T ↵
Select object to offset or [Exit/Undo] <Exit>: (by any selection method)
Specify through point or [Exit/Multiple/Undo] <Exit>: M ↵
Specify through point or [Exit/Multiple/Undo] <Exit>:

Autodesk AutoCAD 2021
Learn CAD With Ease.

                                                          by mouse click
Specify through point or [Exit/Multiple/Undo] <Exit>:
                                                          by mouse click

Erase: This option is used to erase source object after offsetting.
O ↵
Specify offset distance or [Through/Erase/Layer] <Through>:
                                                                E ↵
Erase source object after offsetting [No/Yes]: N ↵

Note: If you enter "yes", when AutoCAD asked to "Erase source object after offsetting", it will erase source object.
Rest of command is same as given in other options.

Layer: This option determines whether offset objects are created on the current layer or on the layer of the source object.

Note: You can easily understand the layer option after completing **Chapter- Layer**.

5.2 Command: Trim
    Alias   : Tr
    Home tab → Modify Panel →Trim.
Use: This command is used to cut extra edges of the drawing created by intersection of two objects.
There are two modes available in the trim command.
These are **Quik mode** and **Standard mode**.

Standard mode: This mode is a standard trimming mode as available in old versions of AutoCAD.
In this option , you have to select cutting edge first to trim objects.
To change trim mode:
Tr ↵
Current settings: Projection=UCS, Edge=None, Mode=Quick
Select object to trim or shift-select to extend or [cuTting edges/Crossing/mOde/Project/eRase]: O ↵
Enter a trim mode option [Quick/Standard] <Quick>: S ↵

Autodesk AutoCAD 2021
Learn CAD With Ease.

After typing or selecting **"Standard"** in **mOde** option as mentioned above you can continue the command.
OR
You can finish the command by pressing **"Esc"** in the keyboard then again activate trim command and follow the steps as given below.

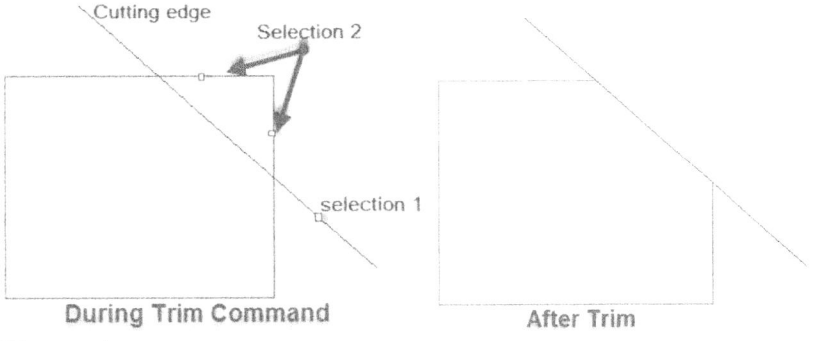

During Trim Command **After Trim**

Tr ↵

Current settings: Projection=UCS, Edge=None, mOde= Standard
Select objects or [mOde] <select all>: by mouse (cutting edge – selection 1)

Select objects: ↵
Select object to trim or shift-select to extend or [cuTting edges/ Fence/Crossing/Project/Edge/eRase/Undo]: (pick the part of the square which you want to trim - selection 2)

Fence: This is a selection method. All objects which crossed by the fence line will be selected. The Fence option is invoked by typing F at the "Select objects" prompt.

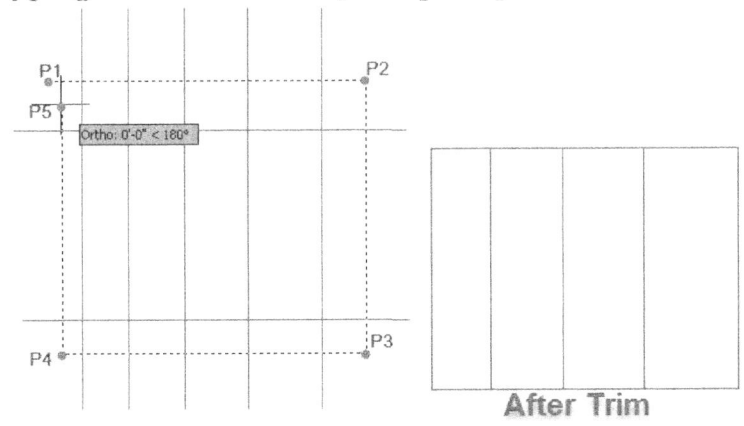

After Trim

Autodesk AutoCAD 2021
Learn CAD With Ease.

Tr ↵

Current settings: Projection=UCS, Edge=None, mOde = Standard
Select objects or [mOde] <select all>: ↵
Select object to trim or shift-select to extend or [cuTting edges/ Fence/Crossing/Project/Edge/eRase/Undo]: F ↵
Specify first fence point: mouse click
Specify next fence point or [Undo]: mouse click (P1).
Specify next fence point or [Undo]: mouse click (P2)
Specify next fence point or [Undo]: mouse click (P3)
Specify next fence point or [Undo]: mouse click (P4)
Specify next fence point or [Undo]: mouse click (P5)

Note: You can activate **select all** option by pressing ↵ in "select objects <select all>" prompt. This will select all objects situated in a drawing area.

Edge: This option is used to trim objects which do not intersect by any other object.
There are two sub options (modes) available in this option.
 i. Extend mode
 ii. No Extend mode.

Extend: By this sub option, you can trim objects which do not intersects by other objects.

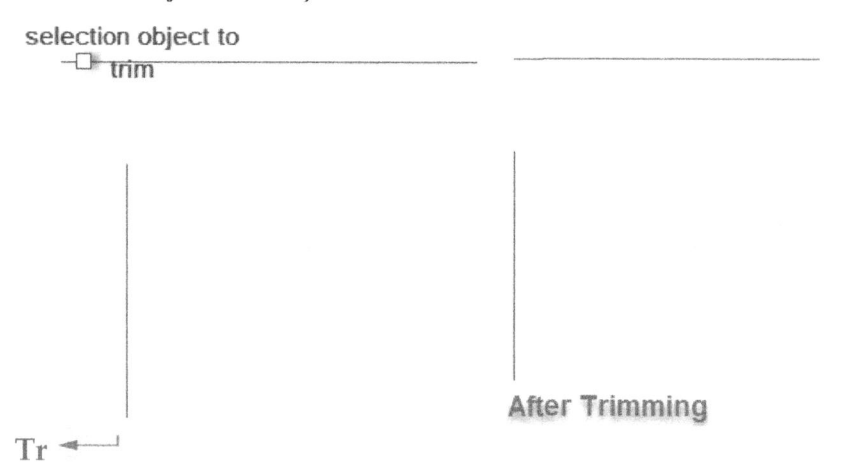

selection object to trim

After Trimming

Tr ↵

Current settings: Projection=UCS, Edge=None
Select objects or [mOde] <select all>: ↵
Select object to trim or shift-select to extend or [cuTting edges/

Fence/Crossing/Project/Edge/eRase/Undo]: E ↵
Enter an implied edge extension mode [Extend/No extend] <No extend>: E ↵
Select object to trim or shift-select to extend or [Fence/Crossing/Project/Edge/eRase/Undo]: (by any selection method)

No Extend: This option is not allowed to trim that objects which didn't intersect to any other object.

eRase: This method is used to delete unneeded objects without leaving the trim command.

Tr ↵
Current settings: Projection=UCS, Edge=None
Select objects or [mOde] <select all>: ↵
Select object to trim or shift-select to extend or [cuTting edges/Fence/Crossing/Project/Edge/eRase/Undo]: R ↵
Select objects to erase or <exit>: Use an object selection method and press ↵ to return to the previous prompt

Undo: This option is used to reverses the most recent change made by the trim command in a drawing.

Quick mode: In this mode, you don't need to select any cutting edge first, you can start trimming directly. Its make trimming very easy.

To change trim mode:

Tr ↵
Current settings: Projection=UCS, Edge=None, Mode=Standard
Select object to trim or shift-select to extend or [cuTting edges/Crossing/mOde/Project/eRase]: O ↵
Enter a trim mode option [Quick/Standard] <Quick>: Q ↵
After typing or selecting **"Quick"** in **mOde** option as mentioned above you can continue the command.
                      OR

Autodesk AutoCAD 2021
Learn CAD With Ease.

You can finish the command by pressing **"Esc"** or ↵ in the keyboard then again activate trim command and follow the steps as given below.

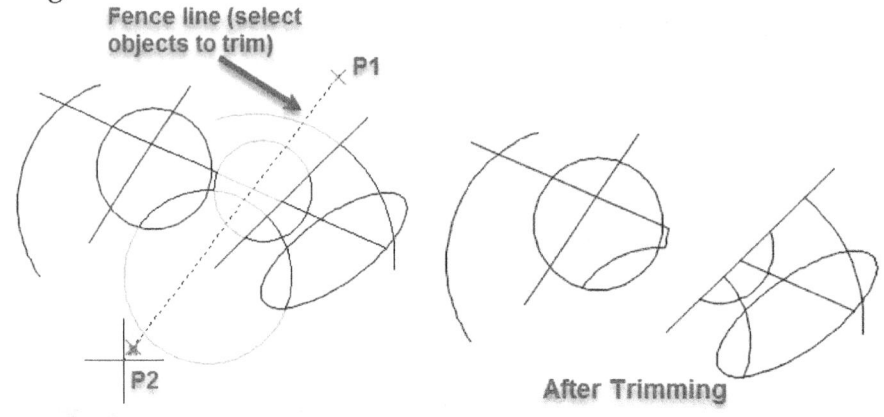

Fence line (select objects to trim)

P1

P2

After Trimming

Tr ↵

Current settings: Projection=UCS, Edge=None, Mode=Quick
Select object to trim or shift-select to extend or [cuTting edges/ Crossing/mOde/Project/eRase]: mouse click P1 in free area
Specify next fence point: mouse click P2
Press **"Esc"** or ↵ to finish command.

Note: There is no need to activate fence option here, when you start selecting object by mouse click, it will create fence line to select object.

Crossing: This option is used to select objects by crossing window selection during trim command.

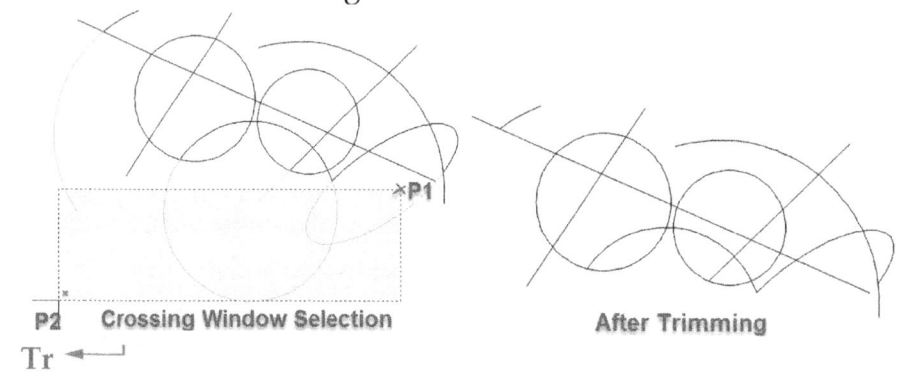

×P1

P2 **Crossing Window Selection** **After Trimming**

Tr ↵

Current settings: Projection=UCS, Edge=None, Mode=Quick
Select object to trim or shift-select to extend or [cuTting edges/ Crossing/mOde/Project/eRase]: C ↵

Specify first corner: by mouse click P1
Specify opposite corner: by mouse click P2
Press **"Esc"** or ↵ to finish command.

cuTting edges: You can use this option, if you want to trim objects in the respect of any cutting edge.

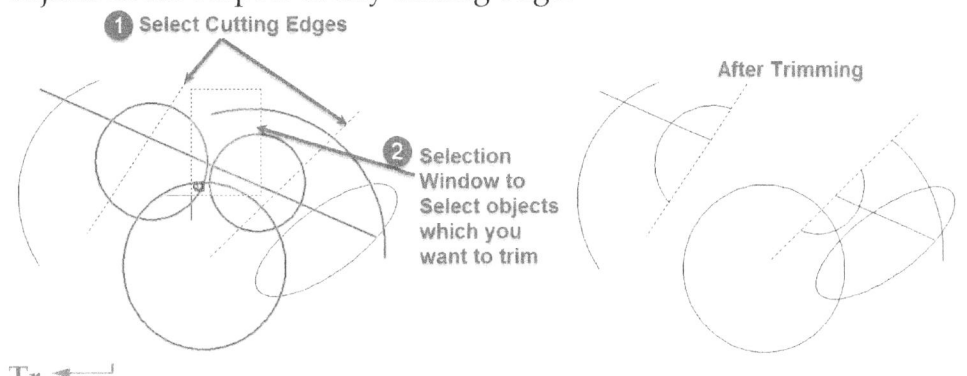

Tr ↵

Current settings: Projection=UCS, Edge=None, Mode=Quick
Select object to trim or shift-select to extend or [cuTting edges/ Crossing/mOde/Project/eRase]: T ↵
Select object to trim <select all>: select cutting edges by mouse.
Select object to trim or shift-select to extend or [cuTting edges/ Crossing/mOde/Project/eRase]: C ↵ (to invoke crossing option)
Specify first corner: by mouse click P1
Specify opposite corner: by mouse click P2
Press **"Esc"** or ↵ to finish command.

Note: You can extend object by trim command for this press shift while selecting object (select object to trim :)

5.3 Command: Extend
   Alias   : Ex
   Home tab → Modify Panel → Extend.

Use: The Extend command can be used to extend a part of an object. In order to extend an object you must draw a second object which forms the "boundary edge". Boundary edges can be lines, x lines, rays, polylines, circles, arcs or ellipses. Blocks and text cannot be trimmed or used as cutting edges.

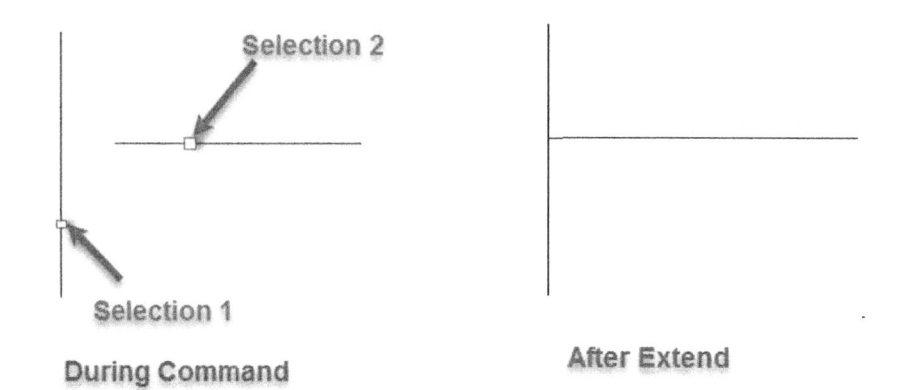

Autodesk AutoCAD 2021
Learn CAD With Ease.

Selection 2

Selection 1

During Command   **After Extend**

Boundary edge :
Ex ←┘
Current settings: Projection=UCS, Edge=None, Mode=Quick
Select object to extend or shift-select to trim or [Boundary edges/ Crossing/mOde/Project]: B ←┘
Select boundary edges ...
Select objects or <select all>: by mouse selection 1
Select objects: by mouse selection 2 (if you click in free space then, it will automatically activate "Fence Selection option")
Select objects: Press Esc or ←┘ to finish command

Note: All options are like trim command.
Note: You can trim objects by using extend command for that press "shift" while selecting object (select object to extend).

5.4 Command: Move
   Alias   : M

Home tab → Modify Panel → Move
Use: To displace object from one location to another location.

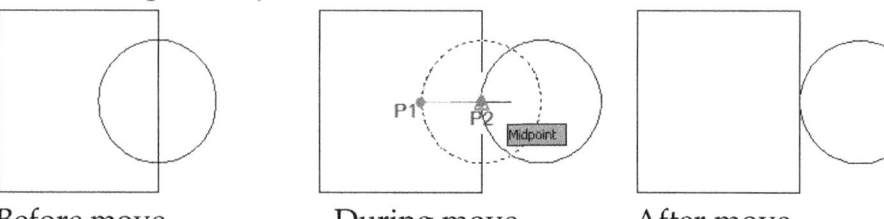

Before move   During move   After move

M ←┘
Select objects: by any selection method
Select objects: ←┘(to end selection)

Autodesk AutoCAD 2021
Learn CAD With Ease.

Specify base point or [Displacement] <Displacement>: by mouse
click P1
Specify second point or <use first point as displacement>: by
mouse click P2 or numerical entry

5.5 Command: Copy
   Alias   : Co

   Home tab→ Modify Panel →Copy

Use: The Copy command can be used to create one or more duplicates of any drawing object or objects which you have previously created. Copy is a very useful and time-saving command because you can create very complex drawing elements and then simply copy them as many times as you like.

Co ←
Current Settings: Copy mode: Multiple
Select objects: by mouse
Select objects: ← (to end selection)

Specify base point or displacement, or [Displacement/mOde]:
pick P1 or (O← for single/multiple copies)
Specify second point or [Array]: by mouse click

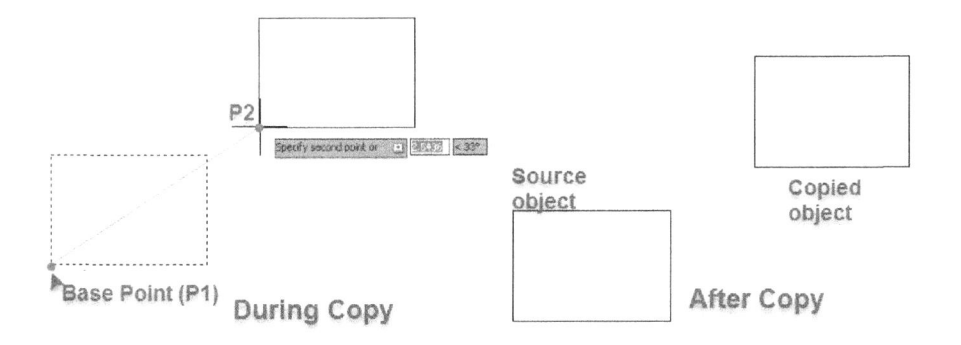

Base Point (P1)   During Copy   Source object   Copied object   After Copy

Mode:
It controls whether the command repeats automatically or not.
a) Single: It creates a single copy of selected objects and ends the command.

60

By Madhumita Kshirsagar

b) Multiple: It overrides the Single mode setting. By this mode you can create multiple copies of selected object in single selection.

Array:

This option is used to arrange a specified number of copies in a linear array.

a) Number of Items to Array

In this you can specify the number of items in the array, including the original selection set.

b) Second Point

It determines a distance and direction for the array relative to the base point. By default, the first copy in the array is positioned at the specified displacement. The remaining copies are positioned in a linear array beyond that point using the same incremental displacement.

CO ↵

Current Settings: Copy mode: Multiple
Select objects: by any selection method

Select objects: ↵ (to end selection)
Specify second point or [Array]: A ↵
Enter number of items to array: 4 ↵
Specify second point or [Fit]: 10 ↵
Specify second point or [Array/Exit/Undo] <Exit>: A ↵
Enter number of items to array or [4]: 3 ↵
Specify second point or [Fit]: 12 ↵
Specify second point or [Array/Exit/Undo] <Exit>: ↵ to finish

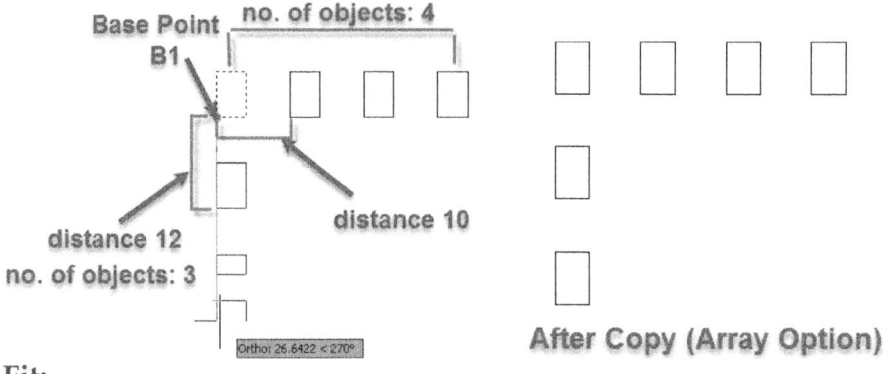

Fit:

It fits number of specified copies between first and last object's base point.

Autodesk AutoCAD 2021
Learn CAD With Ease.

In this option of copy (array), we specify distance between the base point of the source object and the base point of the last object.

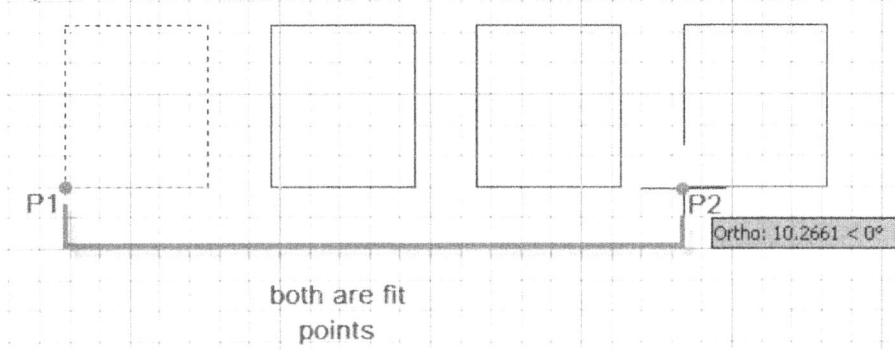

both are fit points

5.6 Command: Mirror
   Alias   : Mi

   Home tab →Modify Panel → Mirror.

 Use: To create mirrored copy of selected object.

MI ↵
Select objects: by any selection method
Select objects: ↵ (to end selection)
Specify first point of mirror line: P1 (mouse click)
Specify second point of mirror line: P2 (mouse click)
Erase source objects? [Yes/No] <N>: N ↵

② Specify first point on mirror line: by mouse click (P1)
③ Specify second point on mirror line: by mouse click (P2)

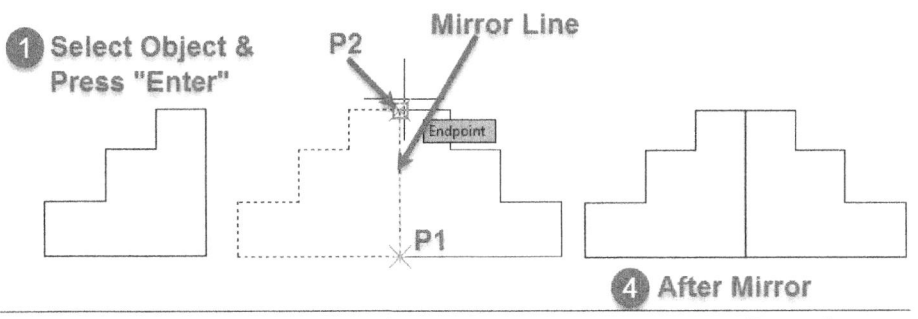

① Select Object & Press "Enter"

Mirror Line

④ After Mirror

Note: If you want to erase object after mirroring, type "Y ↵" in "Erase source objects".

62

By Madhumita Kshirsagar

Autodesk AutoCAD 2021
Learn CAD With Ease.

5.7 Command: Rotate
   Alias   : Ro

Home tab →Modify Panel →Rotate.

Use: The Rotate command allows an object or objects to be rotated about a point selected by the user. AutoCAD prompts for a second rotation point or an angle which can be typed at the keyboard.

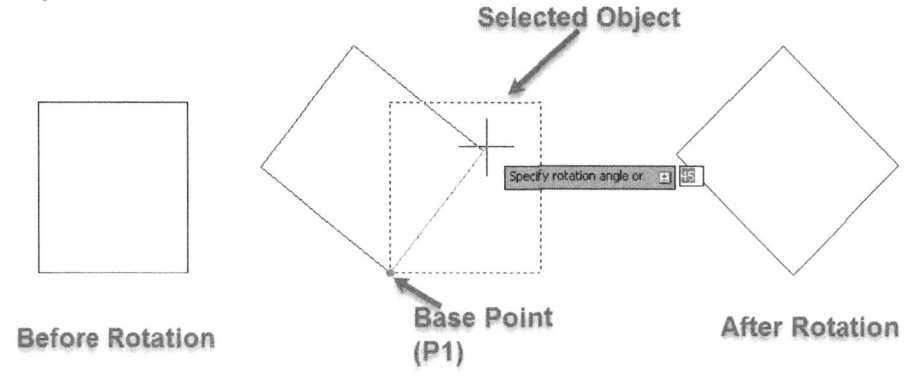

Before Rotation   **Base Point (P1)**   **After Rotation**

Selected Object

RO ↵

Current positive angle in UCS: ANGDIR=counter clockwise ANGBASE=0
Select objects: by any selection method
Select objects: ↵ (to end selection)
Specify base point: P1 (mouse click)
Specify rotation angle or [Copy/Reference] <30>: 45 ↵

Note: Remember, by default, AutoCAD angles start at 3 o'clock or East and increase in an anti-clockwise direction. The "ANGDIR" and "ANGBASE" variables remind you of this. If you want to rotate objects in a clockwise direction you can enter a negative angle by using a minus sign.

Copy: This option is used to create rotated copy of the selected object.

RO ↵

Current positive angle in UCS: ANGDIR=counter clockwise ANGBASE=0
Select objects: by any selection method
Select objects: ↵ (to end selection)

Specify base point: P1 (mouse click)
Specify rotation angle or [Copy/Reference] <30>: C ↵
Specify rotation angle or [Copy/Reference] <30>:45 ↵

① Select Object & press "Enter"
② Specify base point (P1) by mouse click.
③ Type "C" & press "Enter"
④ Specify rotation angle: 45 & press "Enter"

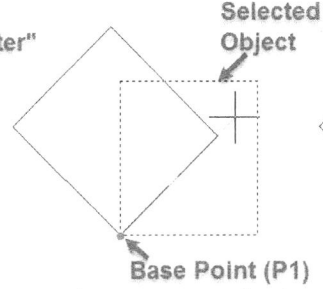

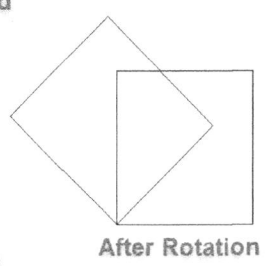

Selected Object
Base Point (P1)
After Rotation

Reference: Rotates objects from a specified angle to a new, absolute angle.
If you don't have rotation angle, rotate object by giving reference angle. For this option, type R ↵ instead of giving rotation angle.

① Select object to rotate & press "Enter"
② Specify base point (P1) by mouse click
③ Type "R" and press "Enter"
④ Specify reference angle by picking point "R1" and "R2" by mouse.
⑤ Specify new angle by click on "N1"

Base Point (P1)
After Rotation

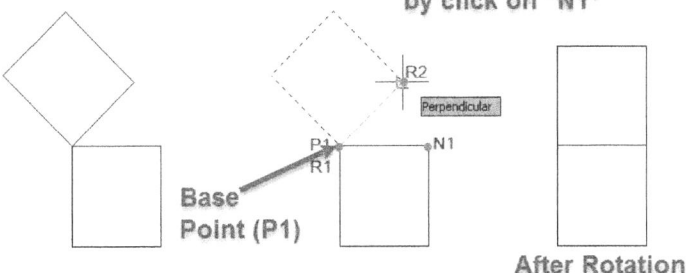

RO ↵
Current positive angle in UCS: ANGDIR=counterclockwise ANGBASE=0
Select objects: by any selection method
Select objects: ↵ (to end selection)
Specify base point: P1 (mouse click)
Specify rotation angle or [Copy/Reference] <30>: R ↵
Specify reference angle: R1 (mouse click) or angle.
Specify second point : R2 (mouse click)
Specify new angle (Points): N1 (mouse click) or angle.

Points: This option is used when two objects are situated at some distance from each other and you want to rotate any one object in the reference of another object.

In this option you can specify new angle by clicking on two points.

RO ↵

Current positive angle in UCS: ANGDIR=counterclockwise ANGBASE=0

Select objects: by any selection method
Select objects: ↵ (to end selection)
Specify base point: P1 (mouse click)
Specify rotation angle or [Copy/Reference] <30>: R ↵
Specify reference angle: R1 (mouse click) or angle.
Specify second point : R2 (mouse click)
Specify new angle (Points): P ↵
Specify first point: N1 (mouse click)
Specify next point: N2 (mouse click)

1. Select object & press "Enter"
2. Specify base point (P1)
3. Specify reference angle by picking point "R1" and "R2" by mouse.
4. Specify new angle by picking point "N1" and "N2" by mouse.

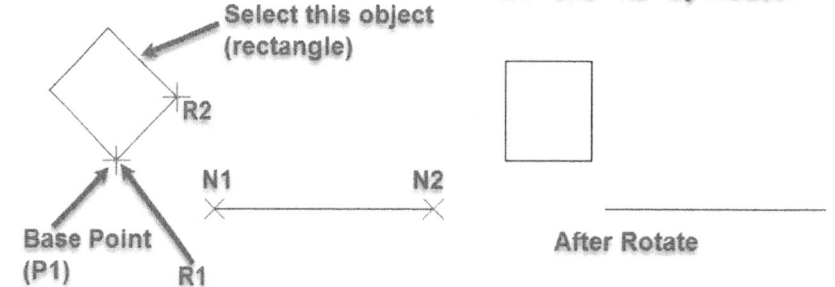

5.8 Command: Stretch
   Alias   : S

Home tab → Modify Panel → Stretch.

Use: To increase or decrease size of object lengthwise or widthwise by stretching.

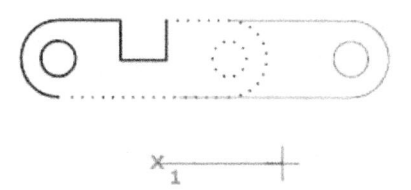

Autodesk AutoCAD 2021
Learn CAD With Ease.

S ←⏎

Select objects to stretch by crossing-window or crossing-polygon...
Select objects: by implied window selection
Select objects: ⏎(to end selection)
Specify base point or [Displacement]: mouse click (1)
Specify second point or <use first point as displacement>: 3 ⏎

5.9 Command: Scale
    Alias   : Sc

  Home tab → Modify Panel → Scale

Use: To enlarge or reduce size of selected object.

Sc ←⏎
Select objects: by any selection method (objects to be scaled)
Select objects: ⏎(to end selection)
Specify base point: by mouse click (P1)
Specify scale factor or [Copy/Reference]: (pick second point P2
                                    or enter scale factor 2 ⏎)

Source Object   Base Point   **P1**   **During Scale**   **After Scale**

Ortho: 1.8542 < 0°

Note: Scale factor less than 1, reduces the size of the selected object and scale factor more than 1, enlarges the size of the selected object.

Copy: This option is used to create scaled copy of the selected object.
Sc ←⏎
Select objects: (pick objects by any selection method)
Select objects: ⏎(to end selection)

66

By Madhumita Kshirsagar

Autodesk AutoCAD 2021
Learn CAD With Ease.

Specify base point: by mouse (P1)
Specify scale factor or [Copy/Reference]: C ↵
Specify scale factor or [Copy/Reference]: 2 ↵

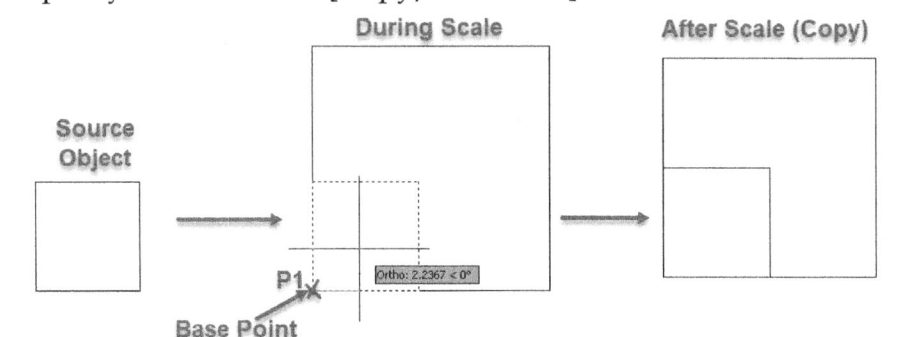

Reference: This option is used for scale object in the reference of other object.

Sc ↵
Select objects: (pick objects by any selection method)
Select objects: ↵ (to end selection)
Specify base point: by mouse (BP)
Specify scale factor or [Copy/Reference]: R ↵
Specify reference length: (pick point by mouse, R1)
Specify second point: (pick point by mouse, R2)
Specify new length (Points): (pick point by mouse, NL)

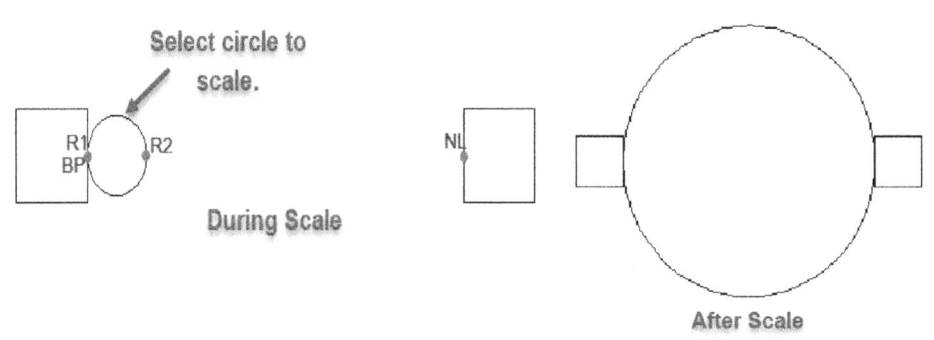

Points: This option is used when two objects are situated at some distance from each other and you want to scale any one object in the reference of another object. **For example:** Let's scale the square in the reference of the line.

Sc ↵
Select objects: (pick objects by any selection method)

Autodesk AutoCAD 2021
Learn CAD With Ease.

Select objects: ↵(to end selection)
Specify base point: by mouse (BP)
Specify scale factor or [Copy/Reference]: R ↵
Specify reference length <1.0000>: (pick point by mouse, R1)
Specify second point: (pick point by mouse, R2)
Specify new length or [Points] <1.0000>: P ↵
Specify first point: (pick point by mouse, N1)
Specify second point: (pick point by mouse, N2)

① Select object by mouse and press "Enter"
② Specify base point by mouse (BP)
③ Type "R" and press "Enter"
④ Specify reference point R1 and R2 by mouse click
⑤ Then type "P" and press "Enter" to activate Points option.
⑥ Specify new length by mouse click on N1 and N2.

Before scale | During Scale

5.10 Command: Break
Alias : Br

Home tab → Modify Panel → Break.

Use: To break selected object in between two points.

selection 1   P2
During Command   After break

BR ↵

Select object: by any selection method (selection 1)
Specify second break point or [First point]: by mouse click or enter value.

First point: Overrides the original first point with the new point that you specify.

selection
P1   P2
During Command   After Break

68

By Madhumita Kshirsagar

Autodesk AutoCAD 2021
Learn CAD With Ease.

BR ←

Select object: by any selection method (selection)
Specify second break point or [First point]: f ←
Specify first break point: mouse click (P1)
Specify second break point: mouse click (P2)

5.11 Command: Join
    Alias   : J
    Home tab → Modify Panel → Join.

Use: This command is used to join similar objects to form a single object like series of collinear lines, open curves, etc.

During command   After Join

J ←

Select source object or multiple objects to join at once: select first line and press ←.
Select objects to join: select second line.
Select objects to join: ←

5.12 Command: Array
    Alias   : Ar
    Home Tab → Modify Panel → Array

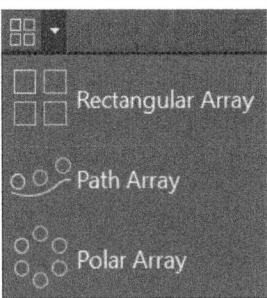

Use: This command is used to create copies of objects in rectangular & polar (circular) arrangement. You can also arrange these copies on a specify path.
Note: You can activate this command by typing "Ar" and then press "Enter" Or by directly click on array drop down menu then select "Rectangular Array, Path Array, and Polar Array".

5.12.1 Rectangular Array: This array is used to arrange copies of selected object in a rows and columns.

Ar ←

Select objects: by any object selection method
Enter array type [Rectangular /PAth /POlar]<Rectangular>: Enter an option and press Enter

Rectangular: Distributes copies of the selected object into any combination of rows, columns, and levels.

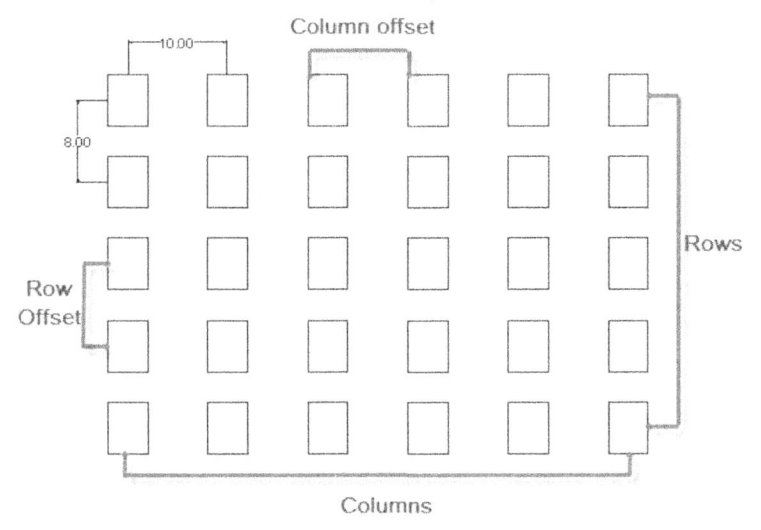

Ar ←

Select objects: by any object selection method
Enter array type [Rectangular /PAth /POlar]<Rectangular>: *R* ←

Type = Rectangular Associative = Yes
Select grip to edit array or [ASsociative/Base point/COUnt/Spacing/COLumns/Rows/Levels/eXit]<eXit>: COL ←
Enter the number of columns or [Expression] <1>: *6* ←
Specify the distance between columns or [Total/Expression] <1.0000>: *10* ←
Select grip to edit array or [ASsociative/Base point/COUnt/Spacing/COLumns/Rows/Levels/eXit] <eXit>: *R* ←
Enter the number of rows or [Expression] <1>: *5* ←
Specify the distance between rows or [Total/Expression] <7.5000>: *8* ←
Specify the incrementing elevation between rows or [Expresson] <0.0000>: ←

Count: In this option you can specify number of rows & columns both.

Array Associativity:

Associative: Arrays are treated as a single array object, which is helpful when you want to modify spacing, angles, or replace or modify the source object.

Autodesk AutoCAD 2021
Learn CAD With Ease.

Non Associative: If an array is non-associative, each copied item is treated as a separate object. Editing one item does not affect the other items.

Spacing: In this option you specify distance between rows, distance between columns.

Note: You can also specify above option like "Rows, Columns, Between, and Associative" by "Array Creation" panel. You can see this panel after activating "type of Array" like "Rectangular, Polar and Path array".

Ar ←

Select objects: by any object selection method
Enter array type [Rectangular /PAth /POlar]<Rectangular>: R ←

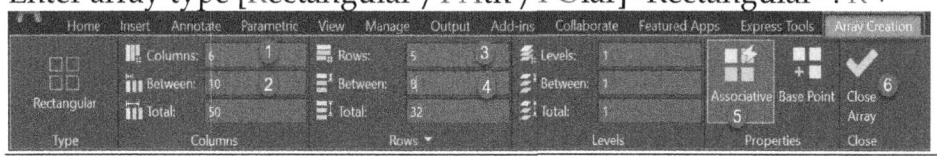

5.12.2 Polar Array: Creates an array by copying the selected objects around a specified center point or axis of rotation.

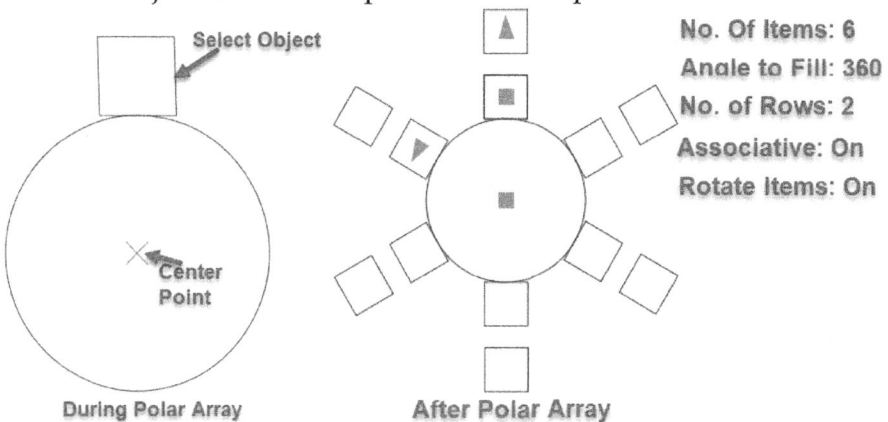

No. Of Items: 6
Angle to Fill: 360
No. of Rows: 2
Associative: On
Rotate Items: On

During Polar Array   After Polar Array

AR ←
Select objects: by using any selection method.
Select objects: ←
Enter array type [Rectangular/PAth/POlar] <Rectangular>:
                                                    PO ←

Autodesk AutoCAD 2021
Learn CAD With Ease.

① Select "Polar Array" by "Array pull-down menu".
② Select object and press "Enter"
③ Specify Center point for Polar Array.

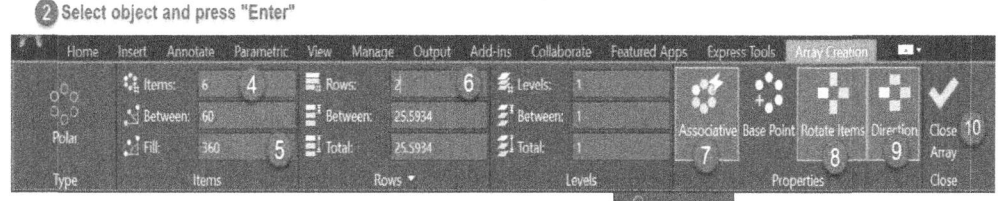

Note: You can directly select "Polar Array" ![Polar Array] from Array pull-down ![icon] available in "Modify Panel".

Note 2: You can also activate polar array by command line, let's take a look:

AR ↵

Select objects: by using any selection method.
Select objects: ↵
Enter array type [Rectangular/PAth/POlar] <Rectangular>: PO ↵
Type = Polar Associative = No
Specify center point of array or [Base point/Axis of rotation]:
                                                by mouse click
Select grip to edit array or [ASsociative/Base point/Items/ Angle between/Fill angle/ROWs/Levels/ROTate items/eXit] <eXit>: I ↵
Enter number of items in array or [Expression] <6>: 6 ↵
Select grip to edit array or [ASsociative/Base point/Items/ Angle between/Fill angle/ROWs/Levels/ROTate items/ eXit]<eXit>: AS ↵
Create associative array [Yes/No] <Yes>: ↵
Enter number of items in array or [Expression] <6>: 6 ↵
Select grip to edit array or [ASsociative/Base point/Items/ Angle between/Fill angle/ROWs/Levels/ROTate items/eXit]<eXit>: ↵

Center Point: Specifies the point around which to distribute the array items. The axis of rotation is the Z axis of the current UCS.
Base Point: Specifies a base point for the array.

Key Point: For associative arrays, specifies a valid constraint (or *key point*) on the source objects to use as the base point.

By Madhumita Kshirsagar

If you edit the source objects of the resulting array, the base point of the array remains coincident with the key point of the source objects.

Axis of Rotation: Specifies a custom axis of rotation defined by two specified points.

Associative: Specifies whether the arrayed objects are associative or independent.
- **Yes:** Contains array items in a single *array object*, similar to a block. With an associative array, you can quickly propagate changes throughout the array by editing the properties and source objects.
- **No:** Creates array items as independent objects. Changes to one item do not affect the other items.

Items: Specifies the number of items in the array using a value or expression.

Note: When defining the fill angle in an expression, the (+ or -) mathematical symbol in the resultant value does not affect the direction of the array.

Angle Between: Specifies the angle between items using a value or expression.

Fill Angle: Specifies the angle between the first and last item in the array using a value or expression.

Rotate Items: Controls whether items are rotated as they are arrayed.

Exit: Exits the command.

5.12.3 Path Array Path Array : This array is used to arrange copies of selected object on a selected path.

During Path Array   After Path Array

Autodesk AutoCAD 2021
Learn CAD With Ease.

After selecting objects to array and a path curve for the objects to follow, you can see the "Create Array visor" or "Array Creation" panel. You can also use the Properties Inspector to set the properties of the new array while it is being created.

Ar ←┘
Select objects: by any selection method (selection 1)
Enter array type [Rectangular /PAth /POlar]<Rectangular>:
PA ←┘
Select path curve: Use an object selection method (selection 2)
Select grip to edit array or [ASsociative /Method/Base point /Tangent direction/Items /Rows /Levels / Align items /Z direction /eXit <eXit>: Select a grip or an option

Path Curve: Specifies the object to use for the path of the array. Select a line, polyline, 3D polyline, spline, helix, arc, circle, or ellipse.

Associative: Specifies whether the arrayed objects are associative or independent.
- **Yes:** Contains array items in a single *array object*, similar to a block. With an associative array, you can quickly propagate changes throughout the array by editing the properties and source objects.
- **No:** Creates array items as independent objects. Changes to one item do not affect the other items.

Method: Controls how to distribute items along the path.
- **Divide:** Distributes a specified number of items evenly along the length of the path.
- **Measure:** Distributes items along the path at specified intervals.

Base Point: Defines the base point of the array. Items in path arrays are positioned relative to the base point.

Key Point: For associative arrays, specifies a valid constraint (or *key point*) on the source objects to align with the path. If you edit the source objects or path of the resulting array, the base point of the array remains coincident with the key point of the source objects.

Tangent Direction: Specifies how the arrayed items are aligned relative to the path.
- **2 Points:** Specifies two points that represent the tangency of the arrayed items relative to the path. The vector of the two points establishes the tangency of the first item in the array. The Align Items setting controls whether the other items in the array maintain a tangent or parallel orientation.
- **Normal:** Orients the arrayed objects with the Z axis of the current UCS.

Items: Depending on the Method setting, specifies the number of items or the distance between items.

- **Number of Items along Path (Available when Method equals Divide is selected):** Using a value or expression, specifies how many items are in the array.
- **Distance between Items along Path (Available when Method equals Measure is selected):** Using a value or expression, specifies the distance between arrayed items. By default, the array is populated with the maximum number of items that fill the path using the distance entered. You can specify a smaller number of items if desired. You can also turn on Fill Entire Path so that the number of items is adjusted if the length of the path changes.

Rows: Specifies the number of rows in the array, the distance between them, and the incremental elevation between rows.
- **Number of Rows:** Sets the number of rows.

- **Distance between Rows:** Specifies the distance between each row, measured from equivalent locations on each object.
- **Total:** Specifies the total distance between the start and end row, measured from equivalent locations on the start and end objects.
- **Incrementing elevation:** Sets the increasing or decreasing elevation for each subsequent row.
- **Expression:** Derives the value based on a mathematical formula or equation.

Levels: Specifies the number and spacing of levels for 3D arrays.
- **Number of Levels:** Specifies the number of levels in the array.
- **Distance between Levels:** Specifies the distance between the levels.
- **Total:** Specifies the total distance between the first and last levels.
- **Expression:** Derives a value using a mathematical formula or equation.

Align Items: Specifies whether to align each item to be tangent to the path direction.
Alignment is relative to the first item's orientation.

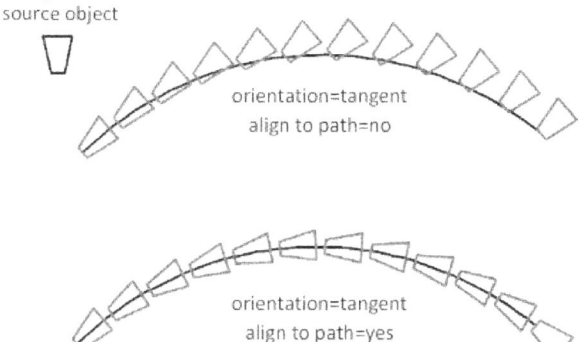

Z Direction: Controls whether to maintain the items' original Z direction or to naturally bank the items along a 3D path.

Exit: Exits the command.

Autodesk AutoCAD 2021
Learn CAD With Ease.

Note: You can also specify these options by "Array Creation" Panel or "Create Array Visor" which appears during array command.

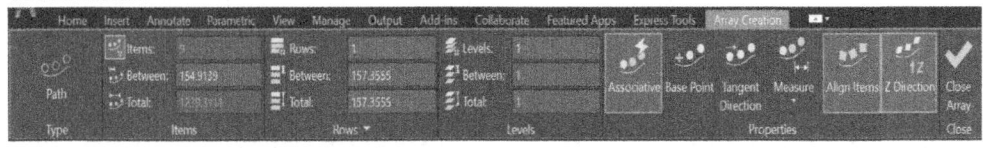

Autodesk AutoCAD 2021
Learn CAD With Ease.

CHAPTER 6
UTILITIES & PROPERTIES

In this chapter you can learn about some utilities commands & some commands related to properties panel. By these commands you will able to measure distance; get ID points, history of drawing file & properties of selected object & many more things.

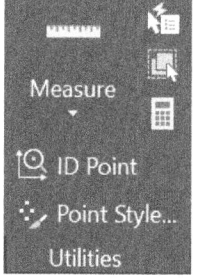

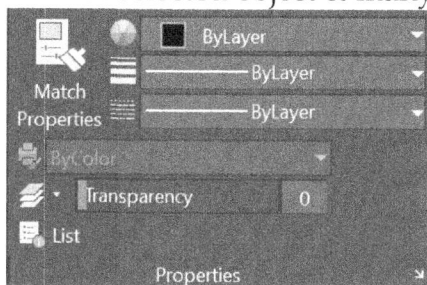

A) Utilities Panel:

6.1 Measure: This group of commands is used to do measurements of different types of objects like line, circle, arc etc.

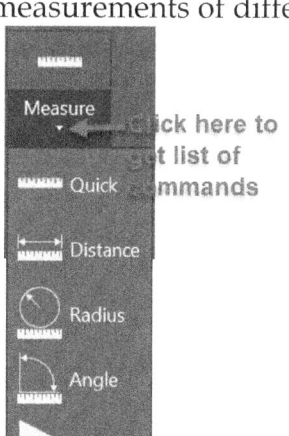

6.1.1 Command: Quick (Measure Geom.)
  Alias   : MEA
Home→Utilities→Measure→Quick
Use: It displays the measurement of the geometry near the cursor when you move the cursor near the object in a 2D plan.

2.5624

During Command

MEA ←┘
Move cursor or [Distance/Radius/Angle/ARea/Volume Mode/eXit] <eXit>: Q ←┘
Move cursor or [Distance/Radius/Angle/ARea/Volume/ Quick/Mode/eXit] <eXit>: move cursor near or on object to get measurement and press Esc/Enter to finish command.

Autodesk AutoCAD 2021
Learn CAD With Ease.

6.1.2 Command: Distance
   Alias   : DI

Home tab →Utilities Panel →Measure →Distance.
Use: To measure distance between two points.

Di ←
Specify first point: by mouse click (P1)
Specify second point or [Multiple points]: mouse click (P2)
Distance = 10.0000, Angle in XY Plane = 0, Angle from XY Plan=0
Delta X = 10.0000, Delta Y = 0.0000, Delta Z = 0.0000

Multiple: If you specify multiple points, a running total of the distance based on the existing line segments and the current rubber band line is displayed in the tooltip. A dynamic dimension is also displayed. The distance is updated as you move the cursor.

6.1.3 Command: Radius (MeasureGeom)
   Alias   : MEA

Home tab → Utilities Panel→ Measure→Radius.

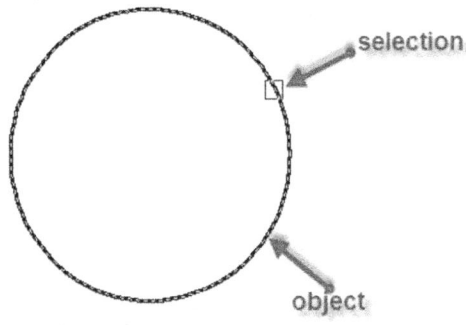

Use: To measure radius of arcs & circles.

Mea ←
Move cursor or [Distance/Radius/Angle/ARea/Volume] <Distance>: R ←
Select arc or circle: by mouse click
Radius = 5.0000
Diameter = 10.0000

6.1.4 Command: Angle (MeasureGeom)
    Alias   : **MEA**

    Home tab → Utilities Panel → Measure → Angle.

Use: To measure angle between two lines.

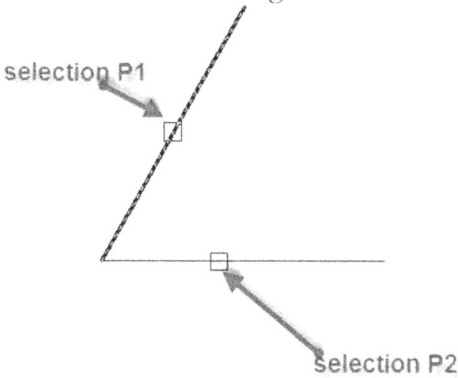

MEA ↵
Move cursor or [Distance/Radius/Angle/ARea/Volume] <Distance>: A ↵
Select arc, circle, line, or <Specify vertex>: select it by mouse click (P1)
Select second line: select it by mouse click (P2)
Angle = 60°

6.1.5 Command: Area (MeasureGeom)
    Alias   : **MEA / AA**

    Home tab → Utilities Panel → Measure → Area.

Use: To measure area of the geometry.

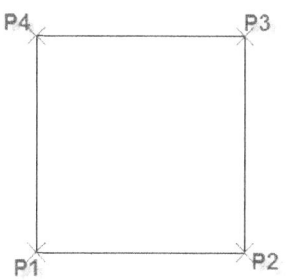

AA ↵
Specify first corner point or [Object/Add area/Subtract area] <Object>: mouse click (P1)
Specify next point or [Arc/Length/Undo]: mouse click (P2)

Autodesk AutoCAD 2021
Learn CAD With Ease.

Specify next point or [Arc/Length/Undo]: mouse click (P3)
Specify next point or [Arc/Length/Undo/Total] <Total>: mouse click (P4)
Specify next point or [Arc/Length/Undo/Total] <Total>: ↵ to end command
Area = 100.0000, Perimeter = 40.0000

Add area: By using this option you can calculate areas & perimeters of individual objects & also calculate their total areas & perimeters.

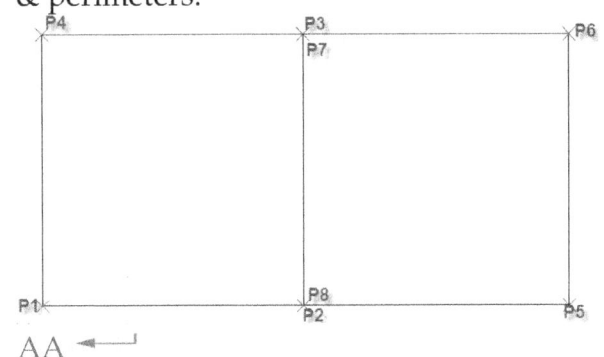

AA ↵

Specify first corner point or [Object/Add area/Subtract area] <Object>: A ↵
Specify first corner point or [Object/Subtract area]: mouse click (P1)
(ADD mode)Specify next point or [Arc/Length/Undo]: mouse click (P2)
(ADD mode)Specify next point or [Arc/Length/Undo]: mouse click (P3)
(ADD mode)Specify next point or [Arc/Length/Undo/Total] <Total>: mouse click (P4)
(ADD mode)Specify next point or [Arc/Length/Undo/Total] <Total>: ↵
Area = 100.0000, Perimeter = 40.0000
Total area = 100.0000
Specify first corner point or [Object/Subtract area]: mouse click (P5)
(ADD mode)Specify next point or [Arc/Length/Undo]: mouse click (P6)
(ADD mode)Specify next point or [Arc/Length/Undo]: mouse click (P7)
(ADD mode)Specify next point or [Arc/Length/Undo/Total] <Total>: mouse click (P8)

Autodesk AutoCAD 2021
Learn CAD With Ease.

(ADD mode)Specify next point or [Arc/Length/Undo/Total] <Total>: ↵
Area = 100.0000, Perimeter = 40.0000
Total area = 200.0000

Subtract area: Similar to the Add Area option, but subtracts areas and perimeters. You can use the Subtract Area option to subtract a specified area from a total area.

You can also specify the area to be subtracted with points. A rubber band line from the first specified point to the cursor is displayed

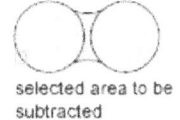

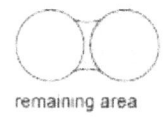

selected area to be subtracted

remaining area

Object: This option is use to calculate the areas of object draw by polylines, or region objects, circles, ellipse, splines by select them.

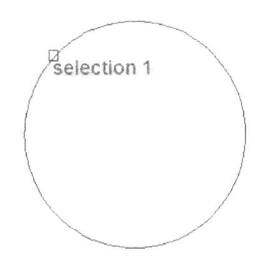

selection 1

AA ↵
Specify first corner point or [Object/Add area/Subtract area] <Object>: O ↵
Select objects: use any selection method
(selection 1)
Area = 46.2087, Circumference = 24.0972

Note: Arc, Length and undo options are used for picking points on different shapes during area command.

6.2 Command: ID Point
Alias   : ID
Home tab → Utilities Panel → ID Point ID Point

Use: To get the UCS co-ordinate values of a specified point.

ID ↵
Specify point: by mouse click

6.3 Command: Point
Alias   : PO
Home tab → Draw Panel → Point

Use: To mark points in a drawing.

Autodesk AutoCAD 2021
Learn CAD With Ease.

PO ←┘

Specify a point: by mouse click

Note: After picking point during "point" command, select point style by "point style" command to see points in a drawing area.

6.4 Command: Point Style
    Alias   : PTYPE

    Home tab → Utilities Panel → Point [Point Style..]

Use: To set point style & size of point.

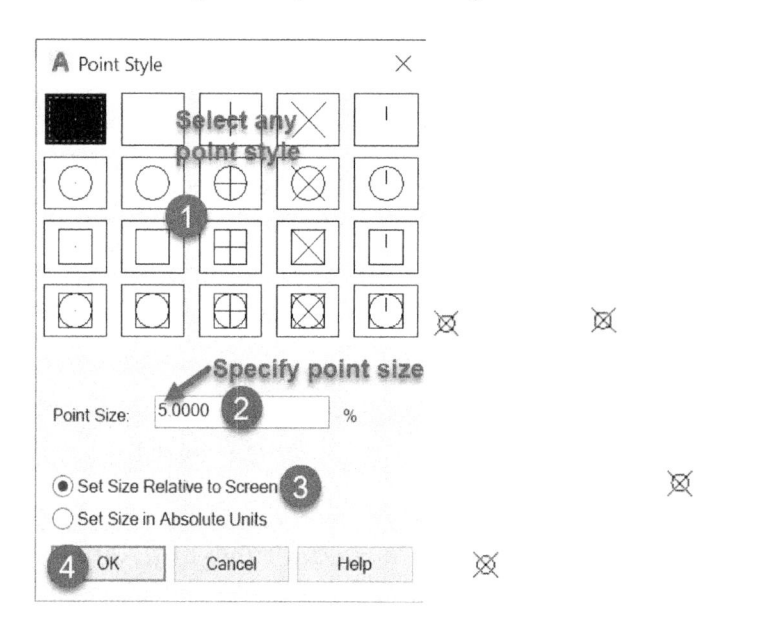

Note: Select point from point style and then activate point command and pick points in a drawing area.

B) Properties Panel:

There are properties related commands available in this panel like color, line type, line weight, list and match properties.

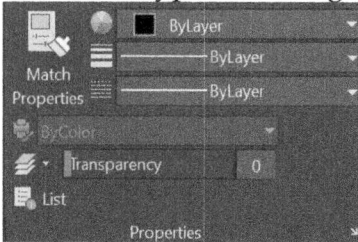

Autodesk AutoCAD 2021
Learn CAD With Ease.

6.5 Command: Color
Alias : Col
Home tab → Properties Panel → Col ByLayer.

Use: Select color to draw colored object or to make previously drawn object colorful.

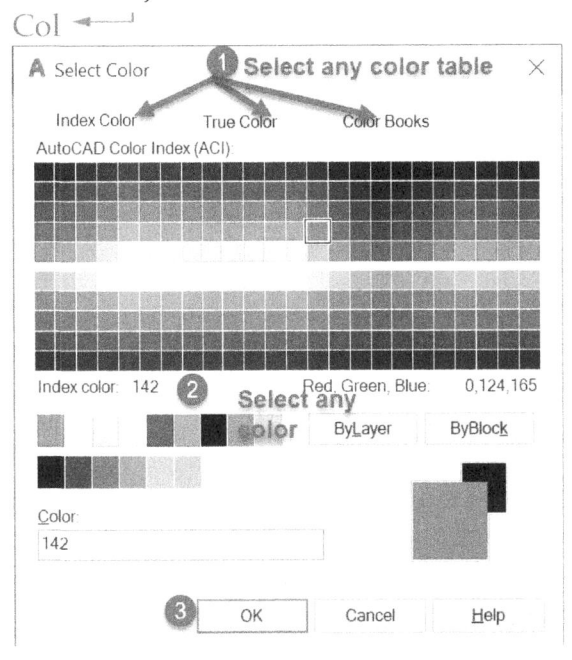

Col ←┘

Follow the steps as given in in a left side given dialog box. After that draw any diagram now your diagram is of selected color.

To assign color in previously drawn object:
For that, select object and then click on ByLayer color pull-down (by layer), it will open color palette.

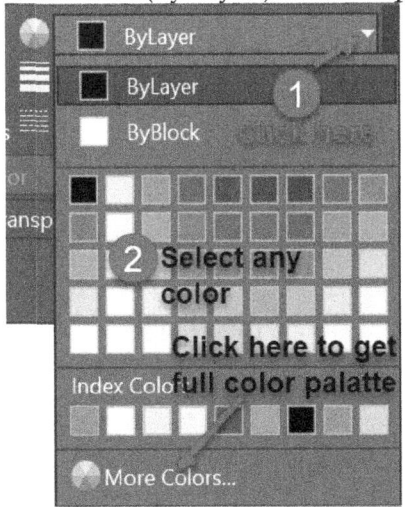

Select any color from palette and press OK.

84

By Madhumita Kshirsagar

Autodesk AutoCAD 2021
Learn CAD With Ease.

6.6 Command: List
   Alias   : Li

   Home tab→ Properties Panel →List List.

Use: To get properties data of selected object. You also get history of selected object.

Li ←

Select objects: by any selection method
Select objects: ← to end command.

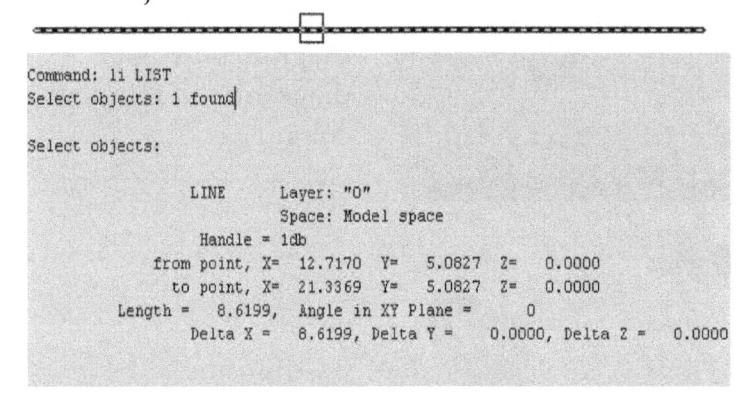

```
Command: li LIST
Select objects: 1 found

Select objects:
                LINE      Layer: "0"
                          Space: Model space
                   Handle = 1db
          from point, X=  12.7170  Y=  5.0827  Z=  0.0000
            to point, X=  21.3369  Y=  5.0827  Z=  0.0000
         Length =   8.6199,  Angle in XY Plane =   0
                 Delta X =  8.6199, Delta Y =  0.0000, Delta Z =  0.0000
```

6.7 Command: Line Type
   Alias   : Lt

   Home Tab→ Properties Panel →Line Type ———ByLayer———

Use: This command is used to select different types of lines like hidden line, center line etc to use them in drawings.

Procedure:
1. Type "Lt" and press "Enter" to invoke line type command. Now it's open "Line Type Manager" dialog box.
2. Click on "Load", its open "Load line type" dialog box.
3. Select line types from list and then click on "OK".
4. Select any line type from loaded line type in the line type manager dialog box.
5. Click on "current" to make selected line type current.
6. Then click on "OK".

Autodesk AutoCAD 2021
Learn CAD With Ease.

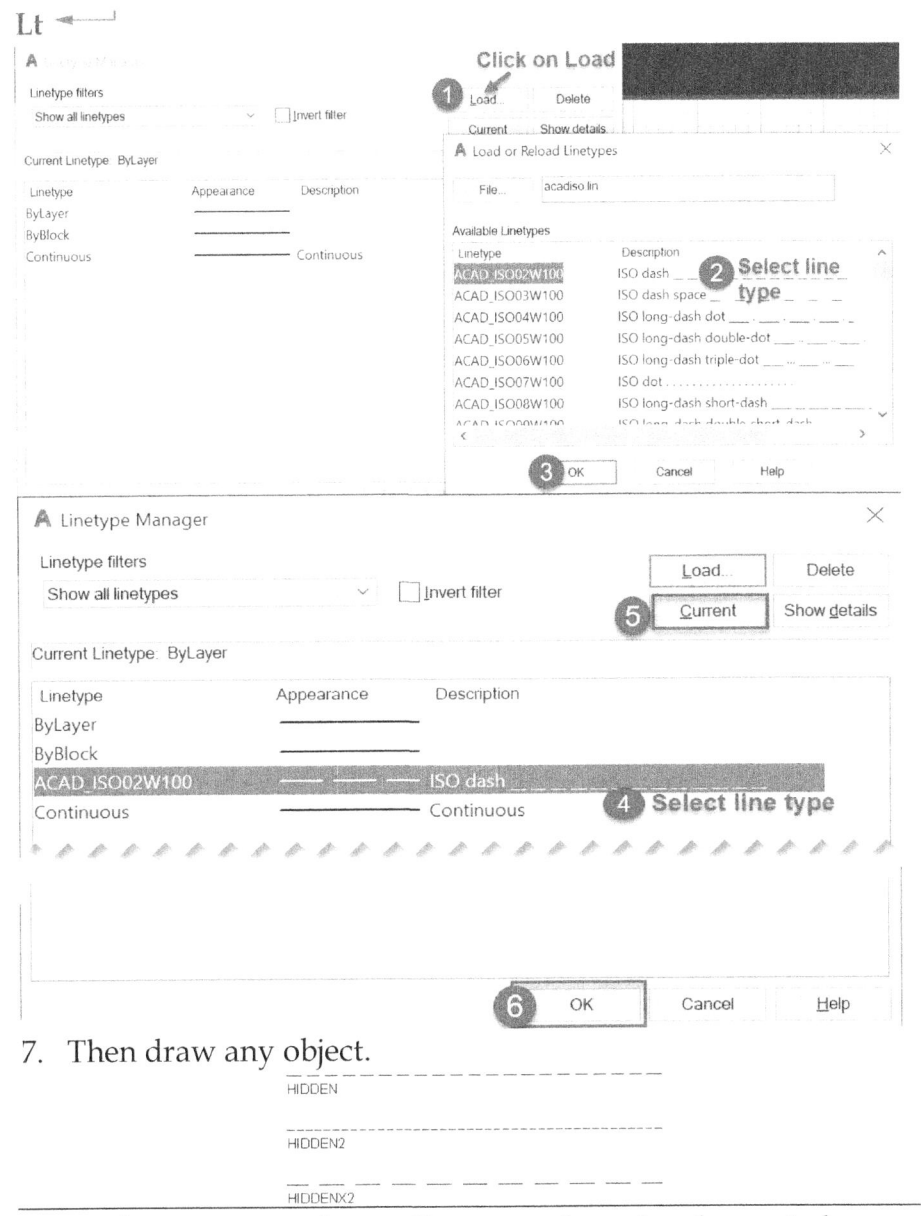

Lt

1. Click on Load
2. Select line type
3. OK
4. Select line type
5. Current
6. OK
7. Then draw any object.

HIDDEN

HIDDEN2

HIDDENX2

Note: If you want to change line type of previously created objects follow these steps:
  i. Select object available in the drawing area.
  ii. Then select click on Line Type (By Layer) and select loaded line type from list.

1. Select the object to change its line type

86

By Madhumita Kshirsagar

Autodesk AutoCAD 2021
Learn CAD With Ease.

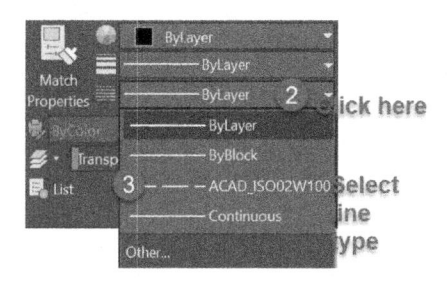

iii. If you want to add more line types in the list, directly from "Properties" panel, click on "Other…" to open "Line Type Manger" dialog box and follow step 2 to step 4 and then click on "OK".

Note: If you want to make any line type current directly from Line type (By Layer).

i. Click on "Line type" drop down.
ii. Select any loaded line type from list.

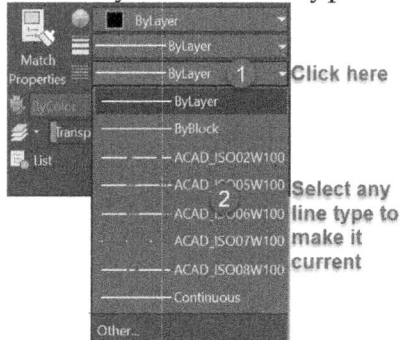

iii. Then draw the object.

6.8 Command: Line Type Scale
    Alias   : LTS

Use: Your line type scale determines how the line type is displayed and plotted. Depending on your line type or original area you set up, you may have to change it.

This is one more reason, why you should set up your drawing properly from the beginning.

If you need to change your line type scale, type in LTSCALE and try different values to get the look you want.

LTS ↵

Enter new linetype scale factor <1.0000>: 2 ↵ (enter scale factor)

Autodesk AutoCAD 2021
Learn CAD With Ease.

Note: You can also change you line type scale from the Line type Manager" dialog box by changing the value in the "Global Scale Factor" box.

Note: You can change the linetype scale separately on each object, but this is not recommended as it can be very difficult to keep track of, and therefore lose consistency.

Here is a single linetype (hidden) with 3 different linetype scales applied. Notice that the line with a LTS of .5 has lines and dashes that are 1/2 the size of line above it. The line with a LTS of 5 has lines and dashes that are 5 times longer.

HIDDEN - LINETYPE SCALE =1

HIDDEN - LINETYPE SCALE = .5

HIDDEN - LINETYPE SCALE = 5

By Madhumita Kshirsagar

Autodesk AutoCAD 2021
Learn CAD With Ease.

6.9 Command: Line Weight
Alias : LW

Home Tab →Properties Panel →Line Weight

Use: This command is used to set line weight of the object to show its intensity in a print.

Here, I am giving some line weights (there are more options in between):

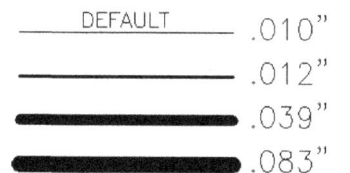

DEFAULT .010"	You can turn on/ off its display on a screen by click on line weight icon.
.012"	
.039"	
.083"	

To apply line weight, activate "Line Weight" and select Line weight from line weights list available in a given diagram. After that press "OK", then draw object.

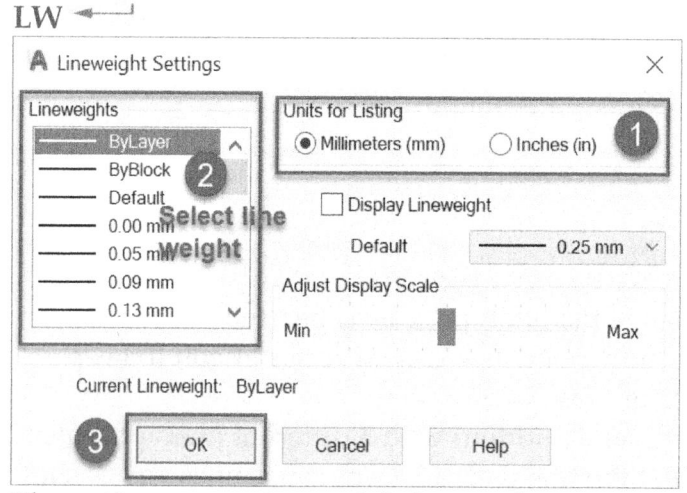

LW ←┘

Lineweight Settings dialog box showing:
- Lineweights list: ByLayer, ByBlock, Default, 0.00 mm, 0.05 mm, 0.09 mm, 0.13 mm (2) Select line weight
- Units for Listing: ● Millimeters (mm) ○ Inches (in) (1)
- Display Lineweight checkbox
- Default: 0.25 mm
- Adjust Display Scale: Min — Max
- Current Lineweight: ByLayer
- (3) OK, Cancel, Help

The options are quite straightforward.

You can turn on/ off its display on a screen by click on
☐ Display Lineweight

You can also apply line weight to previously drawn objects by-
1. Select object
2. Then select Line Weight from Line weight tool available in "Properties Palette".

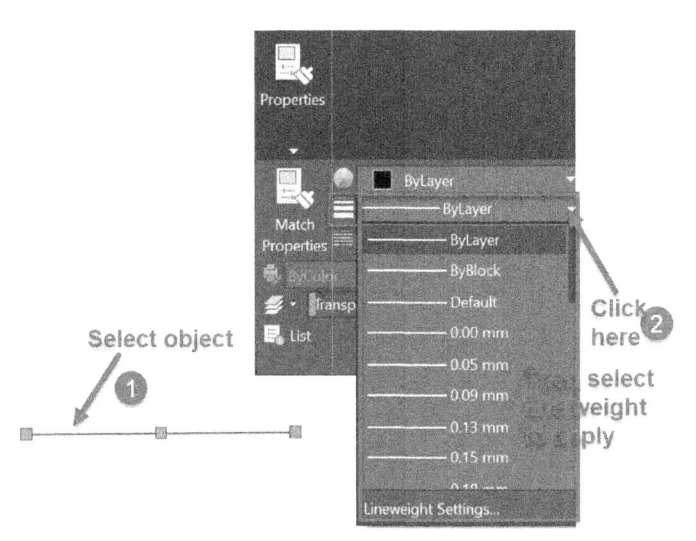

Autodesk AutoCAD 2021
Learn CAD With Ease.

By working with different linetypes & lineweights you can make a drawing clearer.

6.10 Command: **Properties**
    Alias   : Pr OR Ctrl + 1

View Tab → Palettes Panel → Properties

Use: To view properties of selected object.
You can also modify some properties of selected object by using this command.

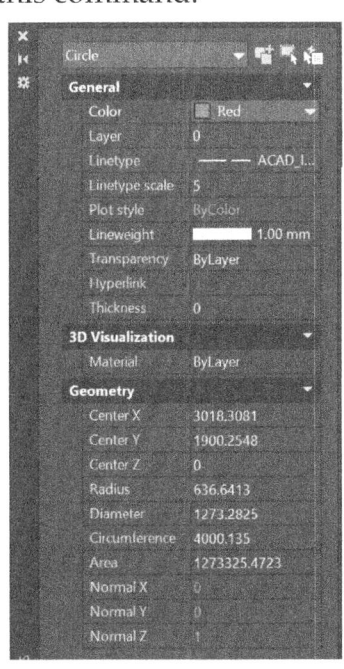

Select object & then right click, select "Properties" from available list.

Select object then right click in the drawing area & select Properties.

90

By Madhumita Kshirsagar

Autodesk AutoCAD 2021
Learn CAD With Ease.

6.11 Command: Match Properties
    Alias   : **Ma**

    Home Tab→ Properties Panel→MatchProperties

Use: To apply properties of selected object to other objects.

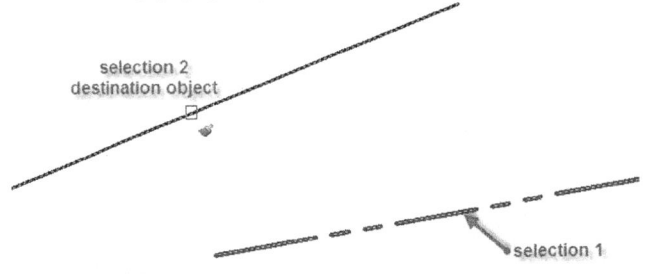

selection 2 destination object

selection 1

MA ↵

Select source object: by any selection method (selection 1)
Current active settings: Color Layer Ltype Ltscale Lineweight Transparency Thickness PlotStyle Dim Text Hatch Polyline Viewport Table Material Shadow display Multileader
Select destination object(s) or [Settings]: by any selection method (selection 2)
Select destination object(s) or [Settings]: ↵ to end command

You can control which properties are matched and which are not by using the **"Settings"** option. The setting option displays a **"Property Setting"** dialog box, shown in the left.
All properties are active or checked by default.

Autodesk AutoCAD 2021
Learn CAD With Ease.

You can deselect whichever properties you don't want to match simply by unchecking the box against that option.
You don't know about many properties given in above dialog box, you will learn about them in next some chapters.

6.12 Command: Quick Calculator
    Alias   : Ctrl+8
    Home tab → Utilities Panel → Quick Calculator

Use: To open & close calculator for calculation.
You can do easy calculations and scientific calculations by this command.

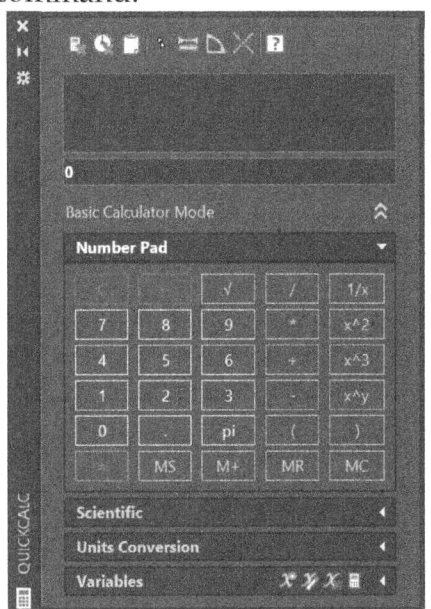

Clear : Clears the Input box.
Clear History : Clears the history area.
Paste Value to Command Line : Pastes the value in the Input box at the Command prompt. When Quick Calc. is used transparently during a command, this button is replaced by the Apply button at the bottom of the calculator.

Get Coordinates : Calculates the coordinates of a point.
Distance Between Two Points : Calculates the distance between two points. The calculated distance always displays as a unit less decimal value.
Angle of Line Defined by Two Points : Calculates the angle of two points.
Two Lines Defined by Four Points : Calculates the intersection of four points.
Scientific: To do scientific calculation.
Unit conversion: To convert any measurement unit in to another measurement unit.

By Madhumita Kshirsagar

Autodesk AutoCAD 2021
Learn CAD With Ease.

Unit type: You can specify unit type here like Length, Area, Volume & Angular.

Convert from: Specify measurement unit which you want to convert.

Convert to: Specify the unit in which you want to convert upper unit.

Value to Convert: Enter the numerical value to convert.

Converted Value: Converts the units entered and displays the converted value.

Calculator Icon: Returns the converted value to the Input box.

Variables Area:
Variables Tree
Stores predefined shortcut functions and user-defined variables. Shortcut functions are common expressions that combine a function with an object snap. The following table describes the predefined shortcut functions in the list.

Shortcut Function	Shortcut For	Description
dee	dist(end,end)	Distance between two endpoints
ille	ill(end,end,end,end)	Intersection of two lines defined by four endpoints
mee	(end+end)/2	Midpoint between two endpoints
nee	nor(end,end)	Unit vector in the XY plane and normal to two endpoints
rad	rad	Radius of a selected circle, arc, or polyline arc
vee	vec(end,end)	Vector from two endpoints
vee1	vec1(end,end)	Unit vector from two endpoints

New Variable Button: Opens the Variable Definition dialog box.
Edit Variable Button: Opens the Variable Definition dialog box so you can make changes to the selected variable.
Delete Variable Button: Deletes the selected variable.
Calculator Button: Returns the selected variable to the Input box.

Autodesk AutoCAD 2021
Learn CAD With Ease.

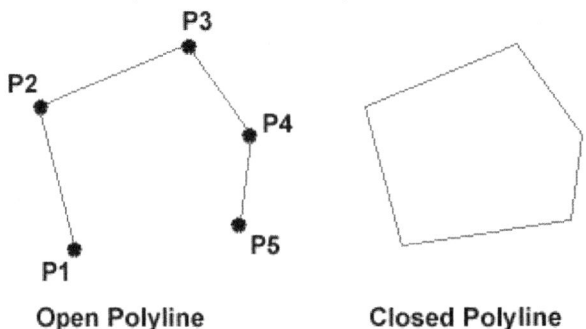

CHAPTER 7
POLYLINES & HATCH

In this chapter you will get knowledge about polyline and hatch. A polyline is a connected sequence of line segments created as a single object. You can create straight line segments, arc segments, or the combination of the both line and arc. Polylines have some unique qualities that make them very useful:
1. They can have width (constant or varying)
2. They can consist of arcs and lines.
3. They can be edited
4. They can be joined together.
5. They can be exploded into individual segments.

7.1 Command: Polyline
   Alias   : Pl

   Home Tab→ Draw Panel →Polyline

PL ←

Specify start point: (pick P1)
Current line-width is 0.0000
Specify next point or[Arc/Halfwidth/Length/Undo/Width]:
(pick P2)
Specify next point or [Arc/Close/Halfwidth/Length/Undo/Width]: (pick P3)
Specify next point or [Arc/Close/Halfwidth/Length/Undo/Width]: (pick P4)
Specify next point or [Arc/Close/Halfwidth/Length/Undo/Width]: (pick P5)
Specify next point or [Arc/Close/Halfwidth/Length/Undo/Width]: ←(or C← to close)

Open Polyline   **Closed Polyline**

Options of polyline:

Half width (h) : This option is used to draw thick line , to draw thick line firstly enter half width of the lines thickness,
for example: if you want to draw 4 mm thick line, enter thickness value 2mm at the starting & ending points.

Half width

PL ↵
Specify start point: by mouse click
Current line-width is 0.0000
Specify next point or [Arc/Halfwidth/Length/Undo/Width]:
H ↵

Specify starting half-width <0.0000>: 2 ↵
Specify ending half-width <2.0000>: 2 ↵
Specify next point or [Arc/Halfwidth/Length/Undo/Width]:
50 ↵

Specify next point or [Arc/Close/Halfwidth/Length/Undo/Width]: ↵

Width(w): This option is also used to draw thick line , to draw thick line firstly enter width of the lines, for example: if you want to draw 4 mm thick line, enter thickness value 4mm at the starting & ending points.

width

PL ↵
Specify start point: by mouse click
Current line-width is 4.0000
Specify next point or [Arc/Halfwidth/Length/Undo/Width]:
W ↵

Specify starting width <4.0000>: 4 ↵
Specify ending width <4.0000>: 4 ↵
Specify next point or [Arc/Halfwidth/Length/Undo/Width]:
50 ↵

Specify next point or [Arc/Close/Halfwidth/Length/Undo/Width]: ↵

Autodesk AutoCAD 2021
Learn CAD With Ease.

Arc (A): This option is used to draw arc or curved lines. This option is same as arc command.

Length (L): This option is used to draw a line segment of a specified length at the same angle as the previous segment. If the previous segment is an arc, the new line segment is drawn tangent to that arc segment.

Specify length of line: Specify a distance and press ↵

7.1.1 Command: Polyline Edit
    Alias   : **Pe**

    Home Tab → Modify Panel → Polyline Edit

Use: To edit polyline.

PE ↵
Select polyline or [Multiple]:
Enter an option [Close/Join/Width/Editvertex/Fit/Spline/Decurve/Ltype gen/Undo]:

a. **Close:** This option is used to close open polylines.

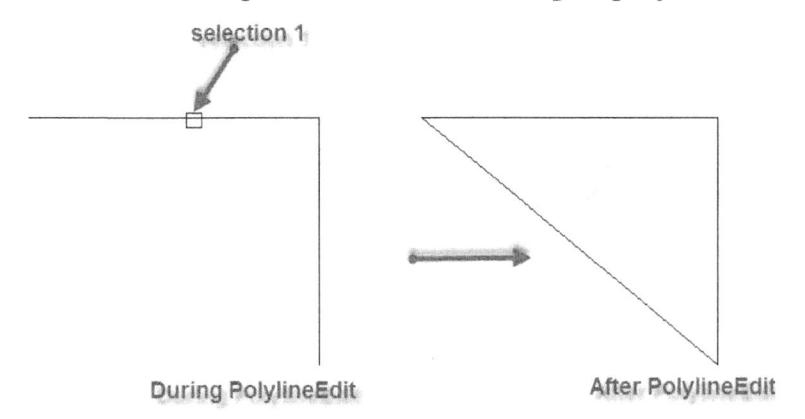

During PolylineEdit   *After PolylineEdit*

PE ↵
Select polyline or [Multiple]: select source polyline (selection 1)
Enter an option [Close/Join/Width/Edit vertex/Fit/Spline/Decurve/Ltype gen/Reverse/Undo]: C ↵
Enter an option [Open/Join/Width/Edit vertex/Fit/Spline/Decurve/Ltype gen/Reverse/Undo]: ↵

b. Join: To join two & more polylines.

PE ↵

Select polyline or [Multiple]: select source polyline
Enter an option [Close/Join/Width/Edit vertex/Fit/Spline/Decurve/Ltype gen/Reverse/Undo]: J ↵
Select objects: select polyline or line to join
Select objects: ↵
Enter an option [Open/Join/Width/Edit vertex/Fit/Spline/Decurve/Ltype gen/Reverse/Undo]: ↵ to end the command.

Width: To give width to polyline.

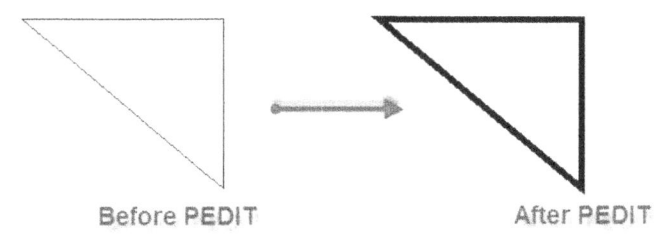

Before PEDIT   After PEDIT

PE ↵

Select polyline or [Multiple]: by any selection method.
Enter an option [Open/Join/Width/Edit vertex/Fit/Spline/Decurve/Ltype gen/Reverse/Undo]: W ↵
Specify new width for all segments: .2 ↵
Enter an option [Open/Join/Width/Edit vertex/Fit/Spline/Decurve/Ltype gen/Reverse/Undo]: ↵ to end the command.

c. Edit Vertex:
This option is used to mark the first vertex of the polyline by drawing an X on the screen. If you have specified a tangent direction for this vertex, an arrow is also drawn in that direction.

Next:
This option of "edit vertex" is used to move the X marker to the next vertex. The marker does not wrap around from the end to the start of the polyline, even if the polyline is closed.

Previous: This option is used to move the X marker to the previous vertex. The marker does not wrap around from the start to the end of the polyline, even if the polyline is closed.

Break:
This option is used to save the location of the marked vertex while you move the X marker to any other vertex.
If one of the specified vertices is at an end of the polyline, the result is one truncated polyline. If both specified vertices are at endpoints of the polyline, or if just one vertex is specified and it is at an endpoint, you cannot use "Break".

Exit: This option is used to exit from "Break" and returns to Edit Vertex mode.

Insert: Adds a new vertex to the polyline after the marked vertex.

Move: This option is used to move the marked vertex.

Regen: Regenerates the polyline.

Straighten: Saves the location of the marked vertex while you move the X marker to any other vertex.

Tangent: Attaches a tangent direction to the marked vertex for use later in curve fitting.

Width: Changes the starting and ending widths for the segment that immediately follows the marked vertex.
You must regenerate the polyline to display the new width.

Exit: Exits Edit Vertex mode.

d. **Fit:** This option is used to create an arc-fit polyline, a smooth curve consisting of arcs joining each pair of vertices. The curve passes through all vertices of the polyline and uses any tangent direction you specify.

Autodesk AutoCAD 2021
Learn CAD With Ease.

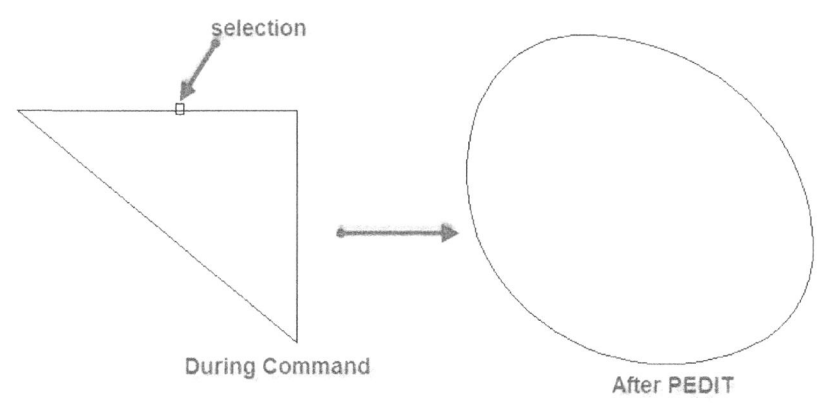

Pe ←

Select polyline or [Multiple]: (select polyline to edit)
Enter an option [Open/Join/Width/Edit vertex/Fit/Spline/Decurve/Ltype gen/Reverse/Undo]: F ←
Enter an option [Open/Join/Width/Edit vertex/Fit/Spline/Decurve/Ltype gen/Reverse/Undo]: ← to end the command.

e. Spline: To create spline fit curve in polylines.

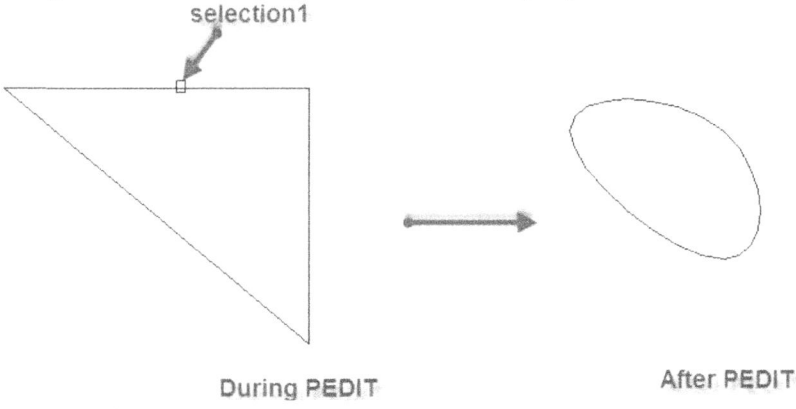

PE ←

Select polyline or [Multiple]: (selection1)
Enter an option [Open/Join/Width/Edit vertex/Fit/Spline/Decurve/Ltype gen/Reverse/Undo]: S ←
Enter an option [Open/Join/Width/Edit vertex/Fit/Spline/Decurve/Ltype gen/Reverse/Undo]: ← to end the command.

Autodesk AutoCAD 2021
Learn CAD With Ease.

f. Decurve: To decurve or remove ARC-FIT curve & SPLINE-FIT curve.

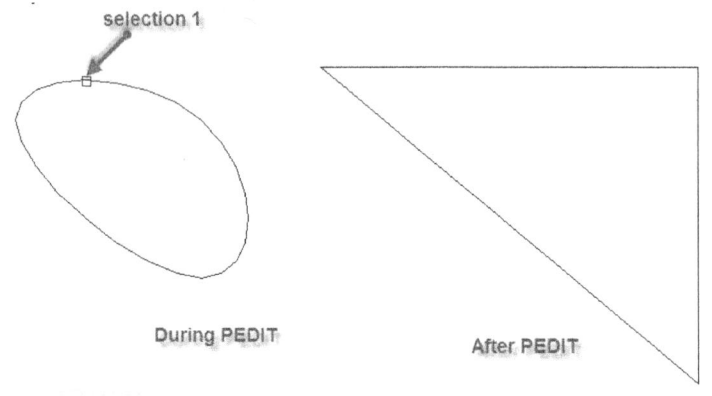

PE ←
Select polyline or [Multiple]: (selection1)
Enter an option [Open/Join/Width/Edit vertex/Fit/Spline/Decurve/Ltype gen/Reverse/Undo]: D ←
Enter an option [Open/Join/Width/Edit vertex/Fit/Spline/Decurve/Ltype gen/Reverse/Undo]: ← to end the command

g. LType Gen: Generates the linetype in a continuous pattern through the vertices of the polyline. When turned off, this option generates the linetype starting and ending with a dash at each vertex. Ltype Gen does not apply to polylines with tapered segments.

PE ←
Select polyline or [Multiple]: (selection1)
Enter an option [Open/Join/Width/Edit vertex/Fit/Spline/Decurve/Ltype gen/Reverse/Undo]: L ←
Enter polyline linetype generation option [ON/OFF]: On ←

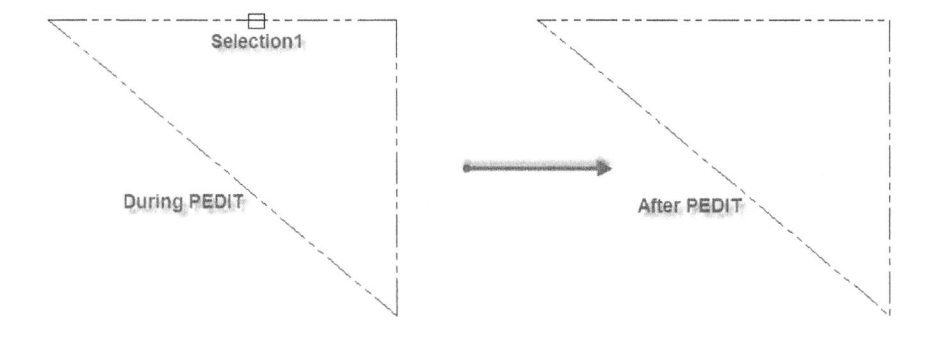

h. Reverse: This option is used to reverse the order of vertices of the polyline. Use this option to reverse the direction of objects that use linetypes with included text.
For example, depending on the direction in which a polyline was created, the text in the linetype might be displayed upside down.

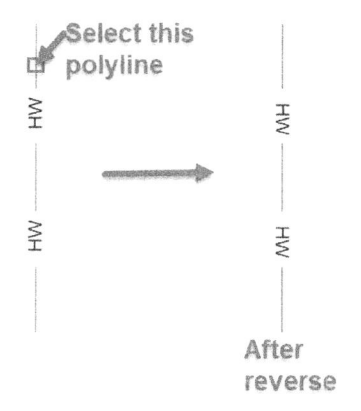

PE ⏎
Select polyline or [Multiple]: select by any selection method
Enter an option [Open/Join/Width/Edit vertex/Fit/Spline/Decurve/Ltype gen/Reverse/Undo]: R ⏎
Enter an option [Open/Join/Width/Edit vertex/Fit/Spline/Decurve/Ltype gen/Reverse/Undo]: ⏎ to end the command

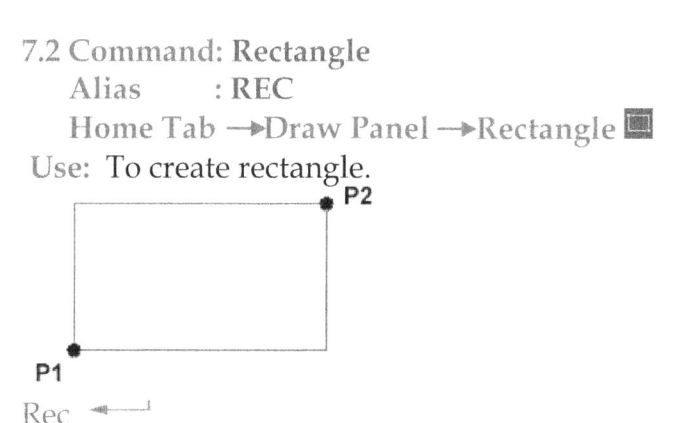

7.2 Command: Rectangle
   Alias   : REC
   Home Tab →Draw Panel →Rectangle
Use: To create rectangle.

Rec ⏎
Specify first corner point or [Chamfer/Elevation/Fillet/Thickness/Width]: (pick P1) by mouse click
Specify other corner point or [Area /Dimensions/Rotate]: (pick P2) by mouse click

Autodesk AutoCAD 2021
Learn CAD With Ease.

Different options available in a rectangle command:

a. Dimension: To draw rectangle by giving dimension.

Rec ←

Specify first corner point or [Chamfer/Elevation/Fillet/Thickness/Width]: pick a point by mouse click
Specify other corner point or [Dimensions]: D ←
Specify length for rectangles <0.0000>: 20 ←
Specify width for rectangles <0.0000>: 10 ←
Specify other corner point or [Dimensions]: (pick a point to fix the orientation)

b. Area: To create rectangle by giving area & any one dimension (length or width).

|—10.0000—|

Rec ←

Specify first corner point or [Chamfer/Elevation/Fillet/Thickness/Width]: pick a point
Specify other corner point or [Area/Dimensions/Rotation]: A ←
Enter area of rectangle in current units <100.0000>: 30 ←
Calculate rectangle dimensions based on [Length/Width] <Length>: l ←
Enter rectangle length <20.0000>: 10 ←

c. Rotate: To create rotated rectangle.

Rec ←

Specify first corner point or [Chamfer/Elevation/Fillet/Thickness/Width]: by mouse click
Specify other corner point or [Area/Dimensions/Rotation]: R ←
Specify rotation angle or [Pick points] <0>: 45 ←
Specify other corner point or [Area/Dimensions/Rotation]: by mouse click or type any option then press ←

Autodesk AutoCAD 2021
Learn CAD With Ease.

d. Chamfer: To draw chamfered rectangle.

Rec ←

Specify first corner point or [Chamfer/Elevation/Fillet/Thickness/Width]: C ←
Specify first chamfer distance for rectangle: 5 ←
Specify second chamfer distance for rectangle: 5 ←
Specify first corner point or [Chamfer/Elevation/Fillet/Thickness/Width]: (pick P1) by mouse click
Specify other corner point or [Area /Dimensions/Rotate]: (pick P2) by mouse click

e. Fillet: To draw filleted rectangle.

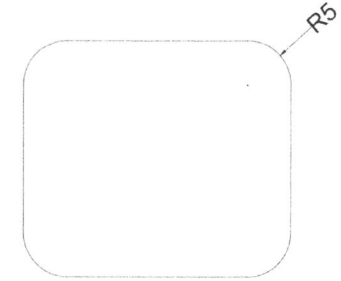

Rec ←

Specify first corner point or [Chamfer/Elevation/Fillet/Thickness/Width]: F ←
Specify fillet radius of rectangle: 2 ←
Specify other corner point or [Area /Dimensions/Rotate]: (pick P2) by mouse click

f. Thickness: To specify thickness of rectangle.

Rec ←

Specify first corner point or [Chamfer/Elevation/Fillet/Thickness/Width]: T ←
Specify thickness for rectangle: 5 ←
Specify first corner point or [Chamfer/Elevation/Fillet/Thickness/Width]: (pick P1) by mouse click
Specify other corner point or [Area /Dimensions/Rotate]: (pick P2) by mouse click

Autodesk AutoCAD 2021
Learn CAD With Ease.

Rectangle with Thickness

Rectangle width = .5

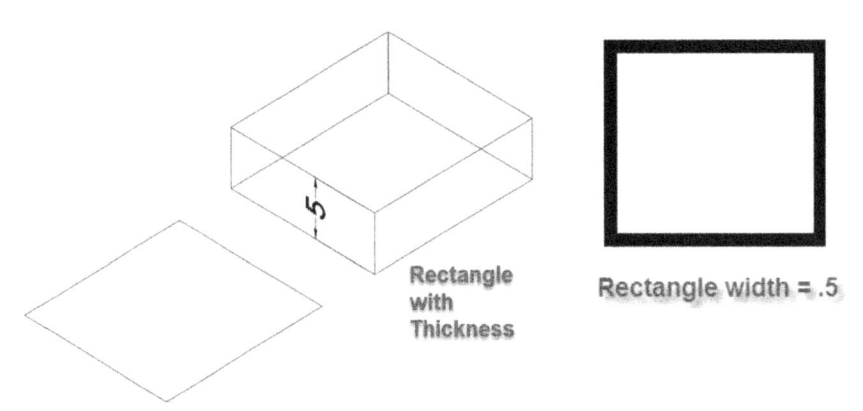

g. **Width:** To specify width of rectangle.

Rec ↵
Specify first corner point or [Chamfer/Elevation/Fillet/Thickness/Width]: W ↵
Specify line width for rectangles <0.0000>: .5 ↵
Specify first corner point or [Chamfer/Elevation/Fillet/Thickness/Width]: by mouse click
Specify other corner point or [Area/Dimensions/Rotation]: by mouse click

h. **Elevation:** To create parallel plane to an object in a z axis.

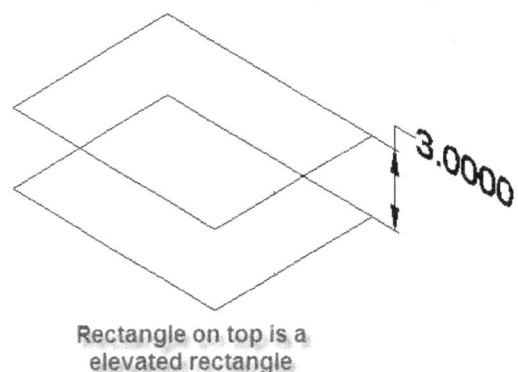

Rectangle on top is a elevated rectangle

Rec ↵
Specify first corner point or [Chamfer/Elevation/Fillet/Thickness/Width]: E ↵
Specify the elevation for rectangles <0.0000>: 3 ↵
Specify first corner point or [Chamfer/Elevation/Fillet/Thickness/Width]: by mouse click
Specify other corner point or [Area/Dimensions/Rotation]: by mouse click

Autodesk AutoCAD 2021
Learn CAD With Ease.

7.3 Command: **Region**
    Alias   : **REG**
   Home Tab → Draw Panel → Region

Use: To convert an object that encloses an area into a region object. It's a dimensional area you create from closed shapes & loops.

REG ←
Select object: by any selection method and press ←

Before Region   **After Region**

7.4 Command: **Explode**
    Alias   : **X**
   Home Tab → Modify Panel → Explode

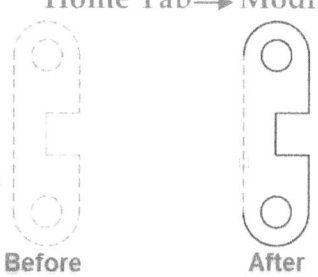

Use: To break a compound object or regioned object in to segmented object.

X ←
Select object: by any selection method and press ←

Before Explode   **After Explode**

7.5 Command: **Hatch**
    Alias   : **H**
   Home Tab → Draw Panel → Hatch

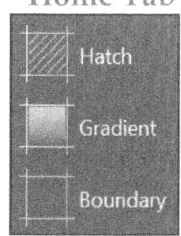

Use: Hatching is used for highlighting a certain area of the drawing according to the standard of which drawing discipline it is used for. It is also used to show the material of the object.

H ←

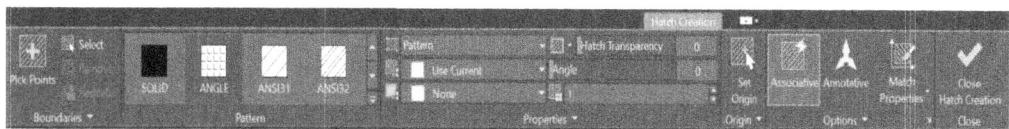

When you type "**H ←**" at the Command prompt "Hatch visor" is displayed as given above and you can also see some options in command prompt.

Autodesk AutoCAD 2021
Learn CAD With Ease.

H ←⎯⎯

Select objects or [picK internal point/Undo/seTtings]:
Choose from several methods to specify the boundaries of a hatch.

Pick Internal Point: Specify a point in an area that is enclosed by objects.
Select objects: Select objects that enclose an area.
Hatch and Gradient Dialog Box:

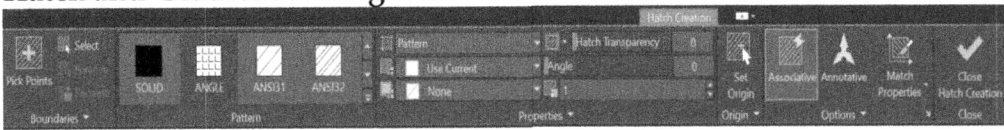

Defines the boundaries, pattern, or fill properties, and other parameters for hatches and fills.
List of Options:
The dialog box includes the following:
- Hatch tab
- Gradient tab
- More Options section
- Add: Pick Points
- Add: Select Objects
- Remove Boundaries
- Recreate Boundary
- View Selections
- Display Boundary Objects
- Options
- Preview

Add: Pick Points :
It determines a boundary from existing objects that form an enclosed area around the specified point.

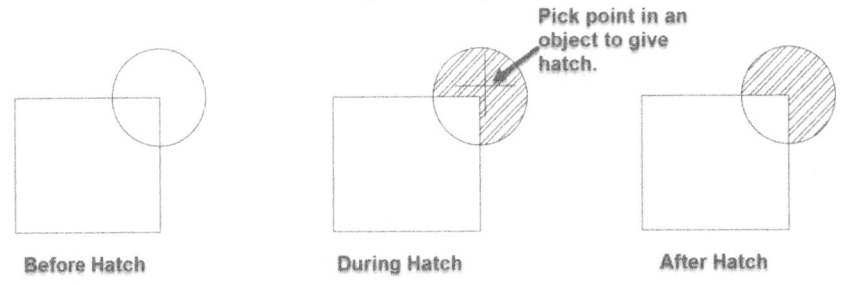

Pick point in an object to give hatch.

Before Hatch   During Hatch   After Hatch

There are some island detection methods available in hatch methods which effects selection of the object during hatch.
Island detection methods (options):

It detects objects according to island detection method.

a. Normal

Hatches or fills inward from the outer boundary. If an internal island is encountered, hatching or filling is turned off until another island within the island is encountered.

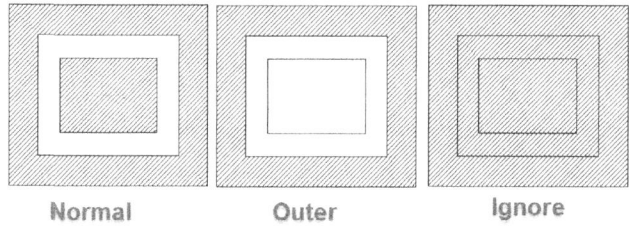

b. Outer (Recommended)

Hatches or fills inward from the outer boundary. This option hatches or fills only the specified area and leaves the internal islands unaffected.

c. Ignore

Ignores all internal objects and hatches or fills through them.

Note: The Normal, Outer, and Ignore options are also available from a shortcut menu by right-clicking in the drawing area while you specify points or select objects to define your boundaries.

Add: Select Objects:-

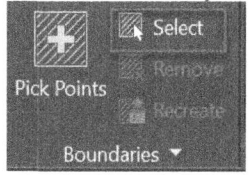

This option is used to determine a boundary from selected objects that form an enclosed area.

Autodesk AutoCAD 2021
Learn CAD With Ease.

Interior objects are not automatically detected. You must select the objects within the selected boundary to hatch or fill those objects according to the current island detection style.
Each time you click Add: Select Objects, HATCH clears the previous selection set.

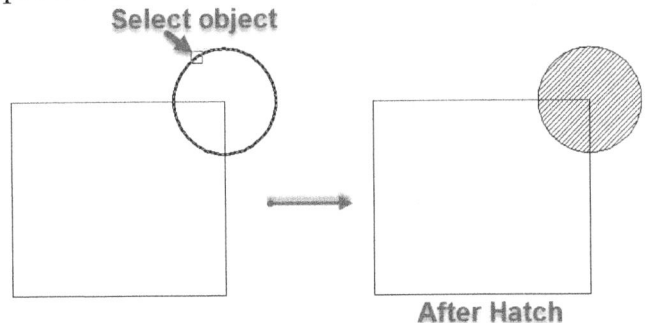

Remove Boundaries:-
It removes from the boundary definition any of the objects that were added previously.

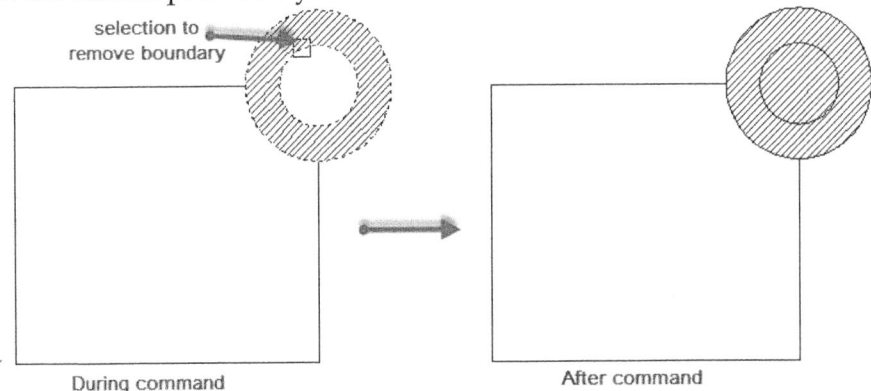

Recreate:
It creates a polyline or region around the selected hatch or fill, and optionally associates the hatch object with it.
Displays the currently defined boundaries with the current hatch or fill settings.
This option is available only when a boundary has been defined.

Display Boundary Objects:
It selects the objects that form the boundaries of the selected associative hatch object. Use the displayed grips to modify the hatch boundaries.

Autodesk AutoCAD 2021
Learn CAD With Ease.

Options:
There are other options of hatch.

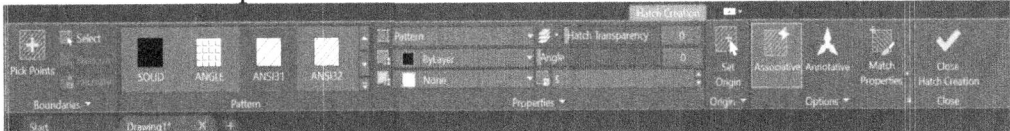

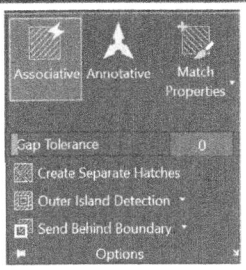

Pattern: You will select different hatch patterns and gradients from this option.
Annotative: Specifies that the hatch is annotative. This property automates the process of scaling annotations so that they plot or display at the correct size on the paper.
Associative: Specifies that the hatch or fill is associative. A hatch or fill that is associative is updated when you modify its boundary objects.
Create Separate Hatches: Controls whether a single hatch object or multiple hatch objects are created when several separate closed boundaries are specified.
Draw Order: Assigns a draw order to a hatch or fill. You can place a hatch or fill behind all other objects, in front of all other objects, behind the hatch boundary, or in front of the hatch boundary.
Layer: Assigns new hatch objects to the specified layer, overriding the current layer. Select Use Current to use the current layer.

Transparency: Sets the transparency level for new hatch or fills, overriding the current object transparency. Select Use Current to use the current object transparency setting.
Match Properties: Hatches or fills specified boundaries using the hatch or fill properties of a selected hatch object.
After selecting the hatch object whose properties you want the hatch to inherit for that just right-click in the drawing area and use the options on the shortcut menu to switch between the Select Objects and Pick Internal Point options.
Preview:
Displays the currently defined boundaries with the current hatch or fill settings.

Autodesk AutoCAD 2021
Learn CAD With Ease.

Click in the drawing area or press Esc to return to the dialog box. Right-click or press Enter to accept the hatch or fill.

You can also do hatch by Hatch & Gradient dialog box.
For this click on arrow given in the diagram available in left hand side.

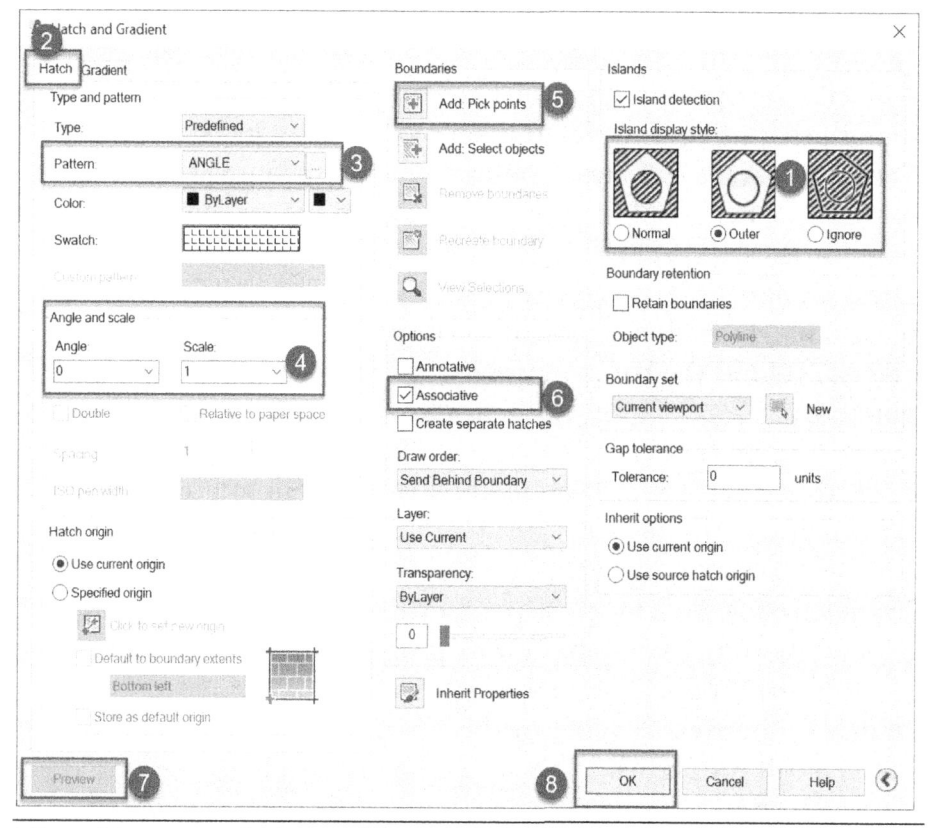

Click here to get "Hatch/Gradient dialog box

Note: You can edit hatch by double click on filled hatch or by "Hatch Edit" command.
Type "He" and press "Enter" then select filled hatch, it will open hatch edit dialog box.

Autodesk AutoCAD 2021
Learn CAD With Ease.

CHAPTER 8
DRAWING SETUP

Among the most important concepts that newcomers to AutoCAD need to get to grips with is *drawing units* & *drawing limits*. You cannot start creating sensible drawings with AutoCAD until you are familiar with units and the commands you use to control them. This lesson discusses these concepts and some other commands related to drawing properties & helpful in making drawings without drafting mistakes.

8.1 Command: Units
    Alias   : UN

    Application menu → Drawing utilities → Units 0.0 .

Use: To set drawing units in which you want to draw your drawing.

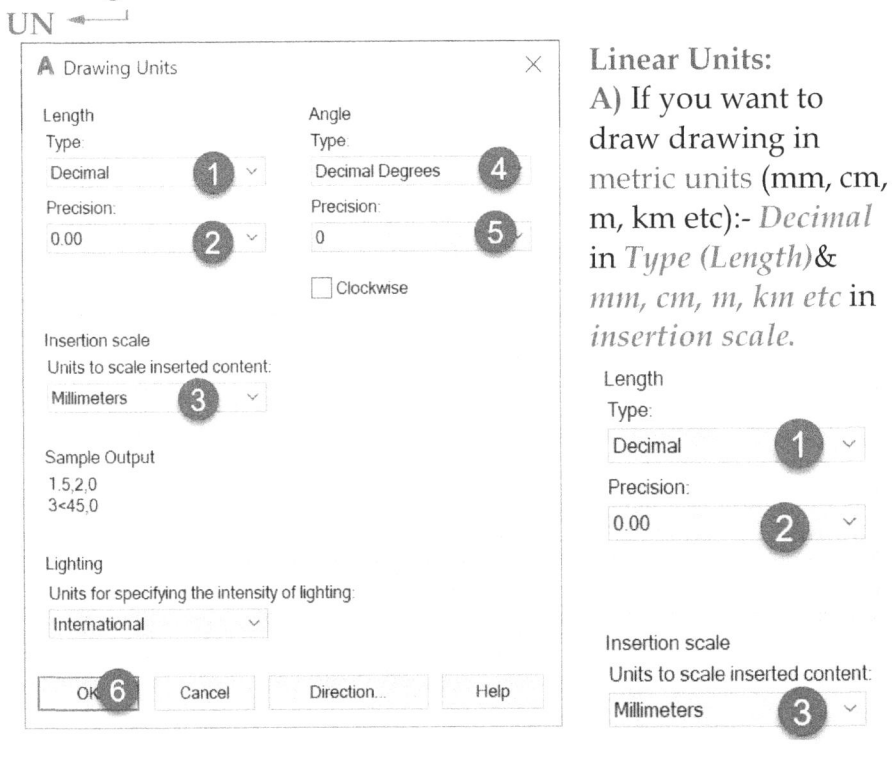

UN ←

Linear Units:
A) If you want to draw drawing in metric units (mm, cm, m, km etc):- *Decimal* in *Type (Length)* & *mm, cm, m, km etc* in *insertion scale*.

B) If you want to draw drawing in Architectural units (feet & inches): *Architectural* in *Type (Length)* & *inches* in *insertion scale*.

Autodesk AutoCAD 2021
Learn CAD With Ease.

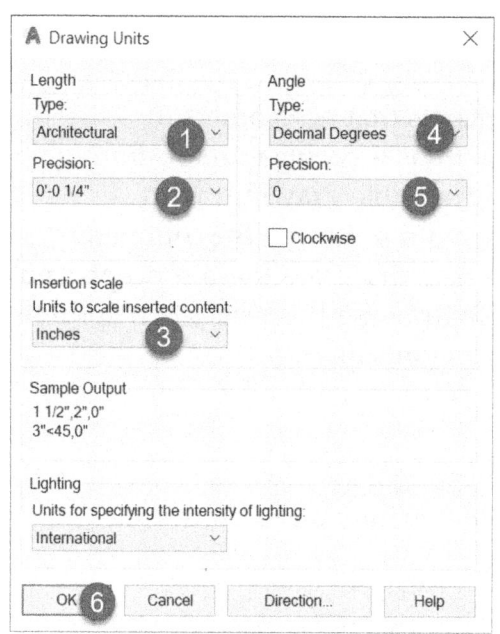

When you change the unit type, it will change the co-ordinate display on the status bar in to current unit type.

Changing the unit type also affects the way of distances, areas and volumes are reported when using the appropriate inquiry command.

Unit Precision: The Drawing Units dialogue box can also be used to set the precision of linear and angular units. By default, AutoCAD sets the linear unit precision to four places of decimal, so distances appear in the form 0.0000. Angular unit precision is set to whole degrees only.

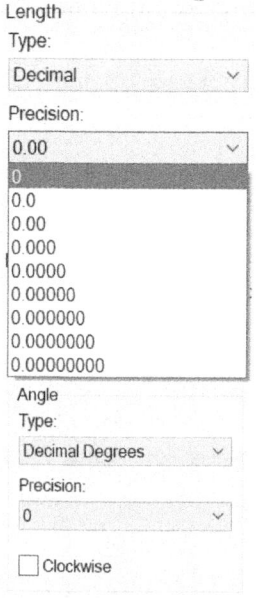

To change the precision with which linear and angular values are displayed, simply click the down arrow against the appropriate drop-down list (see illustration on the left) and select the number of decimal places required. The default setting of four decimal places is usually adequate for linear units. It is, however, often necessary to change the precision for angular units.

Angular Units: Looking at the Drawing Units dialogue box again, you will notice that there is also "angular unit type". The default is decimal degrees, but there are other options available in "Type" like Deg/Min/Sec, Grads, and etc.

Precision in angle is just like precision in **Length**.

Autodesk AutoCAD 2021
Learn CAD With Ease.

Direction:

AutoCAD also allows you to control the direction in which angular units are measured and the position of the start angle. By default, AutoCAD starts with the zero angle at the 3 o'clock position (East) with angles increasing in an anti-clockwise direction.

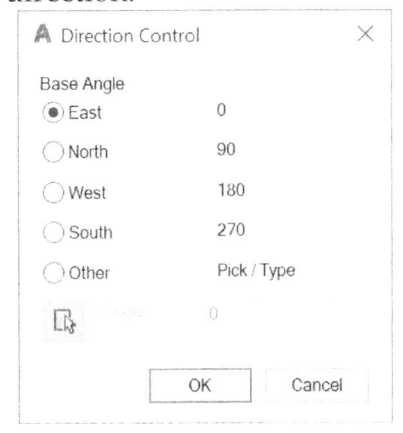

You can select base angle or 0 degree position from "Direction Control" dialog box. For example: If you select North in "Direction Control" dialog box, AutoCAD mark 0 degree in North and calculate further angles in anti clockwise direction from north.
Other: In this option you can give your own base angle and it mark 0 degree on specified angle and calculate further angles from that position.

8.2 Command: Limits
   Alias: None

Use: Sets and controls the limits of the grid display in the current Model or named layout.
The drawing limits are two dimensional points in the world co-ordinate that represents upper-left and lower left boundaries. You cannot impose on the Z direction.
When "limits" checking is turned on (controlled by the on and off option from the first "Limits" prompt), the drawing limits restrict the coordinates you can enter to within the rectangular area.
When plotting a drawing, you can also specify the drawing limits as the area to plot.
You always set limits according to drawing which you want to draw in a viewport.

Autodesk AutoCAD 2021
Learn CAD With Ease.

Limits ←
Specify lower left corner or [ON/OFF] <current>: ←
Specify upper right corner <current>: type x & y distance then ←

On: This option is used to turn on limits checking. When "limits" is on, you cannot specify points outside the grid limits or limit area.

Off: This option is used to turn off limits checking. When "limits" is off, you can specify points anywhere in a drawing area.

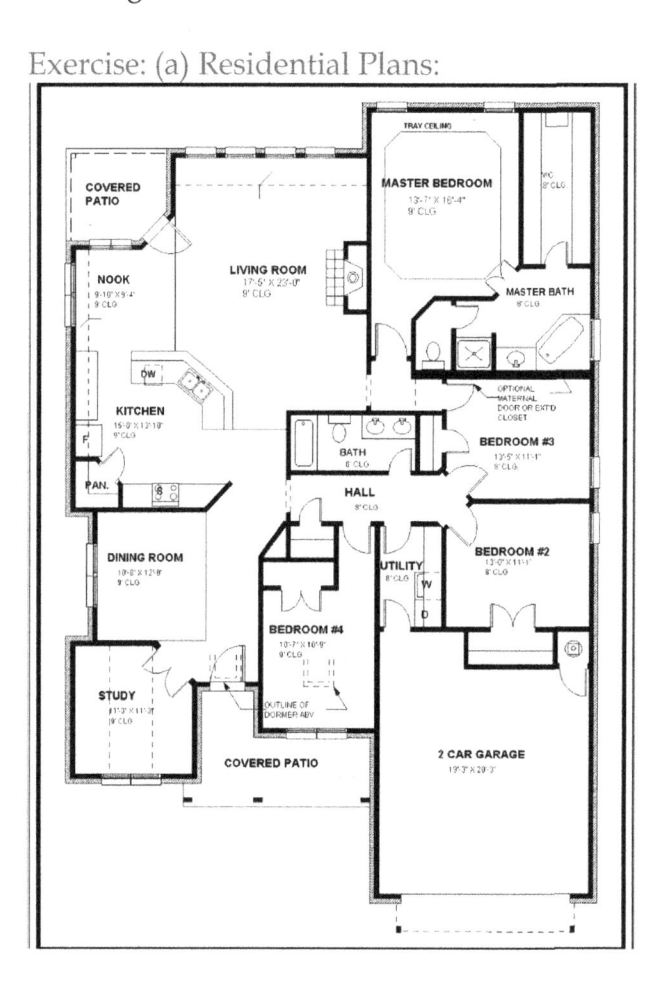

Exercise: (a) Residential Plans:

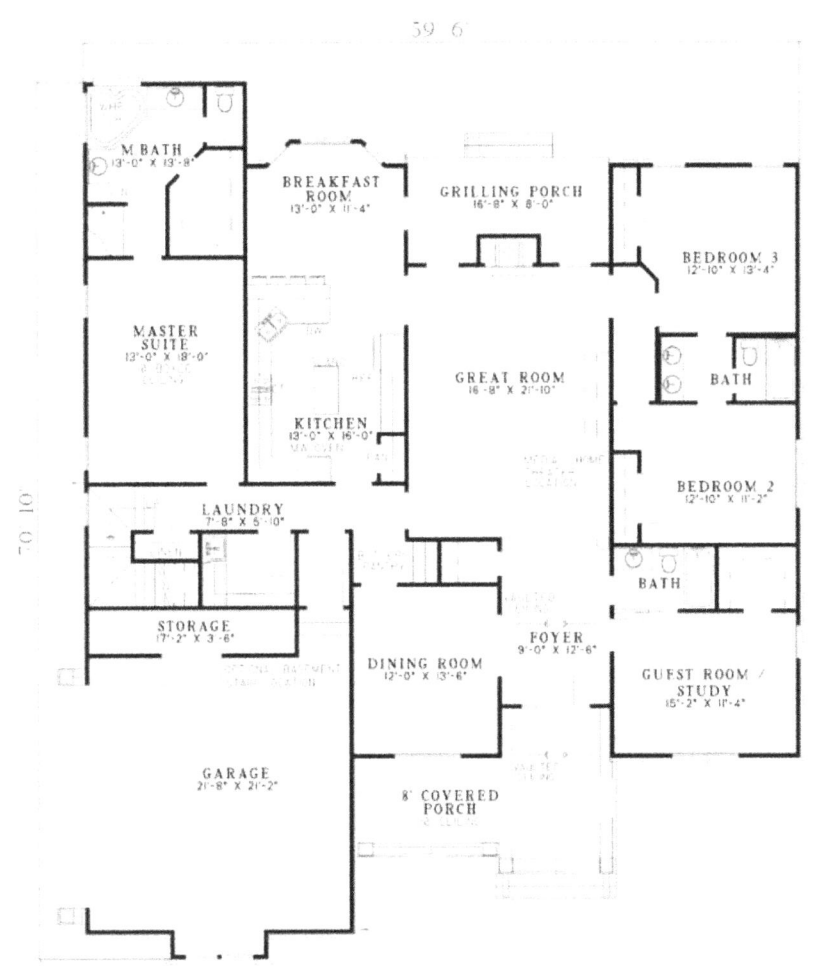

(b) **Mechanical Drawings:**

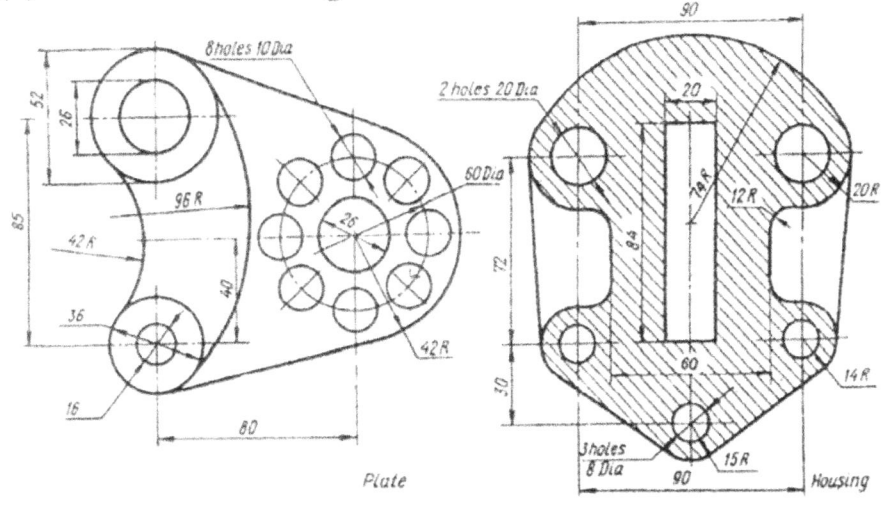

Autodesk AutoCAD 2021
Learn CAD With Ease.

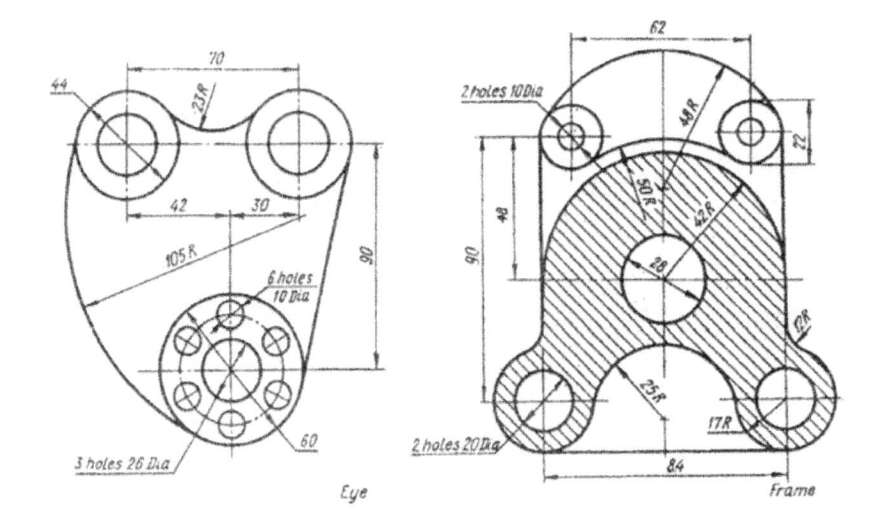

Autodesk AutoCAD 2021
Learn CAD With Ease.

CHAPTER 9
FILLET & CHAMFER

In this chapter you will get knowledge about fillet and chamfer used in an AutoCAD.

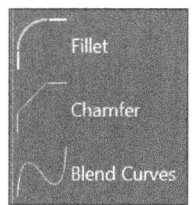

9.1 Command: Fillet
   Alias   : F

   Home Tab→ Modify Panel →Fillet

   Use: To make object's corner round.

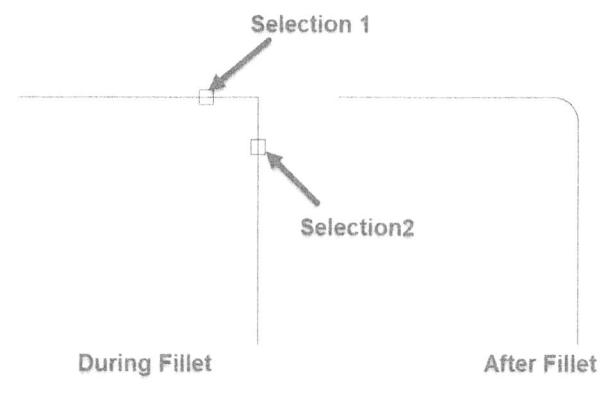

F ↵
Current settings: Mode = TRIM, Radius = 0.0000
Select first object or [Undo/Polyline/Radius/Trim/Multiple]:
                                                              R ↵
Specify fillet radius <0.0000>: 1 ↵
Select first object or [Undo/Polyline/Radius/Trim/Multiple]:
                                                by mouse (selection 1)
Select second object or shift-select to apply corner or [Radius]:
                                                by mouse (selection 2)
Trim mode:
The 'Trim' option allows you to select whether AutoCAD trims the lines back to the fillet radius or leaves them untouched. This option is used in other commands, e.g. **Chamfer**, as well.

By Madhumita Kshirsagar

Autodesk AutoCAD 2021
Learn CAD With Ease.

F ←┘
Current settings: Mode = TRIM, Radius = 1.0000
Select first object or [Undo/Polyline/Radius/Trim/Multiple]:
                                                                       T ←┘
Enter Trim mode option [Trim/No trim] < Trim>: N ←┘
Select first object or [Undo/Polyline/Radius/Trim/Multiple]:
                                          by mouse (selection 1)
Select second object or shift-select to apply corner or [Radius]:
                                          by mouse (selection 2)

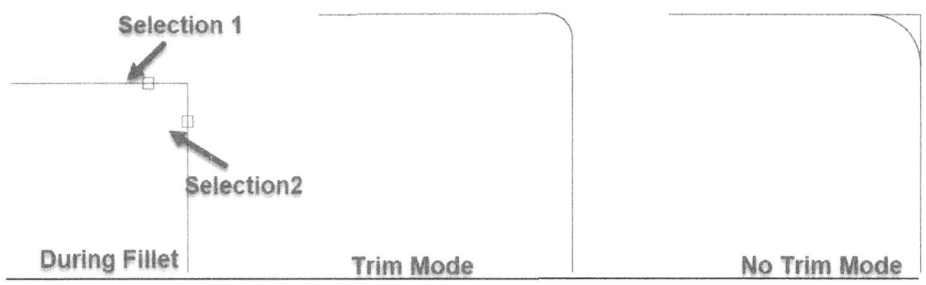

Note: The default value for **Fillet** is to trim the lines.
Type: N ←┘ (to select "No Trim") & Type: T ←┘ (to select "Trim")

Multiple: The 'Multiple' option of the **Fillet** command allows you to do continuous fillets with the current radius setting rather than allow just a single fillet operation.

Polyline: This option is used to fillet object draw by polyline. We shall consider the 'Polyline' option in a later Module. A polyline is just a special group of objects (made up of lines and arcs if so required), which once drawn, are considered one object.

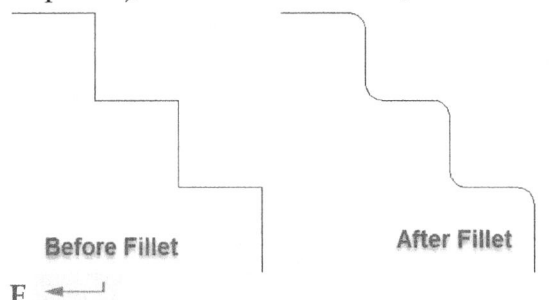

F ←┘
Current settings: Mode = TRIM, Radius = 1.0000
Select first object or [Undo/Polyline/Radius/Trim/Multiple]:R ←┘

Autodesk AutoCAD 2021
Learn CAD With Ease.

Specify fillet radius <1.0000>: 1 ↵
Select first object or [Undo/Polyline/Radius/Trim/Multiple]:
P ↵

Select 2D polyline or [Radius]: by mouse.

Filleting Parallel lines

Not all the lines to be filleted need to have an intersection point or to intersect if they were extended. **Fillet** can also apply an arc to lines that are parallel. Use **Snap** and **Ortho** to draw two parallel lines with different lengths as shown below.

Apply the **Fillet** command to the lines at both right hand ends, picking the shorter one first. The fillet is positioned so that it is trimmed back to the end of the line you picked first regardless of length. The size of the radius is adjusted to join the lines with a semicircle *regardless* of the fillet setting.

Undo the fillet and then re-install the **Fillet** command and apply it again picking the longer line first. This time the radius is positioned at the end of the longer line and the shorter one is extended.

Install the **Fillet** command again to see that the radius used to fillet the parallel lines is only a temporary value and the Current value remains unaltered.
Now, **Fillet** has one more very useful function.

How to create corner by two perpendicular lines using Fillet:
First option is to set the radius to 0 and then Fillet. Draw two lines like those below:

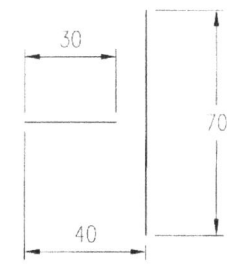

Autodesk AutoCAD 2021
Learn CAD With Ease.

F ←┘
Current settings: Mode = TRIM, Radius = 22.5000
Select first object or [Undo/Polyline/Radius/Trim/Multiple]:
R ←┘

Specify fillet radius <*default value*>: 0 ←┘
Select first object or [Undo/Polyline/Radius/Trim/Multiple]:
Pick the two lines you have just drawn one after the other, picking the vertical line below the horizontal line.

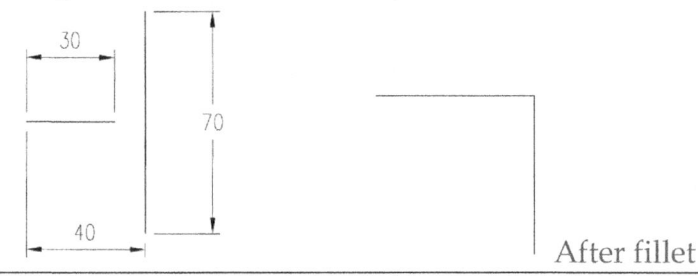

After fillet

Note: If you don't want to change radius to "0" select object with "shift", this will set radius to "0" for current selection only.

9.2 Command: Chamfer
Alias : Cha

Home Tab → Modify Panel → Chamfer

Use: To bevel edges of objects.

The Chamfer command enables you to create a chamfer between any two non-parallel lines as in the illustration below or any two adjacent polyline segments.

During Chamfer   After Chamfer

CHA ←┘
(TRIM mode) Current chamfer Dist1 = 0, Dist2 = 0
Select first line or [Polyline/Distance/Angle/Trim/Method/

mUltiple]: D ↵ *(to set distances)*
Specify first chamfer distance <10.0000>: 1.5 ↵
Specify second chamfer distance <20.0000>:2 ↵
Select first line or [Polyline/Distance/Angle/Trim/Method]:by mouse (selection 1)
Select second line: by mouse (selection 2)

Note: First chamfer distance is on first selected line and second chamfer distance is on second selected line.

Angle: Sets the chamfer distances using a chamfer distance for the first line and an angle for the second line.

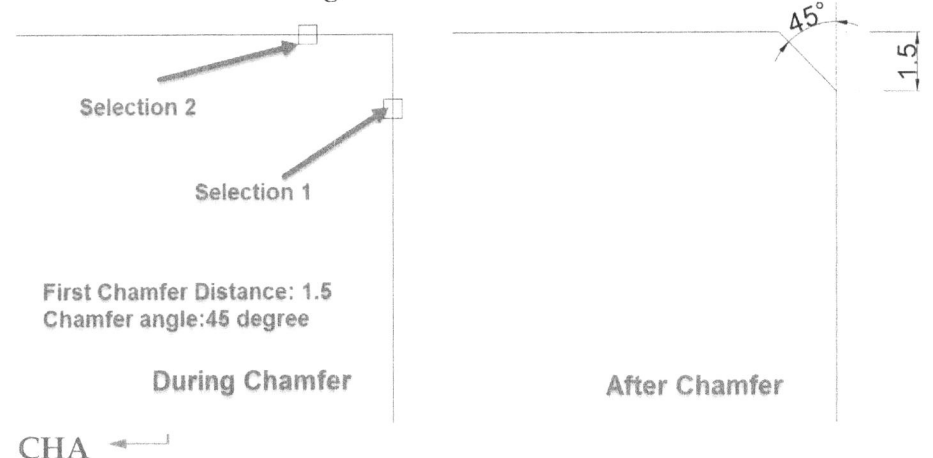

First Chamfer Distance: 1.5
Chamfer angle: 45 degree

During Chamfer | After Chamfer

CHA ↵
(TRIM mode) Current chamfer Dist1 = 0, Dist2 = 0
Select first line or [Polyline/Distance/Angle/Trim/Method/mUltiple]: A ↵ *(to set distances)*
Specify chamfer length on the first line <0.0000>: 1.5 ↵
Specify chamfer angle from the first line <0>: 45 ↵
Select first line or [Polyline/Distance/Angle/Trim/Method]: by mouse (selection 1)
Select second line: by mouse(selection 2)

Multiple: The 'Multiple' option of the **chamfer** command allows you to do continuous chamfer with the current setting rather than allow just a single chamfer operation. Using this option will save exiting and restarting the **Chamfer** command each time you wish to chamfer a set of objects. You must use the 'Enter' or 'Esc' key to end the chamfer command with a 'Multiple' option in force.

Trim: The 'Trim' option allows you to select whether AutoCAD trims the lines back to the chamfer or leaves them untouched. This option is exactly like **Fillet** command.

Polyline: This option is used to chamfer object draw by polyline.

9.3 Command: Blend curves
  Alias   : -

Home Tab → Modify Panel → Blend Curves
Use: This command is used to create a tangent or smooth spline between the end points of the two open curves.

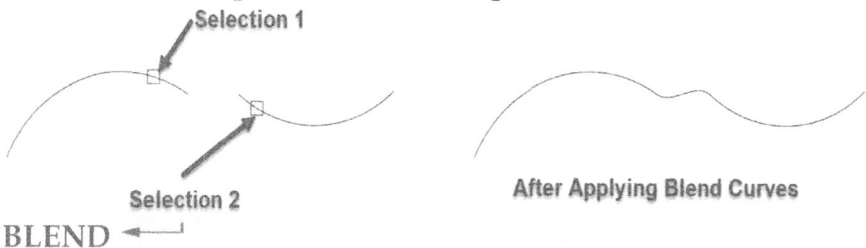

Selection 1
Selection 2
After Applying Blend Curves

BLEND
Continuity = Tangent
Select first object or [CONtinuity]: by mouse (selection 1)
Select second object: by mouse (selection 2)

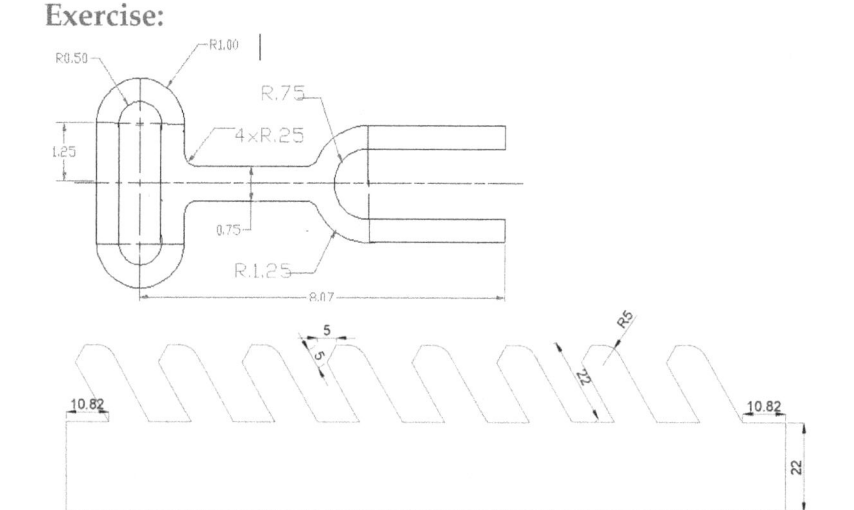

Exercise:

Autodesk AutoCAD 2021
Learn CAD With Ease.

CHAPTER 10
ANNOTATION

In this chapter you will get knowledge about different commands used to give annotation in a drawing.

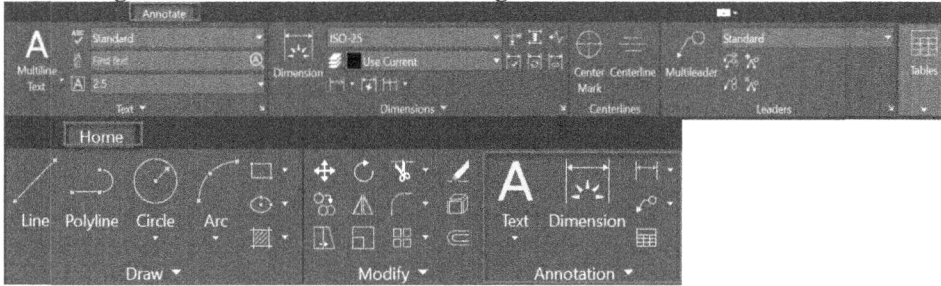

Different things used for annotation of a drawing:
   a. Text
   b. Dimensions
   c. Multileader
   d. Tables

A. **TEXT:** There are two types of text available in an AutoCAD
   a. Single line Text
   b. Multiline Text

10.1 Command: **Text (Single line text)**
   Alias   : Dt
   Home Tab→ Annotation Panel →
                  Single line text
   Annotate Tab→Text Panel→ Single line text

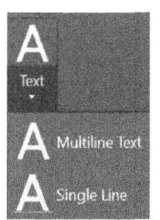

Use: This command is used to write text in the drawing. You can use single-line text to create one or more lines of text, where each text line is an independent object that you can move, format, or otherwise modify.

DT ↵
Current text style: "Standard" Text height: 0.2000 Annotative: No
Specify start point of text or [Justify/Style]: mouse click (P1)
Specify height <0.2000>:1 ↵
Specify rotation angle of text <0>: ↵ or specify angle.

Autodesk AutoCAD 2021
Learn CAD With Ease.

AutoCAD

If you specify rotation angle it rotates the text.

AutoCAD (rotated text at P1)

Justify: Controls justification of the text. You can also enter any of these options at the Specify Start Point of Text.
DT ⏎
Current text style: "Standard" Text height: 0.2000 Annotative: No
Specify start point of text or [Justify/Style]: J ⏎
Enter an option [Align/Fit/Center/Middle/Right/TL/TC/TR/ML/MC/MR/BL/BC/BR]: A ⏎
Specify first endpoint of text baseline: mouse click (P1)
Specify second endpoint of text baseline: mouse click (P2)

Different sub-options of Justify option:

Align: Specifies both text height and text orientation by designating the endpoints of the baseline. The size of the characters adjusts in proportion to their height.
If text string is longer the characters are shorter and they adjusted between two points of the baseline.

AutoCAD 2013 Reference Book (P1 ... P2)

Fit: Specifies that text fits within an area and at an orientation defined with two points and a height. It available for horizontally oriented text only. The height of the characters remains constant.

AutoCAD is a drafting software (P1 ... P2)

Center: Aligns text from the horizontal center of the baseline, which you specify with a point.

AutoCAD (P1)

Autodesk AutoCAD 2021
Learn CAD With Ease.

The rotation angle specifies the orientation of the text baseline with respect to the center point. You can designate the angle by specifying a point. The text baseline runs from the start point toward the specified point. If you specify a point to the left of the center point, the text is drawn upside down.

Middle: Aligns text at the horizontal center of the baseline and the vertical center of the height you specify. Middle-aligned text does not rest on the baseline.

AutoCAD

The Middle option differs from the "MC" option, it uses the midpoint of all text. The MC option uses the midpoint of the height of uppercase letters.

Right: Right-justifies the text at the baseline, which you specify with a point.

AutoCAD

TL (Top Left): Left-justifies text at a point specified for the top of the text.
It's available for horizontally oriented text only.

AutoCAD

TC (Top Center): Centers text at a point specified for the top of the text.
It's available for horizontally oriented text only.

AutoCAD

TR (Top Right): Right-justifies text at a point specified for the top of the text.
It's available for horizontally oriented text only.

AutoCAD

ML (Middle Left): Left-justifies text at a point specified for the middle of the text.
It's available for horizontally oriented text only.

AutoCAD

By Madhumita Kshirsagar

Autodesk AutoCAD 2021
Learn CAD With Ease.

MC (Middle Center): Centers the text both horizontally and vertically at the middle of the text.

It's available for horizontally oriented text only.

AutoCAD

The MC option differs from the Middle option, in that it uses the midpoint of the height of uppercase letters. The Middle option uses the midpoint of all text, including descenders.

MR (Middle Right): Right-justifies text at a point specified for the middle of the text.

It's available for horizontally oriented text only.

AutoCAD P1

BL (Bottom Left): Left-justifies text at a point specified for the baseline.

It's available for horizontally oriented text only.

AutoCAD
P1

BC (Bottom Center): Centers text at a point specified for the baseline.

It's available for horizontally oriented text only.

AutoCAD
P1

BR (Bottom Right): Right-justifies text at a point specified for the baseline.

It's available for horizontally oriented text only.

AutoCAD
P1

Style:

It specifies the text style, which determines the appearance of the text characters.

Text you create uses the current text style.

Entering**?** List the current text styles, associated font files, height, and other parameters.

Note: Firstly you create different types of text styles by Text Style command to use this option.

Autodesk AutoCAD 2021
Learn CAD With Ease.

DT ←┘
Current text style: "style1" Text height: 100.0000 Annotative: No
Justify: Left
Specify start point of text or [Justify/Style]: S ←┘
Enter style name or [?] <style1>: style 1 ←┘
Specify start point of text or [Justify/Style]:
Specify rotation angle of text <0>:
After that, enter text.

10.2 Command: **Text Style**
    Alias   : **ST**
    Home Tab→ Annotation Panel →Text Style
                        &
    Annotate Tab→ Text Panel→Manage Text Styles

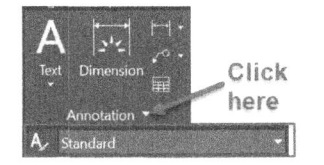

Use: This command is used to create, modify & specify text styles.

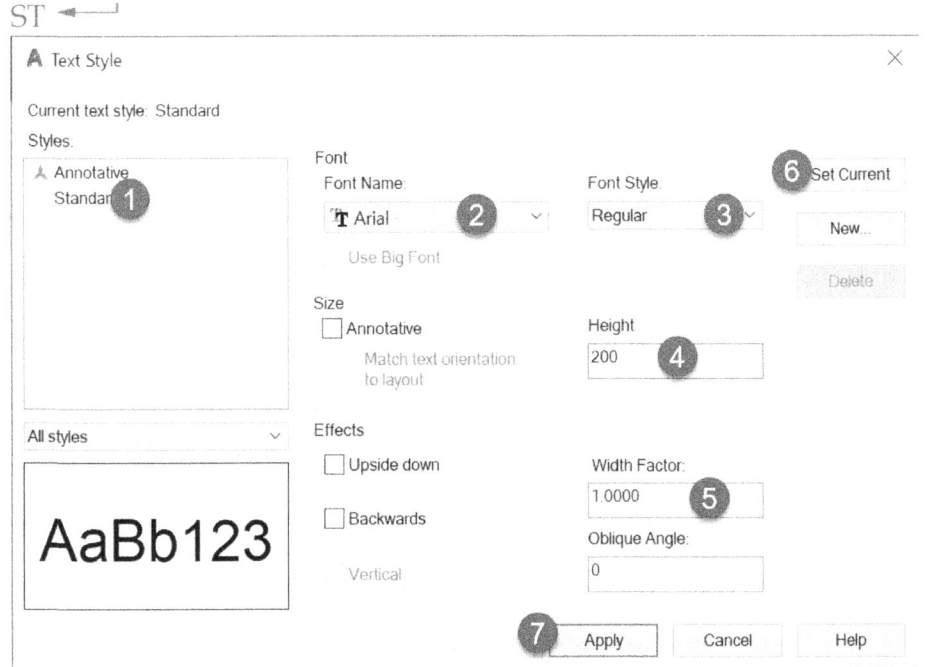

ST ←┘

Font Name: Use to select different types of fonts.

Font style : Use to set font style like *Bold, Italic, Regular.*

128

Autodesk AutoCAD 2021
Learn CAD With Ease.

Height : To specify height of text.

Width Factor : To specify width factor of text.

Upside Down: The effect of *upside down* is given below:

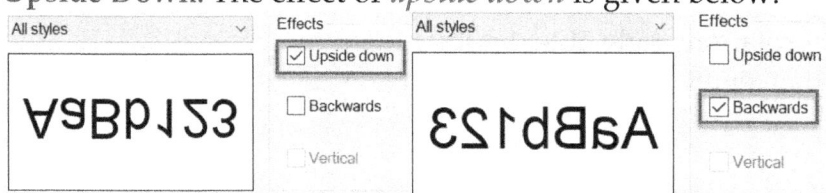

Backwards: The effect of *backwards* is given above:

Oblique Angle: To give angle to a text.

New: This option is used to create new text style.

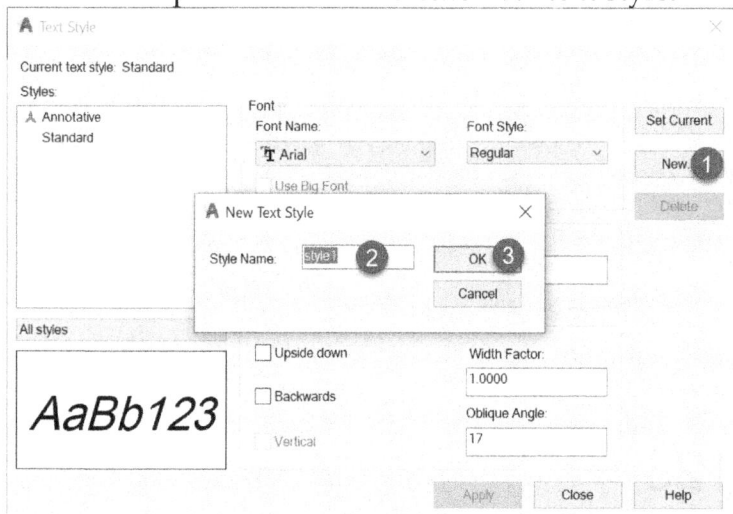

Procedure to create new text style:
1. Activate "Text style" command. (ST ↵).
2. Click on "New" and give "Style Name" and hit "Ok".
3. Select new style name from text list available in "Styles" in "Text Style" dialog box.

Autodesk AutoCAD 2021
Learn CAD With Ease.

4. Set "Font Name", "Font Style", Text Height and etc.
5. Click on "Set Current" to make selected text style current.
6. Then click on "Apply".

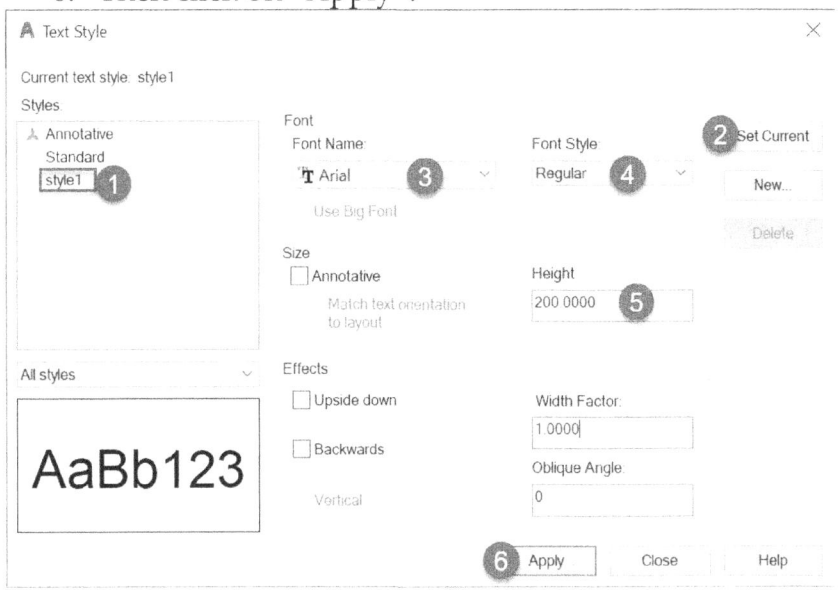

Delete: To delete unnecessary *text style*.

10.3 Command: Multiline Text
    Alias   : **Mt OR T**
    Home Tab→ Annotation Panel →Multiline text

Use: You use *multiline text* for longer notes & labels with internal formatting.

Mt ←

Current text style: "Standard" Text height: 1.0000 Annotative: No
Specify first corner: mouse click
Specify opposite corner or [Height/Justify/Line spacing/ Rotation/Style/ Width/ Columns]: mouse click

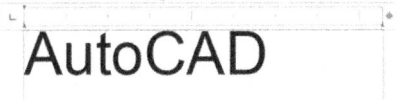

Visor of multiline text:

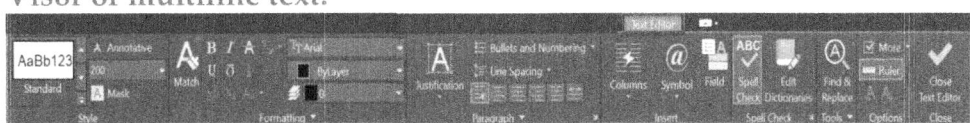

130

By Madhumita Kshirsagar

Autodesk AutoCAD 2021
Learn CAD With Ease.

1) If you want to use a text style other than the default, on the ribbon, click the Annotate tab, Text panel. Select the desired text style from the drop-down list.
2) Enter text.
3) To override the current text style, select text as follows:
   a) To select one or more letters, click and drag the pointing device over the characters.
   b) To select a word, double-click the word.
   c) To select a paragraph, triple-click the paragraph.
4) On the ribbon, make format changes as follows:
   a) To change the font of the selected text, select a font from the list.
   b) To change the height of the selected text, enter a new value in the Height box.
   c) To format text in a TrueType font with boldface or italics, or to create underlined, over lined, or strike through text for any font, click the corresponding button on the ribbon. SHX fonts do not support boldface or italics.
   d) To apply color to selected text, choose a color from the Color list ByLayer.

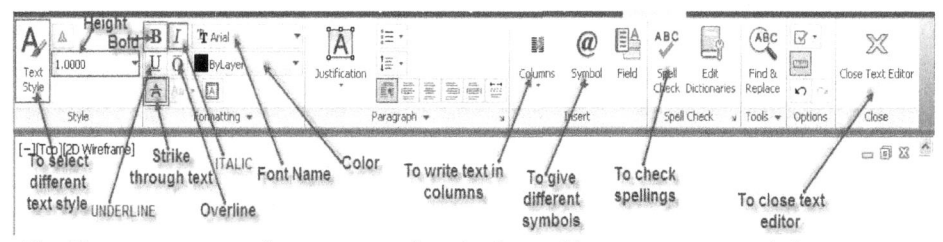

5) To save your changes and exit the editor, use one of the following methods:
   a) On the MTEXT ribbon contextual tab, in the Close panel, click Close Text Editor.
   b) Click in the drawing outside the editor.
   c) Press CTRL+ENTER.

10.4 Command: Text Edit
   Alias   : ED

Use: Edits a selected multiline or single-line text object, or the text in a dimension object.

Autodesk AutoCAD 2021
Learn CAD With Ease.

ED ←┘
MTEDIT
Select an annotation object: *Select a text, mtext, or dimension object.*

Note: You can edit text by double click on text.

10.5 Command: Mirror Text
    Alias   : Mirrtext

Use: This command is used to controls how mirror reflect text.

Have you ever mirrored text and it was backwards and looked as if it was being seen through the rear-view mirror of your car? Well this is how you fix that.

Change the System Variable MIRRTEXT:

- ❖ Mirror text value "0" keeps the text readable after being mirrored by mirror command.

- ❖ Mirror Text value "1" mirrors the text direction after applying mirror command.

Mirrtext ←┘

Enter new value for MIRRTEXT <0>:1 ←┘

AutoCAD | ꓷAƆoɟuA

Mirrtext ←┘

Enter new value for MIRRTEXT <1>:0 ←┘

AutoCAD | AutoCAD

10.6 Command: Scale Text
    Alias   : Scaletext
Annotate Tab→ Text Panel→Scale Text 🅰 Scale

Use: This command is used to scale text.

Autodesk AutoCAD 2021
Learn CAD With Ease.

SCALETEXT ←
Select objects: by mouse
Select objects: ←
Enter a base point option for scaling [Existing/Left/Center/Middle/Right/TL/TC/TR/ML/MC/MR/BL/BC/BR] <Existing>: E ←
Specify new model height or [Paper height/Match object/Scale factor] <2.5>: 4 ←

AutoCAD
Before Applying
Scale Text

AutoCAD
After Applying Scale
Text (Model height=4)

Model Height: By this option you can specify new height for selected text.

Paper Height: This option is used to scale the text height depending on the annotative property.
You can only specify a paper height for annotative objects.

Match Object: Scales the objects that you originally selected to match the size of a selected text object. This option only affects like objects (annotative or non annotative).

Selection 2
AutoCAD   Selection 1   **AutoCAD**
AutoCAD   **AutoCAD**
During Scale Text   After Scale Text

SCALETEXT ←
Select objects: by mouse (selection 1)
Select objects: ←
Enter a base point option for scaling [Existing/Left/Center/Middle/Right/TL/TC/TR/ML/MC/MR/BL/BC/BR] <Existing>: ←
Specify new model height or [Paper height/Match object/Scale factor] <2.5>: M ←
Select a text object with the desired height: by mouse (selection 2)
Height=2.5

Scale Factor:

Scales the selected text objects based on a reference length and a specified new length.

Scaletext ←
Select objects: by mouse
Select objects: ←
Enter a base point option for scaling [Existing/Left/Center/Middle/Right/TL/TC/TR/ML/MC/MR/BL/BC/BR] <Existing>: E ←
Specify new model height or [Paper height/Match object/Scale factor] <2.5>: S ←
Specify scale factor or [Reference] <2>: 2 ←

AutoCAD   **AutoCAD**

Before Scale Text   After Scale Text (Scale :2)

Reference: Scales the selected text objects relative to a reference length and a new length. The selected text is scaled by a ratio of the values that you entered for the new length and the reference length. If the new length is less than the reference length, the selected text objects are reduced in size.

EXERCISE: Write notification in your drawing by using "Text Style" and "Text" Command.

Text Style Settings:- **Font Name: Arial; Font Style: Regular; Text Height: 100mm; Width Factor: 1.**

1. All dimensions are in mm.
2. Dimensions should be read not to be measured.
3. Proposed work shown in black.
4. For R.C.C. detail of "Boxes" refer as design
5. All dimensions and levels should be verified before starting the work.
6. Angle of Level crossing is 44 degrees.
7. All dimensions of structures are tentative shall be finalize after design.

Autodesk AutoCAD 2021
Learn CAD With Ease.

B. DIMENSIONS:

This topic describes the options and commands available for dimensioning drawings and how to use them. The correct use of AutoCAD's dimension tools is the key to producing clear and concise measured drawings. If you just need to quickly find a description of the various dimension commands, click on the appropriate button on the Quick Find toolbar below.

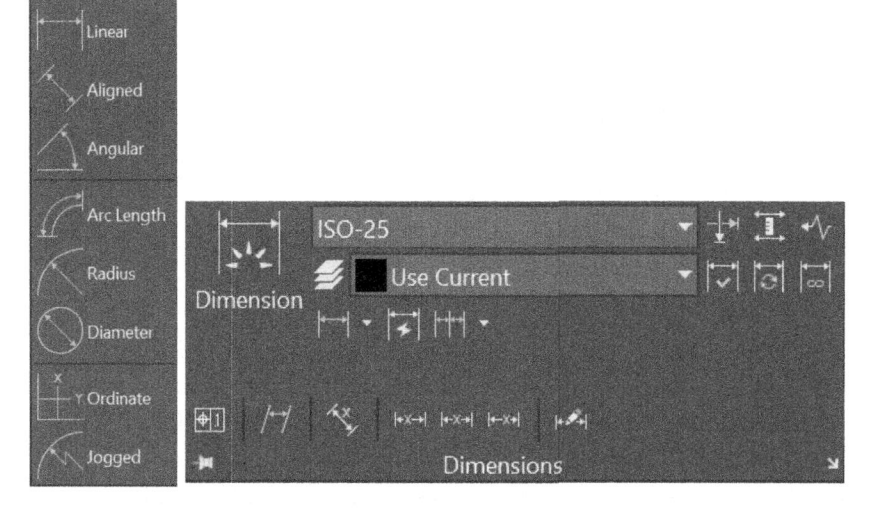

10.7 Command: Linear Dimension
    Alias   : Dimlinear Or Dli
Annotate Tab → Dimension Panel → Linear Dimension
               Or
Home Tab → Annotation Panel → Linear Dimension

Use: Creates a linear dimension with a horizontal, vertical, or rotated dimension line. This command replaces the DIMHORIZONTAL and DIMVERTICAL commands.

Dli ←
Specify first extension line origin or <select object>: mouse click (P1)

Specify second extension line origin: mouse click (P2)
Specify dimension line location or [Mtext/Text/Angle/Horizontal/Vertical/Rotated]: mouse click (P3)
Dimension text = 8
Horizontal: Creates horizontal linear dimensions.

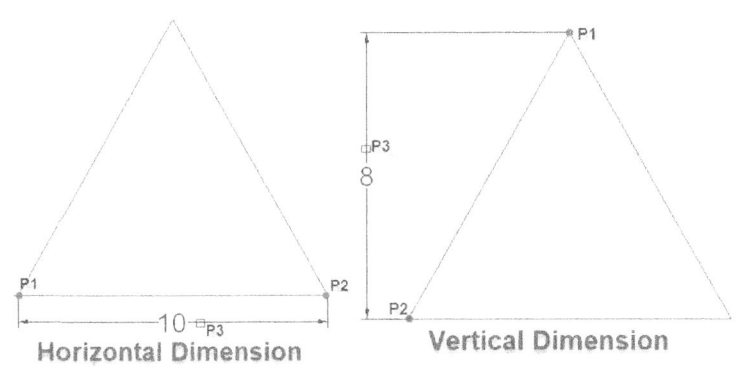

Horizontal Dimension   **Vertical Dimension**

Vertical: Creates vertical linear dimensions.

Dli ↵

Specify first extension line origin or <select object>: mouse click (P1)

Specify second extension line origin: mouse click (P2)
Specify dimension line location or [Mtext/ Text/ Angle/ Horizontal/Vertical/Rotated]: V ↵
Specify dimension line location or [Mtext/Text/Angle]: mouse click (P3)

Dimension text = 10.0000

Rotated: Creates rotated linear dimensions.

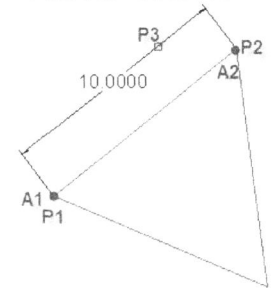

Dli ↵

Specify first extension line origin or <select object>: mouse click (P1)

Specify second extension line origin: mouse click (P2)
Specify dimension line location or [Mtext/ Text/Angle/ Horizontal/Vertical/Rotated]: R ↵
Specify angle of dimension line <0>: mouse click (A1)
Specify second point: mouse click (A2)

Autodesk AutoCAD 2021
Learn CAD With Ease.

Specify dimension line location or [Mtext/ Text/ Angle / Horizontal/ Vertical/ Rotated]: mouse click (P3)
Dimension text = 10.0000

Angle: Changes the angle of the dimension text.

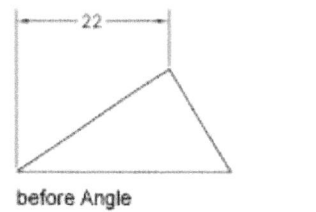

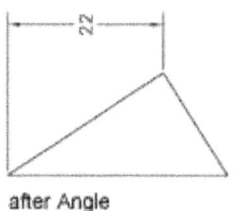

before Angle   after Angle

Mtext: This option is used to display the "In-Place Text Editor", which you can use to edit the dimension text.

DLI ←┘

Specify first extension line origin or <select object>: mouse click (P1)

Specify second extension line origin: mouse click (P2)
Specify dimension line location or [Mtext /Text / Angle / Horizontal/ Vertical/ Rotated]: M ←┘
Specify dimension line location or [Mtext /Text/ Angle/ Horizontal/ Vertical/ Rotated]: mouse click (P3)

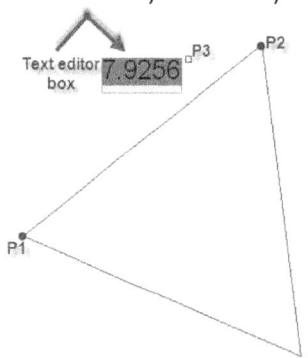

Text: Customizes the dimension text at the Command prompt. The generated dimension measurement is displayed within angle brackets.

DLI ←┘

Specify first extension line origin or <select object>: mouse click
Specify second extension line origin: mouse click

Autodesk AutoCAD 2021
Learn CAD With Ease.

Specify dimension line location or [Mtext/Text/Angle/Horizontal/Vertical/Rotated]: T ↵
Enter dimension text <7.9256>: 8 ↵
Specify dimension line location or [Mtext/Text/Angle/Horizontal/Vertical/Rotated]: specify point for location line
Dimension text = 7.9256 (this is actual dimension)

Select Object:
Automatically determines the origin points of the first and second extension lines after you select an object.

10.8 Command: Aligned Dimension
  Alias   : Dimaligned Or Dal

Annotate Tab → Dimension Panel → Aligned Dimension
            Or
Home Tab → Annotation Panel → Aligned Dimension

Use: Creates a linear dimension that is aligned with the origin points of the extension lines.

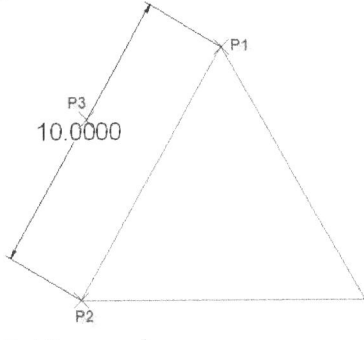

DAL ↵
Specify first extension line origin or <select object>: mouse click (P1)
Specify second extension line origin: mouse click (P2)
Specify dimension line location or [Mtext/Text/Angle]: mouse click (P3)

Dimension text = 10.0000

Note: Mtext, Text, and Angle options are same as linear dimensions.

138

By Madhumita Kshirsagar

Autodesk AutoCAD 2021
Learn CAD With Ease.

10.9 Command: Angular Dimension
Alias : Dimangular Or Dan

Annotate Tab→Dimension Panel→ Angular Dimension

Or

Home Tab → Annotation Panel→ Angular Dimension

Use: Measures the angle between selected objects. Objects that can be selected include arcs, circles, and lines, among others.

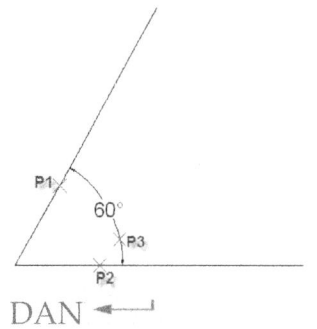

DAN ←⎯

Select arc, circle, line, or <specify vertex>: select by mouse click (P1)

Select second line: select by mouse click (P2)
Specify dimension arc line location or [Mtext/Text/Angle/Quadrant]: mouse click (P3)
Dimension text = 60

10.10 Command: Arc Length
Alias : Dar

Annotate Tab→ Dimension Panel→ Arc Length

Or

Home Tab → Annotation Panel → Arc Length

Use: To measures arc length of arc or the distance along arc & polyline arc segment.

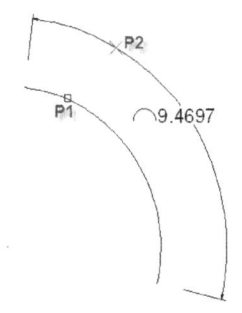

DAR ←⎯

Select arc or polyline arc segment: select by mouse click (P1)
Specify arc length dimension location, or [Mtext/Text/ Angle/Partial/Leader]: mouse click (P2)
Dimension text = 9.4697

Autodesk AutoCAD 2021
Learn CAD With Ease.

Mtext: Displays the "In-Place Text Editor", which you can use to edit the dimension text. By this you can change actual dimension of arc length like dimlinear or other dimension types.

Partial:

This option is used to reduce the length of the arc length dimension. You can give dimension to any part of an arc.

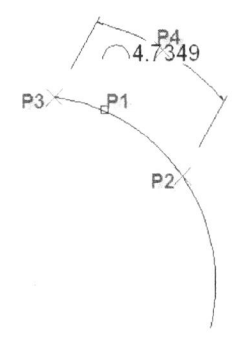

DAR ←┘
Select arc or polyline arc segment: select by mouse click (P1)
Specify arc length dimension location, or [Mtext/Text/Angle/ Partial/Leader]: P ←┘
Specify first point for arc length dimension: mouse click (P2)
Specify second point for arc length dimension: mouse click (P3)
Specify arc length dimension location, or [Mtext/Text/Angle/ Partial]: mouse click (P4)
Dimension text = 4.7349

Angle: Changes the angle of the dimension text.

10.11 Command: Radius

  Alias   : Dimradius Or Dra

  Annotate Tab → Dimension Panel → Radius
          Or
  Home Tab → Annotation Panel → Radius

Use: To give radius of circles & arcs.

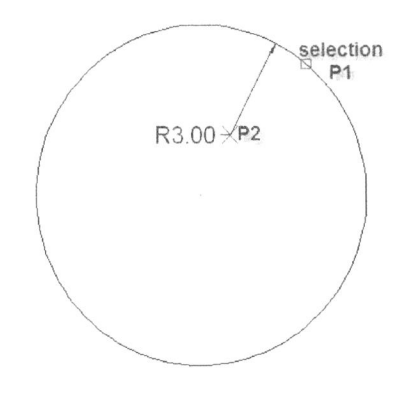

Dra ←┘
Select arc or circle: mouse click (P1)
Dimension text = 3.0000
Specify dimension line location or [Mtext/Text/Angle]: mouse click (P2)

140

By Madhumita Kshirsagar

Autodesk AutoCAD 2021
Learn CAD With Ease.

10.12 Command: Diameter
    Alias : Dimdiameter Or Ddi

Annotate Tab → Dimension Panel → Diameter

Or

Home Tab → Annotation Panel → Diameter

Use: To give diameter of circles & arcs.

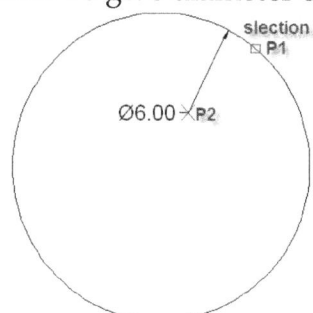

DDI
Select arc or circle: mouse click (P1)
Dimension text = 6.00
Specify dimension line location or [Mtext/Text/Angle]: mouse click (P2)

10.13 Command: Ordinate
    Alias : Dimordinate Or Dor

Annotate Tab → Dimension Panel → Ordinate

Or

Home Tab → Annotation Panel → Ordinate

Use: Ordinate dimensions measure the horizontal or vertical distance from an origin point called the datum to a feature, such as a hole in a part. These dimensions prevent escalating errors by maintaining accurate offsets of the features from the datum.

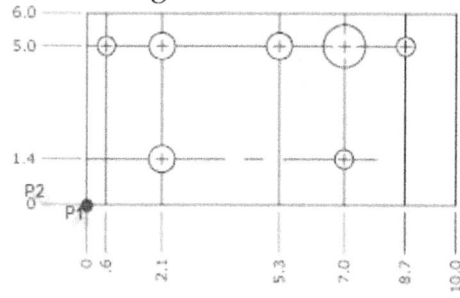

DOR
Specify feature location: mouse click (P1)
Specify leader endpoint or [Xdatum/Ydatum/Mtext/Text/Angle]: mouse click (P2)
Dimension text = 0

Xdatum : To mark X Ordinate on a point.

Autodesk AutoCAD 2021
Learn CAD With Ease.

Specify feature location: mouse click (P1)
Specify leader endpoint or [Xdatum/Ydatum/Mtext/Text/Angle]: X ↵
Specify leader endpoint or [Xdatum/Ydatum/Mtext/Text/Angle]: mouse click (P2)
Dimension text = 10.00

Ydatum: To mark Y Ordinate on a point.

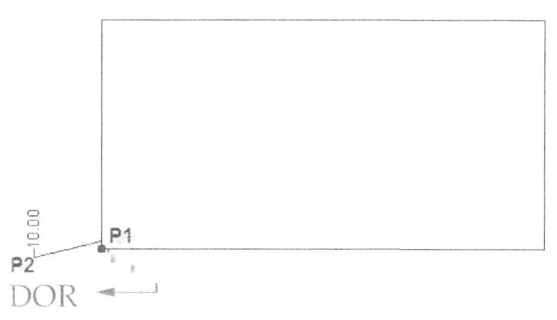

Specify feature location: mouse click (P1)
Specify leader endpoint or [Xdatum/Ydatum/Mtext/Text/Angle]: Y ↵
Specify leader endpoint or [Xdatum/Ydatum/Mtext/Text/Angle]: mouse click (P2)
Dimension text = 15.00

10.14 Command: Jogged
    Alias   : Dimjogged

    Annotate Tab → Dimension Panel → Jogged

    Home Tab → Annotation Panel → Jogged

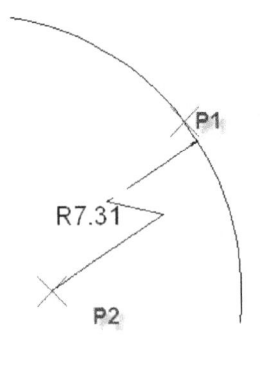

Autodesk AutoCAD 2021
Learn CAD With Ease.

Use: DIMJOGGED measures the radius of the selected object and displays the dimension text with a radius symbol in front of it. The origin point of the dimension line can be specified at any convenient location. It creates jogged radius dimensions when the center of an arc or circle is located off the layout and cannot be displayed in its true location. The origin point of the dimension can be specified at a more convenient location called the center location override.

Dimjogged
Select arc or circle: Select an arc, circle, or polyline arc segment
Specify center location override: Specify a point
Specify dimension line location or [Mtext/Text/Angle]: Specify a point or enter an option

10.15 Command: Baseline
    Alias   : Dimbaseline OR Dba
    Annotate Tab → Dimension Panel → Baseline

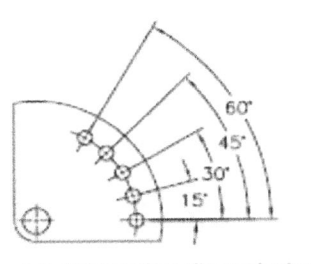

Note: For Baseline dimension you give first dimension by dimlinear or dimaligned & then give command dimbaseline.
You can also apply baseline dimensions with dimangular.

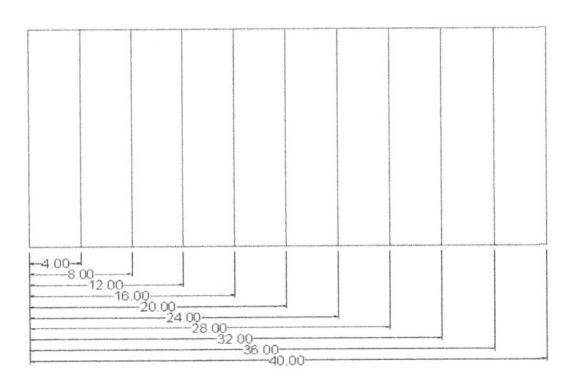

angular baseline dimensioning

Use: To dimension objects from one base points like 1st point to 2nd, 1st to 3rd, 1st to 4th, 1st to 5th. In given example first point is base point.

Autodesk AutoCAD 2021
Learn CAD With Ease.

DBA ←┘

Specify second extension line origin or [Select/Undo] <Select>:
                                  Pick point by mouse
Dimension text = 4.00
Specify second extension line origin or [Select/Undo] <Select>:
                                  Pick point by mouse
Dimension text = 8.00
Specify second extension line origin or [Select/Undo] <Select>:
                                  Pick point by mouse
Dimension text = 12.00
Specify second extension line origin or [Select/Undo] <Select>:
                                  Pick point by mouse
Dimension text = 16.00
Specify second extension line origin or [Select/Undo] <Select>:
                                  Pick point by mouse
Dimension text = 18.00
Specify second extension line origin or [Select/Undo] <Select>:
                            Press "Esc" to finish command.

10.16 Command: Continue
    Alias   : **Dimcontinue OR Dco**

    Annotate Tab → Dimension Panel → Continue

Use: This command is used to give chain dimension.

DCO ←┘

Select continued dimension: Select a linear, ordinate, or angular
                          dimension (P1)

Specify a second extension line origin or [Undo/Select] <Select>:
                                    mouse click(P2)
Dimension text = 8.00
Specify a second extension line origin or [Undo/Select] <Select>:
                                    mouse click(P3)
Dimension text = 8.00
Specify a second extension line origin or [Undo/Select] <Select>:
                                    mouse click(P4)
Dimension text = 8.00
Specify a second extension line origin or [Undo/Select] <Select>:
                                    mouse click(P5)
Dimension text = 8.00

Autodesk AutoCAD 2021
Learn CAD With Ease.

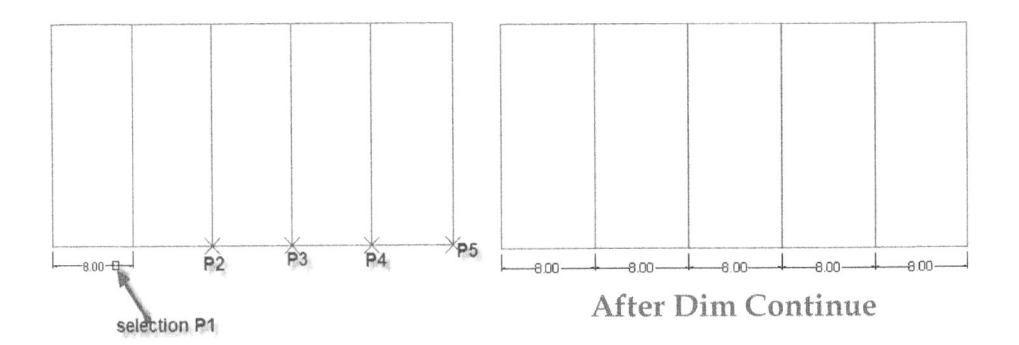

After Dim Continue

selection P1

10.17 Command: Break
     Alias   : Dimbreak OR Dimbr

     Annotate Tab→ Dimension Panel →Break

Use: This command is used to break or restore dimensions and extension lines where they cross other objects. Dimension breaks can be added to linear, angular, and ordinate dimensions, among others.

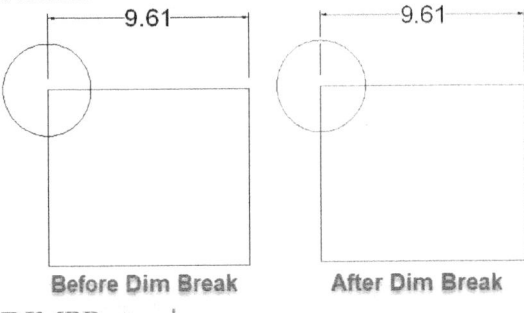

Before Dim Break   **After Dim Break**

DIMBR
Select dimension to add/remove break or [Multiple]: select a dimension, or M ↵ or press ↵
Select object to break dimension or [Auto/Manual/Remove] <Auto>: select an object that intersects the dimension or extension lines of the selected dimension, enter an option, or press ↵

Auto: Places dimension breaks automatically at all the intersection points of the objects that intersect the selected dimension. Any dimension break created using this option is updated automatically when the dimension or an intersecting object is modified.

DIMBR
Select dimension to add/remove break or [Multiple]: select a dimension by mouse.

Select object to break dimension or [Auto/Manual/Remove] <Auto>: A ↵

Manual: Places a dimension break manually. You specify two points on the dimension or extension lines for the location of the break. Any dimension break that is created using this option is not updated if the dimension or intersecting objects are modified. You can only place a single manual dimension break at a time with this option.

DIMBR ↵

Select dimension to add/remove break or [Multiple]: select dimension

Select object to break dimension or [Auto/Manual/Remove] <Auto>: M ↵

Specify first break point: mouse click (P1)
Specify second break point: mouse click (P2)

Remove: Removes all dimension breaks from the selected dimensions.

10.18 Command: Center Mark
    Alias   : **Dimcenter**

    Annotate Tab → Center lines Panel → Center Mark

Autodesk AutoCAD 2021
Learn CAD With Ease.

Use: Creates the center mark or the centerlines of circles and arcs.

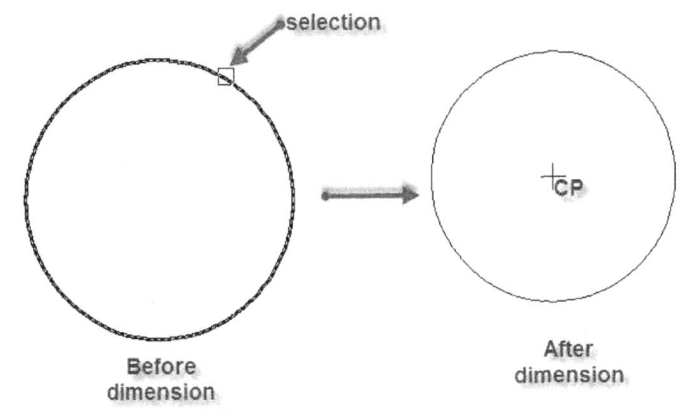

Before dimension → After dimension (CP)

DIMCENTER ↵
Select arc or circle: mouse click on circle

10.19 Command: Inspect
    Alias   : Diminspect

Annotate Tab → Dimension Panel → Inspect

Use: This command is used to add or remove inspection information for a selected dimension.
Inspection dimensions specify how frequently manufactured parts should be checked to ensure that the dimension value and tolerances of the parts are within the specified range.

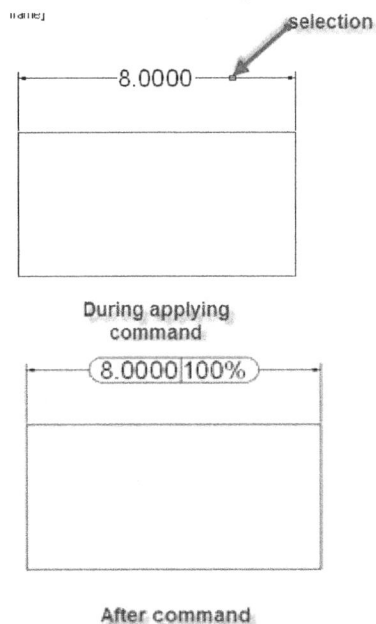

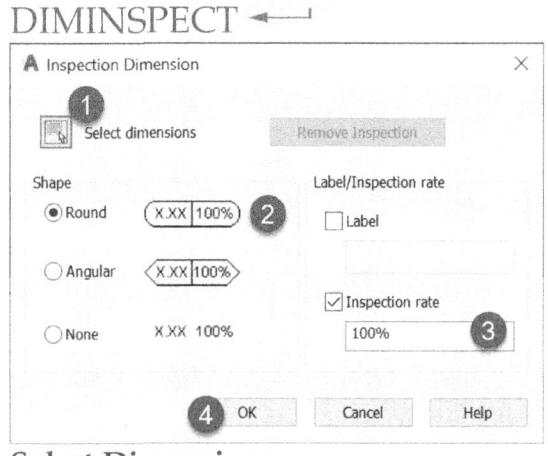

DIMINSPECT ↵

During applying command: 8.0000
After command: 8.0000 100%

Inspection Dimension dialog:
1. Select dimensions / Remove Inspection
2. Shape: Round (X.XX 100%), Angular (X.XX 100%), None (X.XX 100%)
3. Label/Inspection rate: Label, Inspection rate 100%
4. OK / Cancel / Help

Select Dimensions: Specifies the dimensions that an inspection dimension should be added to or removed from.

Autodesk AutoCAD 2021
Learn CAD With Ease.

Remove Inspection: Removes the inspection dimension from the selected dimension.
Shape: Controls the shape of the frame that is drawn around the label, dimension value, and inspection rate of the inspection dimension.
Round: Creates a frame with semi-circles on the two ends; the fields within the frame are separated by vertical lines.
Angular: Creates a frame with lines that form a 90-degree angle on the two ends; the fields within the frame are separated by vertical lines.
None: Specifies that no frame is drawn around the values; the fields are not separated by vertical lines.
Label/Inspection Rate: Specifies the label text and inspection rate for an inspection dimension.
Label: Turns the display of the label field on and off.
Label Value: Specifies the label text.
The label is displayed in the leftmost section of the inspection dimension when the Label check box is selected.
Inspection Rate: Turns the display of the rate field on and off.
Inspection Rate Value: Specifies how frequently a part should be inspected.
The value is expressed as a percentage, and the valid range is 0 to 100. The inspection rate is displayed in the rightmost section of the inspection dimension when the Inspection Rate check box is selected.

10.20 Command: Adjust Space
    Alias   : Dimspace
        Annotate Tab → Dimension Panel → Adjust Space
Use: To adjust space between two linear & angular dimensions

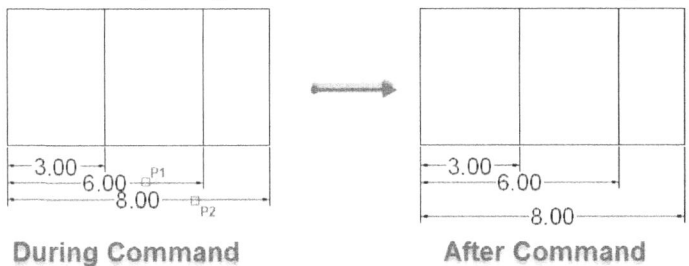

During Command   **After Command**

Autodesk AutoCAD 2021
Learn CAD With Ease.

DIMSPACE ↵
Select base dimension: mouse click (P1)
Select dimensions to space: mouse click (P2)
Select dimensions to space: ↵
Enter value or [Auto] <Auto>: 1 ↵

Notice the second figure, the distance between two dimensions is 1.

Auto:
Calculates the spacing distance automatically based on the text height specified in the dimension style of the selected base dimension. The resulting spacing value is twice the height of the dimension text.

DIMSPACE ↵
Select base dimension: mouse click (P1)
Select dimensions to space: mouse click (P2)
Select dimensions to space: ↵
Enter value or [Auto] <Auto>: A ↵

10.21 Command: Quick Dimension
    Alias   : Qdim

    Annotate Tab → Dimension Panel → Quick Dimension

Use: To create a series of dimensions quickly from selected objects.

QDIM ↵
Associative dimension priority = Endpoint
Select geometry to dimension: by any selection method
Select geometry to dimension: ↵
Specify dimension line position, or [Continuous/Staggered/Baseline/Ordinate/Radius/Diameter/datumPoint/Edit/seTtings] <Continuous>: by mouse click.

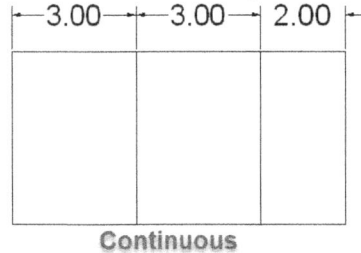

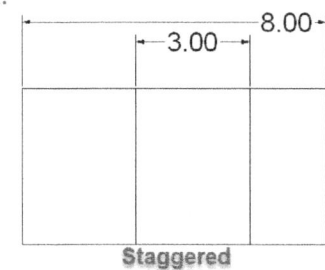

|—3.00—|—3.00—| 2.00 | |—3.00—| 8.00 |

Continuous   **Staggered**

Autodesk AutoCAD 2021
Learn CAD With Ease.

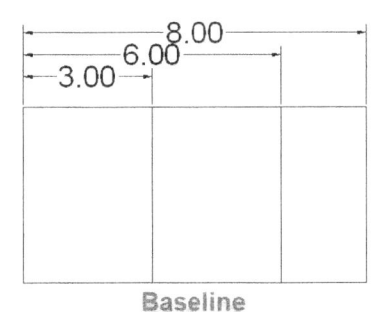

Continuous: Creates a series of continued dimensions

Staggered: Creates a series of staggered dimensions.

Baseline: Creates a series of baseline dimensions.

Ordinate: Creates a series of ordinate dimensions.

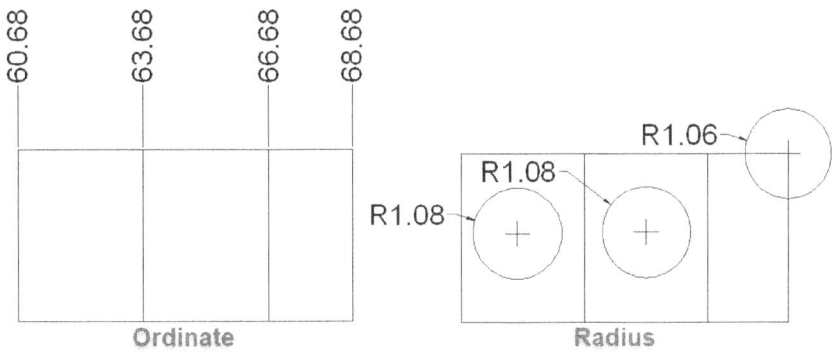

Radius: Creates a series of radial dimensions.

Diameter: Creates a series of diameter dimensions.

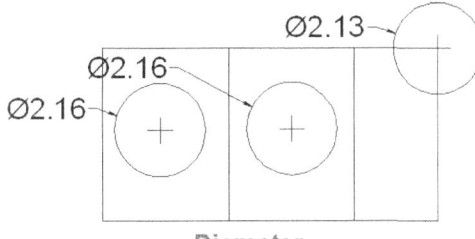

Datum Point: Sets a new datum point for baseline and ordinate dimensions.

Edit: Edits a series of dimensions. You are prompted to add or remove points from existing dimensions.

Settings: Sets the default object snap for specifying extension line origins.

Autodesk AutoCAD 2021
Learn CAD With Ease.

10.22 Command: Tolerance
    Alias   : TOL
    Annotate Tab → Dimension Panel → Tolerance

Use: Creates geometric tolerances contained in a feature control frame.

Geometric tolerances show acceptable deviations of form, profile, orientation, location, and run out. Feature control frames can be created with leader lines using TOLERANCE, LEADER, or QLEADER.

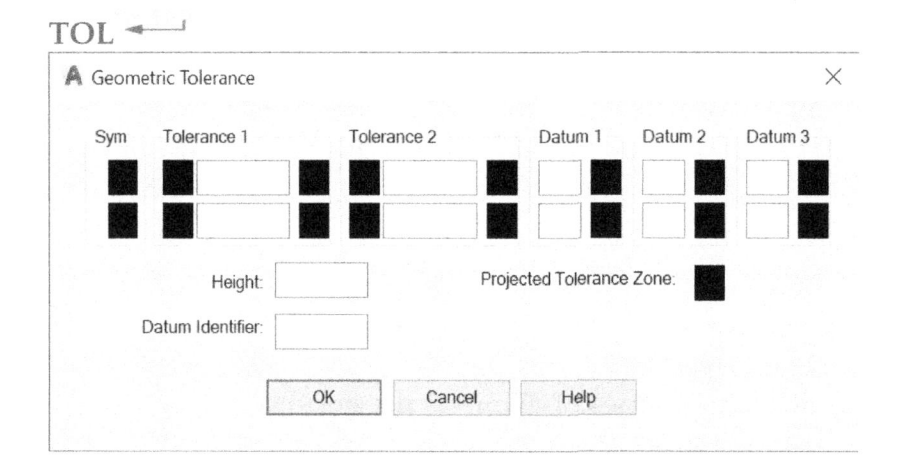

TOL ←

Sym: This option is used to display the geometric characteristic symbol, which you select from the "Symbol" dialog box .The dialog box is displayed when you select one of the Sym boxes.

Tolerance 1: This option is used to create the first tolerance value in the feature control frame. The tolerance value indicates the amount by which the geometric characteristic can deviate from a perfect form. You can insert a diameter symbol before the tolerance value and a material condition symbol after it.

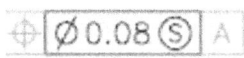

First Box: This option is used to insert a diameter symbol in front of the tolerance value. Click the box to insert the diameter symbol.

Second Box: Creates the tolerance value. Enter a value in the box.

Third Box: Displays the "Material Condition" dialog box, in which you select a modifying symbol.
These symbols act as modifiers to the geometric characteristic and the tolerance value of features that can vary in size.
The symbol is inserted into the MC box for the first tolerance value in the "Geometric Tolerance" dialog box.

Tolerance 2: Creates the second tolerance value in the feature control frame. Specify the second tolerance value in the same way as the first.

Ø0.1 MAX

Datum 1: Creates the primary datum reference in the feature control frame. The datum reference can consist of a value and a modifying symbol. A datum is a theoretically exact geometric reference used to establish the tolerance zone for a feature.

A Ⓜ

First Box: Creates the datum reference value.

Second Box: Displays the "Material Condition" dialog box, in which you select a modifying symbol. These symbols act as modifiers to the datum reference.
The symbol is inserted into the MC box for the primary datum reference in the Geometric Tolerance dialog box.

Datum 2: This option is used to create the secondary datum reference in the feature control frame in the same way as the primary datum reference.

B

Datum 3: This option is used to create the tertiary datum reference in the feature control frame in the same way as the primary datum reference.

C

Height: Creates a projected tolerance zone value in the feature control frame. A projected tolerance zone controls the variation in height of the extended portion of a fixed perpendicular part and refines the tolerance to that specified by positional tolerances.

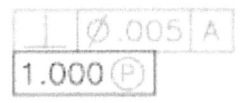

```
  ⊥  | Ø.005 | A |
| 1.000 Ⓟ |
```

Projected Tolerance Zone:
This option is used to insert a projected tolerance zone symbol after the projected tolerance zone value.

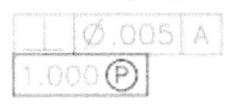

```
  ⊥  | Ø.005 | A |
| 1.000 Ⓟ |
```

Datum Identifier: Creates a datum-identifying symbol consisting of a reference letter. A datum is a theoretically exact geometric reference from which you can establish the location and tolerance zones of other features. A point, line, plane, cylinder, or other geometry can serve as a datum.

| A |

10.23 Command: Dimension Style

Alias : D

Annotate Tab → Dimension Panel → Dimension style

Or

Home Tab → Annotation → Dimension Style

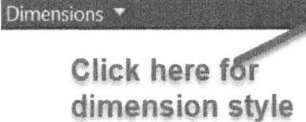

Dimensions ▼

Click here for dimension style

Use: To create new dimension style & modify existing dimension style. A dimension style is a collection of some settings that controls the appearance &format of dimension like:- Primary Units, Alternate Units, Text, Dimension line, Extension line, Tolerance & Fit.

Autodesk AutoCAD 2021
Learn CAD With Ease.

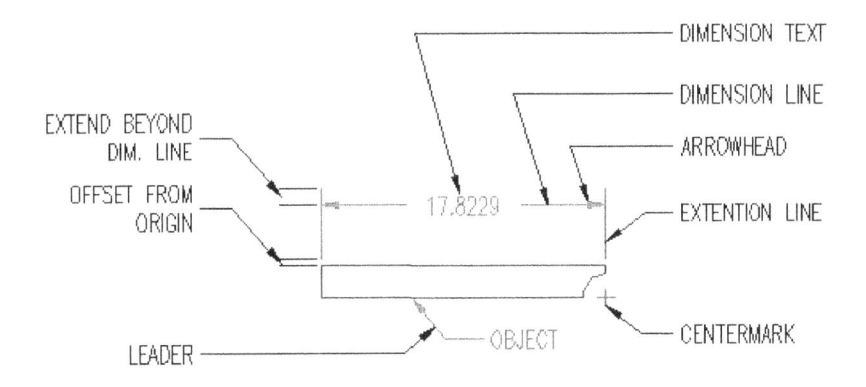

Procedure to modify existing dimension style:

1. D

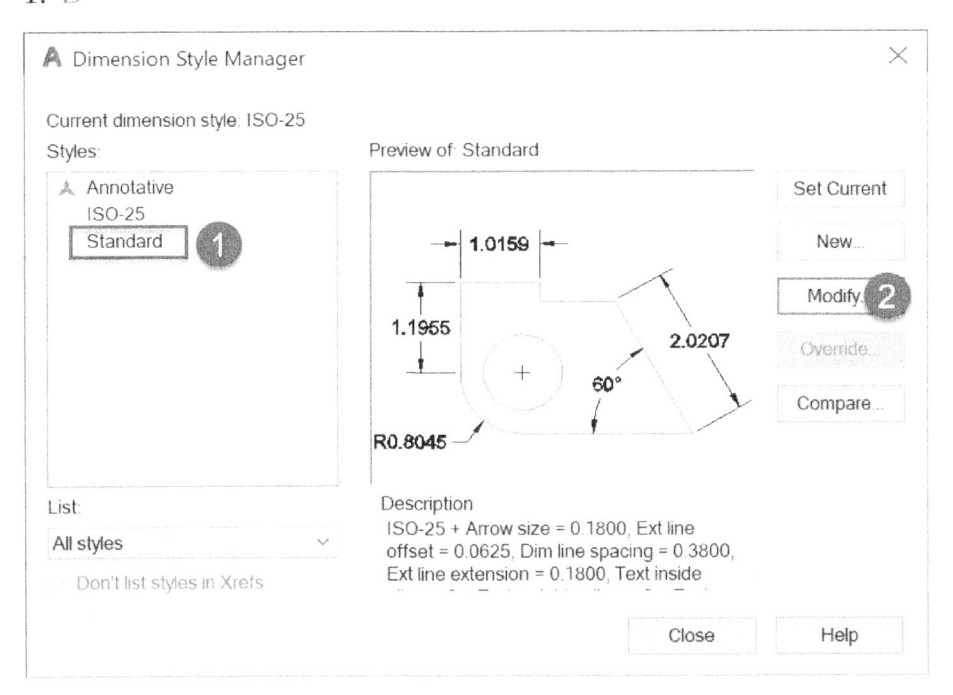

2. Select "Standard" from "Styles" then click on "Modify" to make changes in existing dimension styles.

3. **Primary Units:** In this category you will set primary unit in which you want to give dimensions of the drawing.

Autodesk AutoCAD 2021
Learn CAD With Ease.

i. **Linear Dimensions:** In primary units you enter units in which you want to give dimension of your drawing.

❖ **Unit Format:** If you want to give dimensions in feet & inches you set it **Architectural**.

Modify Dimension Style: Standard

Tabs: Lines | Symbols and Arrows | Text | Fit | **Primary Units** ① | Alternate Units | Tolerances

Linear dimensions
- Unit format: Architectural ②
- Precision: 0'-0 1/8" ③
- Fraction format: Diagonal ④
- Decimal separator: '.' (Period)
- Round off: 0
- Prefix:
- Suffix:

Measurement scale
- Scale factor: 1
- ☐ Apply to layout dimensions only

Zero suppression
- ☐ Leading
- ☐ Trailing
- Sub-units factor: 100
- Sub-unit suffix:
- ☑ 0 feet ⑤
- ☑ 0 inches ⑥

Angular dimensions
- Units format: Decimal Degrees ⑦
- Precision: 0

Zero suppression
- ☐ Leading
- ☐ Trailing

⑧ OK | Cancel | Help

&

Autodesk AutoCAD 2021
Learn CAD With Ease.

If you want to give it in metric units like meter, centimeter, millimeter etc, you set your unit format Decimal.

- ❖ **Precision:** Displays and sets the number of decimal places in the dimension text & in Architectural, it is minimum value in inches.

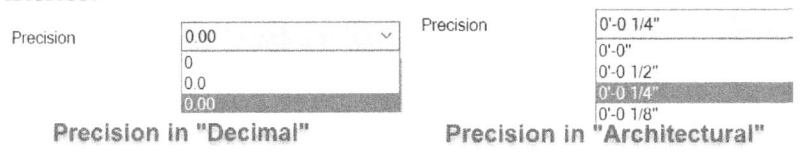

    Precision in "Decimal"   Precision in "Architectural"

- ❖ **Fraction Format:** Sets the format for fractions in "Architectural" primary unit.

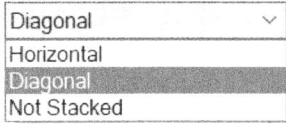

- ❖ Decimal Separator: **Sets the separator for decimal formats.**

156

By Madhumita Kshirsagar

- ❖ Round Off: Sets rounding rules for dimension measurements for all dimension types except Angular. If you enter a value of **0.25**, all distances are rounded to the nearest 0.25 unit. The number of digits displayed after the decimal point depends on the Precision setting.

- ❖ Prefix: Use to add any symbol or alphabet before dimension text.

- ❖ Suffix: Use to add any symbol or alphabet (like mm, cm, m etc) after dimension text.

Prefix:	%%c
Suffix:	mm

⌀10.00mm

ii. **Measurement Scale:**
- ❖ Scale Factor: Sets a scale factor for linear dimension measurements. It is recommended that you do not change this value from the default value of 1.00. For example, if you enter **2**, the dimension for a 10 mm line is displayed as 20 mm.

Measurement scale

Scale factor: 1.0000

☐ Apply to layout dimensions only

- ❖ **Apply to layout dimensions only:** Applies the measurement scale factor only to dimensions created in layout viewports. Except when using non-associative dimensions, this setting should remain unchecked.

iii. **Zero suppression:** Controls the suppression of leading and trailing zeros and of feet and inches that have a value of zero.

- ❖ Leading: Suppresses leading zeros in all decimal dimensions. For example, 0.5000 becomes .5000. Select leading to enable display of dimension distances less than one unit in sub units.

a) **Sub-units factor:** Sets the number of sub units to a unit. It is used to calculate the dimension distance in a sub unit when the distance is less than one unit. For example, enter **100** if the suffix is m and the sub-unit suffix is to display in cm.

b) **Sub-unit suffix:** Includes a suffix to the dimension value sub unit. You can enter text or use control codes to display special symbols. For example, enter cm for .96m to display as 96cm.

❖ **Trailing:** Suppresses trailing zeros in all decimal dimensions. For example, 12.5000 becomes 12.5, and 30.0000 becomes 30.

a) **0 Feet:** Suppresses the feet portion of a feet-and-inches dimension when the distance is less than one foot. For example, 0'-6 1/2" becomes 6 1/2".

b) **0 Inches:** Suppresses the inches portion of a feet-and-inches dimension when the distance is an integral number of feet. For example, 1'-0" becomes 1'.

iv. **Angular dimensions:** To set angular dimension.

❖ **Unit Formats:** You set unit format in Decimal Degrees to give angular dimensions.

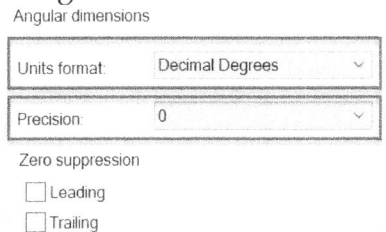

Precision: Sets the number of decimal places for angular dimensions.

4. **Text:** To set font style, height, color etc of dimension text.

i. **Text Appearance:** Controls the dimension text & format.

❖ **Text Style:** Lists the text styles available in the drawing. You can select any one of them.

❖ **Text color:** To set color of text.

Autodesk AutoCAD 2021
Learn CAD With Ease.

- **Fill color:** Sets the color for the text background in dimensions.
- **Text height:** Use to specify height of text in dimension. If you want to use the height set on the Text tab, make sure the text height in the Text Style is set to 0.
- **Fraction height scale:** If you set primary units in architectural this option is turn on. By this option you specify height scale of fractional numbers of dimensions. The value entered here is multiplied by the text height to determine the height of dimension fractions relative to dimension text.
- **Draw frame around text:** If you check out this option a frame is created around dimension text.

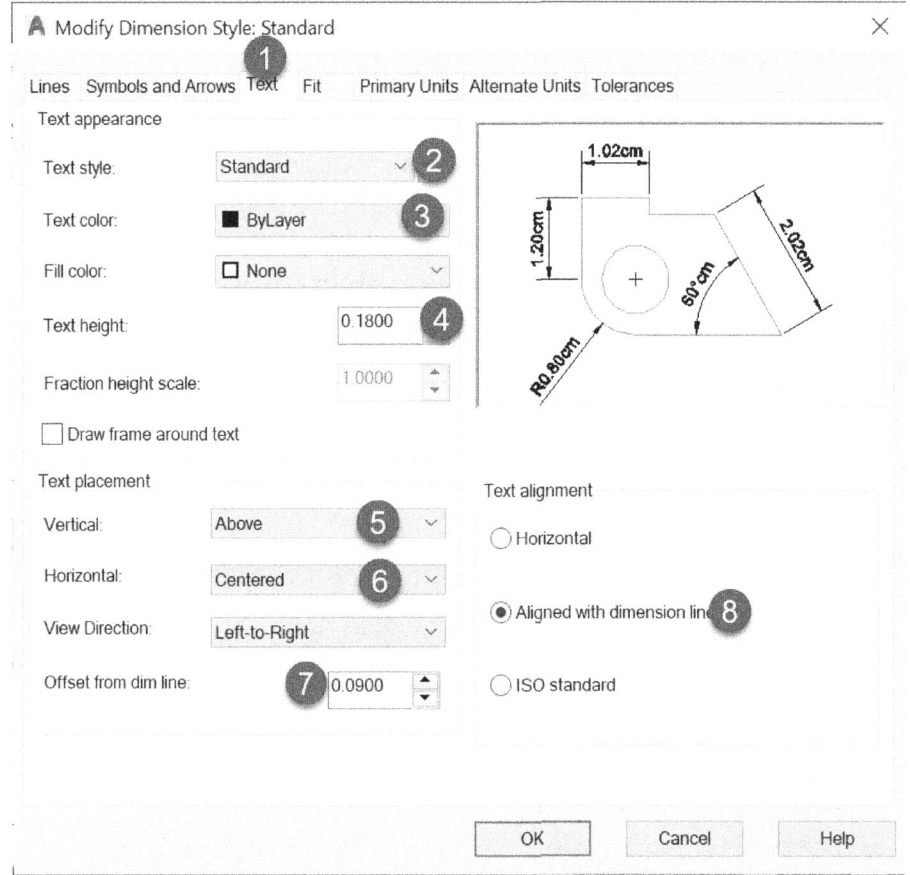

ii. **Text Placement:** Use to control text placement on dimension line.
- **Vertical:** Controls the vertical placement of dimension text in relation to the dimension line.

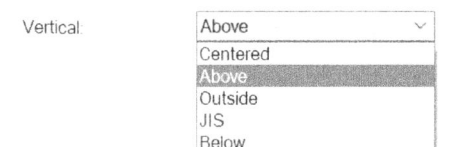

Vertical: [Above ▼]
- Centered
- **Above**
- Outside
- JIS
- Below

Centered: Centers the dimension text between the two parts of the dimension line.

|←———— 5.0000 ————→|

Above: Places the dimension text above the dimension line. The distance from the dimension line to the baseline of the lowest line of text is the current text gap.

|———— 3.9360 ————→|

Outside: Places the dimension text on the side of the dimension line farthest away from the first defining point.

|←———————————————→|
           5.0000

JIS: Places the dimension text to conform to a Japanese Industrial Standards (JIS) representation.

Below: Places the dimension text under the dimension line. The distance from the dimension line to the baseline of the lowest line of text is the current text gap.

|————————————————|
           5.0000

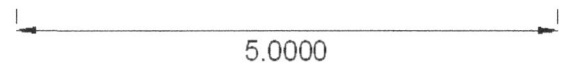

❖ **Horizontal:** Controls the horizontal placement of dimension text in relation to the dimension line.

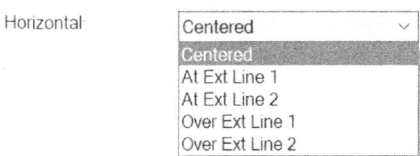

Horizontal: [Centered ▼]
- **Centered**
- At Ext Line 1
- At Ext Line 2
- Over Ext Line 1
- Over Ext Line 2

Centered: Centers the dimension text along the dimension line between the extension lines.

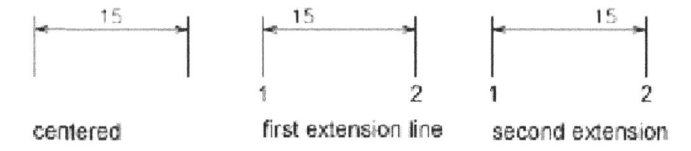

| 1.5 | | 1.5 | | 1.5 |
                    1   2   1   2
centered   first extension line   second extension

At Ext Line 1: Left-justifies the text with the first extension line along the dimension line. The distance between the extension line and the text is twice the arrowhead size plus the text gap value.

At Ext Line 2: Right-justifies the text with the second extension line along the dimension line. The distance between the extension line and the text is twice the arrowhead size plus the text gap value.

Over Ext Line 1: Positions the text over or along the first extension line.

text over first extension line   text over second extension line

Over Ext Line 2: Positions the text over or along the second extension line.

❖ **View Direction:** This option is used to control dimension text viewing direction.

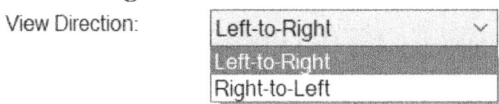

Left to Right: Dimension text read from left to right.

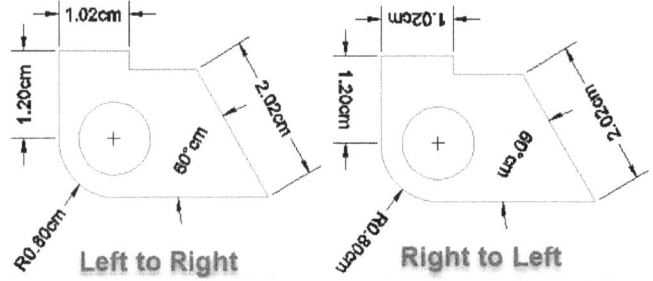

Right to Left: Dimension text read from right to left.

❖ **Offset from dimension line:** Sets the distance between dimension line and text.

iii. Text Alignment: To set orientation of dimension text.
❖ **Horizontal:** In this option the dimension text is unidirectional.

❖ **Aligned with Dimension line:** To align text with dimension line.

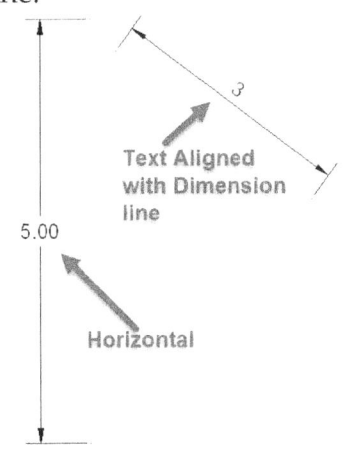

❖ **ISO Standard:** Aligns text with the dimension line when text is inside the extension lines, but aligns it horizontally when text is outside the extension lines.

5. **Symbols & Arrows:** To set arrow heads, size of arrow & center mark size etc in a dimension.

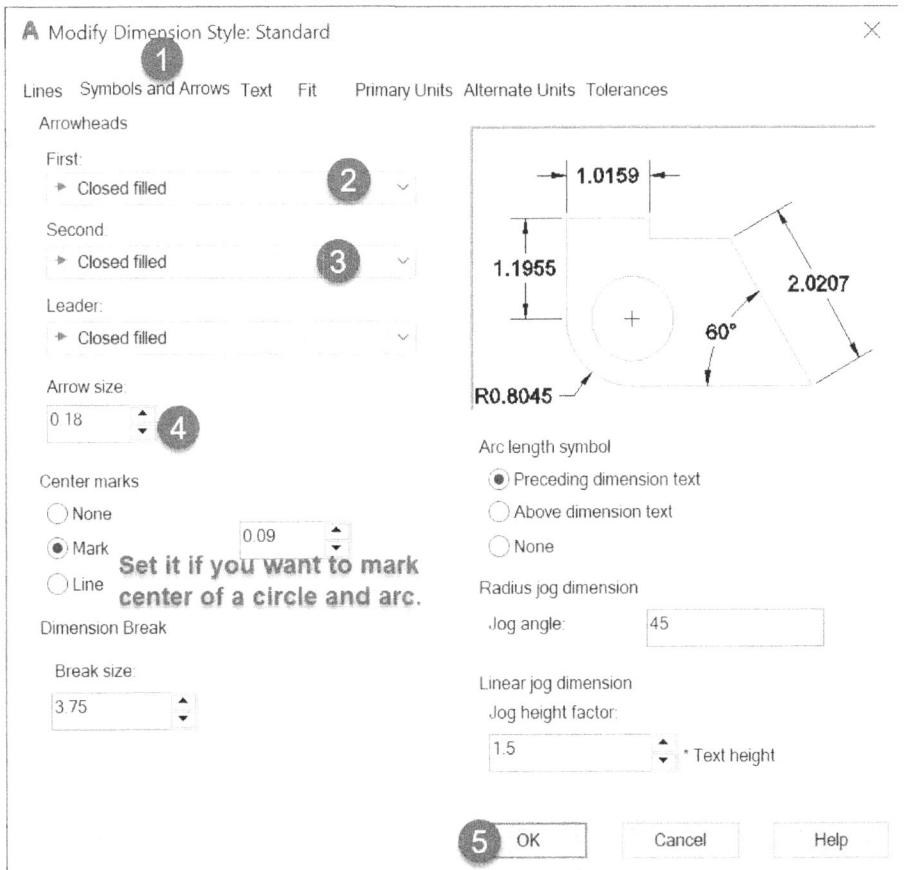

Autodesk AutoCAD 2021
Learn CAD With Ease.

i. **Arrowheads:** Select type of arrowheads for both sides of dimension line.

❖ Arrow size: Specify size of arrows.

ii. **Center marks:** To mark center of circle, arc etc. You can change size of center mark from here.

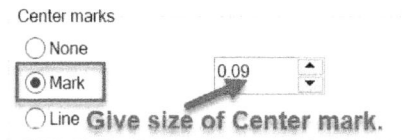

Center marks
○ None
◉ Mark   0.09
○ Line **Give size of Center mark.**

iii. **Dimension break:**
Break size: To specify break size for "Auto" option of "Dimbreak" command.

iv. **Arc length symbol:** Controls the display of the arc symbol in an arc length dimension.

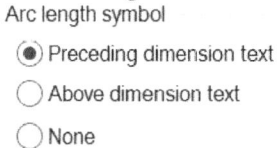

Arc length symbol
◉ Preceding dimension text
○ Above dimension text
○ None

Preceding dimension text: Places arc length symbols before the dimension text.

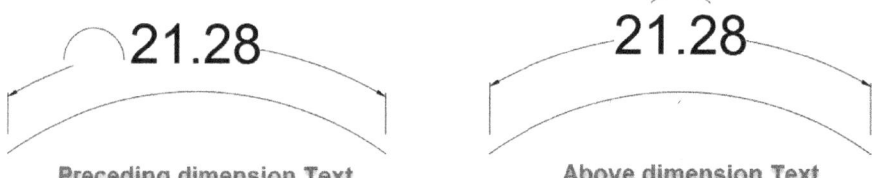

⌒21.28   21.28
Preceding dimension Text   **Above dimension Text**

Above dimension text: Places arc length symbols above the dimension text.

None: Suppresses the display of arc length symbols.

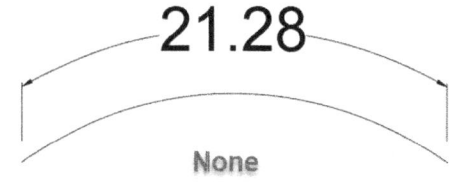

21.28
None

v. **Radius jog dimension:** Controls the display of jogged (zigzag) radius dimensions.

Jogged radius dimensions are often created when the center point of a circle or arc is located off the page.

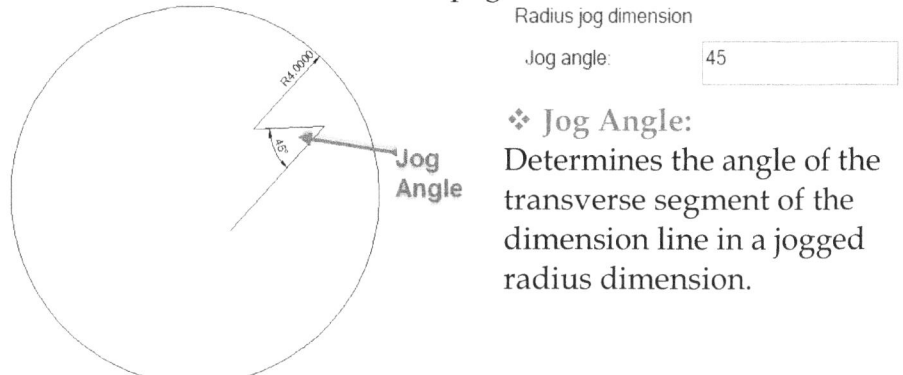

❖ **Jog Angle:** Determines the angle of the transverse segment of the dimension line in a jogged radius dimension.

vi. Linear Jog Dimension: Controls the display of the jog for linear dimensions.

Jog lines are often added to linear dimensions when the actual measurement is not accurately represent by the dimension. Typically the actual measurement is smaller than the desired value.

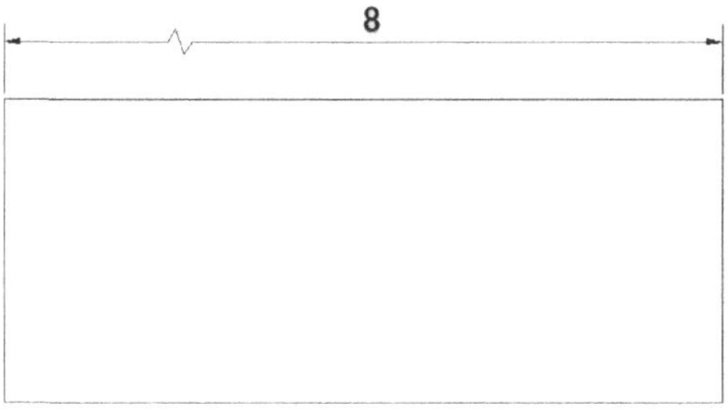

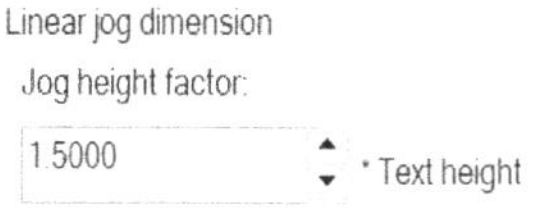

6. **Lines:** You can set different properties related to dimension lines and extension lines from here.
i. **Dimension lines:** To set the properties of dimension lines.

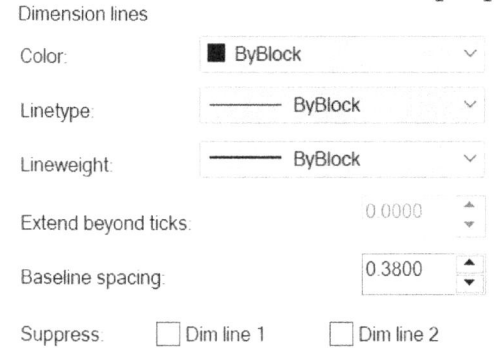

Autodesk AutoCAD 2021
Learn CAD With Ease.

- **Color:** to specify color of dimension line.

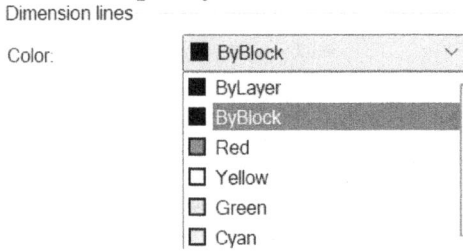

- **Linetype:** to set the linetype of dimension line.

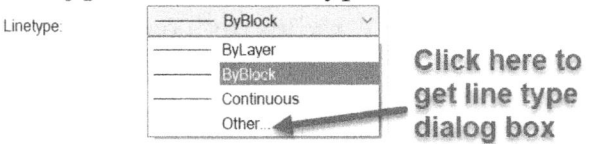

- **Lineweight:** to set lineweight of dimension line to show intensity of dimension line in print.

- **Extend beyond ticks:** This option is turn on when you select **Architectural tick** in **arrowheads** option of **symbols & arrows**. In this option you specify a distance to extend the dimension lines past the extension lines.

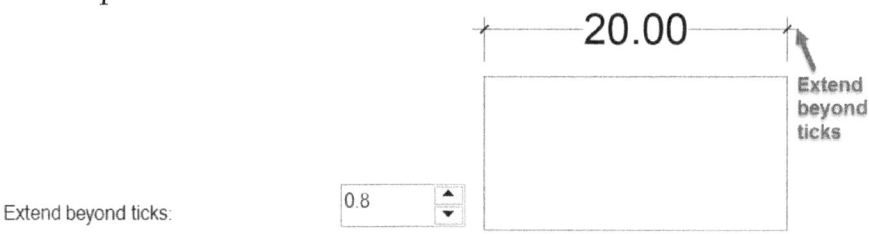

- **Base line spacing:** Specifies distance between dimension lines of baseline dimensions.

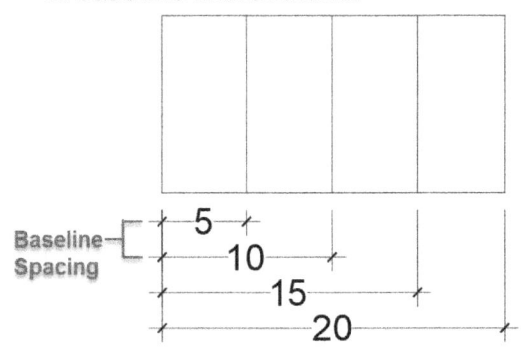

- **Suppress:** Suppresses display of dimension lines. Dimension Line 1 suppresses the first dimension line; Dimension Line 2 suppresses the second dimension line.

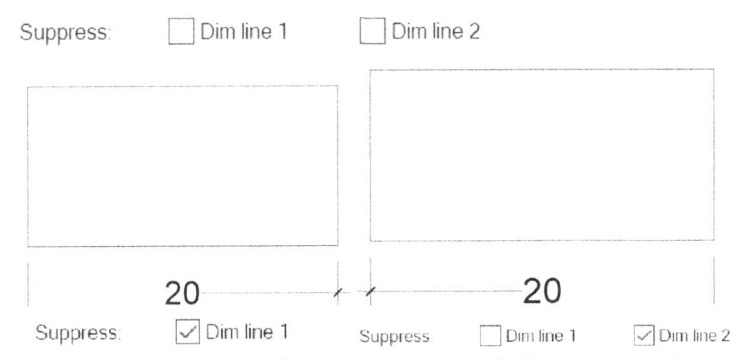

Extension line: to set the properties of dimension lines.

- **Color:** to specify color of extension line.

- **Linetype1:** to set the linetype of first extension line.

- **Linetype2:** to set the linetype of second extension line.

- **Lineweight:** to set lineweight of extension line to show intensity of dimension line in print.

- **Suppress:** Suppresses display of extension lines. Extension Line 1 suppresses the first extension line; Extension Line 2 suppresses the second dimension line.

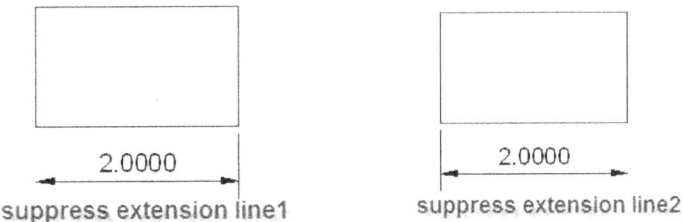

- Extend beyond dimension line: In this option you specify the distance to extend extension line above the dimension line.

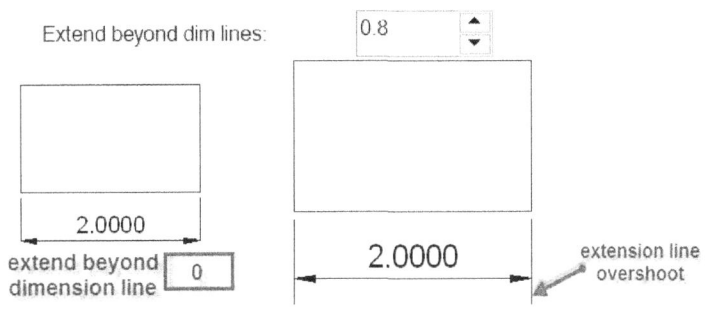

Autodesk AutoCAD 2021
Learn CAD With Ease.

- ❖ **Offset from origin:** Sets the distance to offset the extension lines from the points on the drawing that define the dimension.

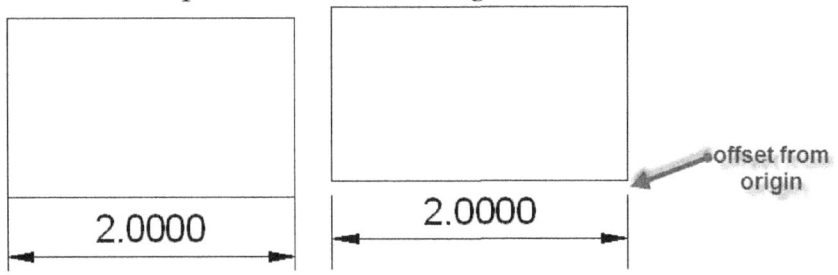

- ❖ **Fixed length extension line:** Enables fixed length extension lines.

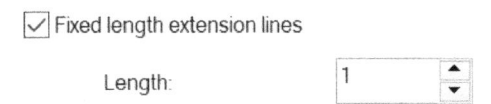

  ☑ Fixed length extension lines

  Length: 1

  Length: Sets the total length of the extension lines starting from the dimension line toward the dimension origin.

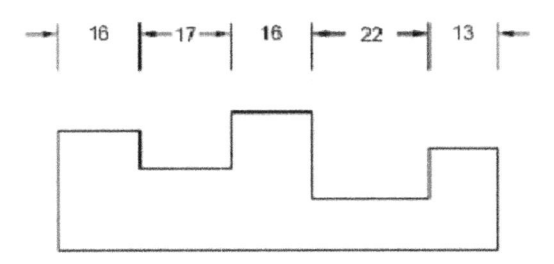

  fixed-length extension lines

7. **Alternate Units:** To give dimensions in another unit with primary units.

- ❖ **Display alternate units:** To turn on alternate unit display. If you want dimension in one more measurement unit, you can check out display alternate units.

  ☑ Display alternate units

i. **Alternate Units:** To set the properties of alternate units for dimensions accept angular.

- ❖ **Unit format:** To select alternate unit for dimensions.

- **Precision:** Sets the number of decimal places for alternate units.

- **Multiplier for alt units:** Specifies the multiplier used as the conversion factor between primary and alternate units. For example, to convert inches to millimeters, enter **25.4**. The value has no effect on angular dimension.

- **Round distance to:** Sets rounding rules for alternate units for all dimension types except Angular. If you enter a value of **0.25**, all alternate measurements are rounded to the nearest 0.25 unit. If you enter a value of **1.0**, all dimension measurements are rounded to the nearest integer. The number of digits displayed after the decimal point depends on the Precision setting.

Note: Prefix, suffix, Zero suppression options are same as **Primary units**.

---

ii. Placement: Controls the placement of alternate units.

- **After primary value:** To place alternate unit after primary value.

- **Below primary value:** To place alternate unit below primary value.

Example 1: If you want to give alternate dimensions in millimeter and your drawing is created in feet inches:

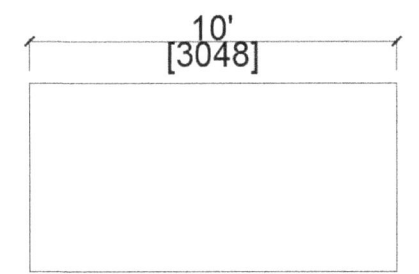

Autodesk AutoCAD 2021
Learn CAD With Ease.

Primary Unit Entries:

Alternate Unit Entries:

If you want type mm in suffix

you can give here 25 because in round off value we consider 1inch= 25 mm

Autodesk AutoCAD 2021
Learn CAD With Ease.

Example 2: If you want alternate dimensions in meters for drawing created in feet inches.

Setting for primary units are same as given in example 1 and settings for alternate units are given below:

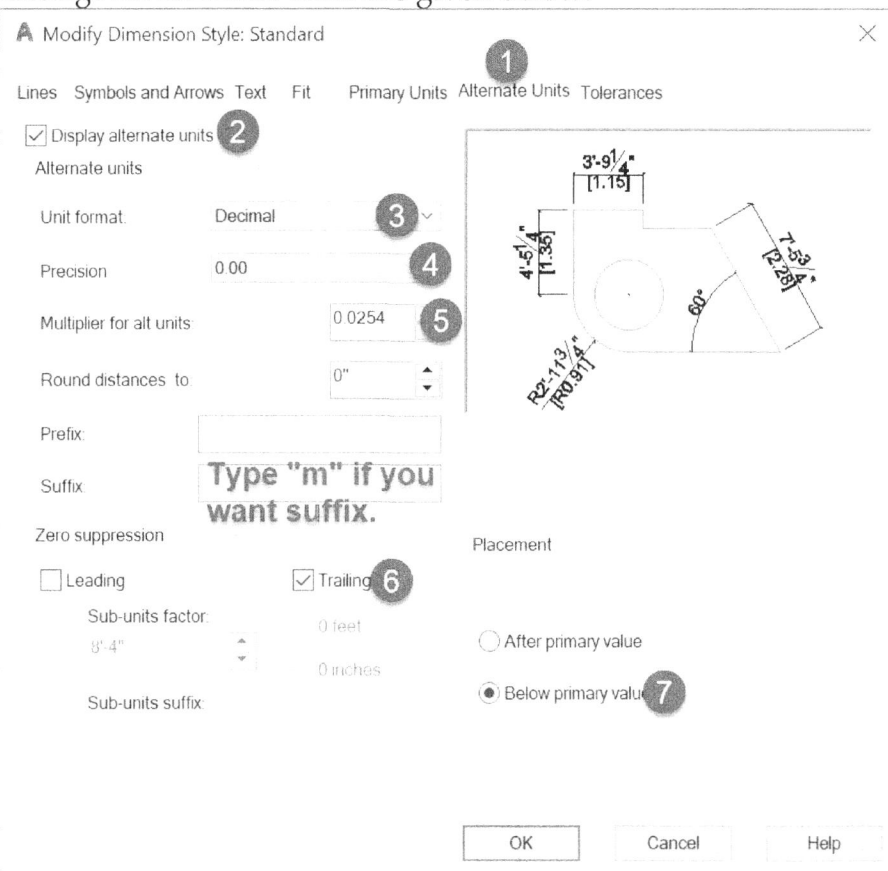

Modify Dimension Style: Standard

Lines Symbols and Arrows Text Fit Primary Units **Alternate Units** Tolerances

☑ Display alternate units

Alternate units

Unit format:	Decimal
Precision	0.00
Multiplier for alt units:	0.0254
Round distances to:	0"
Prefix:	
Suffix:	Type "m" if you want suffix.

Zero suppression

☐ Leading   ☑ Trailing

Sub-units factor: 0 feet
8'-4"   0 inches
Sub-units suffix:

Placement

○ After primary value
● Below primary value

OK   Cancel   Help

Example 3: If you want alternate dimensions in feet inches for drawing created in mm.

Primary Unit Entries:

Linear dimensions

Unit format:	Decimal
Precision	0.00
Fraction format:	Diagonal
Decimal separator:	'.' (Period)
Round off:	0
Prefix:	
Suffix:	

300
[1"]

By Madhumita Kshirsagar

Autodesk AutoCAD 2021
Learn CAD With Ease.

Alternate Unit Entries:

Modify Dimension Style: Standard

Tabs: Lines | Symbols and Arrows | Text | Fit | Primary Units | **Alternate Units** (1) | Tolerances

☑ Display alternate units (2)

Alternate units

- Unit format: Architectural (3)
- Precision: 0'-0 1/4" (4)
- Multiplier for alt units: 0.04 (5)
- Round distances to: 0
- Prefix:
- Suffix:

Zero suppression
- Leading
- Trailing
  - ☑ 0 feet (6)
  - ☑ 0 inches
- Sub-units factor: 100
- Sub-units suffix:

Placement
- ○ After primary value
- ● Below primary value (7)

[OK] [Cancel] [Help]

Example 4: If you want alternate dimensions in feet inches for drawing created in meters.

Setting for primary units are same as given in example 3 and settings for alternate units are given below:

☑ Display alternate units (1)

Alternate units

- Unit format: Architectural (2)
- Precision: 0'-0 1/4" (3)
- Multiplier for alt units: 40 (4)
- Round distances to: 0
- Prefix:
- Suffix:

8. **Tolerance:** Specifies the display and format of dimension text tolerance.

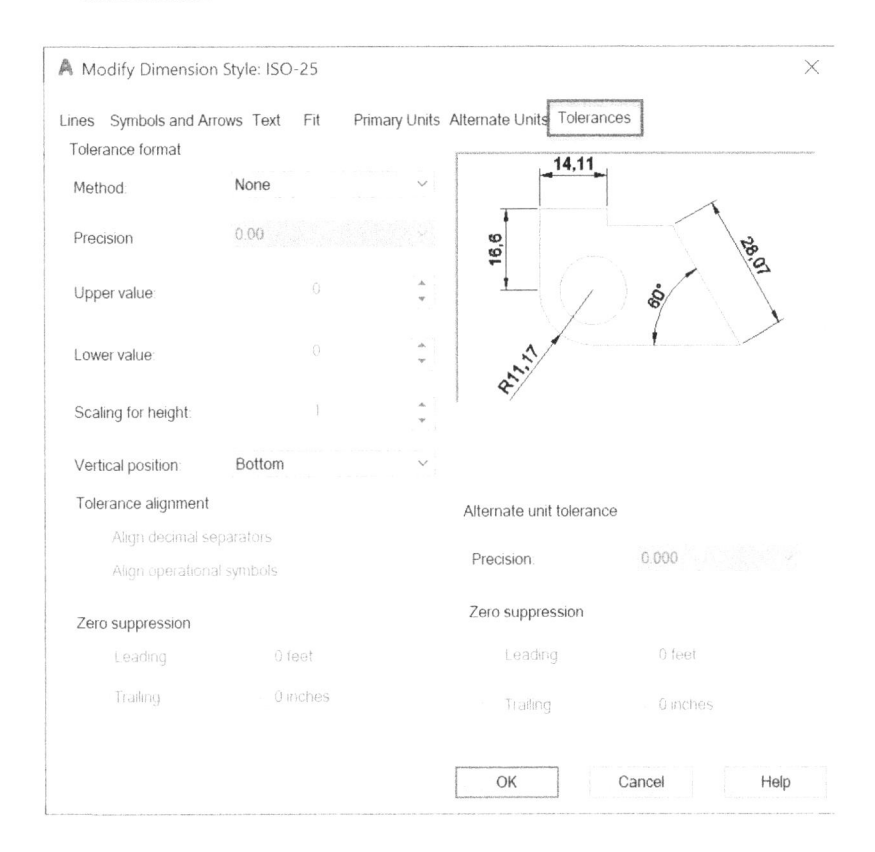

i. **Tolerance Format:** Controls the tolerance format.
   ❖ **Method:** Sets the method for calculating the tolerance.

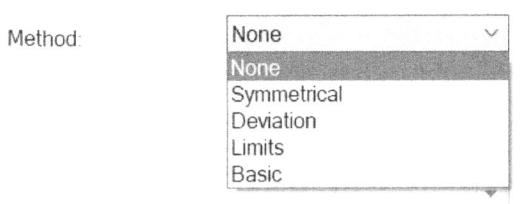

b. **None:** It does not add a tolerance.

c. **Symmetrical:** Adds a plus/minus expression of tolerance in which a single value of variation is applied to the dimension measurement. A plus-or-minus sign appears after the dimension. Enter the tolerance value in Upper Value.

Autodesk AutoCAD 2021
Learn CAD With Ease.

┌─24.00±0.50─┐

Symmetrical Method

Tolerance format

Method: Symmetrical ①

Precision: 0.00 ②

Upper value: 0.5 ③

d. **Deviation:** Adds a plus/minus tolerance expression. Different plus and minus values of variation are applied to the dimension measurement. A plus sign (+) precedes the tolerance value entered in Upper Value, and a minus sign (-) precedes the tolerance value entered in Lower Value.

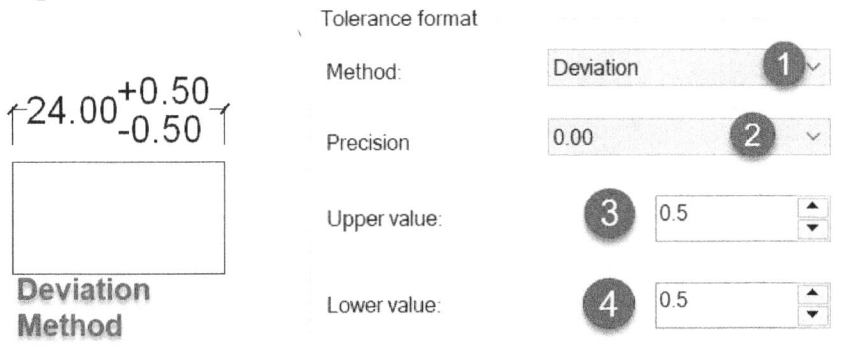

┌─24.00 +0.50 / -0.50─┐

Deviation Method

Tolerance format

Method: Deviation ①

Precision: 0.00 ②

Upper value: ③ 0.5

Lower value: ④ 0.5

e. **Limits:** Creates a limit dimension. A maximum and a minimum value are displayed, one over the other. The maximum value is the dimension value plus the value entered in Upper Value. The minimum value is the dimension value minus the value entered in Lower Value.

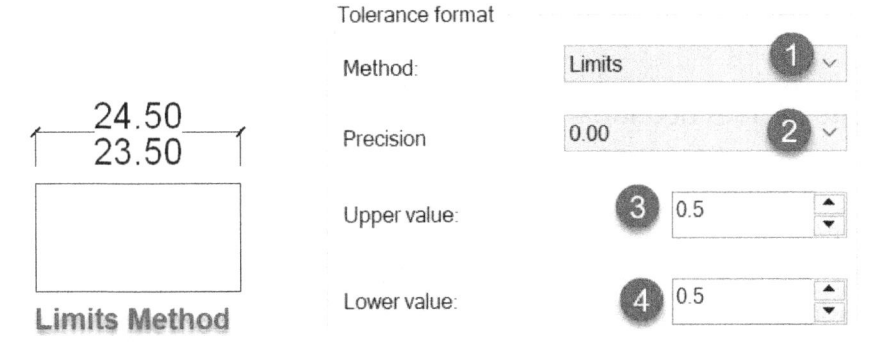

┌─ 24.50 / 23.50 ─┐

Limits Method

Tolerance format

Method: Limits ①

Precision: 0.00 ②

Upper value: ③ 0.5

Lower value: ④ 0.5

f. **Basic:** Creates a basic dimension, which displays a box around the full extents of the dimension.

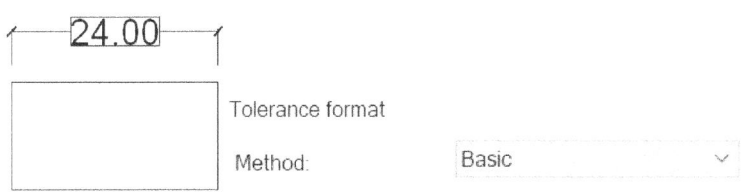

- ❖ Precision: Sets the number of decimal places.

- ❖ Upper Value: Sets the maximum or upper tolerance value. When you select Symmetrical in Method, this value is used for the tolerance.
- ❖ Lower Value: Sets the minimum or lower tolerance value.

- ❖ Scaling for Height: Sets the current height for the tolerance text.

- ❖ Vertical Position: Controls text justification for symmetrical and deviation tolerances.
a. **Top:** Aligns the tolerance text with the top of the main dimension text.
b. **Middle:** Aligns the tolerance text with the middle of the main dimension text.
c. **Bottom:** Aligns the tolerance text with the bottom of the main dimension text.

ii. **Tolerance alignment:** Controls the alignment of upper and lower tolerance values when stacked.
- ❖ Align Decimal Separators:
  Values are stacked by their decimal separators.
- ❖ Align Operational Symbols:
  Values are stacked by their operational symbols.

Example:
In this example, you will set the tolerances to be +/- .05 units and display them at 80% of the primary units. Sound easy? It is. Look at the image below to see how this is done.

Autodesk AutoCAD 2021
Learn CAD With Ease.

Alternate Units Setting:

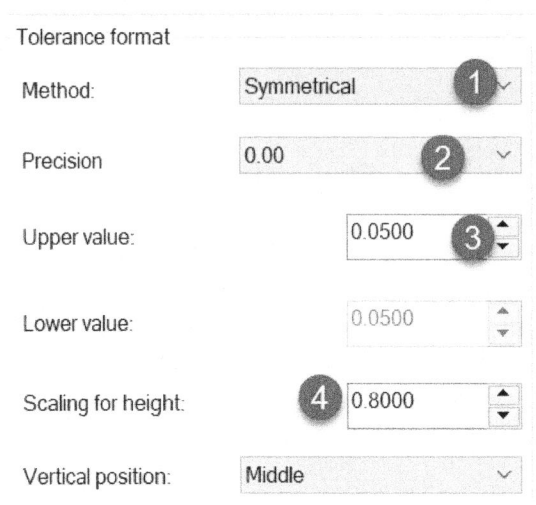

Tolerance format	
Method:	Symmetrical (1)
Precision:	0.00 (2)
Upper value:	0.0500 (3)
Lower value:	0.0500
Scaling for height:	(4) 0.8000
Vertical position:	Middle

Preview available in "Dimension Style Manager" shows you how it will turn out. Click "OK" to close the dialog box. At the original Dimension Style Manger, press the name of your new style, then click the "Make Current" button. Close the dialog box to go back to your workspace.

Draw the wedge shape at the top of the less and dimension it using your new Dimension Style. It should look something like this:

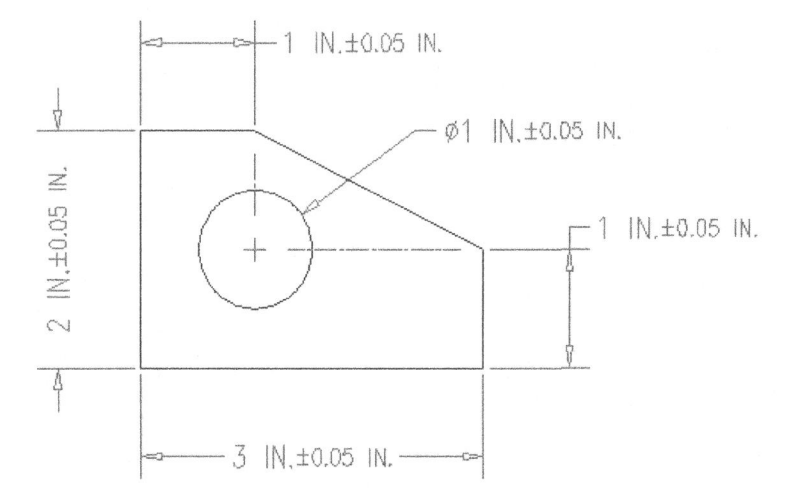

[Drawing showing a wedge shape with a circle, dimensioned as:
- 1 IN.±0.05 IN. (top)
- ⌀1 IN.±0.05 IN. (circle diameter)
- 1 IN.±0.05 IN. (right side)
- 2 IN.±0.05 IN. (left side)
- 3 IN.±0.05 IN. (bottom)]

Now you have the basic understanding of how dimensions work, you can experiment and work with other styles.

Autodesk AutoCAD 2021
Learn CAD With Ease.

Here are some basic rules about dimensioning:

- ❖ Keep them on a separate layer.

- ❖ Dimension towards the end of your project.

- ❖ Use your Osnaps and confirm what you are snapping to.

- ❖ Assign them a unique colour in the drawing, and use that colour in all of your drawings to make it easier to identify dimensions (especially when zoomed in close)

- ❖ After you create your first dimension, AutoCAD creates a new layer called "DEFPOINTS". This is used only for the small points you see at the end of an extension line. This layer will not print - so be sure not to draw on it.

- ❖ Keep even spacing between you dimensions and between your dimension and your object lines.

- ❖ Try not overlap lines (either object or dimension).

- ❖ Use enough dimensions to make sure that all measurements are there - one dimension left out can hold up a project.

- ❖ Try to keep dimensions outside of the objects you are dimensioning.

- ❖ For clarity, don't over-dimension.

- ❖ If you need to override one dimension (perhaps a unique suffix), you can change it in the properties (select > right click > properties)

9. **Fit:** Controls the placement of dimension text, arrowheads, leader lines, and the dimension line.
   Fit Options: Controls the placement of text and arrowheads based on the space available between the extension lines.

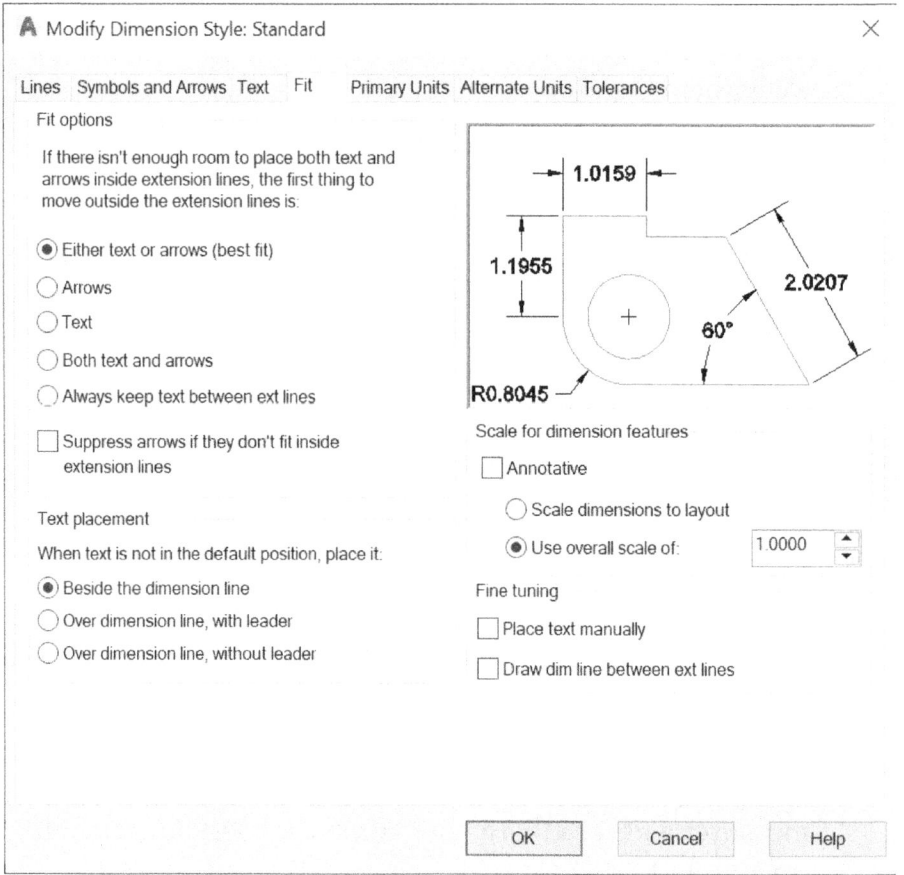

When space is available, text and arrowheads are placed between the extension lines. Otherwise, text and arrowheads are placed according to the Fit options.

- ❖ **Either Text or Arrows (Best Fit):** Moves either the text or the arrowheads outside the extension lines based on the best fit.
  - ➢ When enough space is available for text and arrowheads, places both between the extension lines. Otherwise, either the text or the arrowheads are moved based on the best fit.
  - ➢ When enough space is available for text only, places text between the extension lines and places arrowheads outside the extension lines.
  - ➢ When enough space is available for arrowheads only, places them between the extension lines and places text outside the extension lines.

> When space is available for neither text nor arrowheads, places them both outside the extension lines.

- **Arrows:** Moves arrowheads outside the extension lines first, then text:
  - When enough space is available for text and arrowheads, places both between the extension lines.
  - When space is available for arrowheads only, places them between the extension lines and places text outside them.
  - When not enough space is available for arrowheads, places both text and arrowheads outside the extension lines.

- **Text:** Moves text outside the extension lines first, then arrowheads
  - When space is available for text and arrowheads, places both between the extension lines.
  - When space is available for text only, places the text between the extension lines and places arrowheads outside them.
  - When not enough space is available for text, places both text and arrowheads outside the extension lines.

- **Both Text and Arrows:** When not enough space is available for text and arrowheads, moves both outside the extension lines.

- **Always Keep Text Between Ext Lines:** Always places text between extension lines.

i. **Text Placement:** Sets the placement of dimension text when it is moved from the default position, that is, the position defined by the dimension style.

- **Beside the Dimension Line:** If selected, moves the dimension line whenever dimension text is moved.

- **Over the Dimension Line, with Leader:** If selected, dimension lines are not moved when text is moved.

If text is moved away from the dimension line, a leader line is created connecting the text to the dimension line.
The leader line is omitted when text is too close to the dimension line.

- ❖ **Over the Dimension Line, Without Leader:**
If selected, dimension lines are not moved when text is moved. Text that is moved away from the dimension line is not connected to the dimension line with a leader.

iii. Scale For Dimensions Features: Sets the overall dimension scale value or the paper space scaling.

- ❖ Annotative: Specifies that the dimension is annotative. Click the information icon to learn more about annotative objects.

- ❖ Scale Dimensions To Layout: Determines a scale factor based on the scaling between the current model space viewport and paper space.

- ❖ Use Overall Scale Of: Sets a scale for all dimension style settings that specify size, distance, or spacing, including text and arrowhead sizes. This scale does not change dimension measurement values.

iv. Fine Tuning: Provides additional options for placing dimension text.

- ❖ Place Text Manually: Ignores any horizontal justification settings and places the text at the position you specify at the Dimension Line Location prompt.

- ❖ Draw Dim Line Between Ext Lines: Draws dimension lines between the measured points even when the arrowheads are placed outside the measured points.

- ❖ Preview: Displays sample dimension images that show the effects of changes you make to dimension style settings.

Autodesk AutoCAD 2021
Learn CAD With Ease.

10. Now click on "Ok" and Select dimension style and click on "Set Current" to make selected dimension style current.
11. Then click on "Close" to close "Dimension Style Manager".

If you want to create new dimension style, click on "New".

Procedure to create new dimension style and its settings:

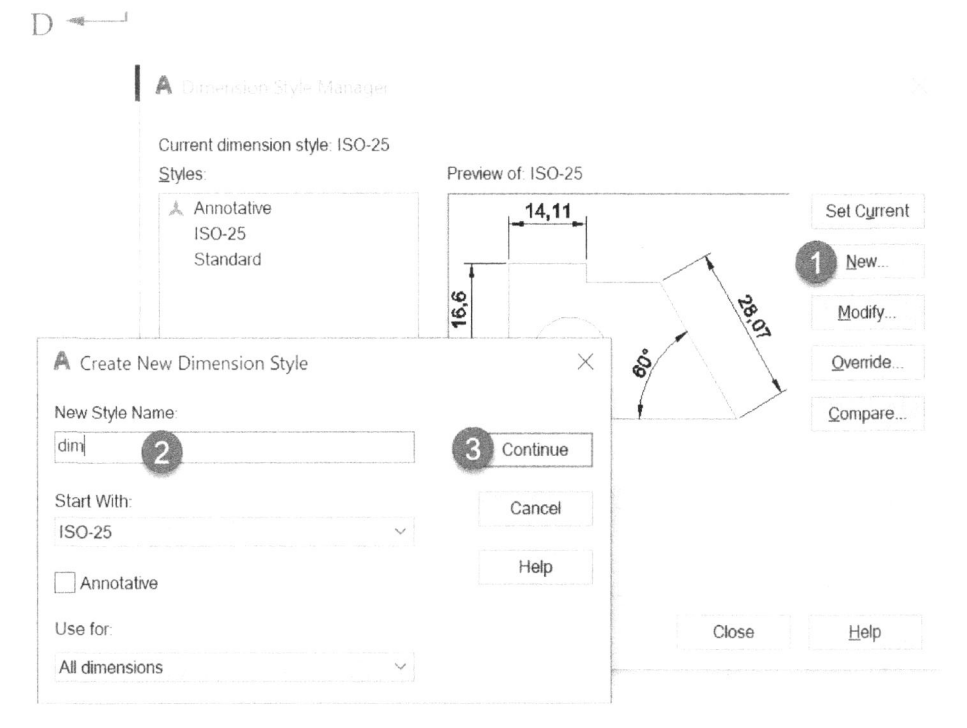

1. Click on "New" in Dimension Style Manager". It opens "Create New Dimension Style" dialog box.

2. Type name of new dimension style in "New Style Name" and click on "Continue".

3. All settings are same in "New" and "Modify".

Set Current: This option is used to make selected dimension style current. For that:

Select dimension style name from "Styles" and click on "Set Current".

Autodesk AutoCAD 2021
Learn CAD With Ease.

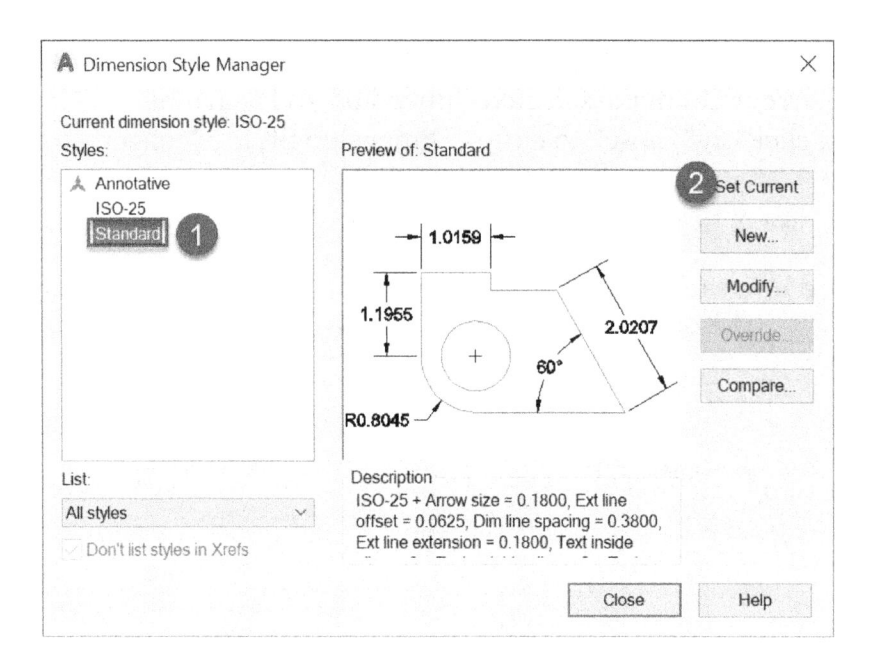

Override: Displays the Override Current dialog box, in which you can set temporary overrides to dimension styles. Dialog box options are identical to those in the New Dimension Style dialog box. Overrides are displayed as unsaved changes under the dimension style in the Styles list.

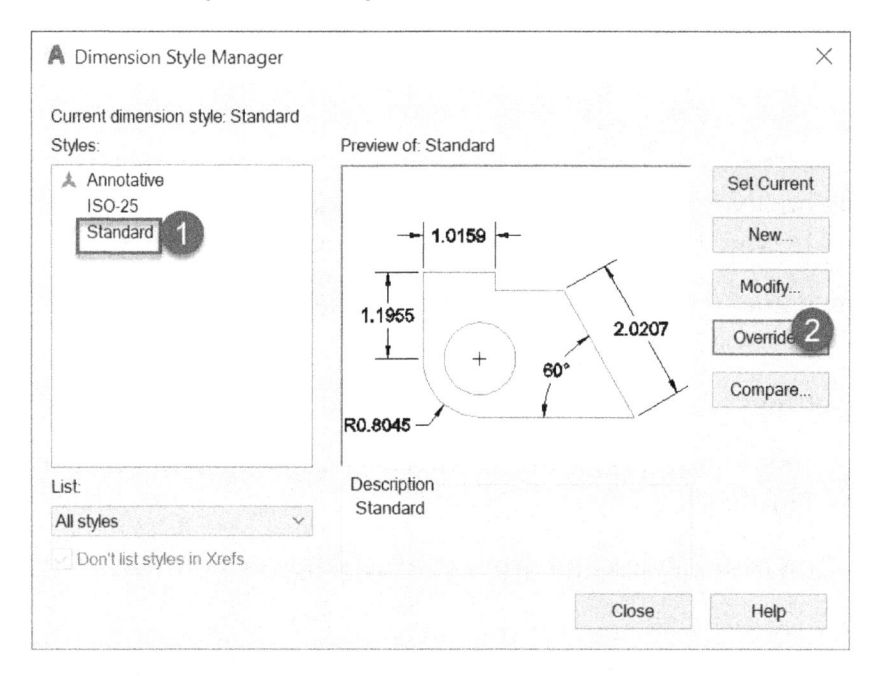

Autodesk AutoCAD 2021
Learn CAD With Ease.

Compares: Displays the Compare Dimension Styles dialog box, in which you can compare two dimension styles or list all the properties of one dimension style.

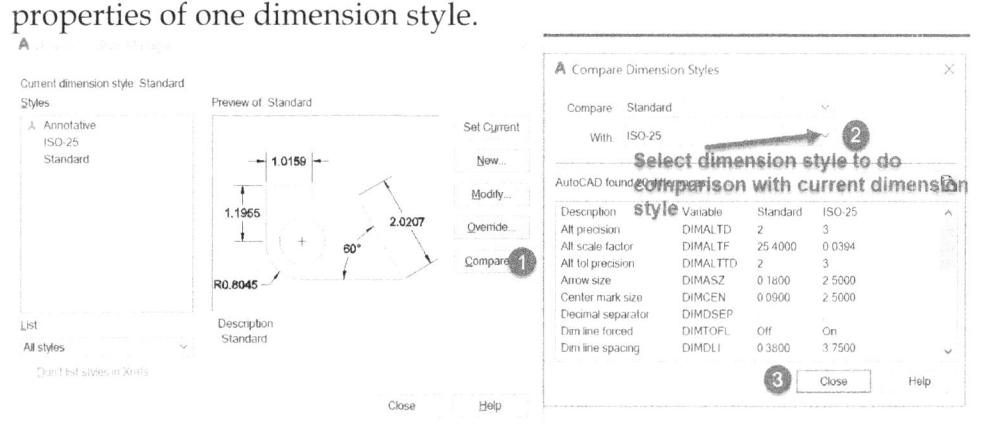

10.24 Command: Dimension Update
    Alias   : -dimstyle

    Annotate Tab → Dimension Panel → Update

Use: The Dimension Update command is used to apply the current dimension style to existing dimensions. You can use this command to change the style of a dimension. Unlike text styles, dimension styles do not automatically update when the style is changed. The UPDATE command must be used to force dimensions to appear in the current text style.

Firstly, select dimension style to make it current (to which you want to match other dimensions).

_-dimstyle

Current dimension style: 1   Annotative: No

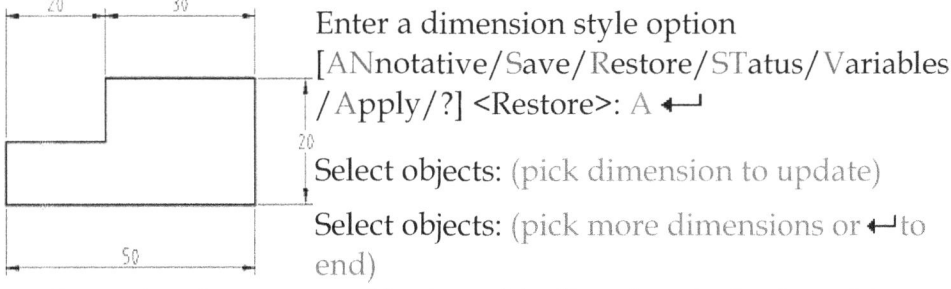

Enter a dimension style option
[ANnotative/Save/Restore/STatus/Variables/Apply/?] <Restore>: A ↵

Select objects: (pick dimension to update)

Select objects: (pick more dimensions or ↵ to end)

If you invoke command by icon, it's directly asked select objects.

Autodesk AutoCAD 2021
Learn CAD With Ease.

Notes:

1. Always attempt to use the least number of dimensions in order to provide the maximum amount of information.

2. Avoid giving duplicate information. For example, if you use a number of running dimensions along the length of an object, it is not necessary to include an additional dimension for the whole length. In the illustration on the right the "50" dimension is unnecessary because it gives no extra information and simply duplicates that which can be inferred from the "20" and "30" dimensions. This will also avoid any ambiguity which may arise from inaccurate dimensioning.

3. Sometimes it may be more appropriate to add notes to your drawing which include dimension information rather than attempt to dimension small or complex items.

4. If you do not include any units information with your dimensions you must always add a note to your drawing such as "All dimensions are in millimeters" to make it absolutely clear.

10.25 Command: Dimension Edit

    Alias   : Ded OR Dimedit

Annotate Tab → Dimension Panel →

Use: To edit dimension text & extension line.

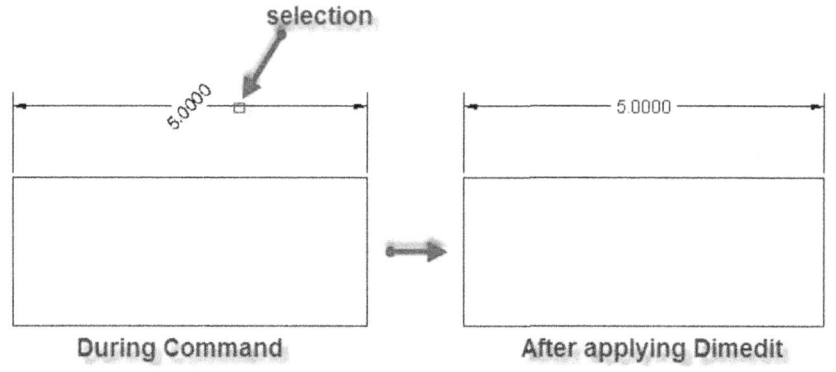

selection

During Command   After applying Dimedit

Home: This option is move rotated dimension text at its default position.

DED ←┘

Enter type of dimension editing [Home/New/Rotate/Oblique] <Home>: H ←┘

Select objects: by mouse click
Select objects: ←┘

New: Its change dimension text by using *In Place Text Editor.*

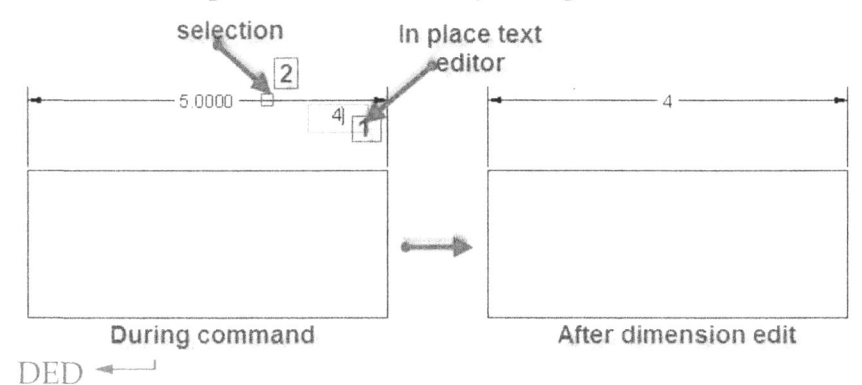

During command → After dimension edit

DED ←┘

Enter type of dimension editing [Home/New/Rotate/Oblique] <Home>: N ←┘

(then its open In PlaceText Editor & you give dimension value& click out of editor box)

Select objects: select dimension.
Select objects: ←┘

Rotate: To rotate dimension text. This option is like *Angle text* command.

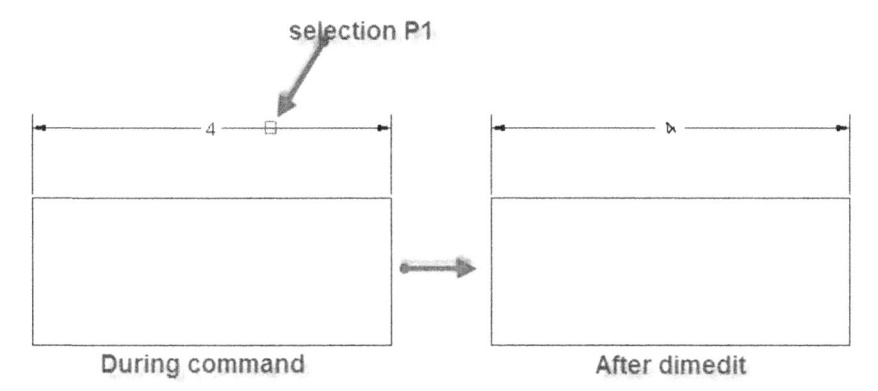

During command → After dimedit

Autodesk AutoCAD 2021
Learn CAD With Ease.

DED ←┘
Enter type of dimension editing [Home/New/Rotate/Oblique] <Home>: R ←┘
Specify angle for dimension text: 45 ←┘
Select objects: select dimension (P1)
Select objects: ←┘

Oblique: The Oblique option is useful when extension lines conflict with other features of the drawing. The oblique angle is measured from the X axis of the UCS.

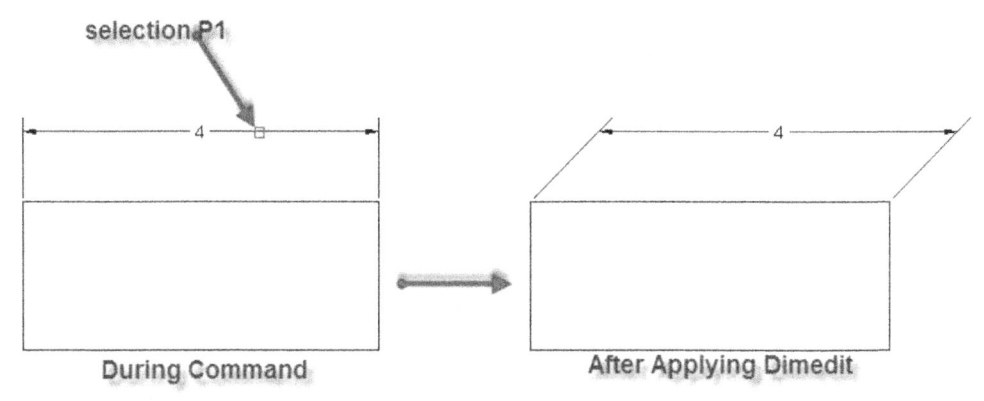

DED ←┘
Enter type of dimension editing [Home/New/Rotate/Oblique] <Home>: O ←┘
Select objects: select dimension (P1)
Select objects: ←┘
Enter obliquing angle (press ENTER for none): 45 ←┘

10.26 Command: Dimension Text Edit
    Alias   : Dimtedit

    Annotate Tab → Dimension Panel →

Use: To edit location of dimension text. This command is only work with *Linear, Radius, Diameter Dimensions.*

DIMTEDIT ←┘
Select dimension: by mouse

Specify new location for dimension text or [Left/Right/Center/Home/Angle]: by mouse click.

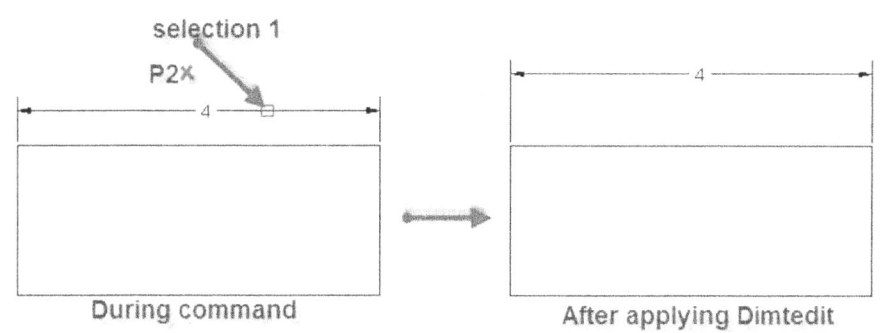

During command → **After applying Dimtedit**

Left: Its change the position of dimension text to left.

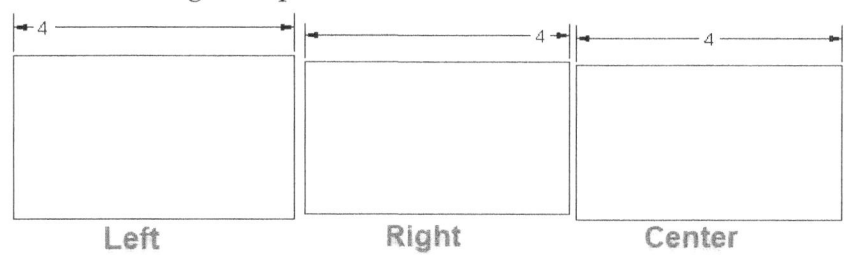

Left | **Right** | **Center**

Right: Its change the position of dimension text to right.
Center: Its change the position of dimension text to center.

10.27 Command: Override

    Alias   : Dov

    Annotate Tab → Dimension Panel → Override

Use: Controls overrides of system variables used in selected dimensions.

Overrides a specified dimensioning system variable for selected dimensions, or clears the overrides of selected dimension objects, returning them to the settings defined by their dimension style.

DOV ↵
Enter dimension variable name to override or [Clear overrides]: dimclrd ↵
Enter new value for dimension variable <BYBLOCK>: 5 ↵
Enter dimension variable name to override: ↵
Select objects: (select dimension)
Select objects: ↵

Autodesk AutoCAD 2021
Learn CAD With Ease.

Before dimoverride → After dimoverride

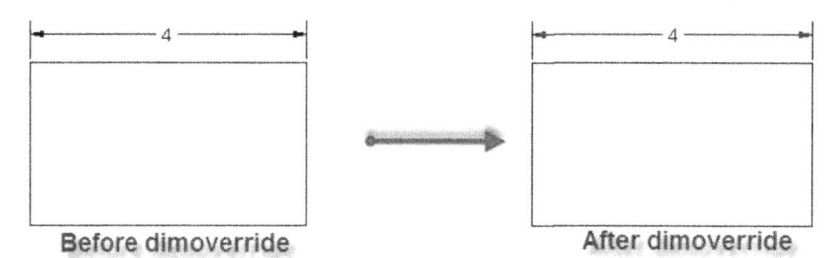

Clear Overrides: Clears any overrides on selected dimensions. The dimension objects return to the settings defined by their dimension style.

Tips:
Different system variable used for different parts of dimension styles in dimension override:

Line:
Dimensionline:
Dimension line color: DIMCLRD
Linetype :   DIMLTYPE
Lineweight: DIMLWD
Extend Beyond Ticks : DIMDLE
Baseline Spacing :DIMDLI
Suppress1: DIMSD1
Suppress1: DIMSD2

Extension Lines
Color :DIMCLRE
Linetype Ext Line 1: DIMLTEX1
Linetype Ext Line 2 :DIMLTEX2
Lineweight: DIMLWE
Suppress:DIMSE1
         DIMSE2
Extend Beyond Dim Lines: DIMEXE
Offset From Origin: DIMEXO
Fixed Length Extension Lines: DIMFXLON
Length: DIMFXL
Symbols and Arrows Tab:
Arrowheads
First: DIMBLK1

Second: DIMBLK2
Leader: DIMLDRBLK
Arrow Size: DIMASZ
Center: DIMCEN
Jog Angle: DIMJOGANG
Arc Length Symbol: DIMARCSYM,
Preceding Dimension Text: DIMARCSYM
Above Dimension Text: DIMARCSYM
None: DIMARCSYM
Text:
Text Style Button: DIMTXSTY
Text Color: DIMCLRT
Fill Color: DIMTFILL, DIMTFILLCLR
Text Height: DIMTXT
Fraction Height Scale: DIMTFAC
Show Text Frame: DIMGAP
Placement:
Vertical: DIMTAD
Horizontal: DIMJUST
View Direction: DIMTXTDIRECTION
Offset from Dim Line: DIMGAP
Alignment: DIMTIH & DIMTOH
Primary Units:
Unit Format: DIMLUNIT, The relative sizes of numbers in stacked fractions are based on the DIMTFAC
Precision: DIMDEC
Fraction Format: DIMFRAC
Decimal Separator: DIMDSEP
Round Off : DIMRND
Prefix: DIMPOST
Suffix: DIMPOST

10.28 Command: **Multileader**
    Alias   : **Mleader**
    Home Tab → Annotation Panel → Multileader
            OR
    Annotate Tab → Leader Panel → Multileader
Use: To create multileaders.

Autodesk AutoCAD 2021
Learn CAD With Ease.

A multileader object typically consists of an arrowhead, a horizontal landing, a leader line or curve, and either a multiline text object or a block.

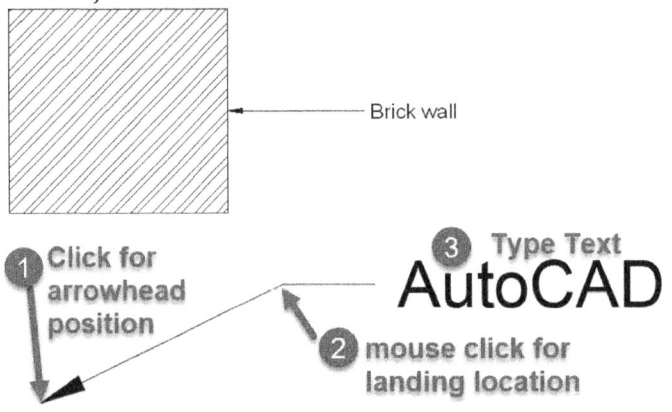

MLD ←┘
Specify leader arrowhead location or [leader Landing first/Content first/Options] <Options>: mouse click
Specify leader landing location: mouse click
Then enter text which you want to write on drawing.

- ❖ **Leader Landing first:** In this option you will specify landing location of leader at first and then you will specify other things like arrowhead position and text.

MLD ←┘
Specify leader arrowhead location or [leader Landing first/Content first/Options] <leader Landing first>: L ←┘
Specify leader landing location or [leader arrowHead first/Content first/Options] <leader arrowHead first>: mouse click
Specify leader arrowhead location: mouse click
Then enter text which you want to write on drawing.

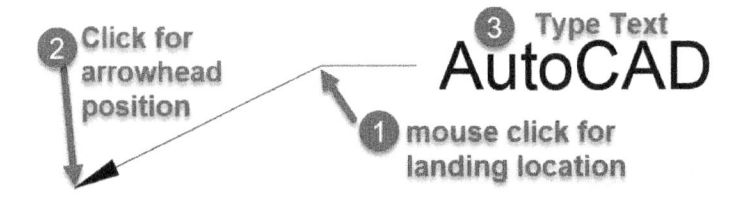

Autodesk AutoCAD 2021
Learn CAD With Ease.

❖ **Content First:** Specifies a location for the text or block associated with the multileader object.

MLD ⏎
Specify leader landing location or [leader arrowHead first/Content first/Options] <leader arrowHead first>: C ⏎
Specify first corner of text or [leader arrowHead first/leader Landing first/Options] <Options>: mouse click to specify first corner of text window
Specify opposite corner: mouse click to specify other corner of text window & enter text, then click outside the window.
Specify leader arrowhead location: by mouse click.

② Click for arrowhead position
① Type Text
AutoCAD

Option: This option is used to specify different options related to leader types, multileader style and text options.

❖ Leader Type: *Straight, Spline, None*
❖ Multileader style
❖ Text options.

Note: You will get knowledge about these options in "Multileader Style" command of this chapter.
You can directly set these settings (Option) by Multileader Style.

10.29 Command: **Add**
    Alias   : **Mle**
    Home Tab → Annotation Panel → Add leader
                OR
    Annotate Tab → Leader Panel → Add leader
Use: To add a leader line to an existing multileader.

190

By Madhumita Kshirsagar

Autodesk AutoCAD 2021
Learn CAD With Ease.

Before Add Leader

After Add Leader

1. select multileader
2. Click here to add leader
3. Click here to add leader

MLE ←┘

Select a multileader: by any selection method
Specify leader arrowhead location or [Remove leaders]: mouse click

10.30 Command: Remove
    Alias   : Mle

    Home Tab → Annotation Panel → Remove leader
         OR
    Annotate Tab → Leader Panel → Add leader

Use: To remove leader from an existing multileader.

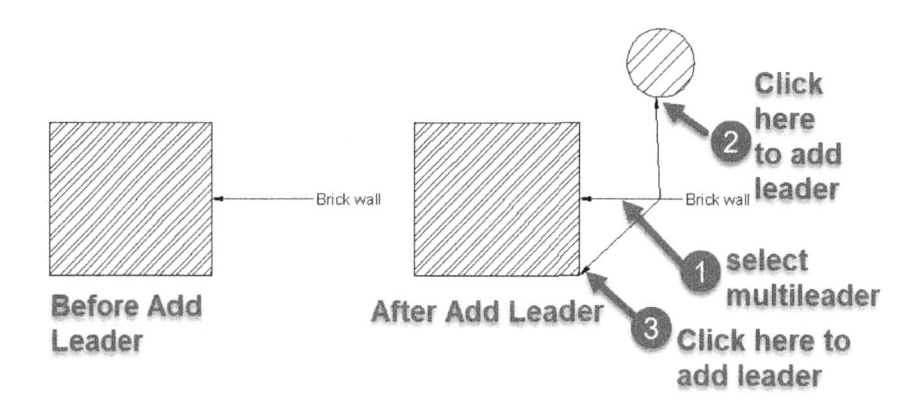

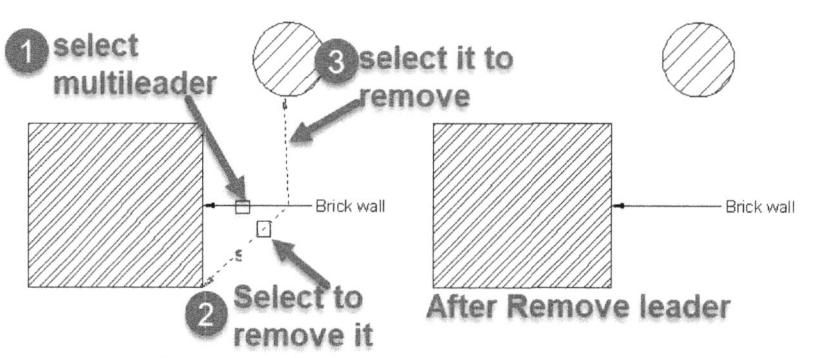

1. select multileader
2. Select to remove it
3. select it to remove

After Remove leader

MLE ←┘

Select a multileader: select multileader from which you want to remove leader
Specify leader arrowhead location or [Remove leaders]: R ←┘
Specify leaders to remove or [Add leaders]: selection 2
Specify leaders to remove or [Add leaders]: selection 2

Autodesk AutoCAD 2021
Learn CAD With Ease.

Note: If you can directly invoke command by clicking on "Remove Leader" icon, select multileader and then directly select leader to remove.

10.31 Command: **Align**
    Alias   : **MLEADERALIGN**
    Home Tab → Annotation Panel → Align Leader
              OR
    Annotate Tab → Leader Panel → Align leader

Use: To align all multileaders of a drawing with each other.

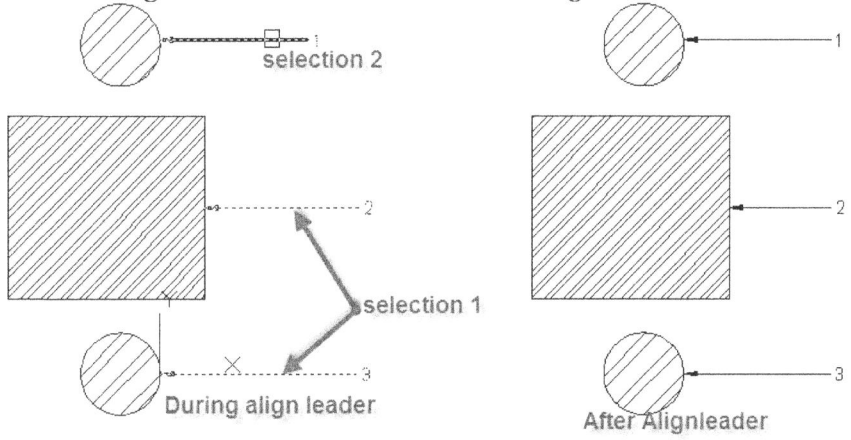

MLEADERALIGN ↵
Select multileaders: (selection 1)
Select multileaders: ↵
Current mode: Use current spacing
Select multileader to align to or [Options]: (selection 2)
Specify direction: by mouse click

10.32 Command: **Multileader Style**
    Alias   : **None**
    Home Tab → Annotation Panel → Multileader Style
              OR
    Annotate Tab → Leader Panel → Multileader Style

Use: To set multileader properties & to create new multileader style.

Autodesk AutoCAD 2021
Learn CAD With Ease.

1. MLS
It will open "Multileader Style Manager" box.
2. Click on "New" to create new multileader style.

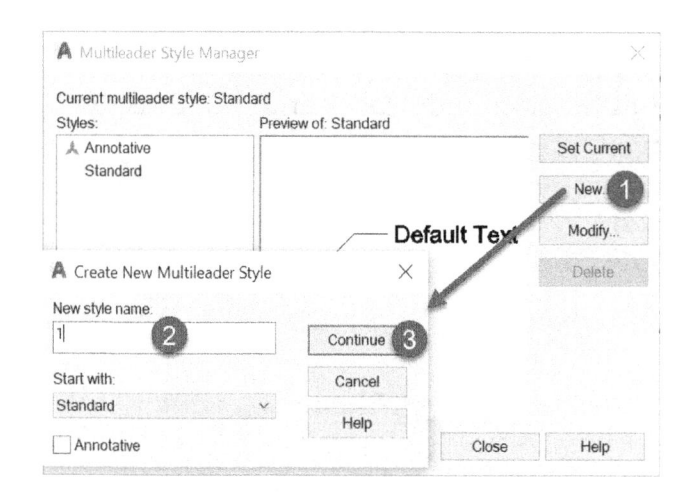

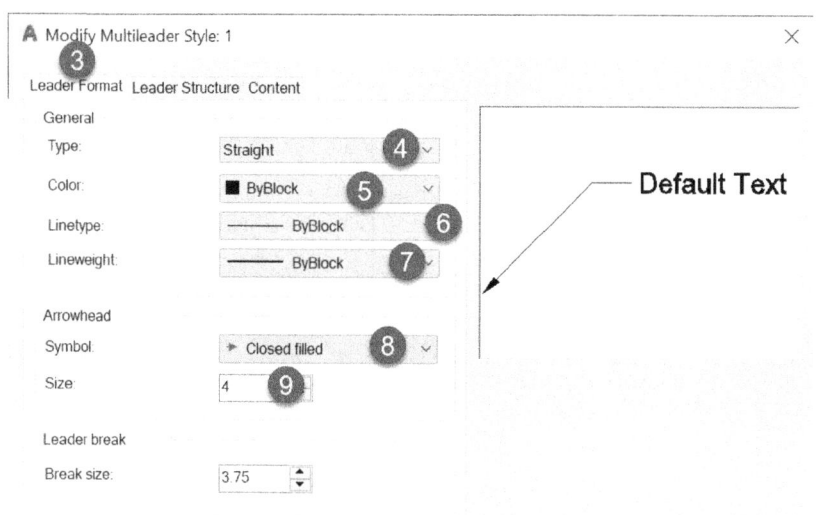

3. Make changes in given options according to your requirements on the basis of description given below.

i. **Leader Format:** To set properties of leader.
❖ **General:** These are general properties of Leader.
a. **Type:** Select type of leader:
  ➢ **Straight:** To create straight leader.
  ➢ **Spline:** To create curve leader.
  ➢ **None:** No leader line available in a multileader.

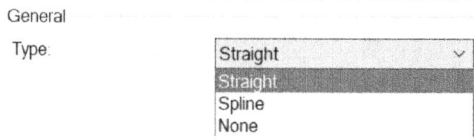

Autodesk AutoCAD 2021
Learn CAD With Ease.

b. **Color:** To specify color of leader.
c. **Line Type:** To select linetype for a leader.
d. **Line weight:** To specify lineweight of leader to show intensity of leader in print.

❖ **Arrowhead:** Controls the appearance of the multileader arrowheads.

Arrowhead
Symbol: ➤ Closed filled
Size: 4

a. **Symbols:** To set the arrowhead symbol for the multileader.
b. **Size:** To set the size of arrowhead.

❖ **Leader Break:** Controls the dimension break to a multileader.
a. **Break Size:** Displays and sets the break size used for the DIMBREAK command when the multileader is selected.

Leader break
Break size: 3.75

ii. **Leader Structure Tab:** Controls the number of leader points, landing size, and scale for the multileader.

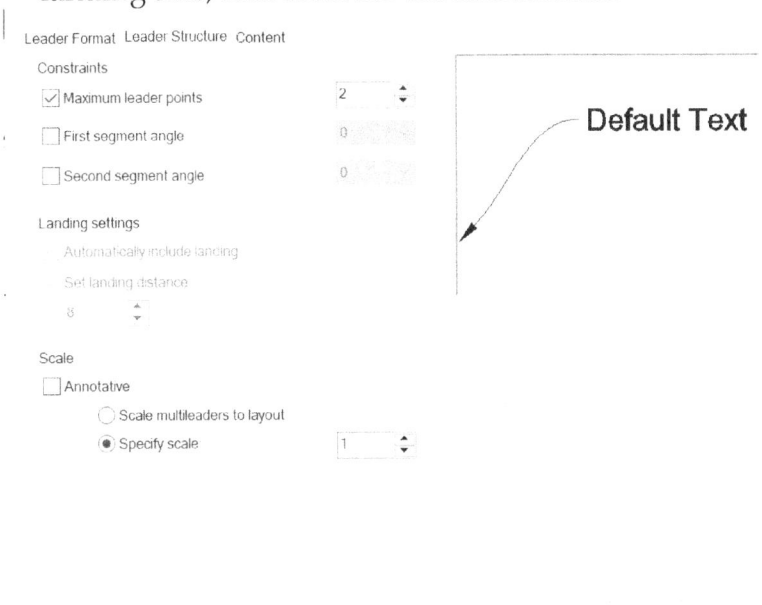

Leader Format Leader Structure Content
Constraints
☑ Maximum leader points   2
☐ First segment angle   0
☐ Second segment angle   0

Landing settings
  Automatically include landing
  Set landing distance
  8

Scale
☐ Annotative
  ○ Scale multileaders to layout
  ● Specify scale   1

― Default Text

    OK   Cancel   Help

❖ **Constrain:** Controls the constraints of the multileader.

194

By Madhumita Kshirsagar

Autodesk AutoCAD 2021
Learn CAD With Ease.

  a. **Maximum Leader Points:** Specifies a maximum number of points for the leader line.
  b. **First Segment Angle:** Specifies the angle of the first point in the leader line.
  c. **Second Segment Angle:** Specifies the angle of the second point in the multileader landing line.

- ❖ **Landing Settings:** Controls the landing settings of the multileader.
  a. **Automatically Include:** Attaches a horizontal landing line to the multileader content.
  b. **Set Distance:** Determines the fixed distance for the multileader landing line.

- ❖ **Scale:** Controls the scaling of the multileader.
  a. **Annotative:** Specifies that the multileader is annotative.
  b. **Scale to Layout:** Determines a scaling factor for the multileader based on the scaling in the model space and paper space viewports.
  c. **Specify Scale:** Specifies the scale for the multileader.

iii. **Content Tab:** Controls the type of content attached to the multileader.

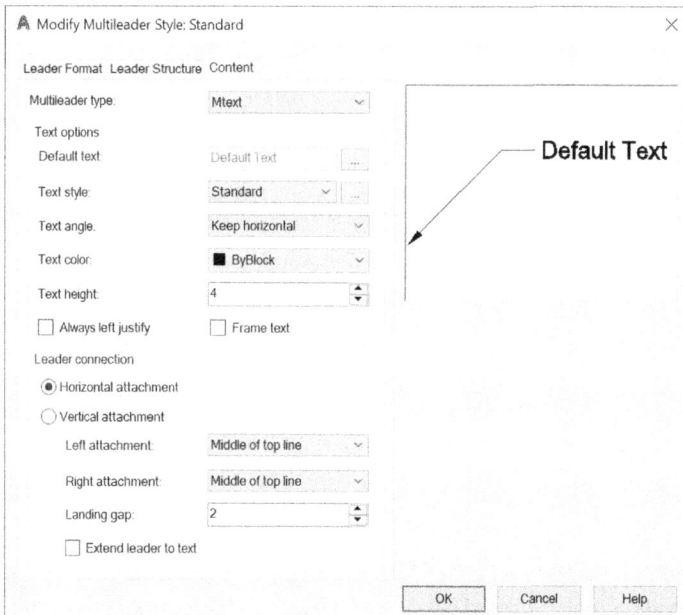

Autodesk AutoCAD 2021
Learn CAD With Ease.

- **Multileader Type:** Determines whether the multileader contains text or a block.
- **Text Options:** Controls the appearance of the text for the multileader.

a. **Default Text:** Sets default text for the multileader content. The [...] button launches the "MTEXT In Place Editor". Type default text which you want with multileader.

b. **Text Style:** Lists the available text styles.

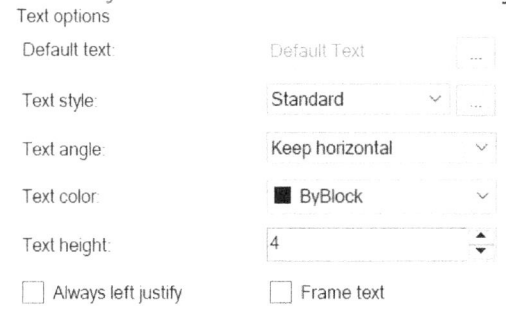

Text options		
Default text:	Default Text	...
Text style:	Standard	...
Text angle:	Keep horizontal	
Text color:	ByBlock	
Text height:	4	
☐ Always left justify	☐ Frame text	

c. **Text Angle:** Specifies the rotation angle of the multileader text.
d. **Text Color:** Specifies the color of the multileader text.
e. **Text Height:** Specifies the height of the multileader text.
f. **Always Left Justify:** Specifies that the multileader text is always left justified.
g. **Frame Text:** Frames the multileader text content with a text box.

Note: You can control the separation between the text and frame by modifying the Landing Gap setting.

- **Leader Connection:** Controls the leader connection settings of the multileader.

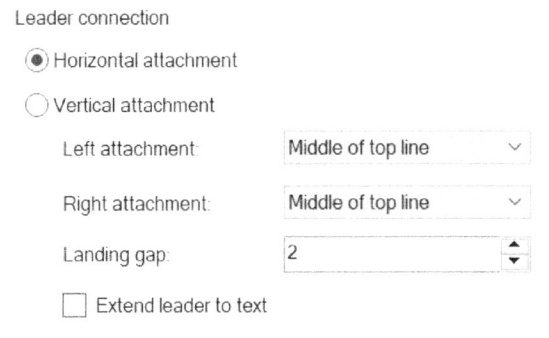

Leader connection	
● Horizontal attachment	
○ Vertical attachment	
Left attachment:	Middle of top line
Right attachment:	Middle of top line
Landing gap:	2
☐ Extend leader to text	

Autodesk AutoCAD 2021
Learn CAD With Ease.

a. **Attachment:** Specifies how the multiline text should be attached to the multileader.
b. **Horizontal:** Inserts the leader to the left or right of the text content. A horizontal attachment includes a landing line between the text and the leader.
c. **Left:** Controls the attachment of the landing line to the multileader text when the text is to the right of the leader.
d. **Right:** Controls the attachment of the landing line to the multileader text when the text is to the left of the leader.
e. **Landing Gap:** Specifies the distance between the landing line and the multileader text.
f. **Extend Leader to Text:** Extends the landing line to end at the edge of the text line where the leader is attached, not at the edge of the multiline text box.

The length of the multiline text box is determined by the length of the longest line of text, not the length of the bounding box.

4. Click on "OK".
5. Select any multileader style from list and click on "Set Current" to make it current.
6. Then click on "Close".
7. Now you do labeling by "multileader" command.

Exercises:

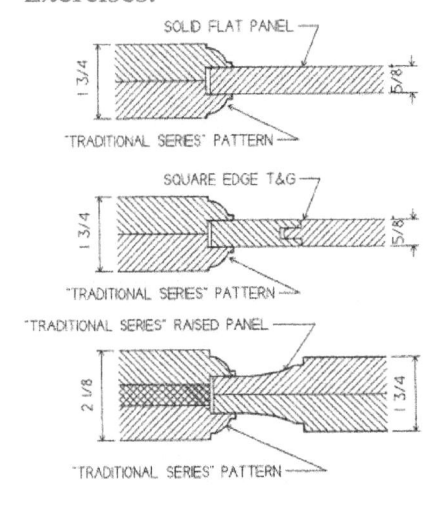

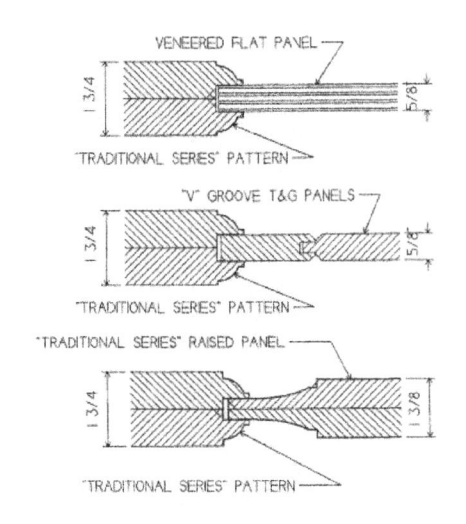

Autodesk AutoCAD 2021
Learn CAD With Ease.

How to create callouts by multileader?
1. Firstly invoke "Multileader Style Manager" and click on "New" to create new multileader style or select any multileader style from "styles" list.
2. Set all options of "Leader Format", "Leader Structure" as mention in "Multileader Style Manager" command.
3. Then "Content" and select "Block" in "Multileader Type"

4. Set Block options as given in above figure:
   ❖ **Source Block:**

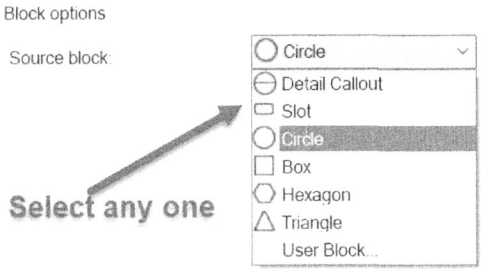

   ❖ **Attachment:** This option is used to specify the way to attach multileader to the block.

198

By Madhumita Kshirsagar

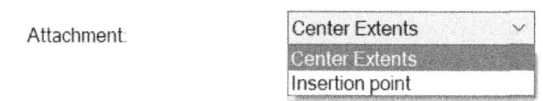

Attachment:
- Center Extents
- Center Extents
- Insertion point

a. **Center Extents:** Attaches the leader line to the **center extent** of the block content.
b. **Insertion Point:** Attaches the leader line to the block content from any point you specify.
❖ **Color:** To give color of the block.
❖ **Scale:** If you want adjust scale of block from here.

5. Click on "Ok" and then click on "Close" to close the "Multileader Manager" dialog box.
6. After that invoke multileader command and click on object for labeling.

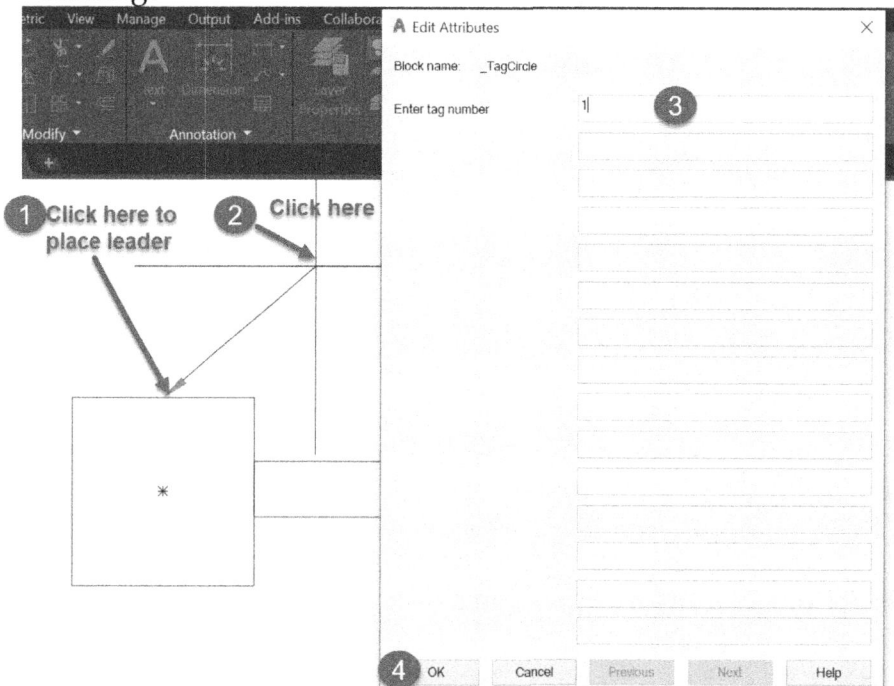

7. It will open **"Edit Attributes"** dialog box.
8. Enter tag number.
9. Then press **OK**.

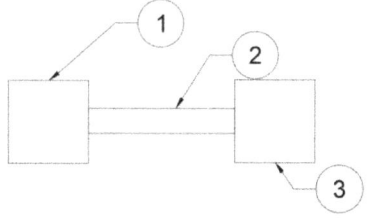

Autodesk AutoCAD 2021
Learn CAD With Ease.

10.33 Command: Multileader Collect
    Alias   : MLC
    Home Tab → Annotation Panel → Multileader Collect
        OR
    Annotate Tab → Leader Panel → Multileader Style

Use: This command is used to organize selected multileaders that contain blocks in to rows and columns and displays the result with a single leader.

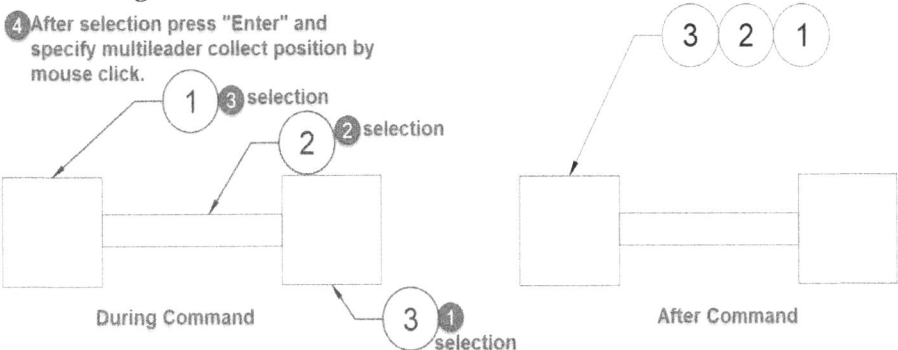

MLC ↵
Select multileaders: by any selection method
Select multileaders: by any selection method
Select multileaders: by any selection method
Select multileaders: ↵
Specify collected multileader location or [Vertical/Horizontal/Wrap] <Horizontal>: by mouse click.

10.34 Command: Table
    Alias   : Tb
    Home Tab → Annotation Panel → Table
        OR
    Annotate Tab → Tables Panel → Table

Use: This command is used to create data tables in a drawing.

In drawings you need to draw some data tables to show different schedules, legends related to drawings. By table command you can easily create tables by specifying number of rows & columns.

A table is a compound object that contains data in rows and columns. It can be created from an empty table or a table style.

Autodesk AutoCAD 2021
Learn CAD With Ease.

When you create a table, the number of columns and rows created is determined by the two points picked to define the size of the table.

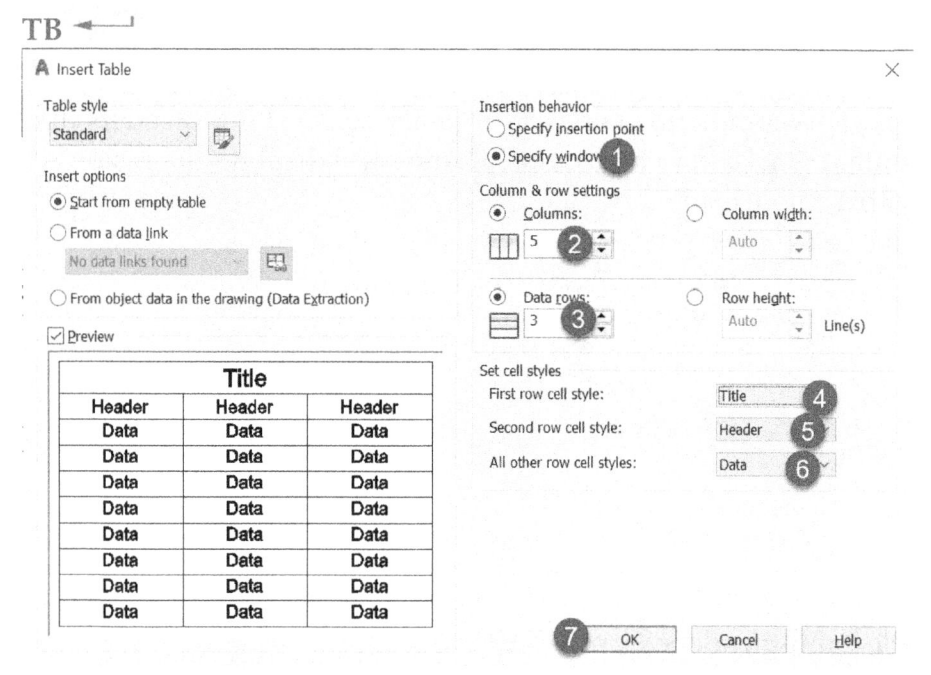

TB

❖ **Insertion Behavior:** There are two types to insert table in a drawing.

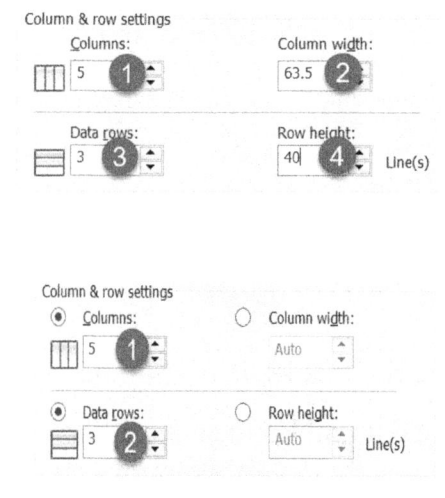

a. **Specify insertion point:** In this type of insertion you can **specify number of rows & columns; column width & row height; set cell styles** & press **OK**. After that you can specify insertion point of table on viewport.

b. **Specify window:** In this type of insertion you can **specify number of rows & columns; set cell styles** & press **OK**. After that you can specify two points on viewport to define size of table.

Autodesk AutoCAD 2021
Learn CAD With Ease.

To create new table style:

1. TB

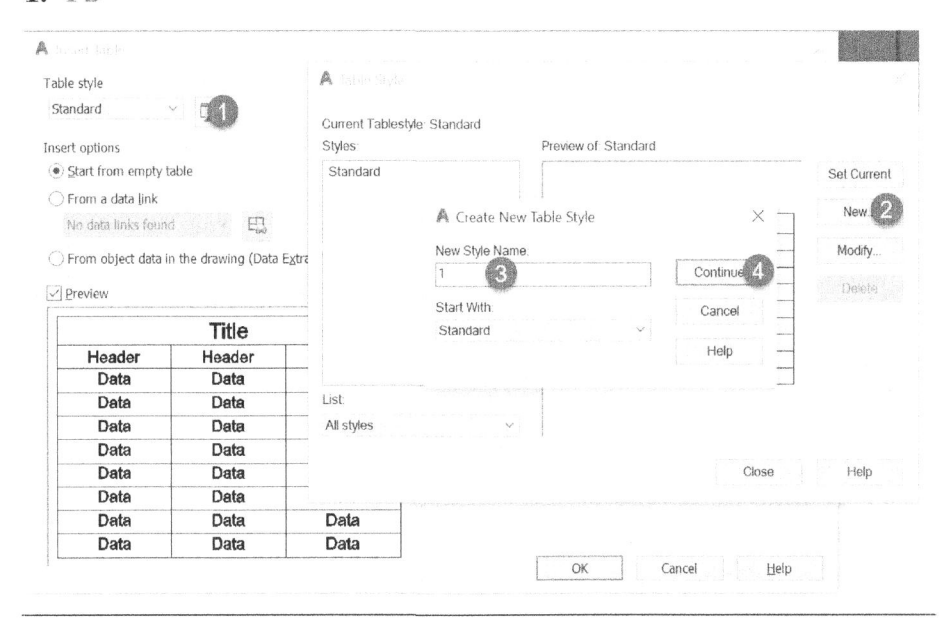

Note: Follow the steps as mention in above figure.

2. Click on "New" and give new style's name in "Create New Table Style" and then click on "Continue".
3. Select Title/Header/Data option in "Cell Styles" and give their properties one by one from "General, Text, and Borders tab.

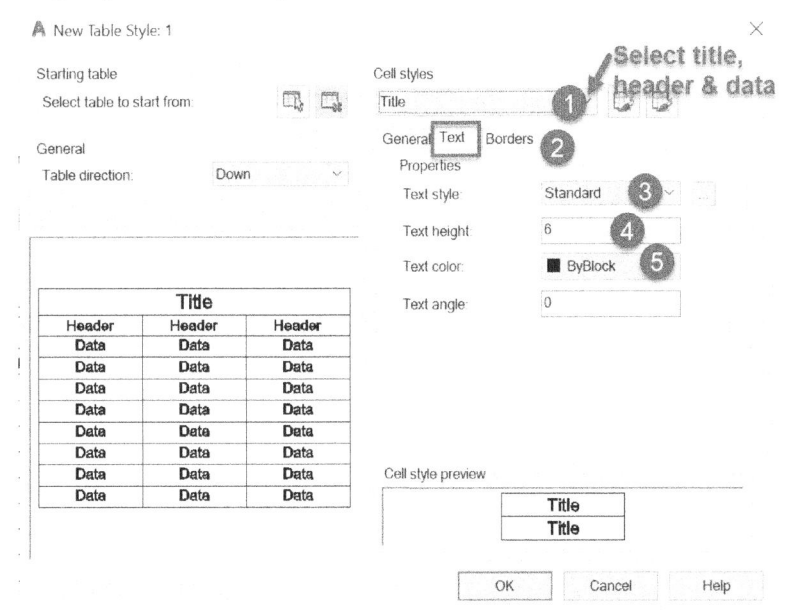

202

Autodesk AutoCAD 2021
Learn CAD With Ease.

(Left dialog) Cell styles: Title — General [6], Borders
Properties:
- Fill color: None
- Alignment: Middle Center
- Format: General
- Type: Label
- Margins — Horizontal: 1.5
- Vertical: 1.5
- ☑ Merge cells on row/column creation

[7] **Specify properties from here**

(Right dialog) Cell styles: Title — General, Text, Borders [8]
Properties:
- Lineweight: ByBlock
- Linetype: ByBlock
- Color: ByBlock
- ☐ Double line
- Spacing:

Apply the selected properties to borders by clicking the buttons above.

[9] **Specify properties of table borders**

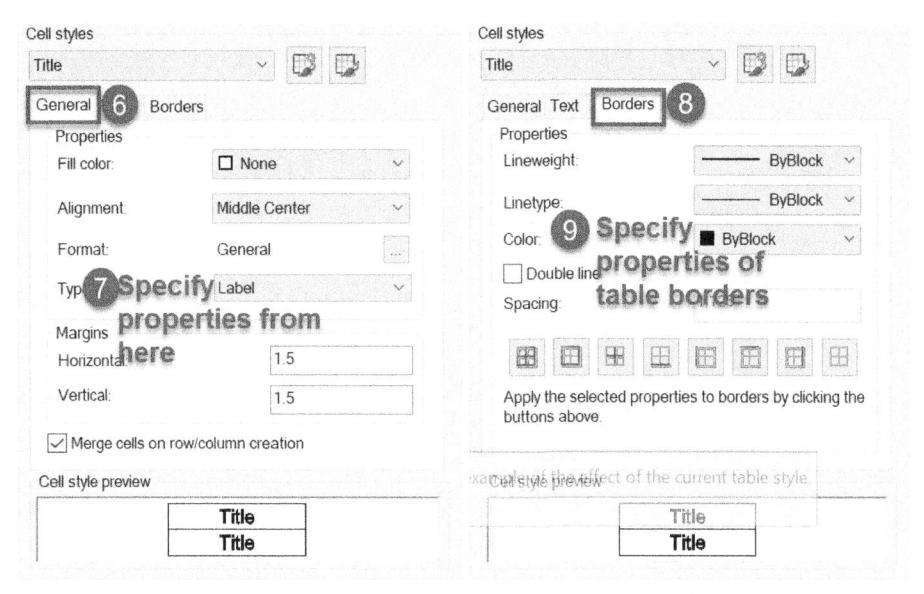

4. After that, click on "OK"
5. Specify "Insertion Behavior" as describe in a "Table" command and set cell styles and then draw table in a drawing area and do different entries in it.

Note 1: You can define the parameters (color, text height, borders, etc.) in your new custom style. This preview is used in the other dialog boxes as well. Make sure you have your **Text Styles** defined first.

So now that you have defined your table style, you can insert one into the drawing and enter data using the Mtext editor and tabbing through the cells. Anyone who has used a simple spreadsheet will be able to use this. One major drawback is that there is no formula function in the table.

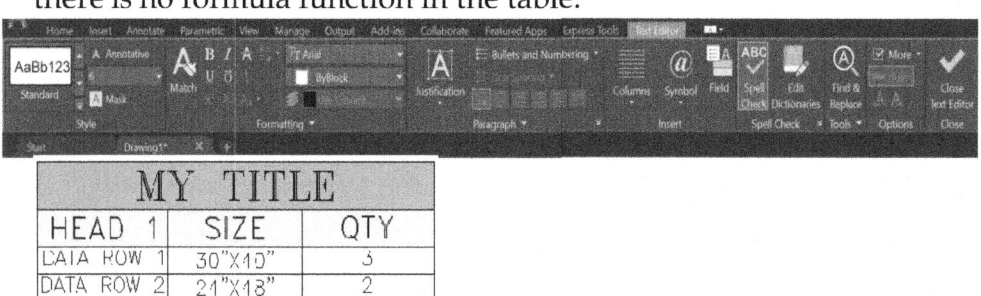

MY TITLE		
HEAD 1	SIZE	QTY
DATA ROW 1	30"X40"	3
DATA ROW 2	21"X18"	2
etc...	etc...	etc...
etc...	etc...	etc...
LAST ROW	60"X72"	8

Autodesk AutoCAD 2021
Learn CAD With Ease.

Note 2: You can modify existing table style by modify option.

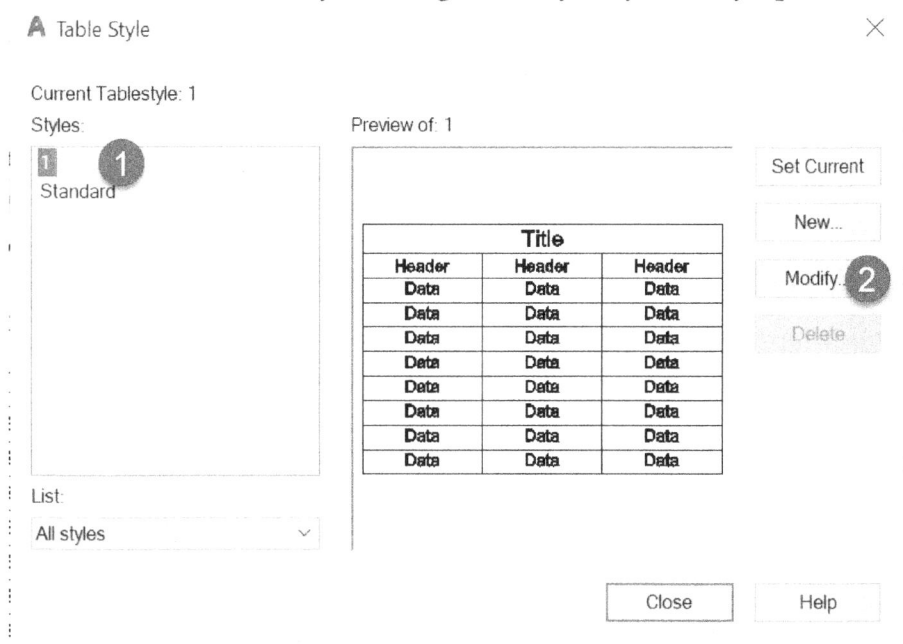

Autodesk AutoCAD 2021
Learn CAD With Ease.

CHAPTER 11
LAYERS

Layers are used to organize different objects of the drawing by assigning them to different layers.

When you work on complex drawings having a large number of objects, it is necessary to work in layers to manage different objects.

You can easily control the visibility and the other properties like line type, color, lineweight, etc of the objects by categorized them into different layers.

The concept of layers is used in other software applications, such as Photoshop programs. For those not aware of the concept, we'll start from the beginning.

When a new AutoCAD drawing is created, everything is drawn on the one default layer, named 0. When creating drawings, the layer 0 shouldn't really be used. New layers should be set up with names corresponding to the content contained on them.

Normally, it is acceptable to have a layer for each different part of a drawing. The layers created for a simple house plan could be as follows:

- Walls
- Partition Walls
- Doors
- Windows
- Text
- Dimensions
- Stairs

Each part of the house plan would be arranged on its relevant layer, for example, main walls should draw in the "Walls" layer, Partition walls in the "Partition walls" layer, and doors in the "Doors" layer.

Remember that layers can be used to manage drawings, for example, in order to see the drawing more clearly, you may want to remove all the text and dimensions from the drawing. All you have to do is tell AutoCAD to not display the "Text" and "Dimensions" layers by turning off the layers in layer manager. The layers can then turned back on again whenever you choose.

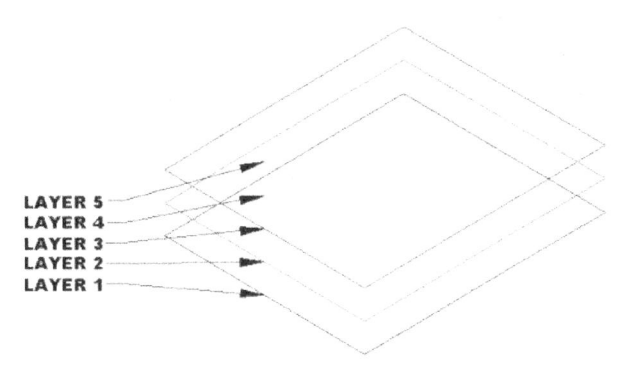

LAYER 5
LAYER 4
LAYER 3
LAYER 2
LAYER 1

11.1 Command: **Layers**
    Alias   : **La**

    Home Tab →Layers Panel→Layer
    Use: To create layers.

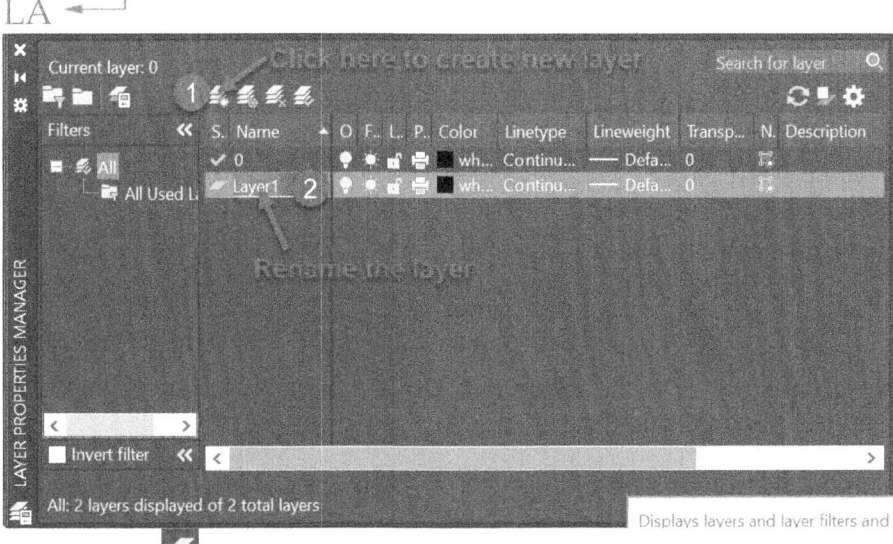

LA

1. Click on icon to create new layer.

Autodesk AutoCAD 2021
Learn CAD With Ease.

2. Rename the new layer. Here I rename it,"Wall".
3. Assign color, line type and line weight to the layer.
4. Select the "wall" layer.
5. Then click on set current icon to make the layer current.

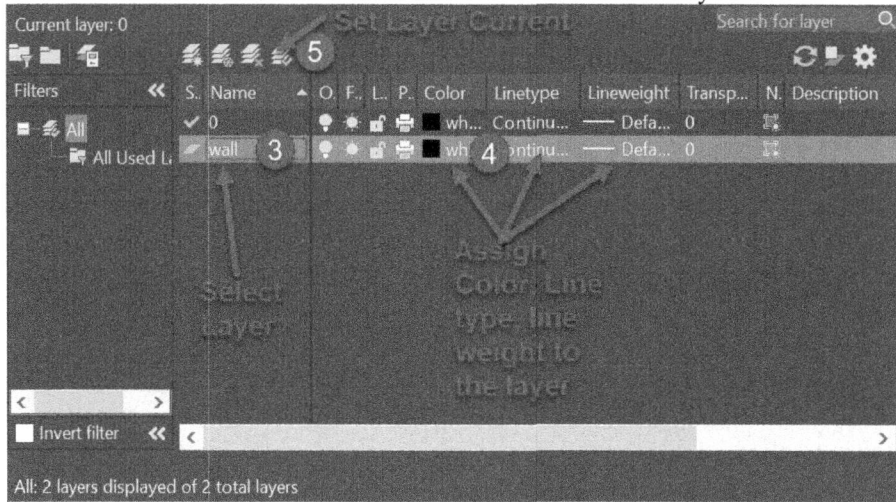

6. Close the layer manager by click on ❌ in left corner.
7. Now, you can draw objects (walls) in the drawing area.

Note: You can create more layers and make them current by following the steps given above to work on them.

New Layer: Press the New button to create a new layer.

Delete Layer: Press the delete button to delete the selected layer.

Set Current layer: Press the current button to set the selected layer current. After that all objects will be drawn on this current layer.

Options of the layers:

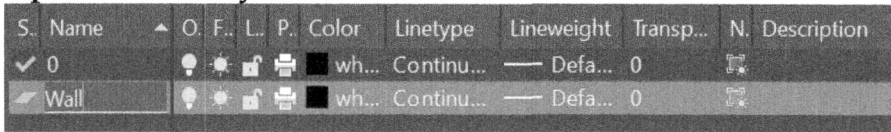

Name: Displays the layer name.

Autodesk AutoCAD 2021
Learn CAD With Ease.

On💡: Controls the on or off of layers. Select the light bulb to turn the layer off on the drawing. When the layer is turned off you can't see object but you can make off layer current.

Freeze❄: Pressing this will freeze the layer in all viewports as well as the current model view. Objects on frozen layers are invisible. In large drawings, freezing unneeded layers speeds up operations involving display and regeneration. In a layout, you can freeze layers in individual layout viewports. You can't make frozen layer current.

Lock🔒: This feature locks a layer and preventing any content of the layer from being modified.

Color⬛: Change this to whichever color you like. All objects drawn on the layer will display the chosen color provided that the objects color setting in the object properties toolbar (shown above) is set to 'By Layer'.

Linetype: Set the default linetype for all objects drawn on the layer. i.e continuous, dashed, dotted etc.

Lineweight: Set the thickness a line appears .Default is no thickness. This option can be toggled on/off on the display by the LWT button above the command console.

Plot 🖨: Select if the layer will be shown when the drawing is plotted (printed).

The current layer, layer color, linetype and lineweight can all be controlled outside of the layer properties manager via the object properties toolbar.

That's it for basic layer controls! Get used to using layers as you will be using them often - especially when you find you need to start managing large drawing files that contain a lot of information.

Autodesk AutoCAD 2021
Learn CAD With Ease.

Layer Property Filter: The good thing about layer naming convention is we can define search criteria by their properties. In AIA standards, we give prefix such as A- for architecture drawing, S- for structural, C- for civil, and so on. So if we want to see Architecture layers only, it is very easy to filter them.

Now let us try to open AutoCAD layer manager. The left column will show you available filters. By default, you will see two available: "ALL" and "ALL USED LAYERS". If you click "ALL USED LAYERS", then you will see only layers containing objects. The unused will be filtered out. "ALL" will show you all layers in the drawing.

Now let's say we want to see only architecture layers. It is easy to filter them, because the layers started with prefix A.

Click on "New Property Filter", it's the left most button at the image below. AutoCAD will open "LAYER FILTER PROPERTIES" dialog box.

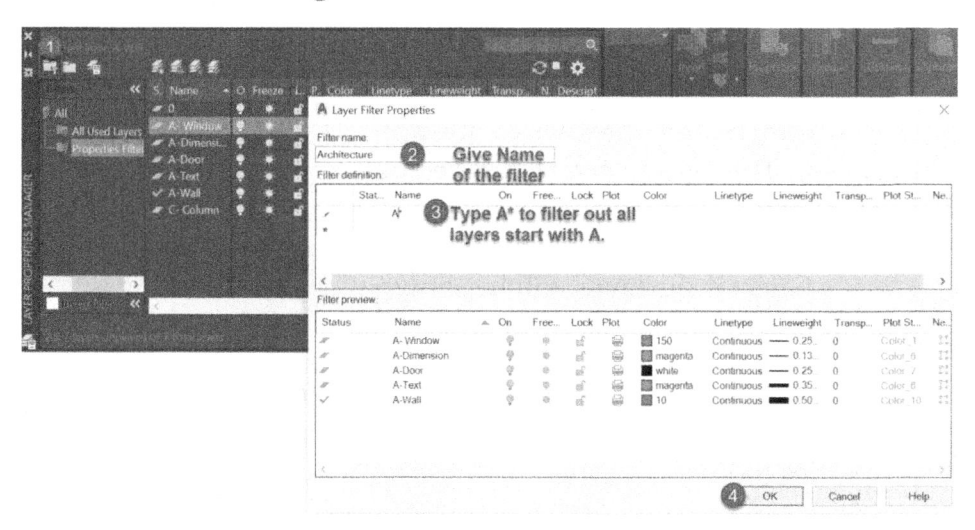

In this dialog, you can define which layers should be included in the list. In this example, we are going to give simple criteria: all layers with prefix A. You can give wildcards (*) so AutoCAD will only include layers that have the characters. Because all architecture layers started with A-, you can add A* or A-* to match all architecture layers criteria.

See the filter preview to see if your search criteria is right.

Click **"OK"** to save this filter. Now make sure the layer filter selected, and you see only architecture layers in the layer list. Now in layer toolbar (or layer panel if you use ribbon) you will see only layers that met the criteria.

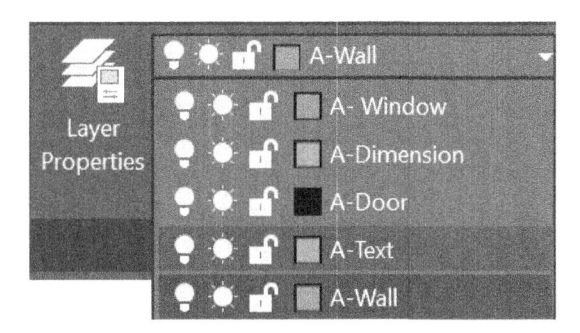

This allows you to see only layers you are using at your current task, and hides all others that you don't need.

Sub Filter Properties: You can filter the layers further by adding more search criteria. Right click on the "Layer Property Filter", then select "New properties filter" from contextual menu.

You need to use contextual menu to define the selected filter as the parent filter. If you click properties filter button, it will create parent level.

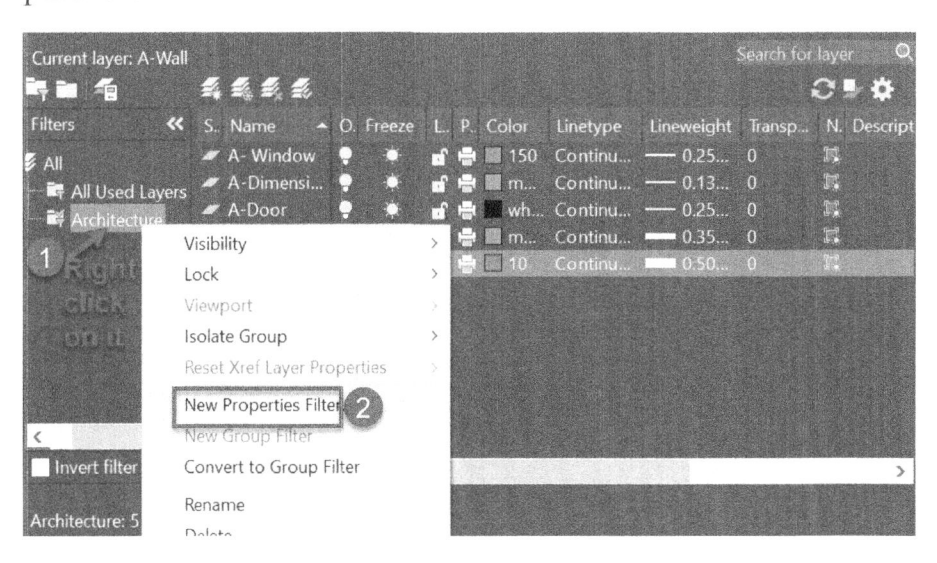

Now when AutoCAD open filter criteria, you will see only layers from its parent filter: architecture layers. Now you don't have to worry about the prefix. In this sample, I give criteria *Win* and

Autodesk AutoCAD 2021
Learn CAD With Ease.

Do in layer name. If there are other layers similar to that name in civil layers with prefix C-, you don't have to worry about them. They will not be included here.

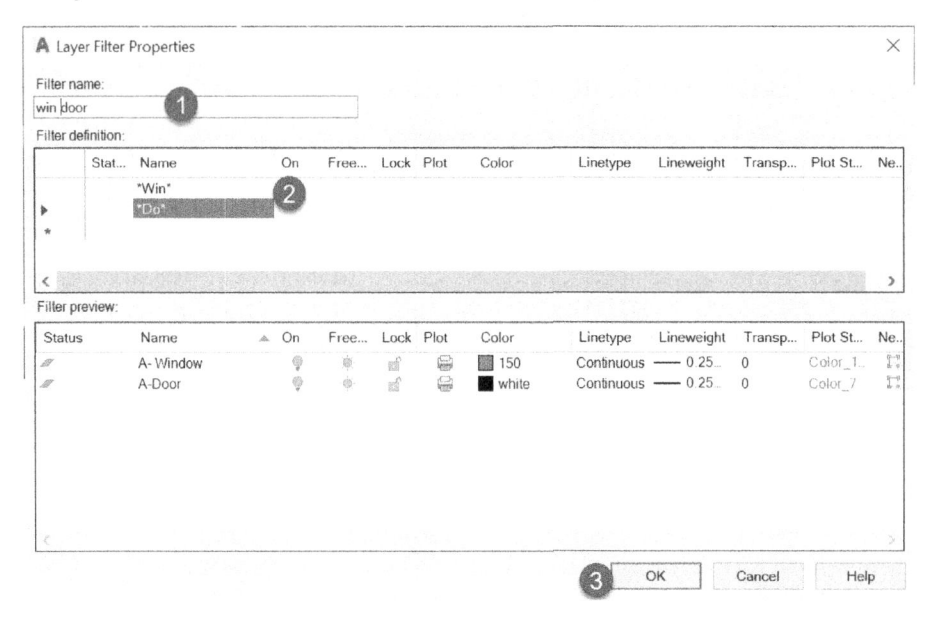

Changing Layer Properties in a Filter: After your layers grouped with filters, you can quickly change all layers properties that criteria. If you want to freeze, lock, or thaw layers, simply right click and choose the option you want in context menu.

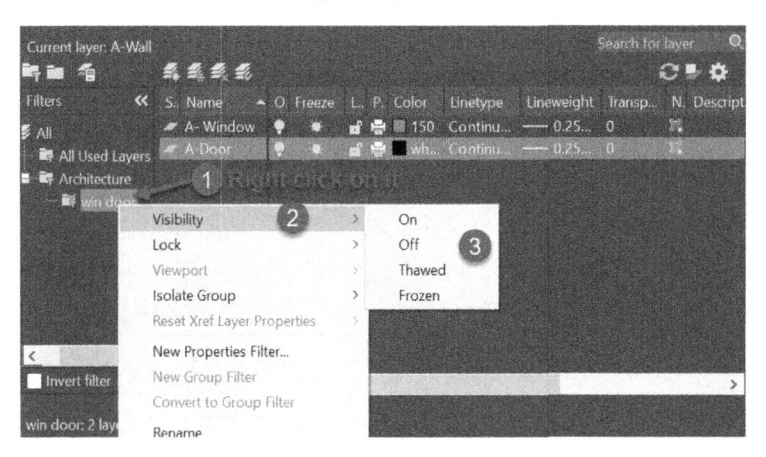

Layer Group Filter: The layer group filter is almost similar to the layer filter, but you don't define the layer criteria in this option. You can add the layers in a group by dragging the layers from the list to the layer group filter, or you can right-click above the

Autodesk AutoCAD 2021
Learn CAD With Ease.

group and choose **Select layers>Add** from the contextual menu. Sometimes you need to group layers from different disciplines or different objects or different objects that can't be defined by search criteria.

Procedure to create "Group Filter":

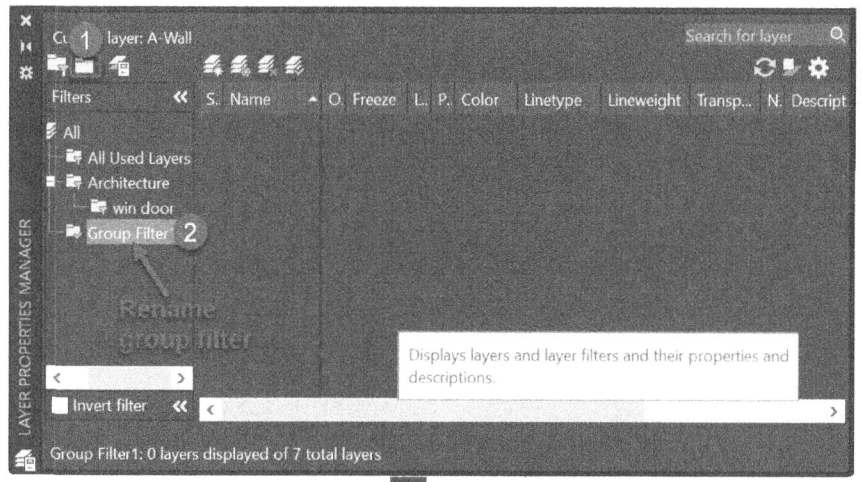

Click on "New Group Filter", then rename new group filter as shown in above figure. I renamed it "Plan".

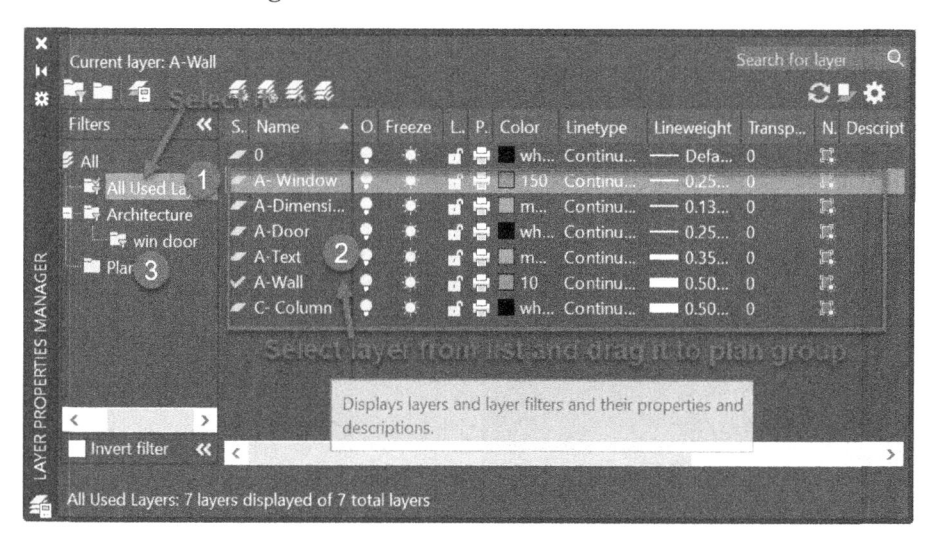

Click on "All used layers" and select layers from list and drag them to the "New Group Filter" named "Plan".

Autodesk AutoCAD 2021
Learn CAD With Ease.

Select "Plan" group filter, you can see layers which you place in a group filter by using above procedure.

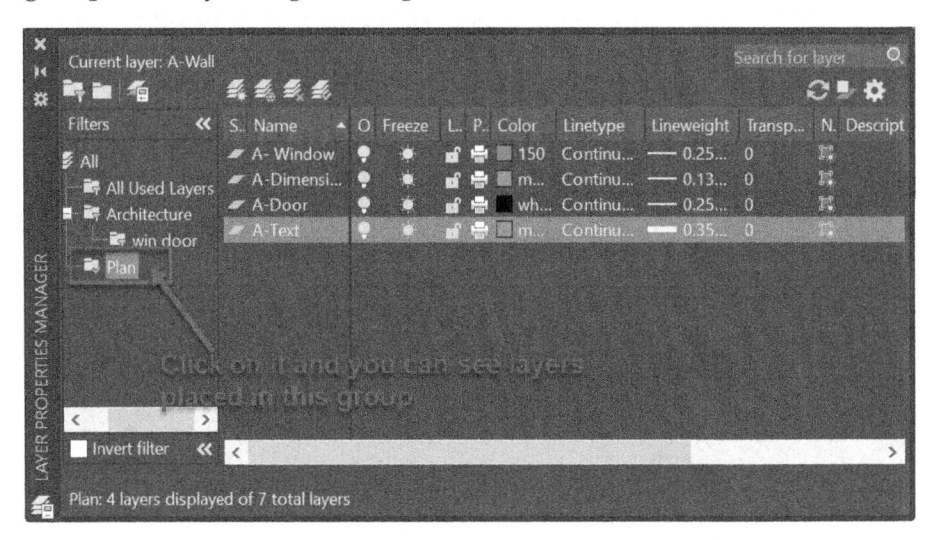

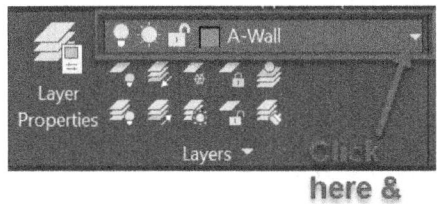

Click on it and you can see layers placed in this group

Note: You can directly make layer current by selecting the name of layer in the "layers" available in a "layer" panel in a "Home" tab.

Click here & select layer to make it current

Different Commands available in the Layer Panel:

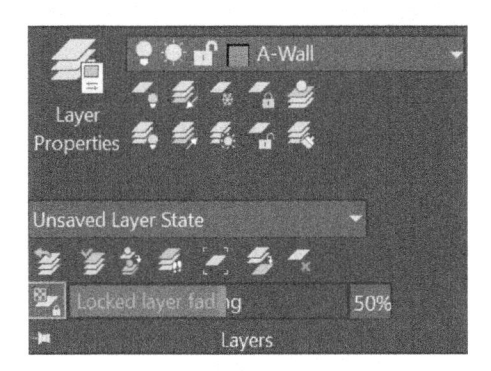

a. **Layer off**: This command is used to turn off the layer.

Click on "Layer Off" and select object on the screen to turn its layer off.

b. **Layer On**: This command is used to turn on all off layers.

c. **Layer Freeze**: This command is used to freeze layer.

Click on "Layer Freeze" and then select object on the screen to freeze its layer.

d. **Layer Thaw**: This command is used to thaw or unfreeze, frozen layers.

e. **Layer Lock**: This command is used to lock layer of selected object.

f. **Layer Unlock**: You can use this command to unlock layer by selecting object situated in locked layer.

Click on "Unlock" icon and select object situated in locked layer.

g. **Layer Isolate**: This command is used to hide or turn off all layers accept layer of selected object.

LAYISO ←

Current setting: Hide layers, Viewports=Vpfreeze

Select objects on the layer(s) to be isolated or [Settings]: by mouse click.

Select objects on the layer(s) to be isolated or [Settings]: S ←

Enter setting for layers not isolated [Off/Lock and fade] <Off>:

O ←

In paper space viewport use [Vpfreeze/Off] <Vpfreeze>: ←

Select objects on the layer(s) to be isolated or [Settings]: ←

Autodesk AutoCAD 2021
Learn CAD With Ease.

Layer WALL has been isolated.

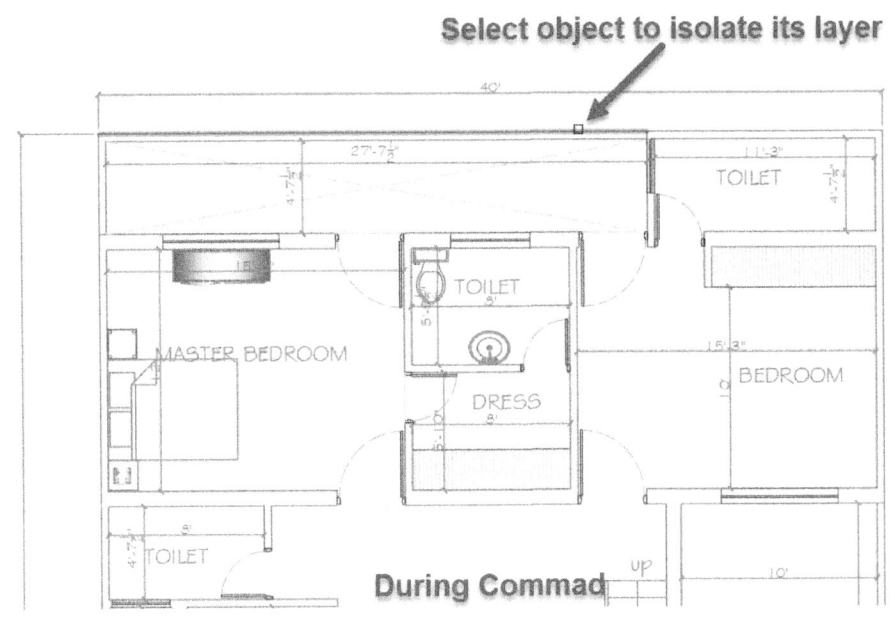

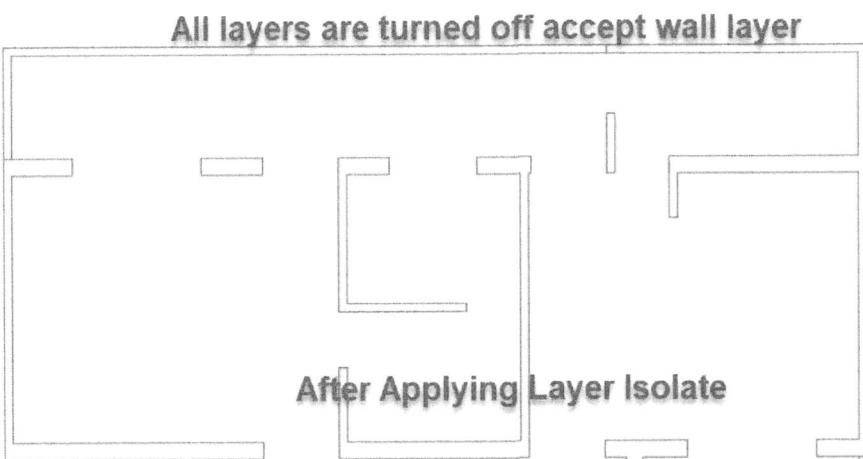

Select object to isolate its layer

During Commad

All layers are turned off accept wall layer

After Applying Layer Isolate

h. **Layer Unisolate**: Click on "Layer Unisolate" icon to restore all the layers that were hidden or locked by the layer isolate command.

i. **Match Layer**: This command is used to change the layer of a selected object to match the destination layer.

If you create an object on the wrong layer and want to change its layer by selecting an object of the destination layer.

Procedure:

Click on "Match Layer" icon to invoke command.

Select objects to be changed: by any selection method

Select objects: 1 found

Select objects: ↵

Select object on destination layer or [Name]: by any selection method.

j. **Change to current Layer**: Changes the layer property of selected objects to the current layer. If any object situated in other layer& you want to shift that object in to current layer from previous layer you can use this command.

LAYCUR ↵

Select objects to be changed to the current layer: by any selection method.

Select objects to be changed to the current layer: ↵

k. **Copy Object's to New Layer**: This command is used to make copies of selected objects on a layer that you specify.

COPYTOLAYER ↵

Select objects to copy: by any selection method (selection1)
Select objects to copy: ↵
Select object on destination layer or [Name] <Name>: select object (selection 2)
1 object(s) copied and placed on layer "Layer1".
Specify base point or [Displacement/eXit] <eXit>: mouse click
Specify second point of displacement or <use first point as displacement>: enter distance or mouse click

Autodesk AutoCAD 2021
Learn CAD With Ease.

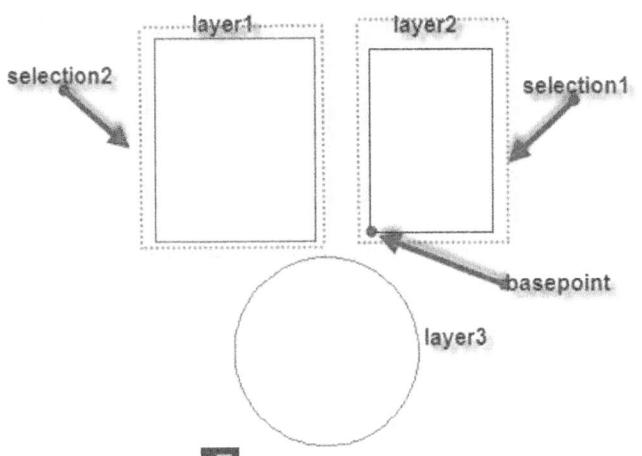

l. **Layer Walk**: Its displays objects situated on selected layers and hides all objects situated on other layers.

Click on "Layer Walk", it will open dialog box given below.

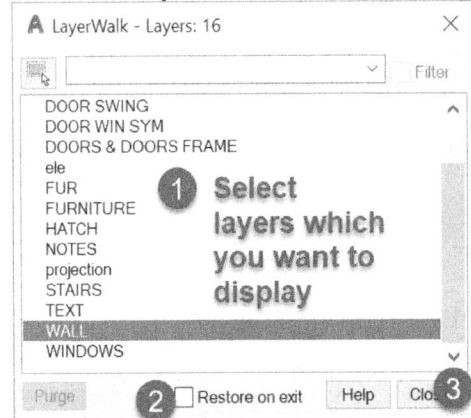

Select layers from list to keep them "On".
Uncheck the option "Restore on exit" and then click on "Close".

Note: Now you can see that all other layers accept selected ones are turned off.

m. **Layer Merge**: Merges selected layers into a target layer, removing the previous layers from the drawing.
You can reduce the number of layers in a drawing by merging them. Objects on merged layers are moved to the target layer, and the original layers are purged from the drawing.

LAYMRG ←

Select object on layer to merge or [Name]: Select an object or type "**n**" and press ← to select a layer from a list of layers

After you selected the layer(s) to merge, the following prompt is displayed:

Autodesk AutoCAD 2021
Learn CAD With Ease.

Select object on target layer [Name]: Select an object or enter "n" and press ↵ to select a target layer from a list of layers

- ❖ Select Object on Layer to Merge: Select an object on the destination layer.

- ❖ Name: Displays a list of layers, where you can select layers to merge.

- ❖ Select Object on Target Layer: Select an object on the target layer.

- ❖ Name: Displays a list of layers onto which you can merge the selected object or layer.

n. Layer Delete: This command is used to delete layers.

LAYDEL ↵
Select object on layer to delete or [Name]: by mouse or type name of layer
Select object on layer to delete or [Name/Undo]: ↵
Do you wish to continue? [Yes/No] <No>: y ↵

o. Layer Previous: This command is used to undo the last change you made in properties of layers.

LAYERP (Layer Previous) does not undo the following changes:
- ❖ Renamed layers: If you rename a layer and change its properties, "Layer Previous" restores the original properties but not the original name.
- ❖ Deleted layers: If you delete or purge a layer, using Layer Previous does not restore it.
- ❖ Added layers: If you add a new layer to a drawing, using Layer Previous does not remove it.

p. Make Current: You can change the current layer by selecting an object on that layer. This is a convenient alternative to specifying the layer name in the Layers palette.

Autodesk AutoCAD 2021
Learn CAD With Ease.

LAYMCUR ←┘

Select object whose layer will become current: by mouse

Aliases or Short Keys of all commands related to layers:

    Layer On: LAYON
    Layer Off: LAYOFF
    Layer Freeze: LAYFRZ
    Layer Thaw: LAYTHW
    Layer Lock: LAYLCK
    Layer Unlock: LAYULK
    Layer Isolate: LAYISO
    Layer Unisolate: LAYUNISO
    Make Layer Current: LAYMCUR
    Match Layer: LAYMCH
    Layer Previous: LAYERP
    Change To Current Layer: LAYCUR
    Layer Walk: LAYWALK
    Layer Merge: LAYMRG
    Delete Layer: LAYDEL

Autodesk AutoCAD 2021
Learn CAD With Ease.

PRODUCTIVITY TOOLS

In this section you will get knowledge of those commands which increases the productivity of drawings. By using those commands you will create better designs faster.

Autodesk AutoCAD 2021
Learn CAD With Ease.

CHAPTER 1
ADVANCE SELECTION METHODS

In this chapter you will get knowledge about some advance selection methods used in the AutoCAD.

These are:
- ❖ Quick Selection
- ❖ Filter
- ❖ Selection Cycle

Let's check these commands.

1.1 Command: Quick Select
   Alias   : QSelect

   Home Tab→ Utilities Panel→Quick Select

Use: To select objects on the basis of properties.
You can invoke Quick Select command by right click on screen.
For example:
If you want to select circles of radius 2, in a drawing you can use *Quick Select* command. The entries are given below:

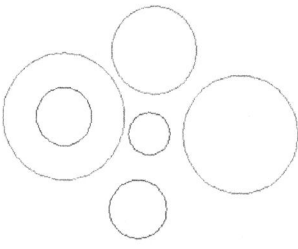

Drawing in which you want to select circle of radius 2.

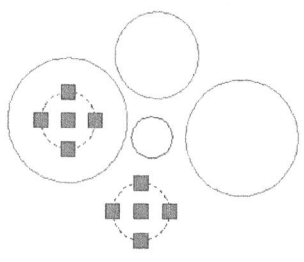

Selection of Circles of Radius 2.

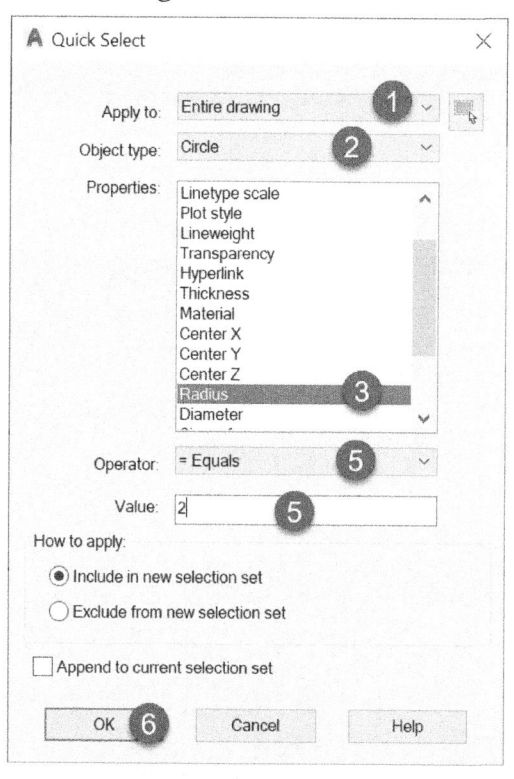

Autodesk AutoCAD 2021
Learn CAD With Ease.

1.2 Command: **Filter**
   Alias   : Fi

Use: This command is used to select objects on the basis of one & more properties.

There are four operators work in Filter command. Every operator has their own conditions according which they select objects.

Operator: Begin And, End And
Properties: 1 and more properties.
Selection: Select objects that fulfill all the properties.

Operator: Begin Or, End Or
Properties: 1 and more properties.
Selection: Select objects that fulfill all the properties and it also select objects that fulfill even one property.

Operator: Begin Not, End Not
Properties: Only one property
Selection: Select objects that not fulfill any property.

Operator: Begin Xor, End Xor
Properties: Only two properties.
Selection: Select objects that fulfill only one property.

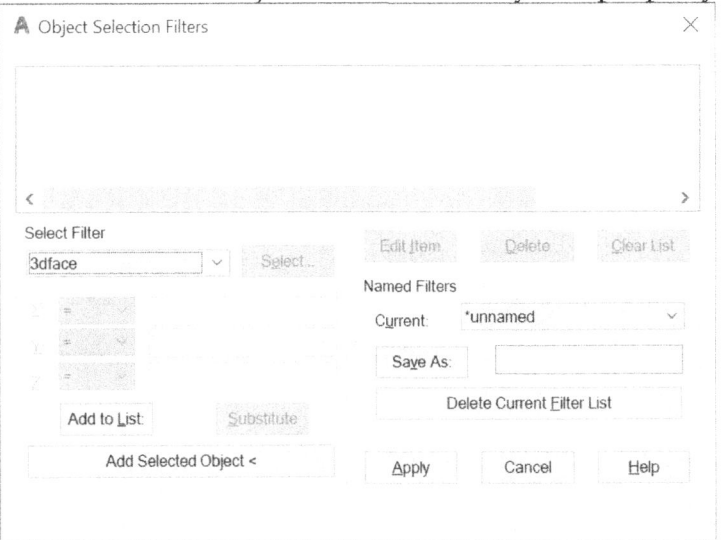

Filter Property List: Displays a list of the filter properties that compose the current filter.

By Madhumita Kshirsagar

Autodesk AutoCAD 2021
Learn CAD With Ease.

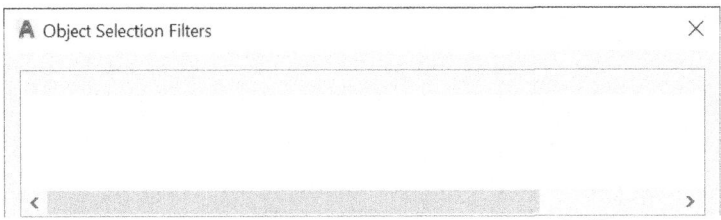

Select Filter: This option is use to select different properties & operators to select or filter objects.

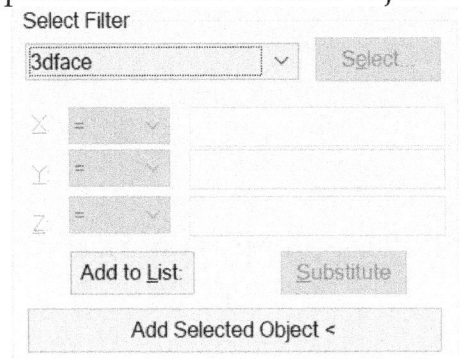

Add to list: To add properties to the filter list.

Substitute: Replaces the filter property selected in the filter property list with the one displayed in Select Filter.

Substitute: Replaces the filter property selected in the filter property list with the one displayed in Select Filter

Add selected object: This option is use to add all properties of one object in the filter list, which you selected directly from viewport.

Edit items: To edit or change items of filter list.

Delete: To delete items from filter list.

Clear List: To delete all the properties from current filter list.

Clear List: To delete all the properties from current filter list.

Named Filter: This section is used to display, save, and delete filters.

Current: Displays saved filters. Select a filter list to make it current. The named filter and its list of properties are loaded from the default file, *filter.nfl*.

Autodesk AutoCAD 2021
Learn CAD With Ease.

Save As: Saves a filter and its list of properties. The filter is saved in the *filter.nfl* file. Names can contain up to 18 characters.

Delete Current Filter List: Deletes a filter and all its properties from the default filter file.

Apply: Exits the dialog box and displays the Select Objects prompt, where you create a selection set. The current filter is used on the objects you select.

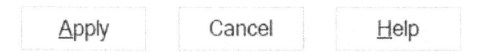

If you want to select circles of blue color with radius 2, you will apply filter as given below.

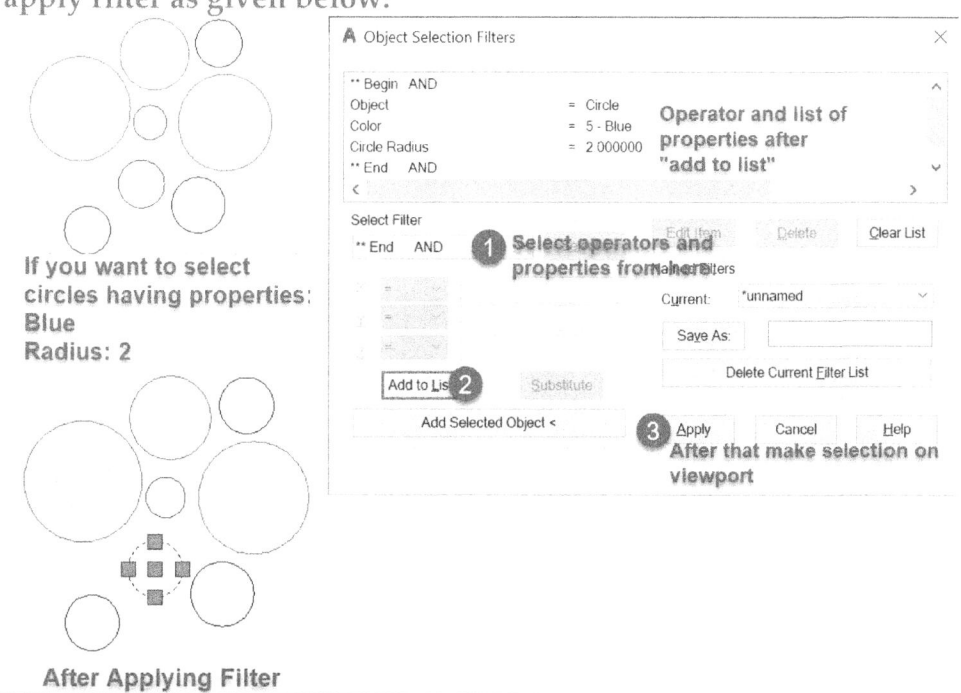

After Applying Filter

Note: You can apply other operators exactly like **Begin And, End And** operator.

224

By Madhumita Kshirsagar

Autodesk AutoCAD 2021
Learn CAD With Ease.

1.3 Command: Selection Cycling

Use: Another great addition to 2011 is the Selection Cycling (SC) toggle found on the Status Bar (drafting setting buttons). If you have objects that are overlapping and you want to select one of them, your only option was to hold SHIFT and hit the spacebar while hovering over the stacked objects. You can still do this method but there is this (SC) toggle that will come in handy.

With Selection Cycling turned on:

- ❖ Hover over the overlapped objects and you will see a blue icon that appears next to your cursor.

- ❖ Click on the overlapped objects and a "Selection" box appears that shows the color of the objects and what the object is made of (line, circle, polyline)…

- ❖ You can either click the desired object from this list or use the up & down arrows to highlight the object, then hit enter to select it.

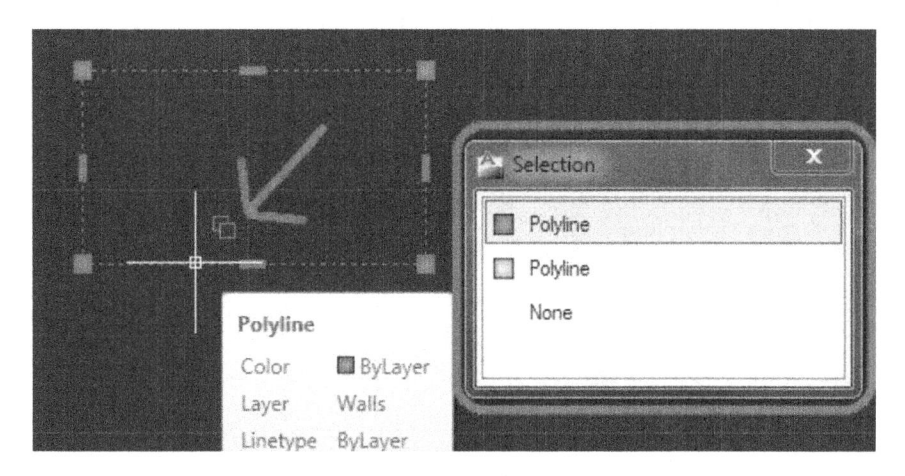

Note: When you are zoomed out and hovering over objects, the SC icon appears, so I wouldn't suggest that this be toggled on all of the time.

Autodesk AutoCAD 2021
Learn CAD With Ease.

CHAPTER 2
BLOCKS & ATTRIBUTE

In this chapter you will get knowledge about placement, making, and editing of reusable contents in the AutoCAD.

Commands cover in this chapter:
- Design Center
- Create Block
- Insert Block
- Block Editor
- Dynamic Blocks
- Divide
- Measure
- Attribute
- Edit Attribute
- Attribute Display
- Block Attribute Manager

2.1 Command: Design Center
Alias   : Ctrl + 2

View Tab →Palettes Panel→Design Center

Use: This command is use to manage & insert blocks, xrefs etc. Design Centre is the library part of AutoCAD that includes mechanical symbols, architectural symbols, and electrical symbols& different other symbols related to different fields.

Path of design centre:

My Computer ▶ Cdrive ▶ Programme/ProgrammeFiles ▶ AutoCAD ▶ Sample ▶ EnUS ▶ DesignCenter

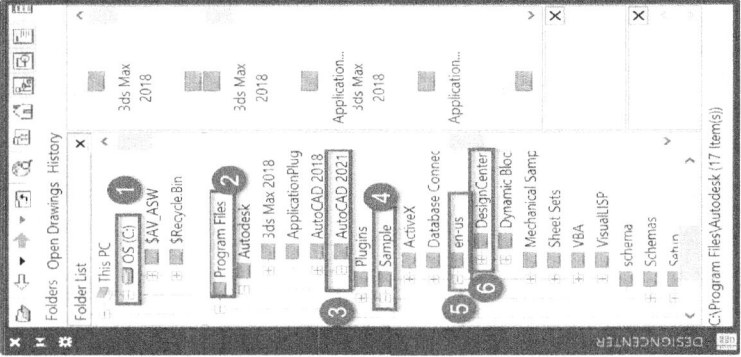

If you want to place symbols in a drawing:
- ❖ Ctrl + 2
- ❖ Open design Center according to given path.

Autodesk AutoCAD 2021
Learn CAD With Ease.

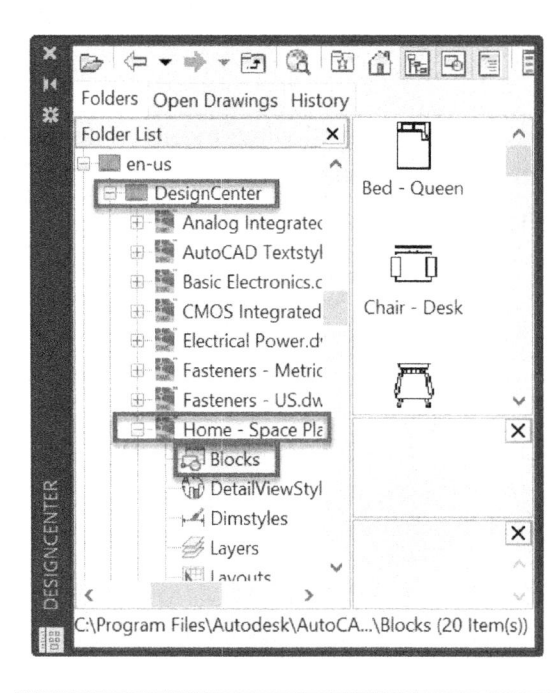

- ❖ Select any file according to your stream like mechanical, architecture, civil, electrical.
- ❖ Click on Block Now you can see different blocks(symbols)
- ❖ Select any one of them & drag it on viewport to place it.

Note:
- ❖ The second method to place symbol is rightclick on it & get insert block to insert symbol in a drawing.
- ❖ You can also transfer Layers, Table styles, Multileader styles, Layouts, Dimension styles, Linetypes, Xrefs etc by DesignCenter like blocks.

2.2 Command: Tool Palettes
    Alias   : Ctrl + 3

    Insert Tab → Content Panel → Tool Palettes

Use: This command is also used to place reusable contents in a drawing. It is easier than design center.

Procedure to place blocks by tool palettes:
- ❖ Type Ctrl+3 to invoke tool palettes command.
- ❖ Select any type of block group or tool palettes like "Architectural, Mechanical, Annotation" and etc from tabs available in the left of the tool palettes.
- ❖ Now you will see blocks related to selected tool palette in the right side.
- ❖ Select block and drag it in the drawing to place it.

Autodesk AutoCAD 2021
Learn CAD With Ease.

List of Different tool palettes
- Modeling
- Constraints
- Annotation
- Architectural
- Mechanical
- Electrical
- Civil
- Structural
- Hatches and Fills
- Tables
- Command Tool Samples
- Leaders
- Draw
- Modify
- Generic Lights
- Fluorescent
- High Intensity Discharge
- Incandescent
- Low Pressure Sodium
- Cameras
- Visual Styles

Click Here to get many more Tool Palettes.

Select tool palettes here

Imperial samples:
- Door - Imperial
- Window - Imperial
- Aluminum Window (Ele...)
- Fluorescent (Recessed) -...
- Stud - Imperial
- Toilet - Imperial
- Trees - Imperial

You can get different blocks related to selected tool palette here. Select blocks and drag them in the drawing to place them.

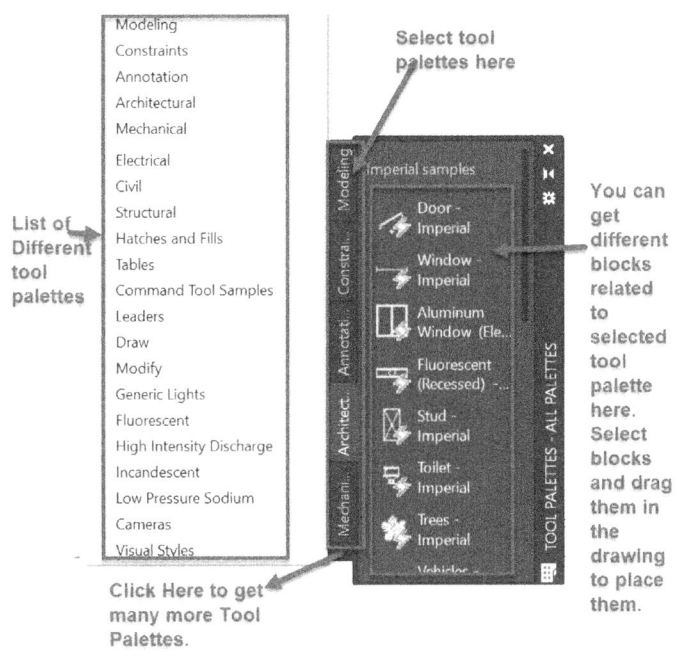

2.3 Command: Create Block
   Alias   : B

   Insert Tab → Block Definition Panel → Create Block
   Draw Tab → Block Panel → Create Block

Use: This command is used to create blocks of objects which you want to use regularly in the different drawings.

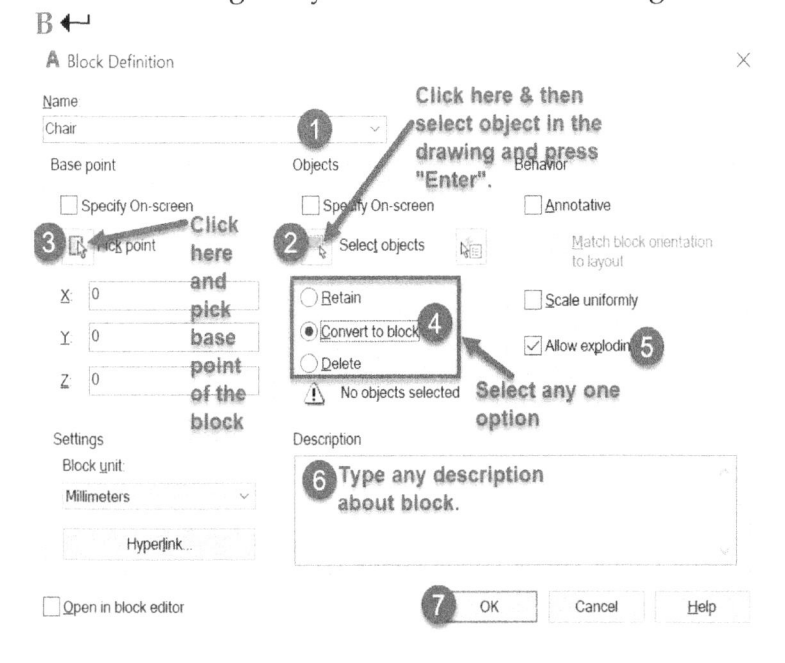

B ↵

Block Definition dialog:
- Name: Chair ①
- Base point
  - ③ Click here and pick base point of the block
  - Pick point
  - X: 0
  - Y: 0
  - Z: 0
- Objects
  - ② Click here & then select object in the drawing and press "Enter".
  - Select objects
  - ④ Select any one option:
    - Retain
    - Convert to block
    - Delete
  - No objects selected
- Behavior
  - Annotative
  - Match block orientation to layout
  - Scale uniformly
  - ⑤ Allow exploding
- Settings
  - Block unit: Millimeters
  - Hyperlink...
- Description
  - ⑥ Type any description about block.
- Open in block editor
- ⑦ OK | Cancel | Help

228

By Madhumita Kshirsagar

Autodesk AutoCAD 2021
Learn CAD With Ease.

Options of block dialog box:

a. **Name:** Specify name of block here.

b. **Objects:**
Select objects: You can select object by this option. When you click on **select object,** the block definition dialog box close temporarily & after selecting object press Enter to return to dialog box.
Retain: Retains the selected objects as distinct objects in the drawing after you create the block.
Convert to block: To convert object in to a block.
Delete: It deletes objects after you create block.

c. **Base point**: Specifies insertion base point for the block.
Specify on Screen: It prompts you to specify the base point when the dialog box is closed.
Pick Point: You can specify base point directly on the object by mouse click.
X: You can specify "x" co-ordinate value of the insertion base point here.
Y: You can specify "y" co-ordinate value of the insertion base point here.
Z: You can specify "z" co-ordinate value of the insertion base point here.

d. **Behavior:**
Annotative: It makes the block annotative.
Make block orientation to layout: This option is used to match block orientation to the layout orientation.
Allow exploding: It allows block to explode after or while you insert it in a drawing.
Scale uniformly: If you check out this option you can't give different scale factor in X scale factor, Y scale factor, Z scale factor while you insert block in a drawing.

There are many advantages to using blocks, here the major ones:

i. Blocks are a single entity. You can modify (move, copy, rotate) a block by selecting only one object in it.

ii. You can build up a library of blocks consisting of the parts that you require many times in your workday. These blocks can be stored in a separate folder and even on a network so that all drafters have access to them.

iii. Using blocks can help keep your file size down. AutoCAD stores block definitions in its database. When you insert a block, AutoCAD only stores the name of the block, its location (insertion point), scale and rotation. This can be very noticeable in a large drawing.

iv. If you need to change something, you can redefine a block. For example, you draw a chair and turn it into a block. Later, you're told that the size of the chair has changed. Since you used a block you can redefine the block and all of your chairs are updated automatically. If you had drawn (or copied) 100 chairs in your drawing, you would have to manually change each one.

v. Blocks can also contain non-graphical information. This means text objects called attributes. For example, you have made blocks of different chairs. You can add information to the block such as manufacturer, cost, weight, etc. This information stays with the block, but can also be extracted to a database or spreadsheet. This would be useful for things such as a bill of materials. Attributes can also be visible or invisible in your drawing. Another good use of attributes could be a title block. (You can get knowledge about attributes later in this chapter).

vi. You can even easily add internet hyperlinks to blocks so you can connect a block to a page on a supplier's online catalogue.

vii. You can also use these blocks in other drawings.

Autodesk AutoCAD 2021
Learn CAD With Ease.

2.4 Command: Insert Block
   Alias   : I

   Insert Tab →Block Panel →Insert
   Home Tab →Block Panel →Insert

Use: This command is used to insert blocks in a drawing.

Procedure to insert blocks in a drawing:
Type "I ↵" to invoke insert block command
Than select block from insert dialog box and click in a drawing to place it.
Note: Always check on "Insertion Point" option available in "Insertion options".

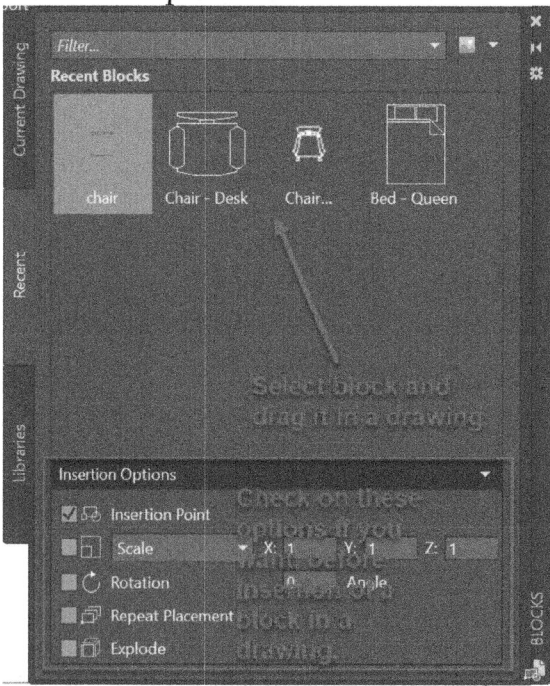

Insertion Point: This option is used to specify insertion point of a block in a drawing.
Scale: This option is used to specify x, y, z scale factor of a block to reduce and enlarge size of a block.
Rotation: This option is used to specify rotation angle of a block on a screen during its placement in a drawing.
Angle: This option is used to specify rotation angle of a block before its insertion in a drawing.

Autodesk AutoCAD 2021
Learn CAD With Ease.

Repeat Placement: Check on this option for repetitive insertion of a block in a drawing.
Explode: This option is used to explode block.

2.5 Command: Block Editor
    Alias   : BE
    Insert Tab →Block Panel →Insert
    Home Tab →Block Panel→Insert

Use: This option is used to open block editor dialog box to edit blocks & it also used to convert blocks in to Dynamic Blocks.

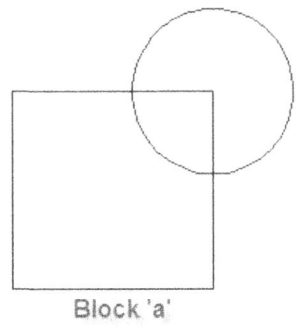

To edit this block apply Block edit command (BE ↵) or double click on it.
Then the new window for editing (Edit Block Definition) is open as given in figure given below.
Select block name in "Block to create or edit and press OK.

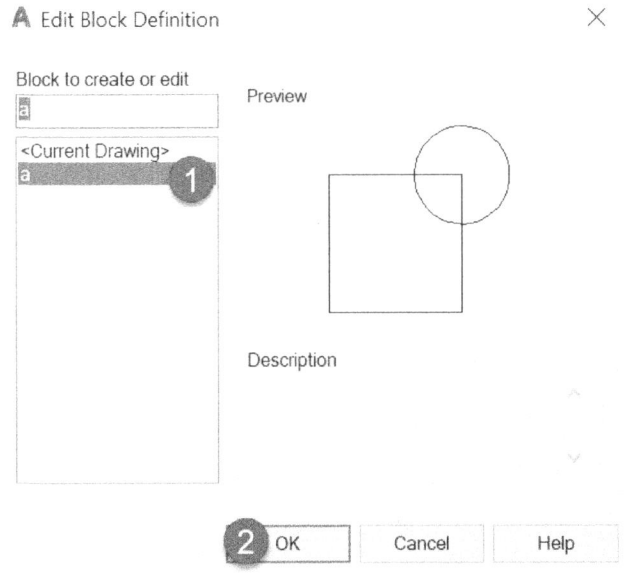

Then it will open Block editor screen.
Now, edit block here I apply hatch in intersecting part in the block.
And click on close Block editor.

After that, you will see a notification to save block after editing. Click on "Save the changes to a block".

232

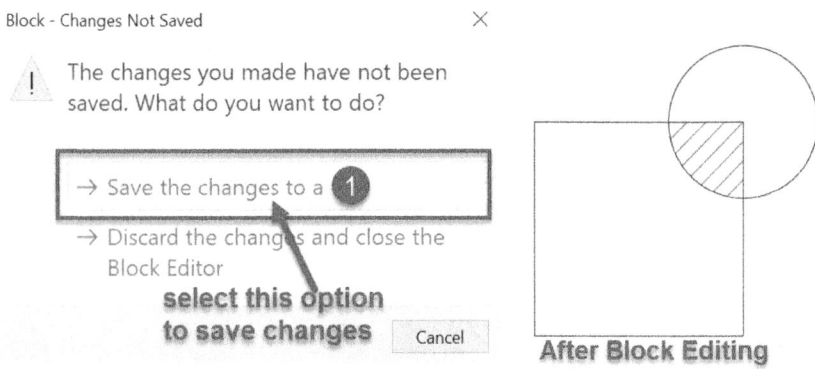

Autodesk AutoCAD 2021
Learn CAD With Ease.

2.5.1 Dynamic Blocks: Dynamic block is a very important feature to add some dynamic parameters to a block.

Parameters and Actions:

Different than the standard blocks, dynamic blocks have the properties of parameters and actions. More than one parameter or action can be assigned to any block. In general, parameters define the dimensions and location of the block. On the other side, actions define how the parameter to which it is assigned will operate and do the work that it is supposed to do. As an exception, ALIGNMENT parameters do not necessarily be assigned with an action.

If you want to create a dynamic block of a door symbol, you can create a block by the "Create block" command as we discussed previously in this chapter.

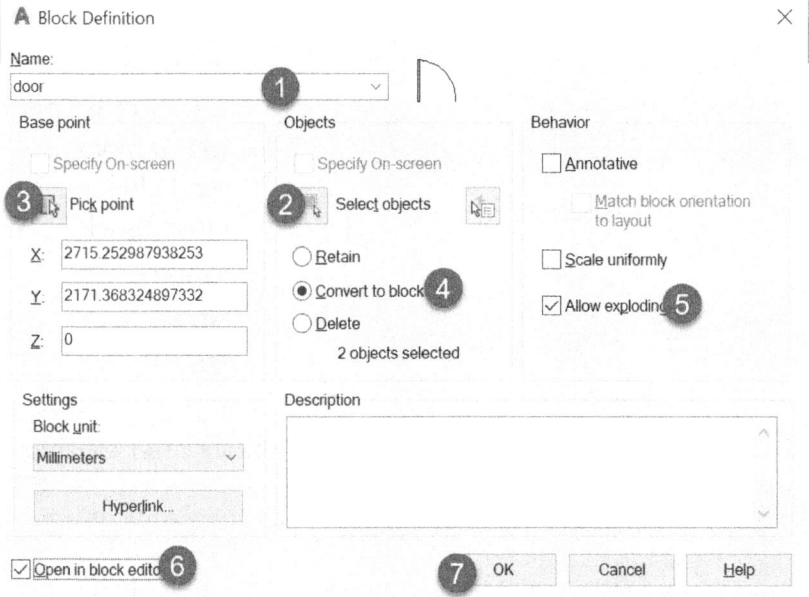

Autodesk AutoCAD 2021
Learn CAD With Ease.

Check on the "Open in block editor" option before pressing "Ok" in "Block Definition" dialog box to open a block editor window to create a dynamic block.

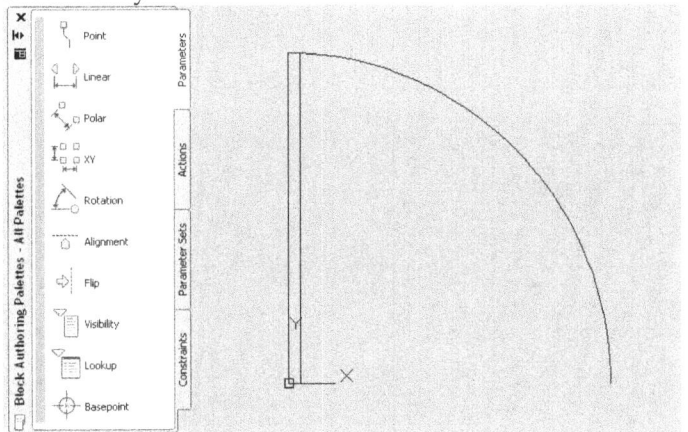

Now you can see a block editor screen, in a left side there is a **Block Authoring Palettes**.
You can use "Parameters" option to add parameters to the block and "Actions" option to apply actions to the block.
a. If you want to flip this door symbol in a drawing, you can do it by "Flip" parameter.

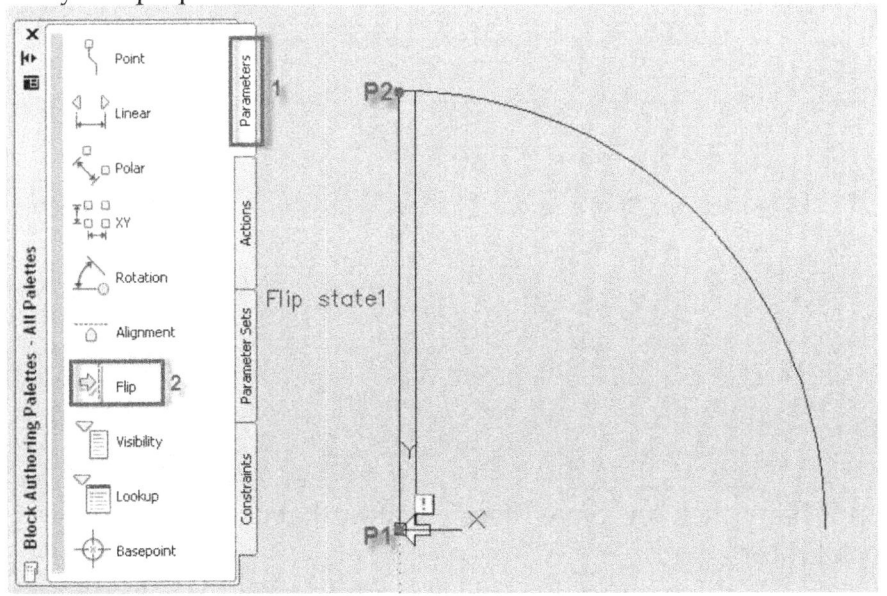

Step 1: Select **FLIP** parameter &specify first base point of reflection line .After that specify second point or end point of reflection line.

234

By Madhumita Kshirsagar

Autodesk AutoCAD 2021
Learn CAD With Ease.

Step 2: Specify label location (Flip state 1).
Step3: Click on **Actions** & select **Flip.**

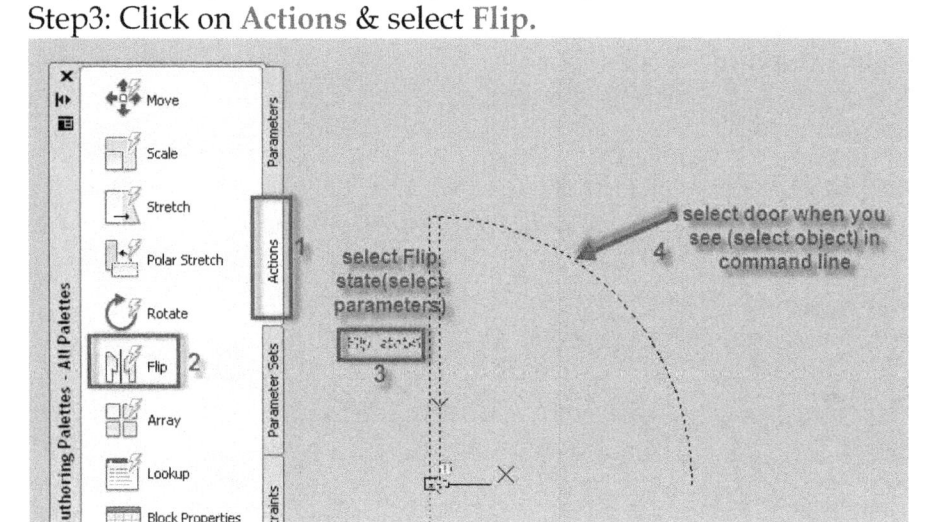

Step 4: Select "Flip state" when you see select parameter in command line.
Step 5: Then select whole object when you see select object in command line.
Step 6: After that press ENTER to end the command.

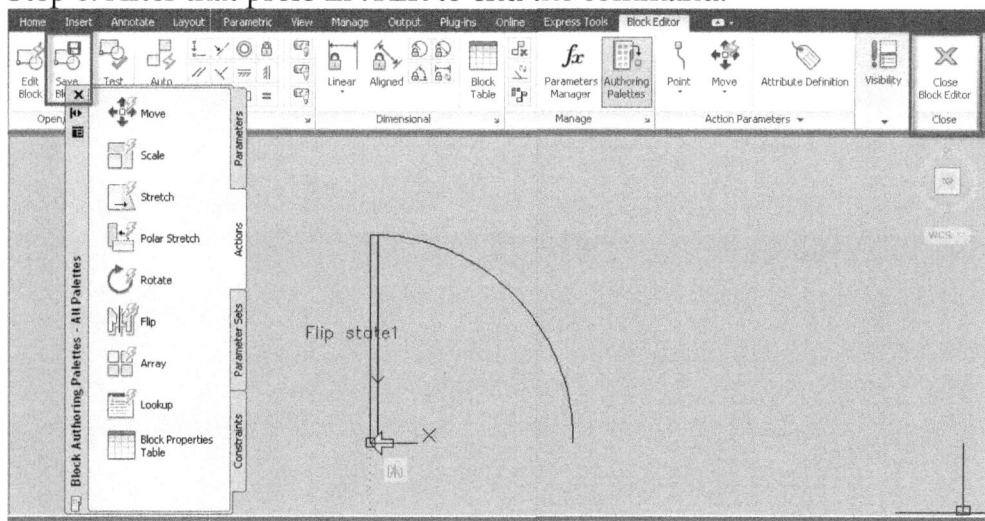

Step 7: Now click on "Save Block" & after that click on "Close Block Editor".

Now your door block is ready to flip. Click on flip arrow to flip the door.

b. The simplest example is that you can move an entity inside a block free from the block itself. In order to do this, you can use a POINT parameter and a MOVE action that is assigned to this point. When you insert a block that is prepared having these properties, then the POINT parameter that you have defined will be seen just like ENDPOINT, MIDPOINT etc. So that, when you select and drag this point, then the entity that you attached to this point will move freely from the block.

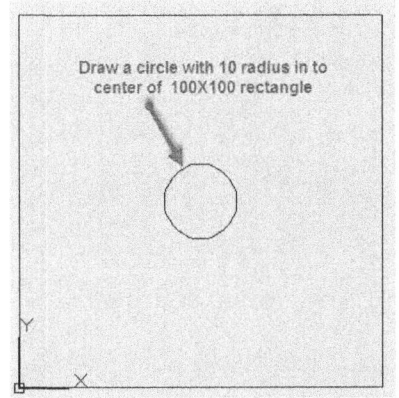

Step1: Firstly draw a circle with 10radius inside a square with 100×100 dimensions & create its block (give block's name hole).After that open it in Block Editor.

Step 2: Let's select Parameters tab from the tool palette from the left side and use POINT PARAMETER from there. Insert the point just at the center of circle. Actually, this is not necessary but, this will look more logical while using it. After inserting the point, change POSITION LABEL property from PROPERTIES tool palette as center. '!' that you see near the point means that this parameter has not been assigned to any action yet.

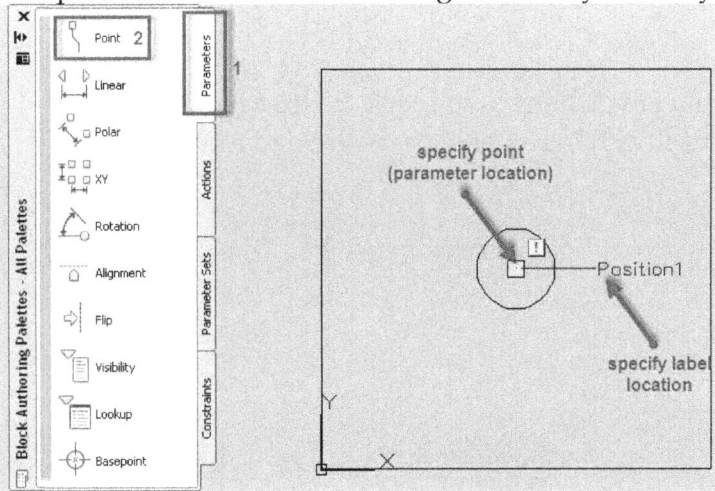

Autodesk AutoCAD 2021
Learn CAD With Ease.

Step 3: After that select **Actions** tab from tool palette select **Move** Action & then select parameter.

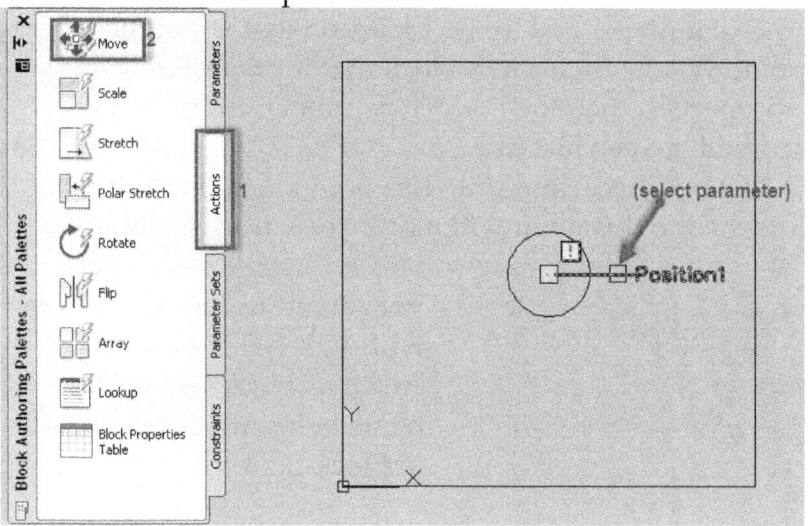

Step 4: Then select circle (select object). Now move action is properly applied to a block.

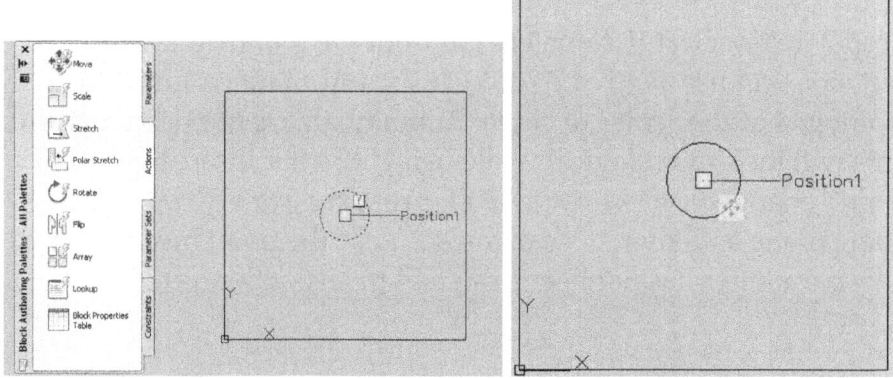

Step 5: After that save changes to block & close block editor. Now you can easily change position of circle in a block.

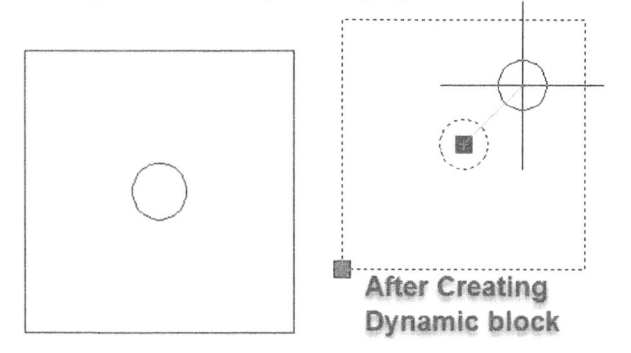

After Creating Dynamic block

Autodesk AutoCAD 2021
Learn CAD With Ease.

c. The goal is to create a Chair block that can be easily rotated to orientate it to a desk.

Step 1: Draw the Chair below on the Zero layer.

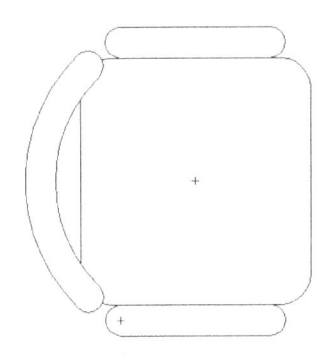

Start the same Block command to create block and check out option open in block editor.

Step 2: As mentioned earlier, our goal is to create a block that we can easily rotate. First you will need to add a parameter to the block, followed by an action.

Click on the "Rotation Parameter" icon in the palette. Then check the command line for prompts (as usual). Use the entries below:

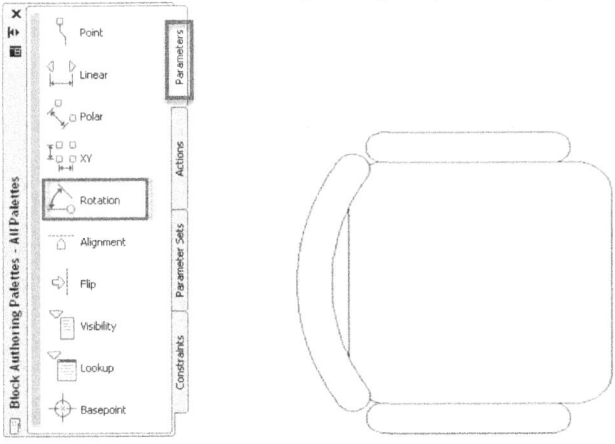

Specify base point or [Name/Label/Chain/Description/Palette/Value set] : click on midpoint of the seat
Specify radius of parameter: 9
Specify default rotation angle or [Base angle] <0>:

Step3: After defining the parameter, you then need to apply an action to the parameter. Select the tab on the palette that says "Actions". You will need to select the "Rotate Action" (makes sense). You will be asked to select the parameter that you want to apply the action to (select the parameter you just drew).

238

By Madhumita Kshirsagar

Autodesk AutoCAD 2021
Learn CAD With Ease.

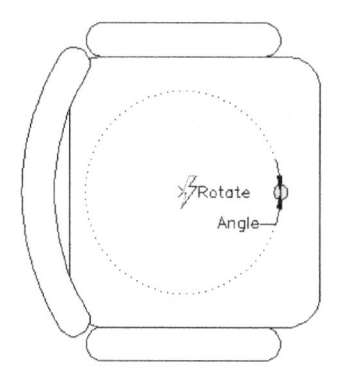

Finally, select the location of the Action)- once again select the center of the seat, and then the objects that you want the action to act on (in this case, all of them). Your block should now look like figure given at left side.

Step 4: Now, you can select the "Close Block Editor" at the top of the drawing screen. You will be returned to the regular drawing screen, and your block will be created. Click on it, and you should see the entire objects highlight, and the grip for the block's **Pick Point**. You will also see a grip for the block's dynamic rotation parameter.

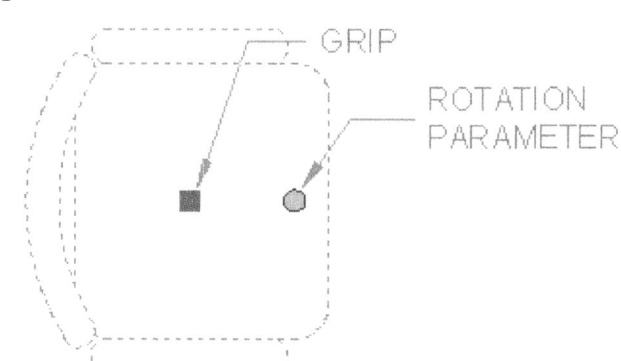

Now click on Rotation Parameter Grip and rotate the block.

d. How to make a smart block which determines the angle of the line over which the block is placed and aligns itself to that angle?

Step 1: Firstly draw a wash basin & create its block, after that open it in block editor.

Step 2: Select Alignment Parameters from parameter tab in the tool palettes.

While assigning the parameter, mark the ALIGNMENT TYPE as TANGENT. If you select PERPENDICULAR here, then your block will be perpendicular to the entity over which it is placed.

Autodesk AutoCAD 2021
Learn CAD With Ease.

During Applying Alignment Parameter

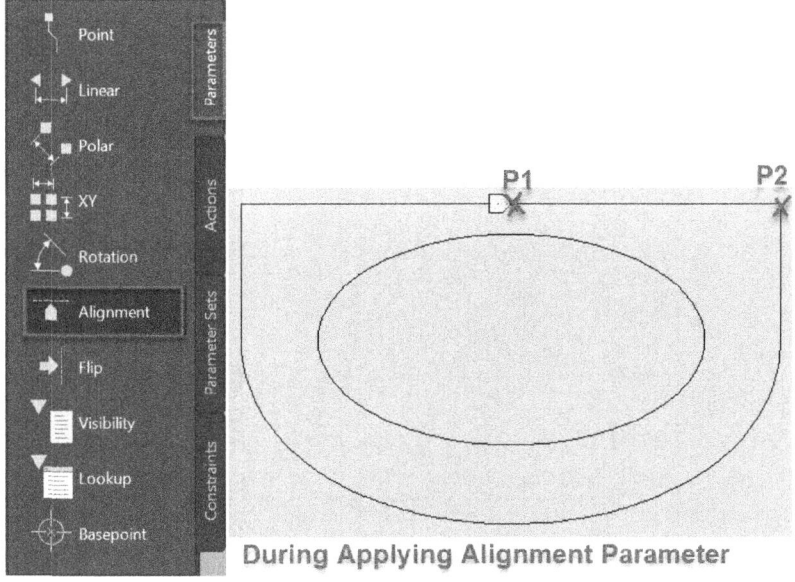

Command invoke in command line:
BParameter Alignment
Specify base point of alignment or [Name]: mouse click P1
Alignment type = Perpendicular
Specify alignment direction or alignment type [Type]: T ↵
Enter alignment type [Perpendicular/Tangent] <Perpendicular>:
T ↵
Specify alignment direction or alignment type [Type] <Type>:
0 ↵ or mouse click P2

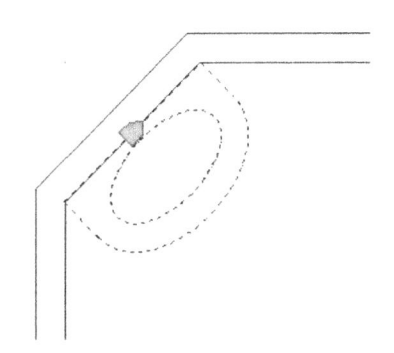

Now insert block on angled line, you can see block is aligned on that line as shown in a figure of a wash basin.

e. If you want to stretch block you will apply Linear Parameter & Stretch Action.
Step1: Firstly create rectangle with dimensions 100 X 80 and then make block of it.

240

By Madhumita Kshirsagar

Autodesk AutoCAD 2021
Learn CAD With Ease.

Step 2: Open this block in block editor.

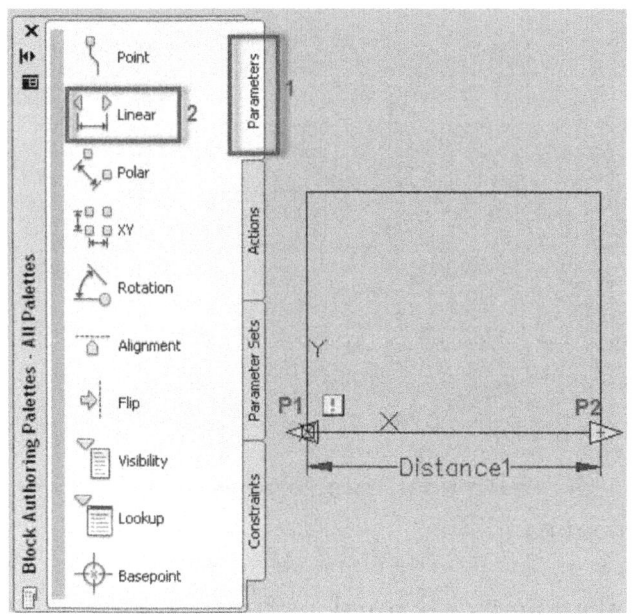

Step 3: Select **Linear parameter** from parameters tab.
Step 4: Specify start point (P1) after that Specify end point (P2).
Step 5: Then Specify label location (location of Distance 1).

Step 6: Select Distance1 & right click, select Grip Display (select 1 grip).

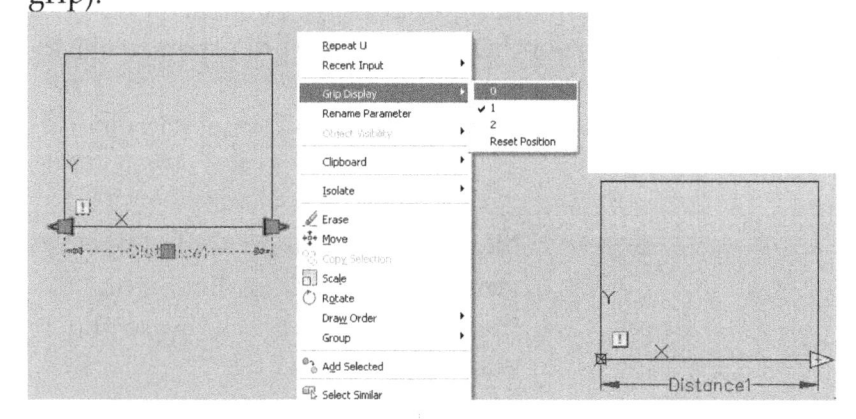

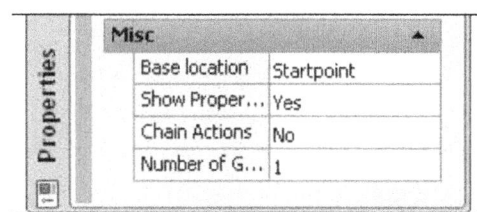

Note: If you select only one GRIP point, then you must set the side where GRIP point will be on, by using 'Base Location' property.

Autodesk AutoCAD 2021
Learn CAD With Ease.

Step 7: Then apply Stretch Action on a block .

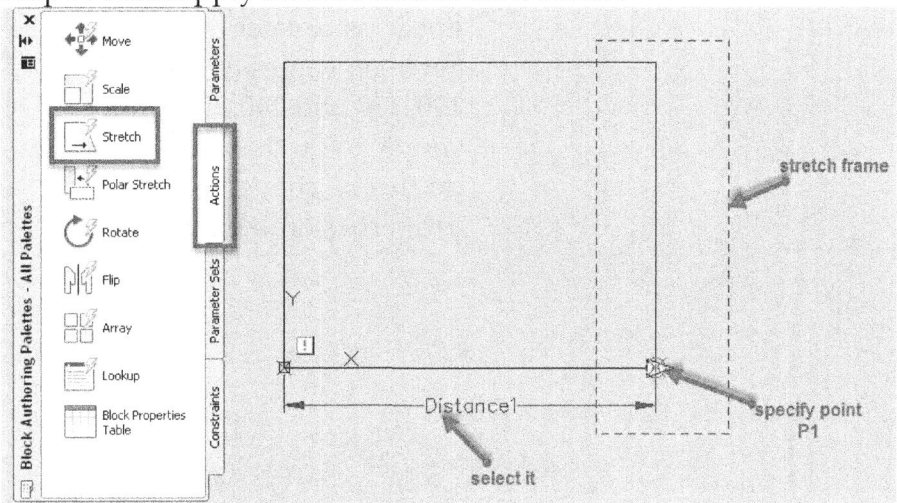

Follow the command line:

BActionTool Stretch
Select parameter: (select distance1)
Specify parameter point to associate with action or enter [sTart point/Second point] <Second>: mouse click (P1)
Specify first corner of stretch frame or [CPolygon]: mouse click
Specify opposite corner: mouse click
Specify objects to stretch: by any selection method and press ↵

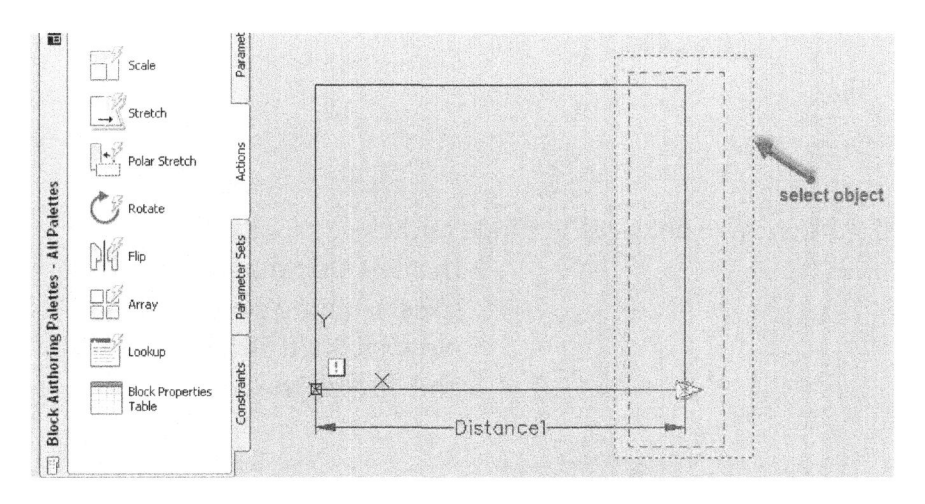

Autodesk AutoCAD 2021
Learn CAD With Ease.

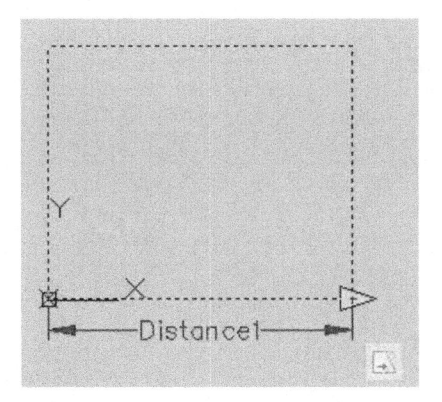

STEP 8: However, you want your linear parameter to change in between values of 90, 100, 110, 120, 130 and 140. It is quite simple to do this. You can easily do this by changing the properties of linear parameter.

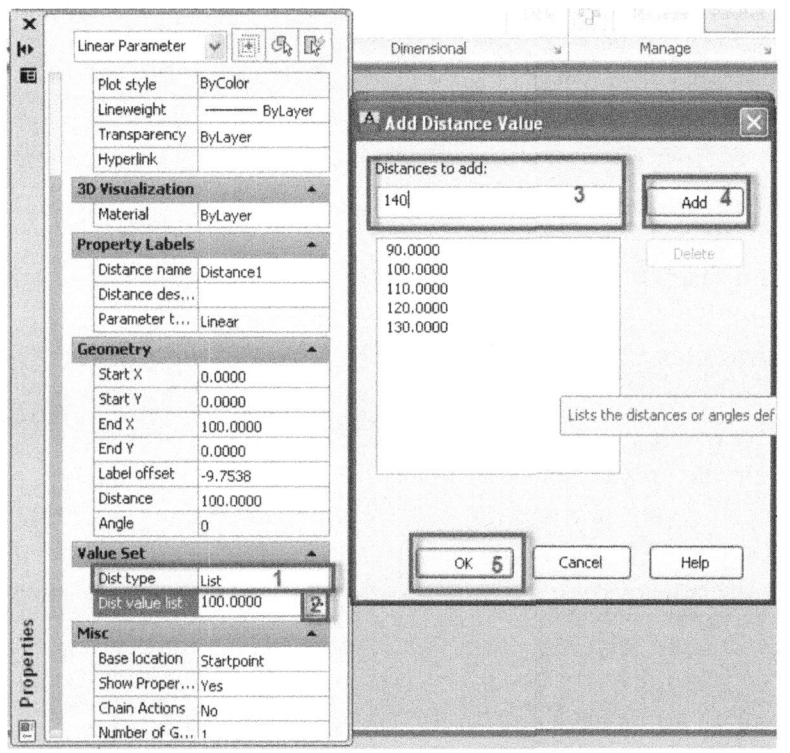

Step 9: Now save changes in block and close block editor.

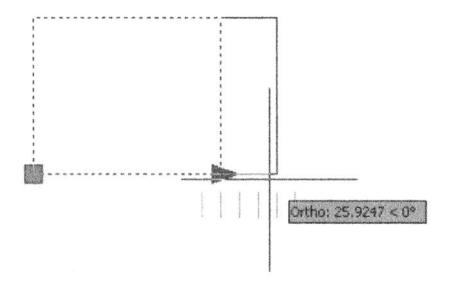

In a left side diagram you can see stretching points.
Now click on stretching grip and stretch the object.

Autodesk AutoCAD 2021
Learn CAD With Ease.

f. If you want to control visibility of blocks you can use Visibility Parameter.

Adds a visibility parameter to the dynamic block definition and defines a custom visibility property for the block reference. With visibility parameter, you can create visibility states and control the visibility of objects in the block. A visibility parameter always applies to the entire block and needs no action associated with it. In a drawing, click on the grip to display a list of visibility states available for the block reference. In the Block Editor, a visibility parameter displays as text with an associated grip.

For example control visibility of different drawings of chair.

Step 1: Firstly draw Plan, front elevation & side elevation of a chair.

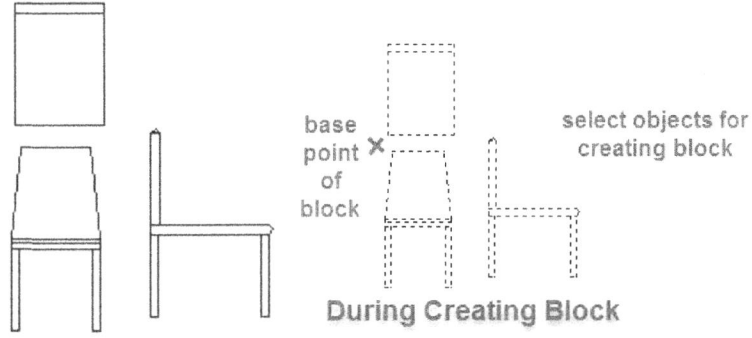

Step 2: Create block of all three drawings together & give the block name Chair.

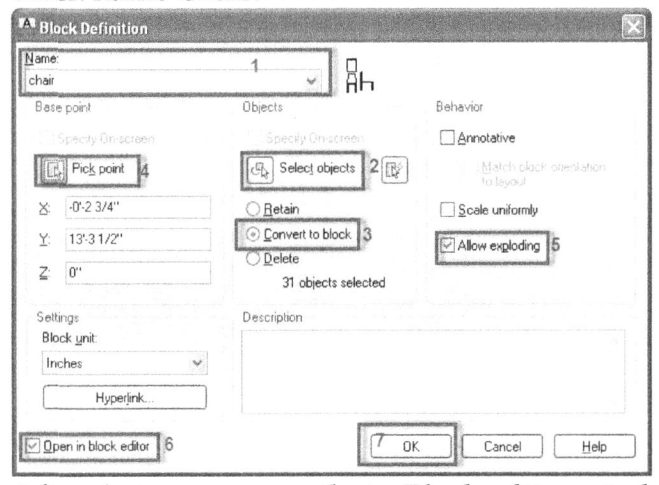

After that you can see that a Block editor window is automatically open.

Autodesk AutoCAD 2021
Learn CAD With Ease.

Step 3: Now you will apply Visibility Parameters to it. For this select Visibility Parameter from parameters tab click on drawing where you want to place mark of visibility parameter.

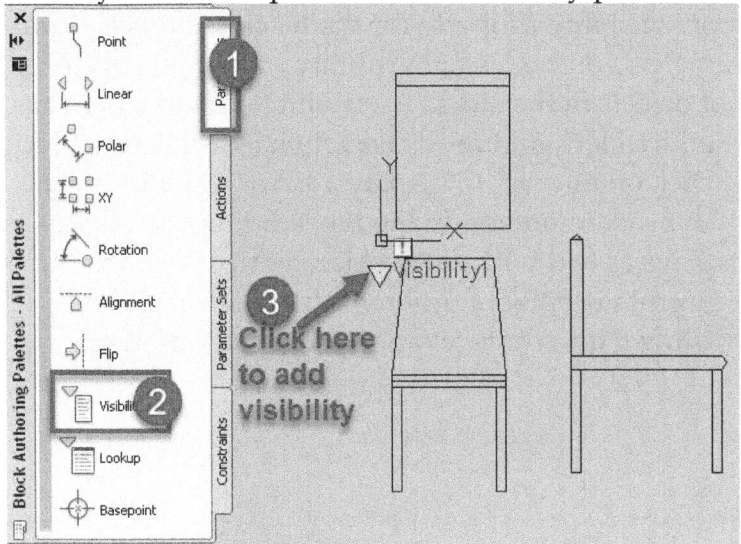

Step 4: To set visibility of object you will click on visibility option top right of screen.

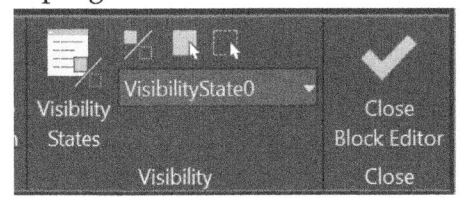

Step 5: Select plan of chair & click on visibility states, you can see Visibility State 0 Select it & rename it (plan chair), after that click on OK.

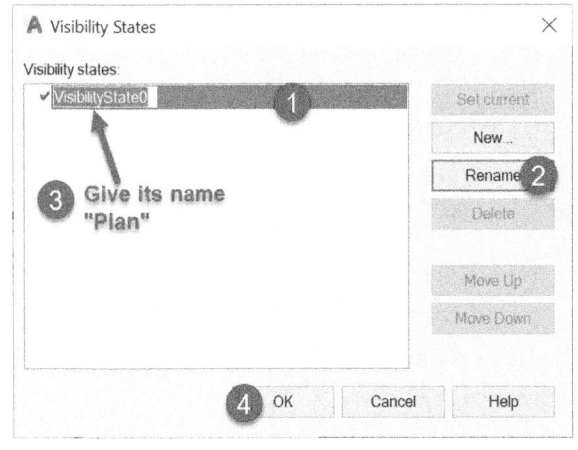

Step 6: In next step you will make both elevations invisible by click on make invisible.

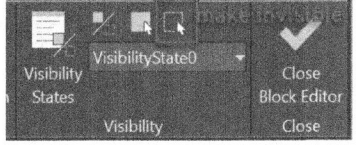

Autodesk AutoCAD 2021
Learn CAD With Ease.

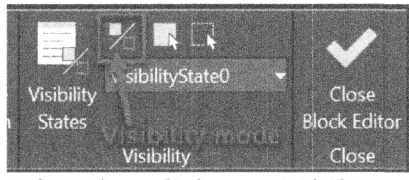

After that click on visibility mode, now you can see both elevations look faded.

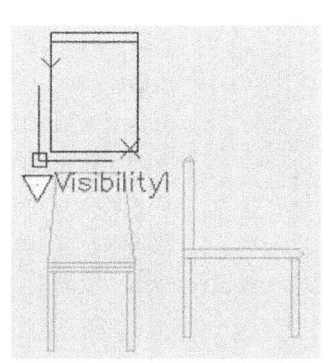

Step 7: Select Front Elevation of chair, click on visibility state you will see visibility states window, then click on New to create new visibility state & rename it (front elevation), after completing this work click on OK.

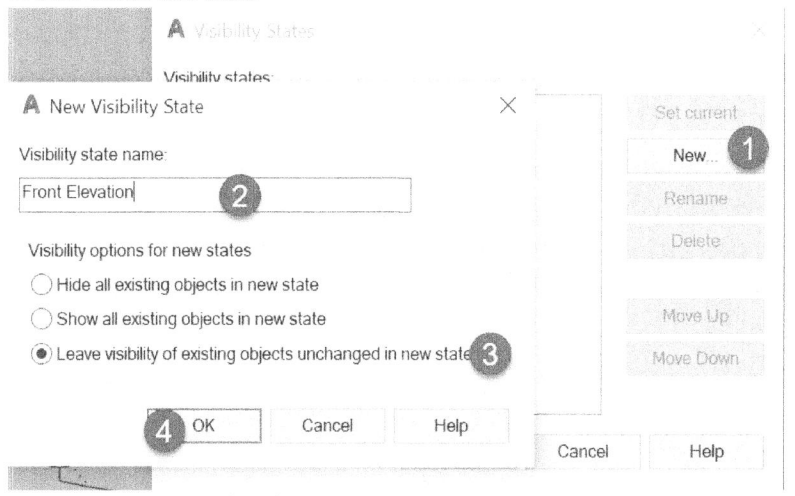

Step 8: Then make front elevation visible by Make visible option, and hide plan, side elevation of chair by option Make invisible. Click on Visibility mode to show hidden objects faded.

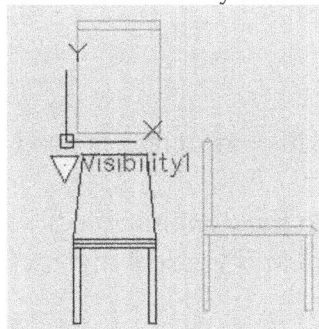

Step 9: Select side elevation of chair in drawing then click on Visibility State & create new visibility state and rename it (Side elevation).

246

By Madhumita Kshirsagar

Autodesk AutoCAD 2021
Learn CAD With Ease.

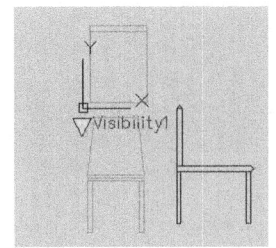

Step 10: Click on Make visible option to make side elevation visible after that select front elevation and click on Make invisible to make front elevation invisible, after that click on Visible mode to show hidden object faded.

Step 11: Click on Save block & then click on Close Block Editor.

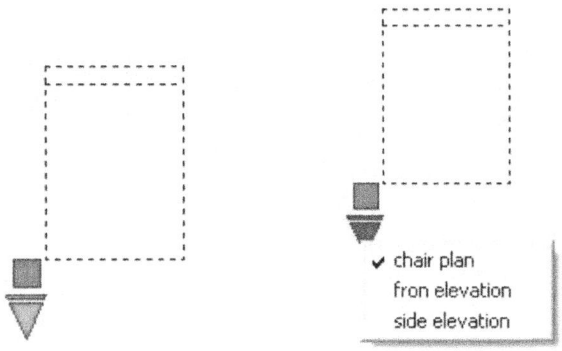

Step 13: Select that block you will see a blue triangle mark (visibility mark) in drawing. If you click on that mark you will see list of other objects of a chair block.

Step 14: Now you can show any object of a block by selecting it from the list.

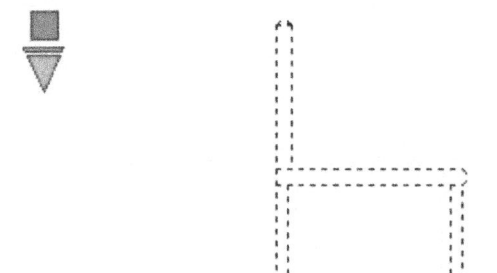

g. Base point Parameter: This parameter is used to change base point of a block.

h. XY Parameter: Adds an XY parameter to the dynamic block definition and defines custom horizontal and vertical distance properties for the block reference.

An XY parameter shows the X and Y distances from the base point of the parameter. In the Block Editor, an XY parameter displays as a pair of dimensions (horizontal and vertical). These dimensions share a common base point.
You can use this parameter for dynamic scaling of block (Action – Scale) & for dynamic Array of a block (Action - Array).

2.6 Command: Divide
    Alias   : DIV

Home Tab → Draw Panel → Divide

Use: Creates evenly spaced point or blocks along the length or perimeter of an object.
In other words this command is used to divide object in equal parts. To show division points firstly change point style by using **POINT STYLE** (ddptype) command, select point style from window &check on set size relative to screen. Then select object & enter number of segments. It also shows division by blocks.

Div ←

Select object to divide: (by any selection method)
Specify number of segments (Blocks):5 ←

During Divide command   After Divide command

Block: If you want to show blocks in the place of these division points you can use block option of Divide command. For this firstly draw object for a block & create its block give it name (A).

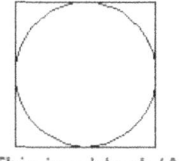

This is a block (A)

DIV ←

Select object to divide: (by any selection method)
Enter the number of segments or [Block]: B ←

Autodesk AutoCAD 2021
Learn CAD With Ease.

Enter name of block to insert: A ↵
Align block with object? [Yes/No] <Y>: ↵
Enter the number of segments: 5 ↵

2.7 Command: Measure
    Alias   : Me
    Home Tab → Draw Panel → Measure

Use: Creates point objects or blocks at measured intervals along the length or perimeter of an object.
Use DDPTYPE to set the style and size of all point objects in a drawing.

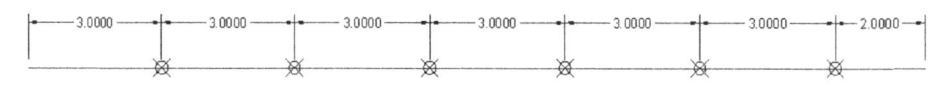

ME ↵
Select object to measure: mouse click (by any selection method)
Specify length of segment or [Block]: 3 ↵

Block option: If you want to show division points by blocks, firstly make a block. Here we use block which we create previously for divide command.

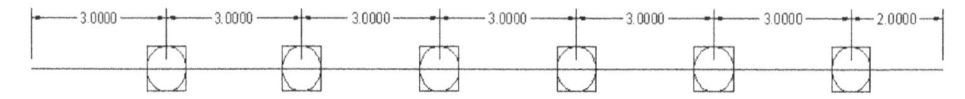

ME ↵
Select object to measure: mouse click (by any selection method)
Specify length of segment or [Block]: B ↵
Enter name of block to insert: A ↵
Align block with object? [Yes/No] <Y>: ↵
Specify length of segment: 3 ↵

2.8 ATTRIBUTE:
So far in using AutoCAD you have created geometry: lines, circles, etc. You have also added things such as text and dimensions. All of these things could also be done by hand, so what else does CAD have to offer?

Autodesk AutoCAD 2021
Learn CAD With Ease.

As noted at the beginning, AutoCAD is also a database of information. Most of that database contains the information for reproducing what you have drawn, but you can also add information that is non-graphical. One of the easiest ways of adding non-graphical information is to use attributes. An attribute is a text that can be attached to a block that conveys more information than just the geometry on its own could convey.

Look at the two drawings below for an example:

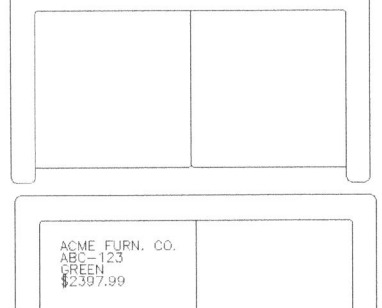

The first example shows some lines and arcs that could be anything.

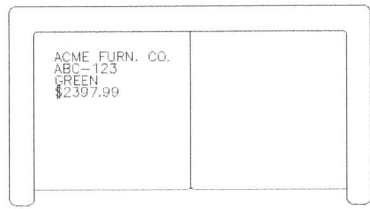

The second example shows the same geometry with the attributes visible so that you see what the shapes represent.

The pictures above show a couch. The attributes describe what the model number, color and cost are as well as the manufacturer. From this simple example, you can see that AutoCAD has a useful tool for showing more than just geometry.

This example shows information about furnishings in an office. Once you have drawn the floor plan, you could insert blocks of furniture that have information about the manufacturer, price, weight, and any other information you may need.

This information can then be extracted out of AutoCAD and then used in a spreadsheet or other program which could generate a Bill of Materials. Although you won't normally use the more advanced features of Attributes in your daily work, it's good to know how they work.

In this lesson you will be creating attributes and attaching them to the computer block that you made previously. Like everything you do in AutoCAD, there are particular steps involved when you work with attributes.

First you have to define (or create) the attribute.
Next you will create the block with attributes.

Autodesk AutoCAD 2021
Learn CAD With Ease.

Finally, when you insert the block you will give it the specific information

Command: Define Attribute
Alias   : Att
Home Tab → Block Panel → Define Attribute
                    OR
Insert Tab → Block Definition Panel → Define Attribute

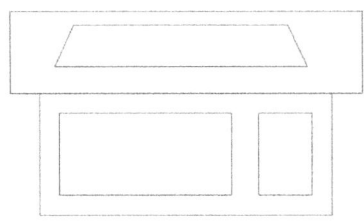

Use: This command is used to create an attribute definition for storing data in a block.
Firstly draw the computer on the viewport and apply Define Attribute command.

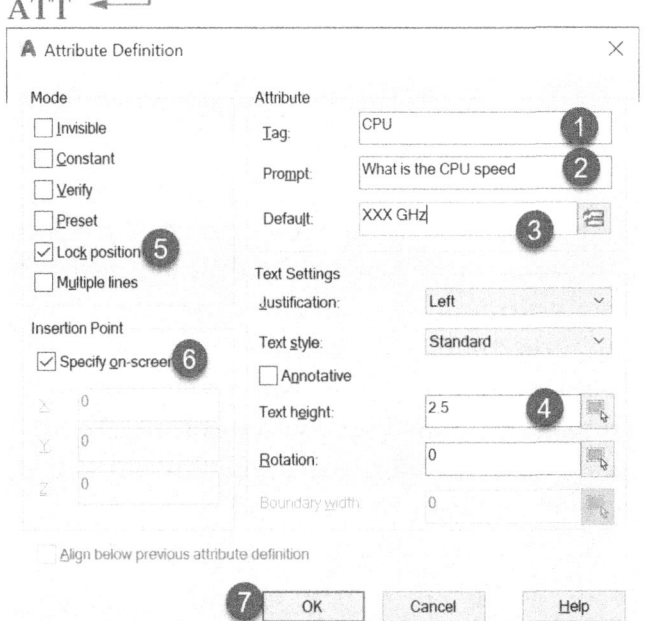

What you did is give the attribute its definition - a name (tag), a prompt to help the user while they're inserting it, and a (default) value for the prompt.
Once everything is entered, select the **OK** button.
When you are back on the drawing screen, pick a point near the middle of the computer block. When you are done, the dialog box comes back so press **OK**.

Add the following attributes the same way, except instead of picking a point, check off the **"Align below previous attribute"** checkbox.

TAG	PROMPT	VALUE
MONITOR	What is the MONITOR SIZE?	XX"
HDD	What capacity is the Hard Drive?	X.XXGB
RAM	How much RAM is installed?	XXXMB
STATION	What station is this	XXX

Once all the attributes are created you should have something like this:

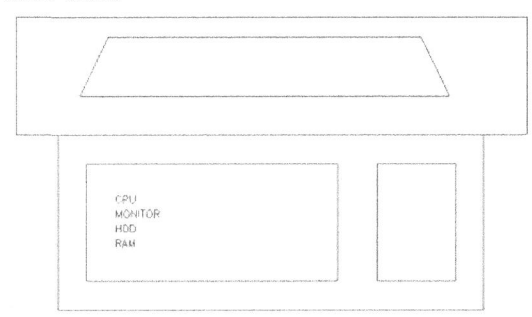

Next you will create a block that includes your four attributes. Start up the **BLOCK** command and create its block. When you are asked for the block name, give it the name COMP-AT.

Insert the block and you will get a dialog box where you can enter the values for the tags. You will be prompted to provide answers to the prompts that you defined in the attributes.

Command: I (INSERT) ↵

Specify insertion point or [Scale/X/Y/Z/Rotate/PScale/PX/PY/PZ/PRotate]: mouse click

What is the CPU Speed <XXX GHz>: 2.5 GHz ↵
What is the monitor size <XX">: 21" ↵
What is the capacity of the Hard Drive <XXX Gb>: 60Gb ↵
How much ram is installed <XXX Mb>: 512Mb ↵
What station is this? <XXX>: 104 ↵

After inserting the block and answering all the prompts, your block should look like this:

Autodesk AutoCAD 2021
Learn CAD With Ease.

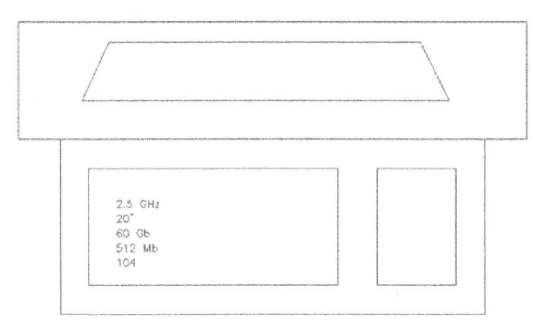

Now by looking at the drawing, you can see exactly what type of computer it is and what station (location) it is. This is just one application, but you can see how it can be used in any discipline of drafting. You can either insert more blocks, or copy the one that is in the drawing.

Different Modes of Attribute:

Mode: Sets options for attribute values associated with a block when you insert the block in a drawing.

Invisible: Specifies that attribute values are not displayed or printed when you insert the block. ATTDISP overrides Invisible mode.

Constant: Gives attributes a fixed value for block insertions.

Verify: Prompts you to verify that the attribute value is correct when you insert the block.

Preset: Sets the attribute to its default value when you insert a block containing a preset attribute.

Lock Position: Locks the location of the attribute within the block reference. When unlocked, the attribute can be moved relative to the rest of the block using grip editing, and multiline attributes can be resized.

Multiple Lines: Specifies that the attribute value can contain multiple lines of text. When this option is selected, you can specify a boundary width for the attribute.

Note: In a dynamic block, an attribute's position must be locked for it to be included in an action's selection set.

Autodesk AutoCAD 2021
Learn CAD With Ease.

2.9 Editing Of Attributes

Of course, in any project, the data is subject to change. In this example, the company may decide that it cannot afford 24" monitors. You can easily change the value of attributes within a single block insertion by double-clicking on the block. That will bring up this dialog box:

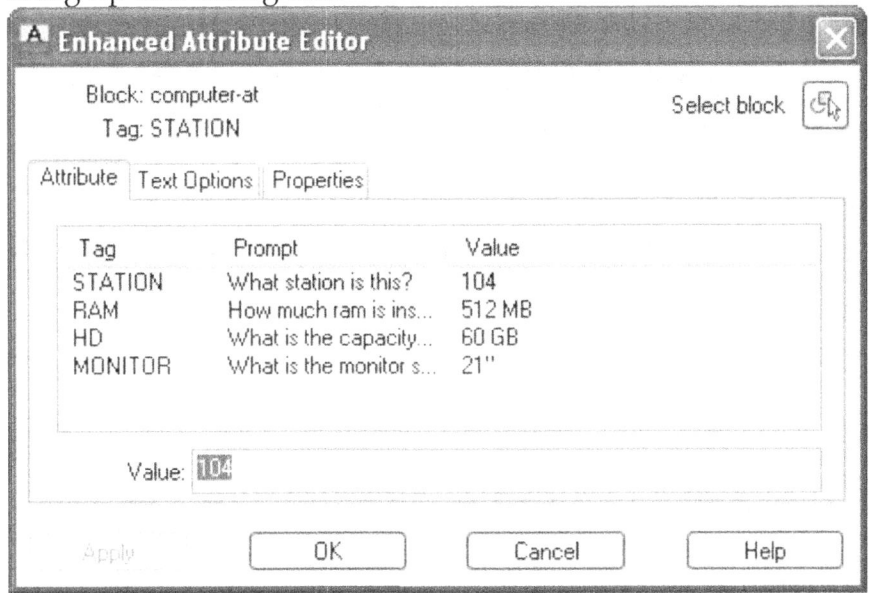

```
Enhanced Attribute Editor
    Block: computer-at                     Select block
    Tag: STATION

Attribute | Text Options | Properties

Tag         Prompt                  Value
STATION     What station is this?   104
RAM         How much ram is ins...  512 MB
HD          What is the capacity... 60 GB
MONITOR     What is the monitor s... 21"

Value: 104

Apply    OK       Cancel      Help
```

For editing purpose you can also use Edit Attribute command.
Command: Edit Attribute
Alias   : EATTEDIT

Insert Tab→ Block Definition Panel→Edit Attribute
Use: This command is used to edit attributes.

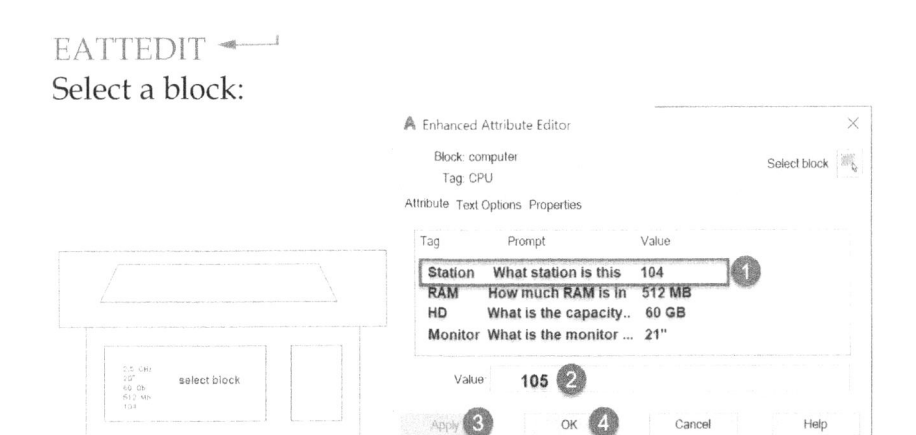

EATTEDIT
Select a block:

```
Enhanced Attribute Editor
    Block: computer                        Select block
    Tag: CPU

Attribute  Text Options  Properties

Tag         Prompt              Value
Station     What station is this  104    ①
RAM         How much RAM is in    512 MB
HD          What is the capacity.. 60 GB
Monitor     What is the monitor... 21"

Value:  105  ②

Apply ③   OK ④    Cancel     Help
```

254

By Madhumita Kshirsagar

Autodesk AutoCAD 2021
Learn CAD With Ease.

2.10 Command: **Attribute display**
    Alias   : **Attdisp**
    Insert Tab →Block Panel→Attribute Display

Use: Sometimes you don't want to see the attribute values displayed (say for plotting). You can turn them off. This can be done by typing in the command line ATTDISP and then OFF. To turn them back on again, type ATTDISP and ON. It can't get much easier.

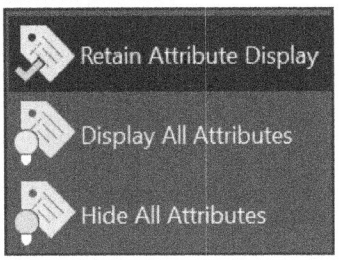

- Retain Attribute Display
- Display All Attributes
- Hide All Attributes

2.11 Command: **Block Attribute Manager**
    Alias   : **Battman**
    Insert Tab →Block Definition Panel→Block Attribute Manager

Use: While editing the title blocks, here we used the Block Attribute Manager for a different purpose: The ordering of the attributes in the Enhanced Attribute Editor.

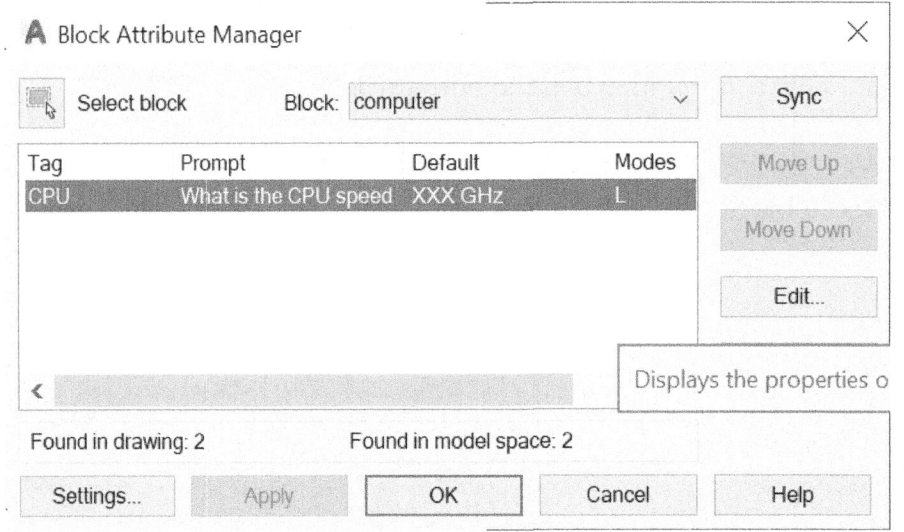

Tag	Prompt	Default	Modes
CPU	What is the CPU speed	XXX GHz	L

Block: computer

Found in drawing: 2   Found in model space: 2

Buttons: Select block, Sync, Move Up, Move Down, Edit..., Settings..., Apply, OK, Cancel, Help

Displays the properties o

When you have an attributed block, when you double-click on that block, the Enhanced Attribute Editor opens. If you have several attributes, there's a possibility the order of the attributes may not be in a logical order. To order the attributes in a block definition, use BATTMAN.

Tips on using the Block Attribute Manager:
Click the Select Block button in the upper left corner so you can select the block containing the attributes you wish to order.
Select the attributes one at a time, and then use the Move Up or Move Down buttons.
If you have several block references (locations) of the same block definition, use the Sync button to synchronize the new attribute order to all of the block definitions in the drawing. You will need to use the Sync button if you remove attributes, too.

Note: You can also edit constant attribute by this command.

Autodesk AutoCAD 2021
Learn CAD With Ease.

CHAPTER 3
GROUP & EDITING COMMANDS

3.1 Command: Group
   Alias   : G

Home Tab→ Groups Panel→Group

Use: To create group of selected objects.
A group is a saved set of objects that you can select and edit together or separately as needed.

Groups provide an easy way to combine drawing elements that you need to manipulate as a unit. You can create them quickly and with a default name, or you can use the Group Manager to assign a name from the start.

You can change the components of groups as you work by adding or removing objects.

In some ways, groups resemble blocks, which provide another method of combining objects into a named set. For example, the groups you create are saved from session to session. However, you can edit individual objects in groups more easily than you can edit them in blocks, which must be exploded first. Unlike blocks, groups cannot be shared with other drawings.

You can easily understood Group by study an example given below:

Creating a Group:

We'll make two groups, one of the red channel and the other of the green clip.

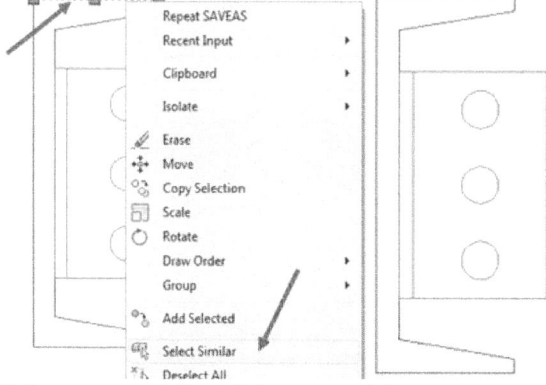

Select one of the objects making up the red channel.
Right-click and choose Select Similar from the menu.

Autodesk AutoCAD 2021
Learn CAD With Ease.

All the objects making up the channel are selected because they have similar properties.
Select the **Group** command (Home>Groups).

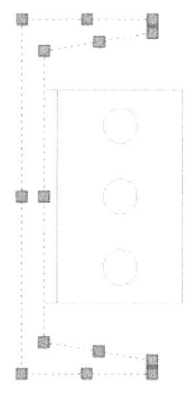

Managing Groups:

The Group Manager displays a list of the groups in the drawing and performs various functions like rename, delete and explode.
Select Group Manager (Home>Groups>).
The group just created is unnamed. By default unnamed groups are not listed in the Group Manager.

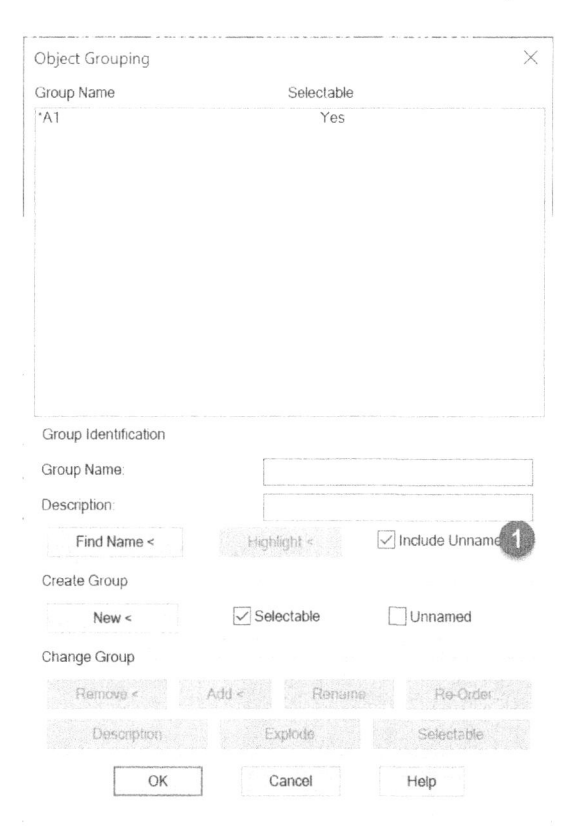

Click the Include Unnamed box to display all groups, including unnamed groups.
Now that the unnamed group is listed, it can be renamed.
Select the unnamed group from the list (it may have a different designation)

258

By Madhumita Kshirsagar

Autodesk AutoCAD 2021
Learn CAD With Ease.

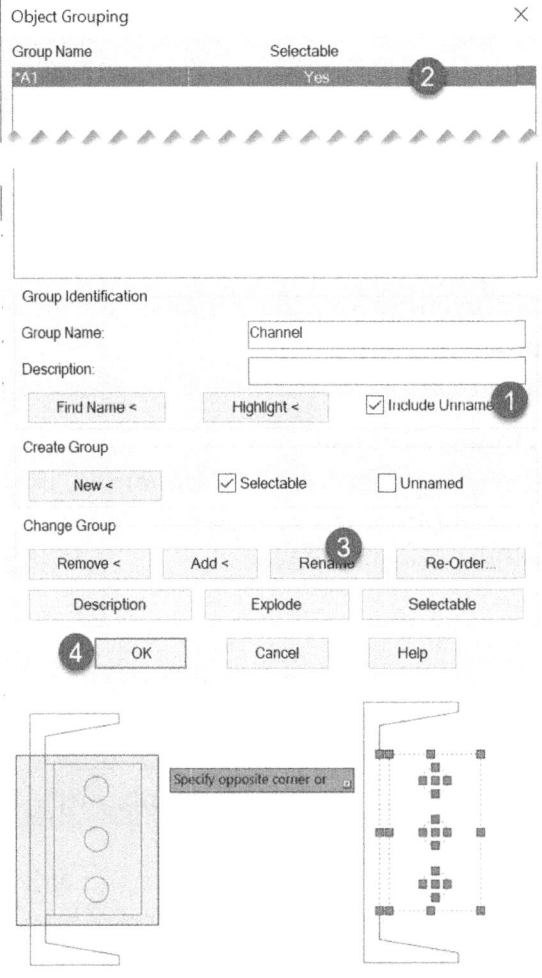

Type **Channel** in the **Group Name:** box. Click the **Rename** button and click **OK**.

Select the clip objects with a window selection.
Select the Group command (Home>Groups>Group).

Group Bounding Box.
By default, groups are indicated with a bounding box.

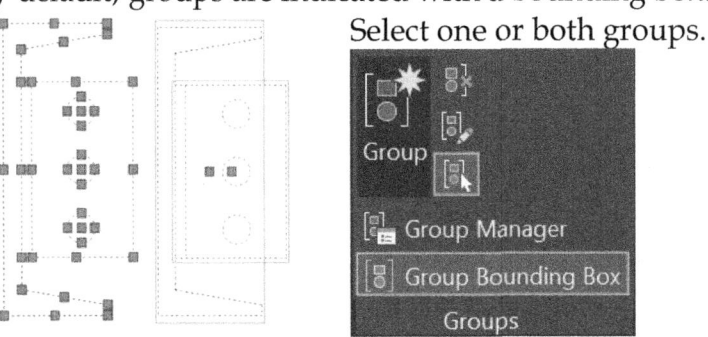

Select one or both groups.

Autodesk AutoCAD 2021
Learn CAD With Ease.

Select Group Bound Box On/Off ▣(Home>Groups) to toggle the display type of groups.

Manipulating Group Objects:

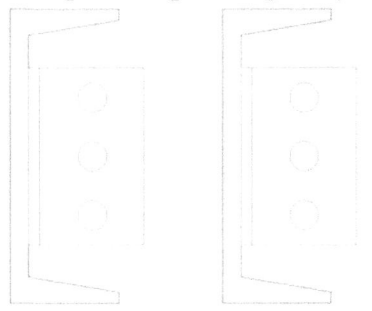

Make a copy of the channel and clip.
The new channel and clip are to be stretched 2" to create a new attachment.
You can turn off grouping to change individual objects belonging to a group.

Choose Group Selection On/Off ▣ (Home>Groups).

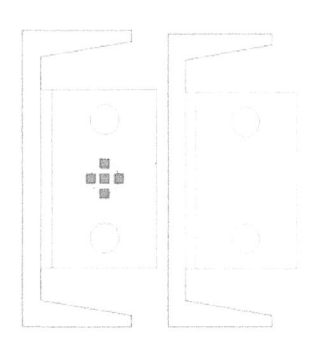

Delete the center circle.
Stretch the object upward by using stretch command according to diagram given below.

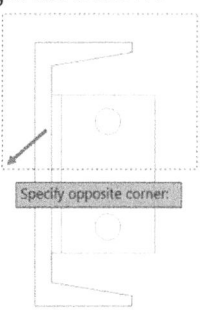

Then create three more circles in a clip.

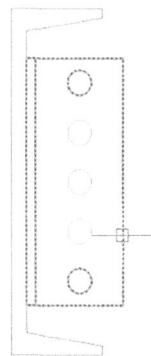

Now the changes are complete, turn Group Selection On (Home>Groups>▣).
Notice that the three circles are not part of this group since they did not exist when the group was created.

Autodesk AutoCAD 2021
Learn CAD With Ease.

Adding to a Group:

Select GROUPEDIT (Home>Groups>).

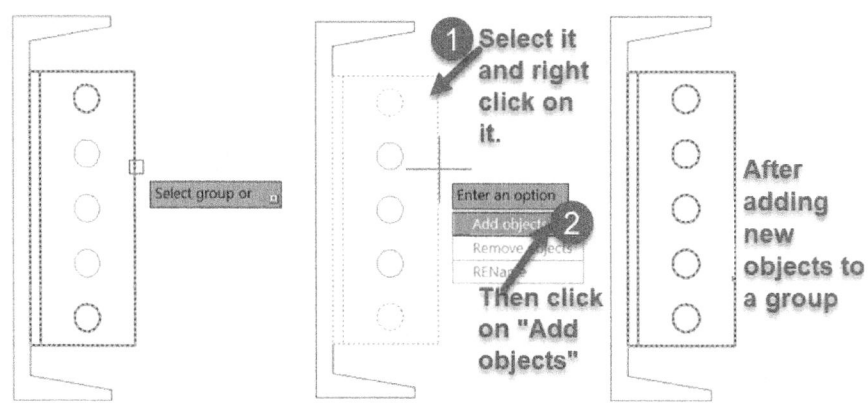

Select any portion of the clip group and right click on it and then select Add objects option to add new objects to an existing group. Then select three new circles to add them to a group and press "Enter".

Now it is compulsory to get knowledge about all options of Group Manager which we used in above example. In that example you get complete knowledge about other options of Group command accepting Group Manager.

Group Manager:

Group Name:
Display the names of existing groups.
Selectable:
Specify whether a group is selectable. When a group is selectable, selecting one object in the group selects the whole group. Objects on locked or frozen layers are not selected.

When the **PICKSTYLE** system variable is set to 0, no groups are selectable.

Group Identification: Display the name and description (if any) of the group selected in the Group Name list.

Group Name: Specify the group name. Group names can be up to 31 characters long and can include letters, numbers, and the special characters dollar sign ($), hyphen (-), and underscore (_) but not spaces. The name is converted to uppercase characters.

Description: Display the description of the selected group, if there is one. You can also give description about group here.

Find Name: Lists the groups to which an object belongs. The Group Member List dialog box is displayed, showing the groups to which the object belongs.

Highlight: Show the members of the selected group in the drawing area.

Include Unnamed: Specify whether unnamed groups are listed. When this option is cleared, only named groups are displayed.

Create Group: Specifies properties of new groups.

New: Creates a new group from the selected objects, using the name and description under Group Name and Description.

Selectable: Specifies that a new group is selectable.

Unnamed: Indicates that a new group is unnamed. A default name, *An, is assigned to unnamed groups. The n represents a number that increases with each new group.

Change Group: Modifies existing groups.

Remove: Removes objects from the selected group. To use this option, clear the Selectable option.

Autodesk AutoCAD 2021
Learn CAD With Ease.

If you remove all the group's objects, the group remains defined. You can remove the group definition from the drawing by using the Explode option.

Note: When you remove objects from a group and then later add them back during the same drawing session, they are returned to their previous position in the numerical order of the group.

Add: Adds objects to the selected group.

Note: Group names are displayed in alphabetical order.

Rename: Renames the selected group to the name entered in Group Name under Group Identification.

Re-Order: Displays the Order Group dialog box, in which you can change the numerical order of objects within the selected group. Objects are numbered in the order in which you select them for inclusion in the group. Reordering is useful when creating tool paths. For example, you can change the cut order for the horizontal and vertical lines of a tool path pattern.
You can either change the numerical position of individual group members or ranges of group members or reverse the order of all members. The first object in a group is number 0, not number 1.

Description: Updates the selected group's description to the name that you enter in Description. You can use up to 64 characters for a description name.

Explode: Deletes the definition of the selected group. The group's objects remain in the drawing.

Selectable: Specifies whether the group is selectable.

Autodesk AutoCAD 2021
Learn CAD With Ease.

3.2 About Using Clipboard:

Cut, copy, copy with base point, paste, paste as block, paste to original co-ordinate are commands used in this category.

These commands are used to copy object one drawing file to another drawing file.

To get these commands select object and then right click and select "Clipboard".

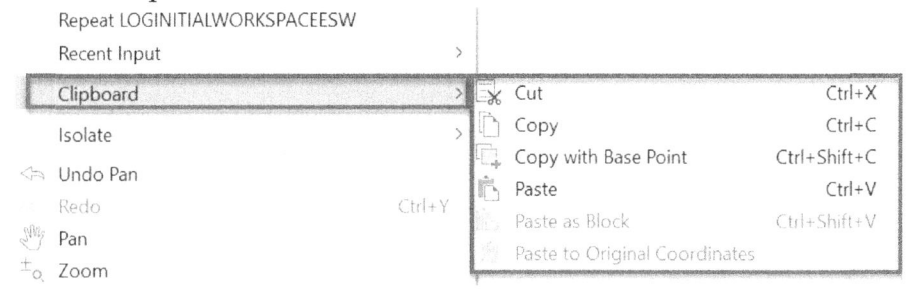

```
Repeat LOGINITIALWORKSPACEESW
Recent Input                    >
Clipboard                       >   Cut                        Ctrl+X
Isolate                         >   Copy                       Ctrl+C
Undo Pan                            Copy with Base Point       Ctrl+Shift+C
Redo                    Ctrl+Y      Paste                      Ctrl+V
Pan                                 Paste as Block             Ctrl+Shift+V
Zoom                                Paste to Original Coordinates
```

Cut (Ctrl+X): To cut drawing from an AutoCAD file& paste it to another file, drawing is deleted from one file & pasted to another.

Copy (Ctrl+C): To copy drawing from an AutoCAD file& paste it to another file, drawing is copied in another drawing file.

Copy with basepoint (Ctrl+Shift+C): By using this command you asked to pick base point on object for copy object.

Paste (Ctrl+V): To paste copied object to another drawing file.

Paste as Block (Ctrl+Shift+V): This command is used to paste object like a block.

Paste to original co-ordinates : By using this command you are able to paste object at its original situation or original co-ordinates.

By Madhumita Kshirsagar

Autodesk AutoCAD 2021
Learn CAD With Ease.

CHAPTER 4
LINKINGS & REFERENCES

In this chapter, you will get knowledge about linking & reference commands of AutoCAD. These commands help you to do your work in less time.

After completing this chapter you will be able to do:

❖ **Linking commands:**
   Hyperlink
   Data Link
   Ole objects
   Data Extraction

❖ **Reference commands:**
   External reference
   Attach (image)
   Adjust
   Clip
   eTransmit

4.1 Command: Hyperlink
   Alias   : Ctrl+K
   Insert Tab → Data Panel → Hyperlink 🌐

Use: A hyperlink can link any drawing object or objects to a URL, any file, or a location in a file (such as a named view in another drawing) to AutoCAD drawing. If you haven't been using hyperlinks, consider doing so, as they offer lots of possibilities. For example you can link AutoCAD files to other files like, bills of materials, price lists, detail drawings, part specifications, etc. When you create hyperlinks in your drawing to these other documents, your drawing can become almost like a Web page.

Procedure:

Step1. To creates a hyperlink, select an object and use the HYPERLINK command. (You can also press Ctrl+K or choose Insert tab> Data panel> Hyperlink.) The Insert Hyperlink dialog box opens.

Autodesk AutoCAD 2021
Learn CAD With Ease.

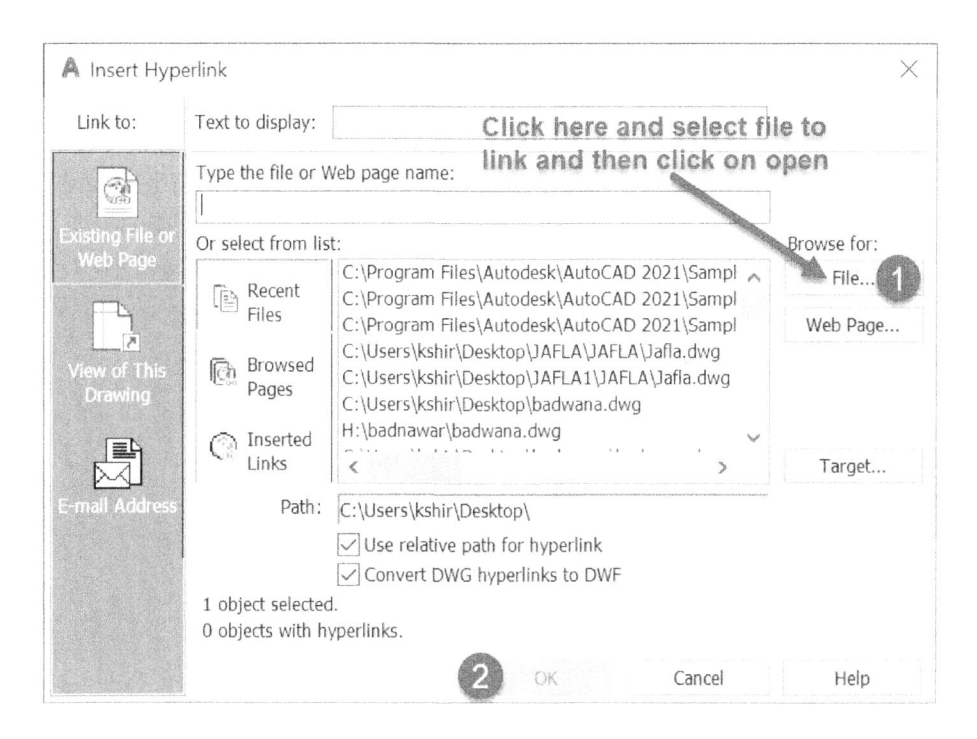

Step2. To link to a file, click the File button, select the file, and click Open. You can also type a URL, or browse to it using the Web Page button.

Step3. Now, when you keep the cursor near the object, you see a web cursor.
Using a hyperlink in a drawing is a little different from using one on the Internet. In a drawing, if you click the hyperlink, you just select the object.
There are two ways to open the hyperlink:
Press Ctrl and click on linked object, but this doesn't bring the new file to the fore, so you have to find it on the Windows taskbar.
Select the object, right-click and choose Hyperlink> Open. This brings the new file to the fore.

4.2 Command: Data Extraction
    Alias   : Eattext
    Insert Tab⟶ Linking & Extraction Panel⟶ Data Extraction

266

By Madhumita Kshirsagar

Autodesk AutoCAD 2021
Learn CAD With Ease.

Use: This command is used to extract drawing data and merges data from an external source to a data extraction table or external file.
To understand this command properly see example given below:
In this example we are going to create some schedules like door schedule, column schedule, and a wall schedule by using this command.

Procedure:

Step1. Firstly create a floor plan. In this plan doors, columns and walls are created by dynamic block.

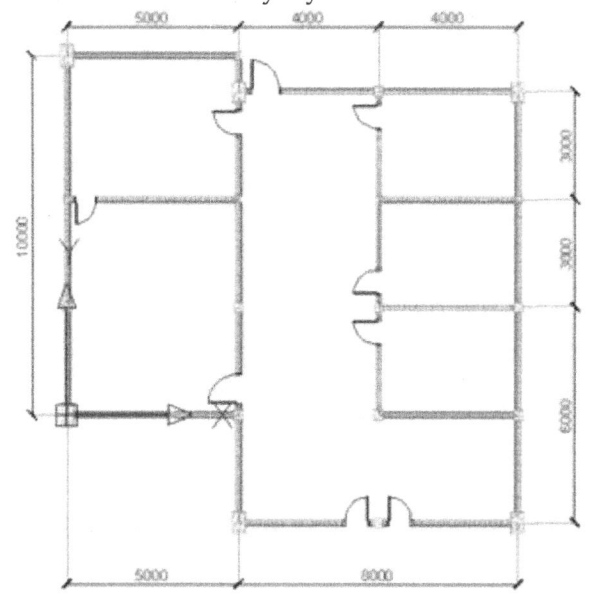

Step2. Now we create a door schedule by using data extraction. It's on your ribbon bar> **Insert> Linking & Extraction> Extract Data.**

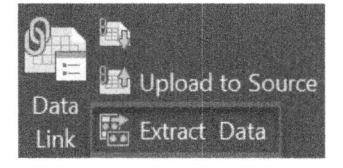

This will open data extraction wizard.

Autodesk AutoCAD 2021
Learn CAD With Ease.

Step3. This is the first time we use data extraction, so use "**Create a new Data Extraction**". Click "**Next**", and when AutoCAD ask you for file name, give it door schedule.dxe. You can use this file again later when you need to create another door schedule. Save it.

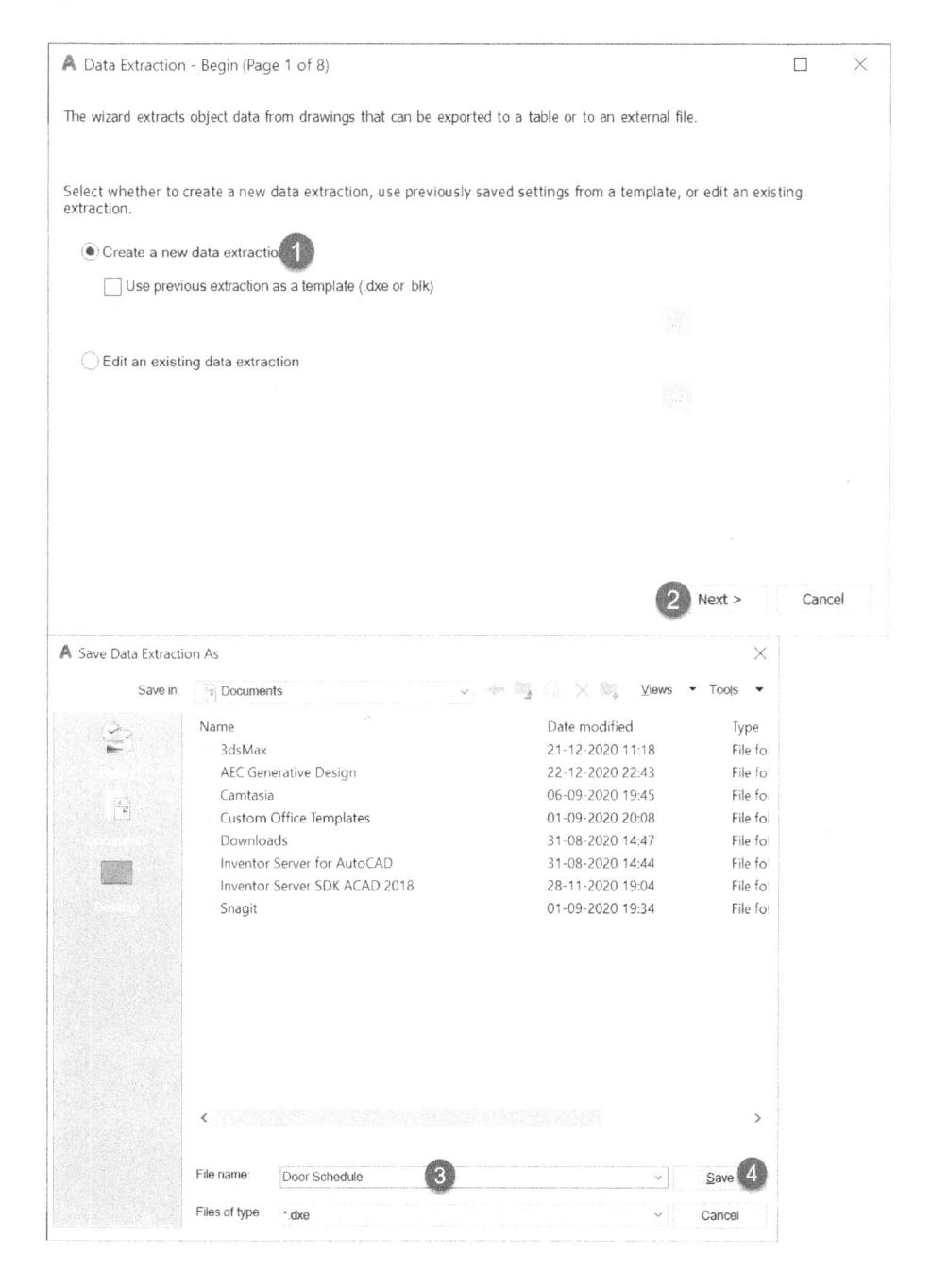

Autodesk AutoCAD 2021
Learn CAD With Ease.

Step4. AutoCAD gives you a choice: you want to create a data extraction from file(s) or from some objects in your drawing.
If you have several floor plans in one drawing, you can select them separately. But now let's just use "**Drawing/Sheetset**". Then click on "**Next**".

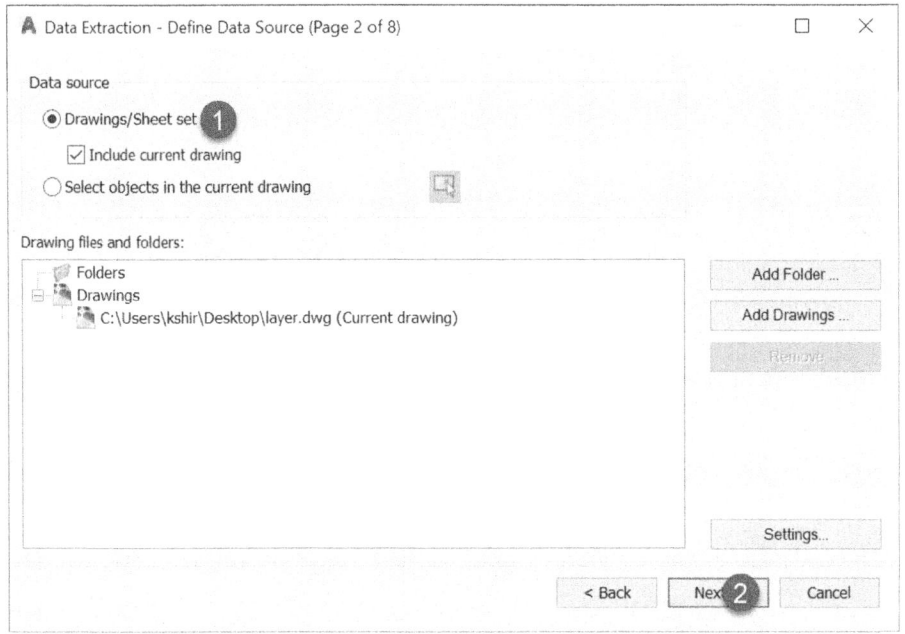

Step5. AutoCAD will recognize all type of objects you have in your drawing. Now we need to filter what kind of objects to be included in the schedule. Let's just select the **Door**, and left the rest unchecked. Click "**Next**".

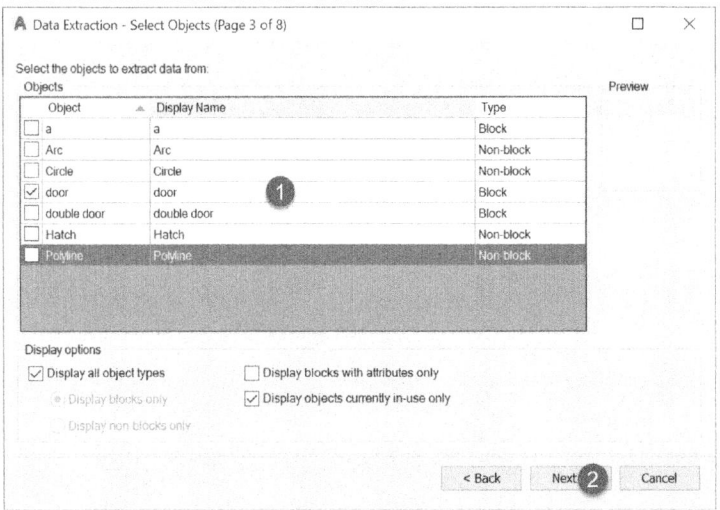

Autodesk AutoCAD 2021
Learn CAD With Ease.

Step6. This time we will need to define which properties we want to be included in our report. We only need the door width. Let's filter it first.
On the right column, category filter, uncheck everything except Dynamic Block. Now it should be only 3 properties left. Check only Width.

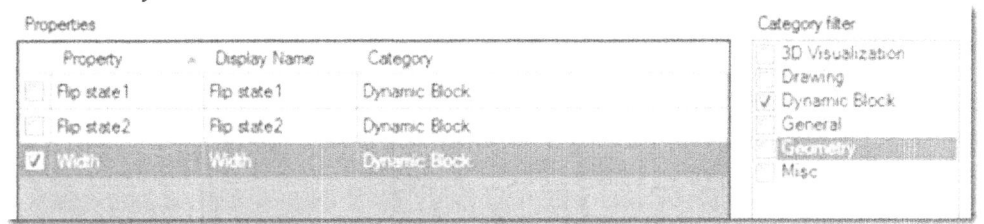

Where's this width property come from? You get it by dynamic block.

Step7. In this page you will see your schedule preview.
Click "**Next**".
Step8. Then you specify output option:

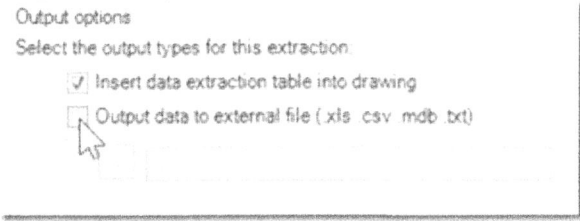

Check on "Insert data extraction table into drawing" to place table in a drawing.
Or if you want to save data in an excel sheet click on "Output data to external file".

Step8. If you use your own drawing, you might not yet set your table style. Type the table title "**Door Schedule**". Click "**Next**".

Step9. It's just telling you you're done. Click "**Finish**". Now place your table to your drawing. Or if you choose external file, then you're done.
Column and Wall Schedule: Try to create these schedules by yourself. You can easily create them by above given process.

270

By Madhumita Kshirsagar

Autodesk AutoCAD 2021
Learn CAD With Ease.

Pay attention to door and column schedule. Remember we have only one door block and one column block. But in this schedule, we can see 3 door type and 3 column type their size are different. Data extraction can recognize it.

Door Schedule

Name	Width	Count
SingleDoor	600.0000	1
SingleDoor	650.0000	6
SingleDoor	800.0000	2

Column Schedule

Name	h	w	Count
column	200	200	5
column	300	300	9
column	600	400	6

Wall Schedule

Count	Name	Length
1	brickwall	2750.0000
1	brickwall	2600.0000
1	brickwall	3650.0000
1	brickwall	600.0000
1	brickwall	2750.0000
1	brickwall	2750.0000
1	brickwall	3700.0000
1	brickwall	2700.0000
1	brickwall	4800.0000
1	brickwall	3650.0000
1	brickwall	3800.0000
1	brickwall	3700.0000
1	brickwall	4700.0000
1	brickwall	2700.0000
1	brickwall	2550.0000
1	brickwall	2700.0000
1	brickwall	3650.0000
1	brickwall	3650.0000
1	brickwall	2550.0000
1	brickwall	3600.0000
1	brickwall	2600.0000
1	brickwall	4650.0000
1	brickwall	2550.0000
1	brickwall	2750.0000
1	brickwall	2750.0000

Unfortunately for wall schedule, we can't sum them all and only list wall with the same name. It will only group wall with the same length and name.

4.3 Command: Data Link
Alias   : None

Insert Tab→ Linking & Extraction Panel→Data Link

Use: This command is use to link Microsoft excel sheet to AutoCAD. You will place this excel file in AutoCAD viewport with the help of table command.

To understand this command you have to follow the given procedure:

Autodesk AutoCAD 2021
Learn CAD With Ease.

Procedure:

Step1. Click on **Data link** icon.
This will open **"Data Link Manager"** dialog box.
Step2. Click on **"Create a new Excel Data Link"** for linking.
Step3. Enter Data link name and press **OK**.

Step4. Click on "Browse for a file……" and select excel file and press **OK**.

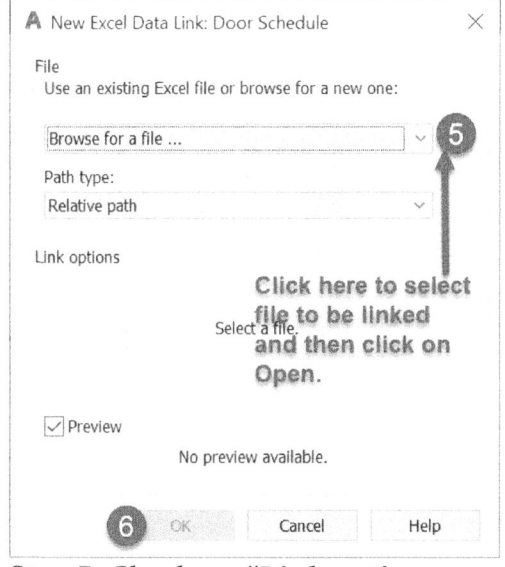

Step 5: Check on **"Link entire sheet"** and press **"OK"**. Then click on **"OK"** again in window to finish linking.

Step6. Now, invoke TABLE command:

Autodesk AutoCAD 2021
Learn CAD With Ease.

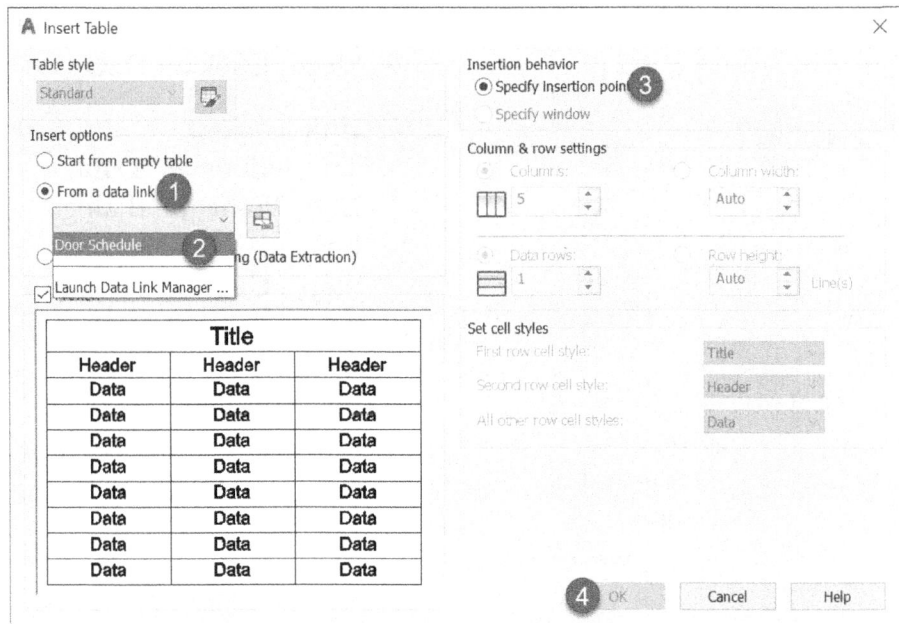

Step6. Select "**Door Schedule**" in "**From a data link**" (Insert option) and press "**OK**".

Step7. Check on "**Specify insertion point**" and press "**OK**". Now specify insertion point by mouse click on viewport.

4.4 Command: OLE Object
   Alias   : IO
   Insert Tab → Data Panel → Ole Object

Use: This command is used to insert linked or embedded objects.

Procedure:
Step1. Select Ole Object from **Insert Menu** or type **IO** ↵ . This will open Insert Object dialog box.

Autodesk AutoCAD 2021
Learn CAD With Ease.

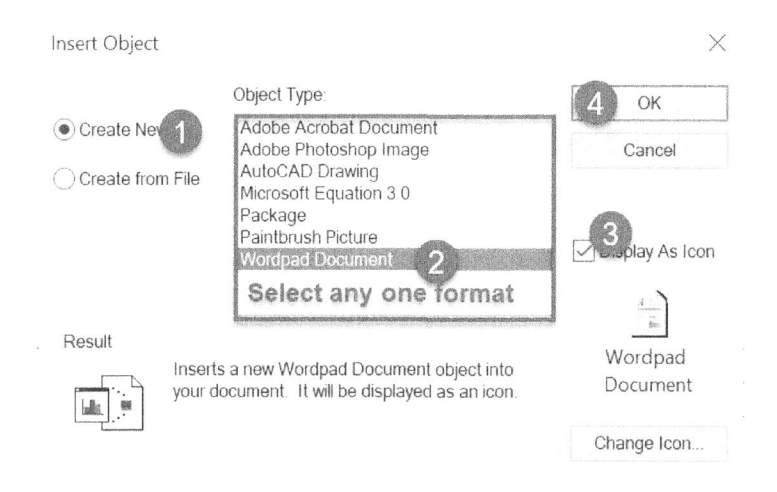

Step2. Click on **"Create New"** to create new file in any software listed in **"Object Type"**. Here we select **Wordpad Document**.
Step3. Click on **"Display As Icon"** and press **OK**.
It will open new Wordpad file in AutoCAD and now you can work on it and close it.
If you want to save file outside the AutoCAD save it by "File> Save Copy As".

Create New: Opens the application that's highlighted in the Object Type list so that you can create a new object to insert.

Object Type: Lists available applications that support linking and embedding. To create an object to embed, double-click an application to open it.
On the application's **"File menu"**, the Save option is replaced with a new Update option. Choosing Update inserts the object into the drawing or updates it.

Display as Icon: Displays the source application's icon in the drawing. Double-clicking the icon displays the embedded information.

Create from File: Specifies an existing file to link or embed.
Follow the given diagram to link file by "Create from file" option.

Autodesk AutoCAD 2021
Learn CAD With Ease.

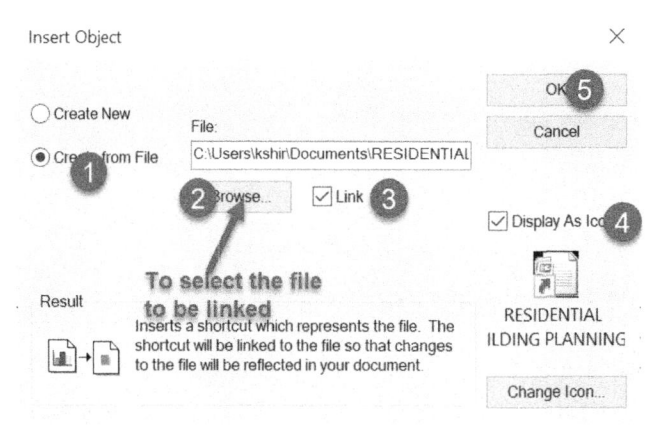

Always check on "Link" when you link the file with "Create from Files" option.

Link: This option is used to link source file and inserted file. Links can be set to be updated either automatically or manually when information in the linked document changes. By default, links are updated automatically. Use OLELINKS to specify automatic or manual updating.

4.5 Command: External References OR Attach
   Alias   : X-Ref

   Insert Tab→Reference Panel →Attach

Use: An X-ref is an 'external reference' to another AutoCAD drawing file. One file can reference many other files and display them as if they were one. These are used in larger projects for many reasons:
They keep the file sizes down.
They allow many users to work on individual components of a project.
Every time an X-ref is loaded, it is the most recent version of the drawing.
X-ref's can be updated, added, or unattached from the main drawing at any time.
You can X-ref drawings that they themselves X-ref other drawings (nesting).
To understand Xref properly follow the procedure given below.
Procedure:
Step1. Open AutoCAD drawing file.

Autodesk AutoCAD 2021
Learn CAD With Ease.

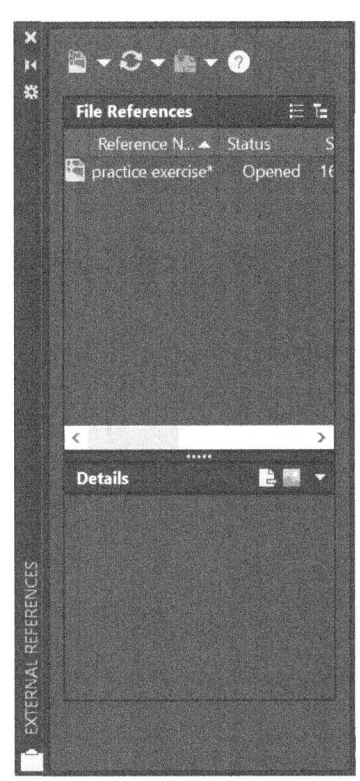

Step2. Type Xref in a command line and press ENTER.
Or
Click on Insert Tab> Reference Panel> Attach.

Step3. If you invoke command by X-ref, Xref dialog box appears on screen.

Step4. Click on Attach drawing or Attach image.

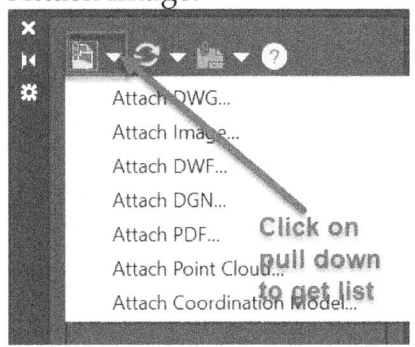

Step5. Click on **"Browse"** and select any drawing or Image file and click on **"Open"**.

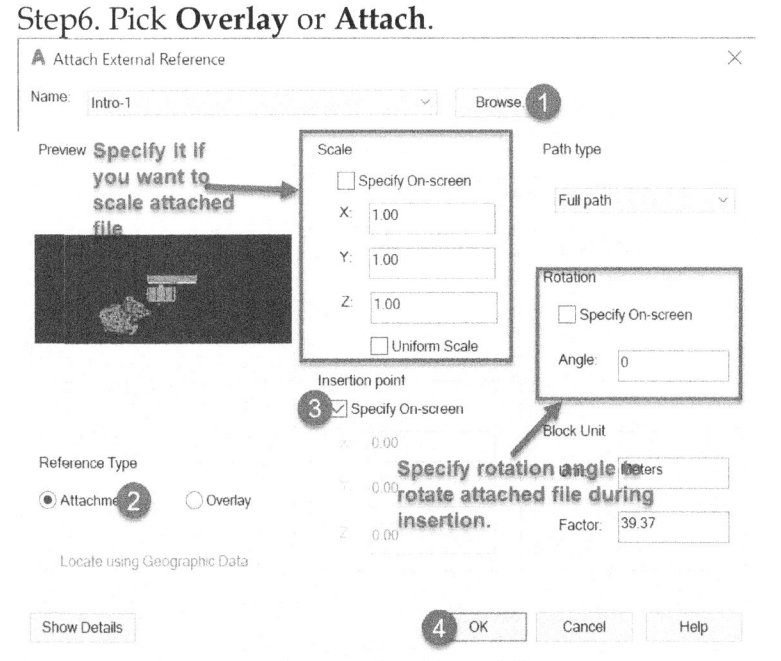

Step6. Pick **Overlay** or **Attach**.

Step7. **Path Type:** choose **"Full path"**.

276

By Madhumita Kshirsagar

Autodesk AutoCAD 2021
Learn CAD With Ease.

Step8. **Insertion point:** scale and rotation: leave them unchecked.
Step9. Click **OK** and close the dialogue box then click on viewport to insert reference drawing file.
Now that you have an X-ref, there are more options for you if you right-click the filename of the Xref.

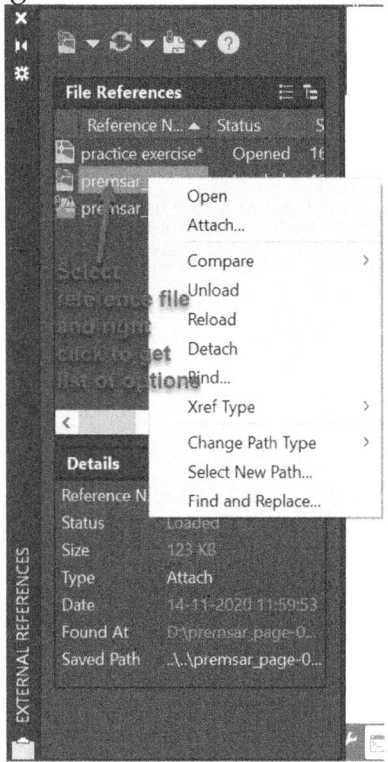

Attach: Attaches another X-ref.
Detatch: Detaches the selected X-ref.
Reload: Updates the selected X-ref - use this if the Xref was changed.
Unload: Removes the X-ref, but retains the reference for future use.
Bind: Permanently attaches a loaded X-ref, so that it is part of the drawing.

Now, let us become more practical here. Let us assume you have three drawings: sheet 1, sheet 2 and sheet 3 (see images below).

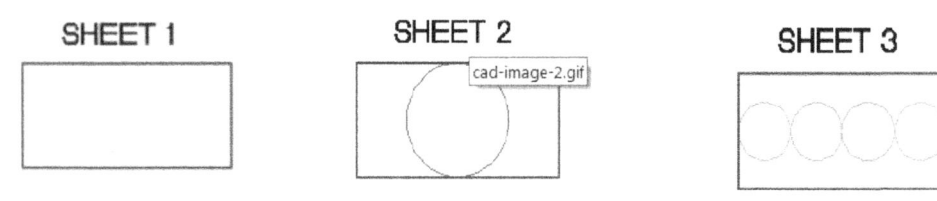

SHEET 1   SHEET 2   SHEET 3

Sheet 1 shows a rectangle. But it could be anything else. The two other sheets have circles, etc., but they both have one thing in common: a rectangle. So instead of drawing that rectangle twice, it would be wise to draw it once and xref it to both drawings. Some of you might think: What if I draw it once and then copy it to each drawing?

Autodesk AutoCAD 2021
Learn CAD With Ease.

If you copy the drawing you will have to copy it again if you want to make changes to that rectangle. Let us say you want to make it larger or want to chamfer the edges. Do you want to copy again? Or do you want to just change the xref and that is it.
The idea here is to reduce steps and time by drawing anything in common once. And that is when the xref comes in handy.
There are two types of xrefs: Overlay and Attachment.

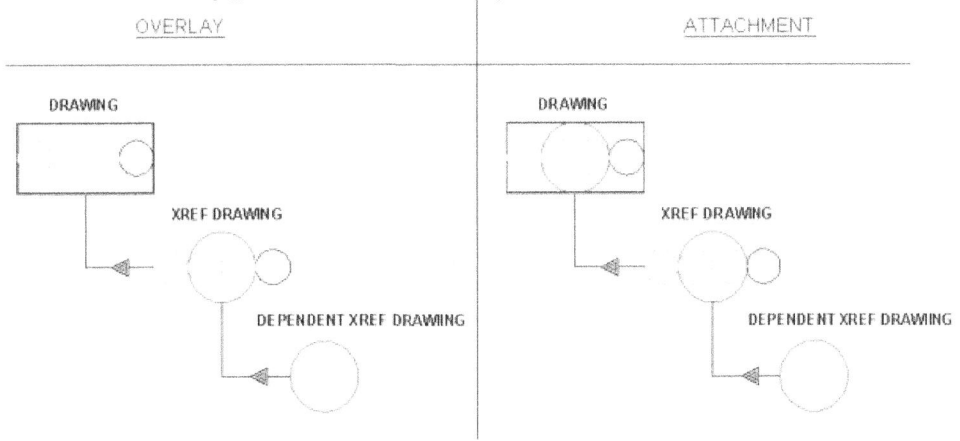

Overlay only brings what you draw inside that xref sheet. No other dependent. In other words, if you were to look at a tree diagram, it only goes one level deep (see image above on the left). Attachment xrefs bring unlimited dependent xrefs and levels (see image above on the right).
Apply Xref like above mentioned steps. (Step1 to Step9)

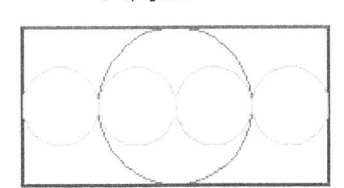

Your xref drawing should be inserted inside the current drawing like the above image.

4.6 Command: XClip OR Clip
    Alias   : Clip

Insert Tab→Reference Panel→Clip

Autodesk AutoCAD 2021
Learn CAD With Ease.

Use: Xrefs are frequently used to import large drawings for reference or backgrounds. Multiple Xrefs, such as a floor plan, column grid layout, and site-plan drawing, might be combined into one file. One drawback to multiple Xrefs in earlier versions of AutoCAD was that the entire Xref was loaded into memory even if only a small portion of it was used for the final plotted output. For computers with limited resources, multiple Xrefs could slow the system to a crawl.

AutoCAD offers two tools that help make display and memory use more efficient when using Xrefs: the Clip command and the Demand Load option in the Options dialog box.

XCLIP

Select Object to clip: by any selection method
Enter clipping option [ON/OFF/Clipdepth/Delete/ generate Polyline/New boundary] <New>: N ↵
Outside mode - Objects outside boundary will be hidden.
Specify clipping boundary or select invert option [Select polyline/Polygonal/Rectangular/Invert clip] <Rectangular>: P ↵
Specify first corner: Specify opposite corner: by mouse click

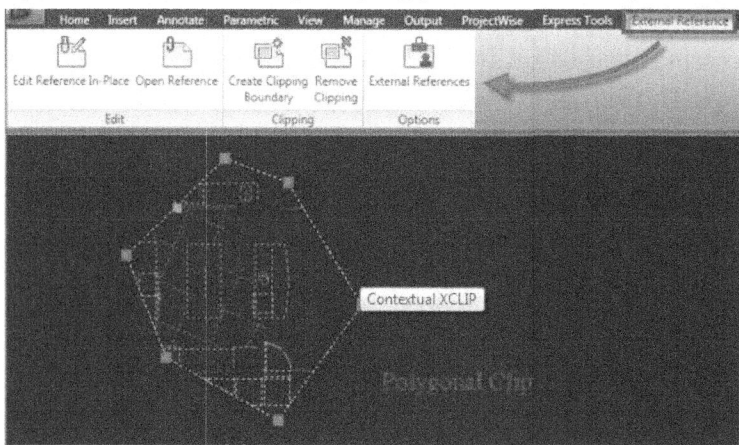

Clipping Options:
On: Displays the clipped portion of the external reference or block in the current drawing.
Off: Displays all of the geometry of the external reference or block in the current drawing, ignoring the clipping boundary.

Clipdepth: Sets the front and back clipping planes on an xref or block. Objects outside the volume defined by the boundary and the specified depth are not displayed. Regardless of the current UCS, the clip depth is applied parallel to the clipping boundary.

New Boundary Options:
Select Polyline: Defines the boundary with the selected polyline. The polyline can be open but must consist of straight line segments and cannot intersect itself.
Polygonal: Defines a polygonal clipping boundary with three or more points that you specify for the vertices of a polygon.
Rectangular: Defines a rectangular boundary with the points that you specify for opposite corners.
Invert Clip: Inverts the mode of the clipping boundary: objects are clipped either outside the boundary or inside the boundary.

4.7 Command: Adjust
   Alias   : None

   Insert Tab → Reference Panel → Adjust

Use: This command is use to adjust brightness, contrast, fadedness of image files and drawing files which we link by reference commands.

Procedure:
Step1. Insert an image in AutoCAD by "Attach" command.
Step2. Then apply Adjust command:
   Insert Tab >Reference Panel>Adjust
Step3. After that set brightness, contrast and fadedness of image.

You can also do it, without invoking "Adjust" command for that: Select image file and then you will see adjust panel on screen at the top left corner.

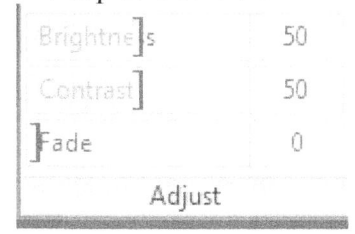

Brightness	50
Contrast	50
Fade	0
Adjust	

Autodesk AutoCAD 2021
Learn CAD With Ease.

Before adjust command

After change in brightness, contrast and fade

4.8 Command: eTransmit
   Alias   : None

Application Menu→Publish→ eTransmit

Use: The eTransmit feature helps you to send drawings to others by collecting all of a drawing's associated files. It's also an excellent tool when you simply want to move drawings. You can create a folder (use this option for moving files), a ZIP file, or an .EXE file that is a self-extracting compressed format. You can automate the process of sending an e-mail with the transmittal attached.

Procedure:
Step1. Save your drawing. If there are any unsaved changes, you'll see a message telling you that you need to save your drawing first.
Step2. Choose Application menu >Publish >eTransmit. The "**Create Transmittal**" dialog box opens.
Step3. If you want, enter a note to the recipient in the text box at the lower-left corner of the dialog box. If you send an e-mail, the note will become part of the body of the e-mail. If you create an EXE or ZIP file, the note becomes part of the transmittal report, which is a separate file included with the drawing and other files.

Autodesk AutoCAD 2021
Learn CAD With Ease.

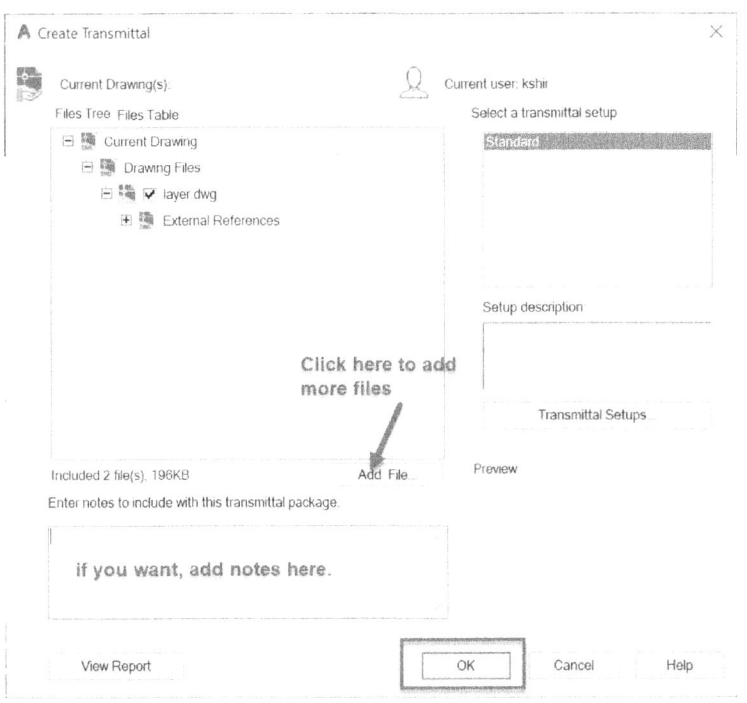

Step 4: Click on **OK** and save zip folder including all referenced files.

Other Options:
Step5. Use the Select a Transmittal Setup box to choose a saved transmittal, if you've saved one from previous etransmittals. Otherwise, click Transmittal Settings to open the Transmittal Setups dialog box. Click on "**New**", name the transmittal and click Continue to create a new transmittal. If you have a saved transmittal that you want to change, choose it, and click **"Modify"**. Either way, you end up in the Modify Transmittal Setup dialog box.

Step6. From the Transmittal Package Type drop-down list, choose Folder, Self-extracting Executable, or Zip.

Step7. From the File Format drop-down list, you can choose an earlier release of AutoCAD. Use this feature if your recipient has an earlier release.

Autodesk AutoCAD 2021
Learn CAD With Ease.

Step8. In AutoCAD, there's a checkbox, **Maintain Visual Fidelity for annotative objects**. This is checked by default, which saves each scale representation as a separate block on its own layer.

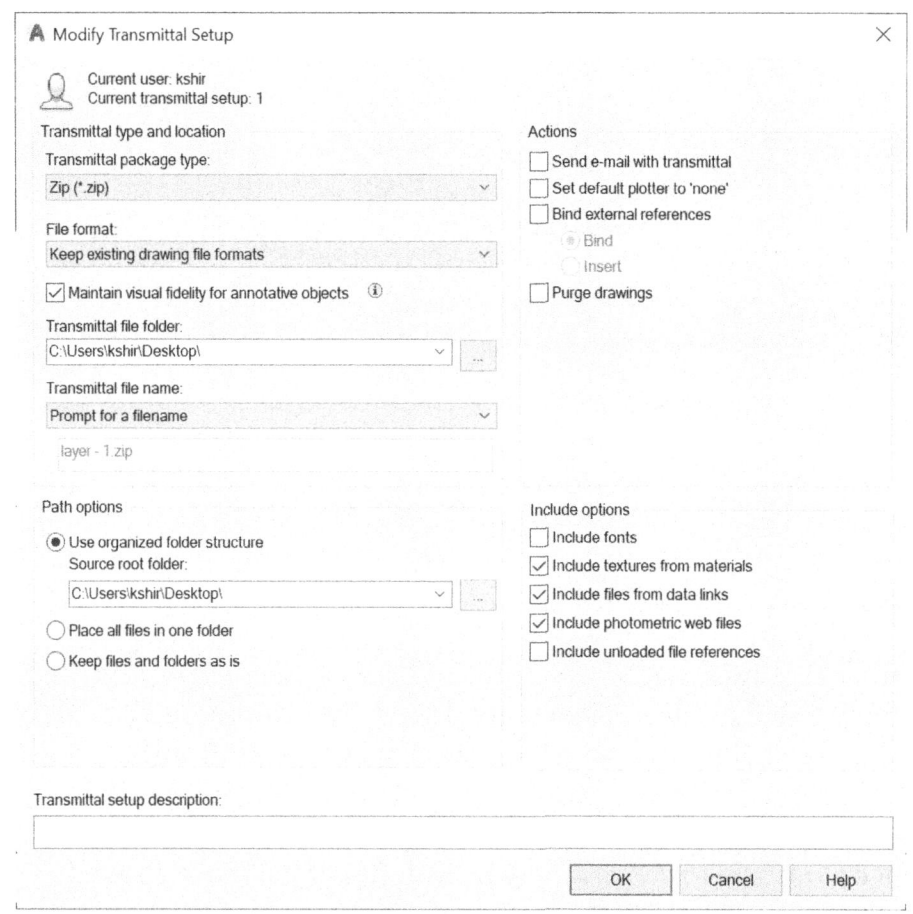

Recipients with earlier versions can then choose which representation they want by turning off the unwanted layers or deleting the unwanted blocks.

Step9. From the Transmittal File Folder drop-down list, enter a location or click Browse to navigate to a location for the transmittal file. If you leave this blank, the files are saved in the same folder as the current drawing. (If you're transmitting a sheet set, the file goes in the same folder as the DST file.

Autodesk AutoCAD 2021
Learn CAD With Ease.

Step10. In the Transmittal File Name drop-down list, you can choose to be prompted for a file name, let AutoCAD assign a name (overwriting any existing file with that name), or let AutoCAD assign an incremental file name.

Step11. In the Transmittal Options section, choose one of these options:

Path options:

Use organized folder structure: To create a hierarchical folder structure based on the structure of the files.

Place all files in one folder: To do just that.

Keep files and folders as is: Recreates the exact paths of the existing files.

Include options:

Include Fonts: Check **the Include Fonts** check box to include AutoCAD fonts used. Choose this if you have created your own AutoCAD fonts that the recipient might not have. This option does not include TrueType fonts.

Include Textures from Materials: Check the **Include Textures from Materials** check box to include texture files.

Include files from data links: In AutoCAD, check the **Include Files from Data Links** check box to include Excel or CSV files that the drawing links to.

Include photometric web files: In AutoCAD, check the **Include Photometric Web Files** check box to include web files that you have used for photometric data for lights.

Actions:

Send E-mail with Transmittal: Check the **Send E-mail with Transmittal** check box to open your e-mail program, create a new message, insert the note in the body of the message, and attach the transmittal file.

Autodesk AutoCAD 2021
Learn CAD With Ease.

Default plotter to 'none': Check the **Default plotter to 'none'** check box to do just that. If your recipient will plot the drawing and has a different plotter, this is a good idea.

Bind External References: Use the Bind External References check box to bind xrefs, rather than keeping them as separate files.

Prompt for Password: Use the Prompt for Password check box to let you specify a password after you save the transmittal file. You then give this password to the recipient, to make sure no one else can open the drawing.
If you want, add a description at the bottom that describes the choices you have made.

Click **OK** to return to the Transmittal Setups dialog box. Select the transmittal that you want and click **Close**. You're now back in the **Create Transmittal** dialog box.
You can click the Files Table tab to check which files will be included in the transmittal file. Note that eTransmit does not include files that you hyperlinked to.
Click the View Report button to see the Transmittal Report, which includes your note and instructions to the recipient, depending on the choices you made. You can choose Save As to make a copy for yourself.

Click **OK** to create the transmittal. If you chose to send an e-mail, your e-mail program opens.

Autodesk AutoCAD 2021
Learn CAD With Ease.

CHAPTER 5
PARAMETERIC CONSTRAINTS

In this chapter you will get knowledge about parametric constraints available in AutoCAD. These parametric constraints are affects editing of drawing. Parametric involves constraining drawing objects so they are related to each other. Changing or moving one object will affect all its siblings.

After completing this chapter you are able to apply:

* Geometrical Constraints to a drawing.
* Dimensional Constraints to a drawing.
* Parameter Manager.

Now let's start parametric constraints.
There are two types of Parametric Constraints:
* Geometric Constraints
* Dimensional Constraints

5.1 Geometric Constraints: Firstly we study about Geometric Constraints.

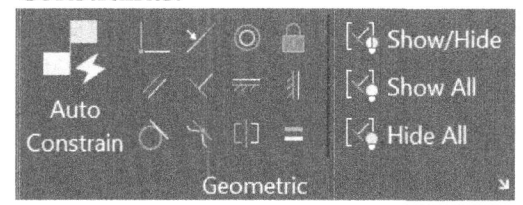

Parametric Tab→Geometric Panel →Geometric Constraints.

Geometric Constraints: **Geometric constraints** are sticky object snaps. In standard AutoCAD, a Tangent object snap exists only for the split-second interval while the location is being calculated. In parametrics, however, the line remembers that it is tangent to the arc and vice versa. If you change or move one object, then the other will adjust itself to remain tangential.

As well as the usual object snaps, additional geometric constraints are available such as Equal (length or radius), Symmetric, Collinear, Coincident, and so on.

Autodesk AutoCAD 2021
Learn CAD With Ease.

Objects don't need to touch for geometric constraints to work. A line in a front view can be equal in length to a line in the top view so that changing one line will change the other, and one end of the front-view line always can be vertical to the end top-view line. Now the views will stay in step if anything changes.

Let's start with a quick exercise to see this in operation. Draw two line segments with Ortho and Polar turned off and with gaps between the ends of the lines, as shown in the figure below.

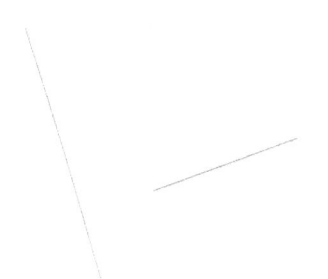

Next, click on the Parametric tab on the Ribbon. The Geometric panel (see figure below) shows the different types of constraints that can be applied.

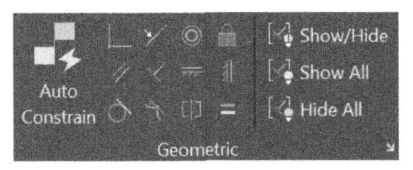

5.1.1 Coincident : This command is used to constrain two points to coincide or a point to lie anywhere on an object or the extension of an object. The constraint points on objects vary based on the object type. For example you can connect the midpoint and the endpoint of the lines.

Click on coincident icon to invoke coincident command.

Select first point on the first line and then select second point on the second line to coincide them.

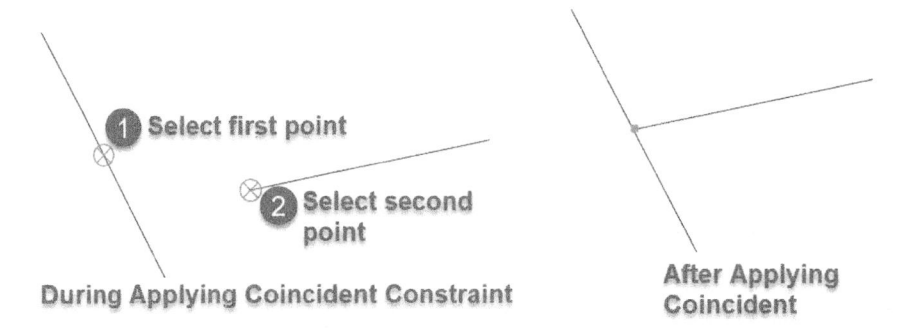

During Applying Coincident Constraint

After Applying Coincident

The Coincident constraint connects two points together.

Autodesk AutoCAD 2021
Learn CAD With Ease.

5.1.2 Horizontal Constraints: This constraint is used to make angled line horizontal.
For that, click on Horizontal constraint and then select line to make it horizontal.

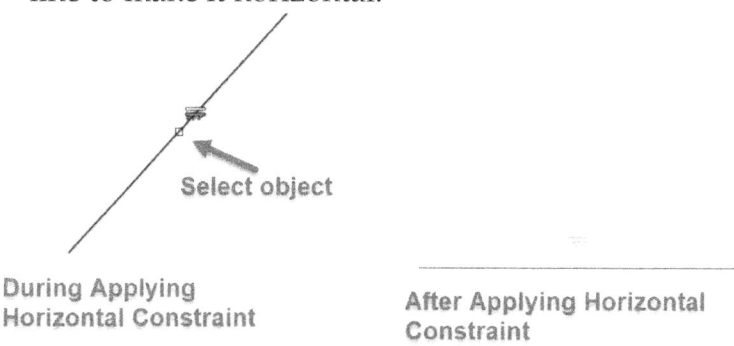

Select object

During Applying Horizontal Constraint

After Applying Horizontal Constraint

5.1.3 Perpendicular Constraint:
Draw two lines as shown in figure given below and then apply perpendicular constraint on them.

    i.   Click on perpendicular constraint.
   ii.   Select lower line (first line) and then select second line.

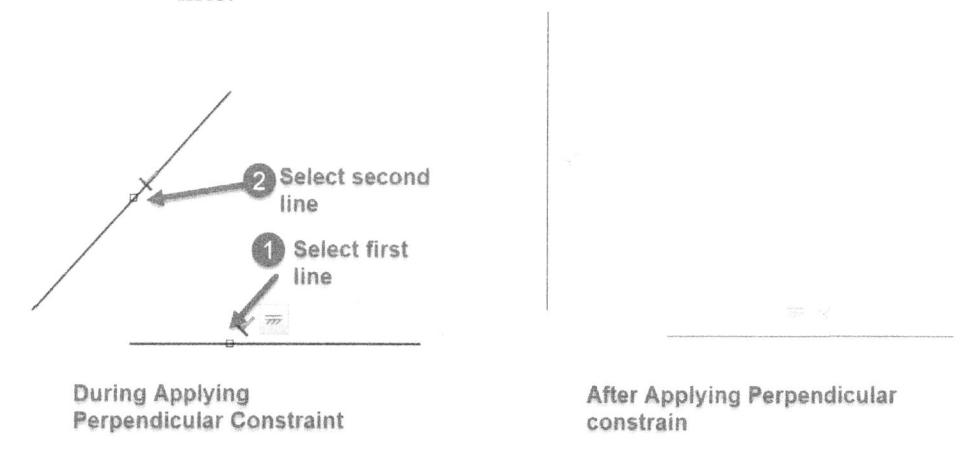

② Select second line
① Select first line

During Applying Perpendicular Constraint

After Applying Perpendicular constrain

Note: Here, Firstly I apply Horizontal constraint to the lower line (first line) to make it horizontal and then apply perpendicular constraint.

Horizontal and Perpendicular constraints have been added to the drawing.

5.1.4 Vertical Constraint: Causes lines or pairs of points to lie parallel to the Y axis of the current coordinate system.

Autodesk AutoCAD 2021
Learn CAD With Ease.

Before Applying Vertical Constraint

After Applying Vertical Constraint

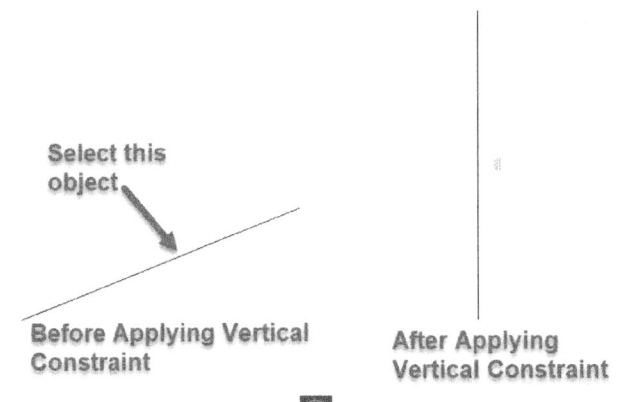

5.1.5 Concentric Constraint:
This constraint is use to constrains two arcs, circles, or ellipses to the same center point.
Here we have two circles in a diagram given below:

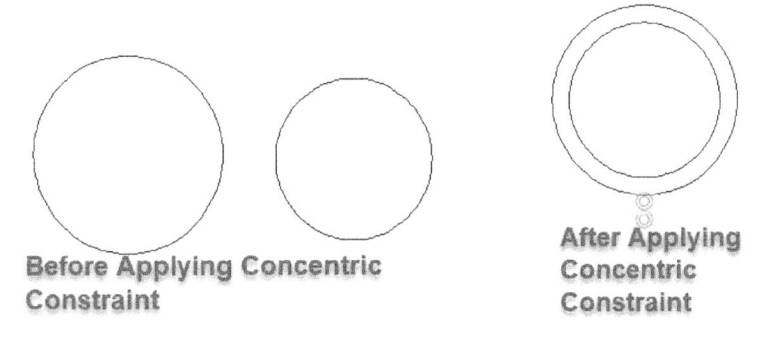

Before Applying Concentric Constraint

After Applying Concentric Constraint

For giving them same center point we will apply concentric constraint, for that:

i. Click on **Concentric Constraint**.
ii. Select big circle and then select small circle.

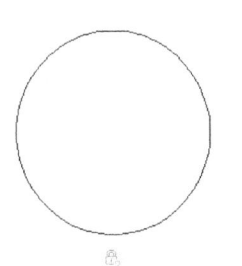

5.1.6 Fixed Constraint: This constraint is used to lock the position of a point and object.

For that: Select object to fix; now you can't move the object.

5.1.7 Collinear Constraints:

It constrains two lines to lie on the same infinite line. The second selected line is made collinear with the first line.

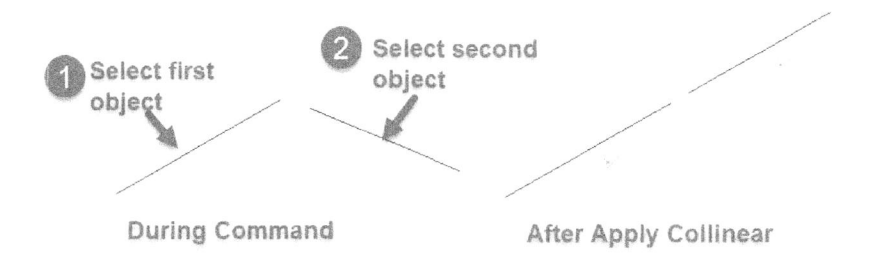

5.1.8 Parallel Constraint:

It constrains two lines to maintain the same angle. The second selected object is made parallel to the first.

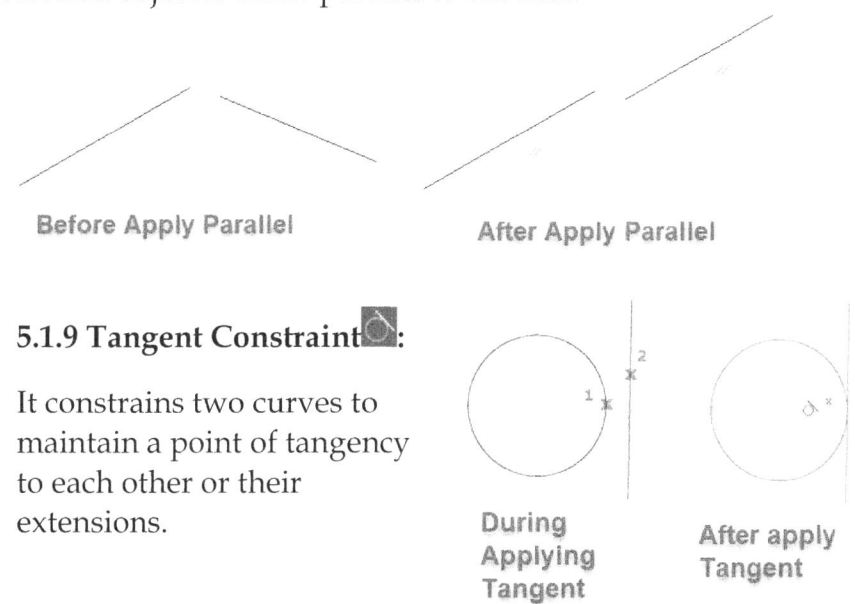

5.1.9 Tangent Constraint:

It constrains two curves to maintain a point of tangency to each other or their extensions.

5.1.10 Smooth Constraint:

It constrains a spline to be contiguous and maintain G2 continuity with another spline, line, arc or polyline.

The first object selected must be a spline. The second selected object is made G2 continuous with the first line.

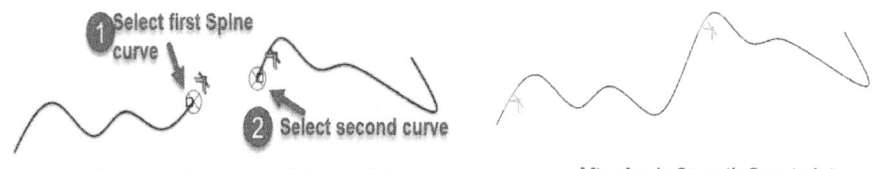

Autodesk AutoCAD 2021
Learn CAD With Ease.

During Applying Smooth Constraint

After Apply Smooth Constraint

5.1.11 Symmetric Constraint:

It constrains two curves or points on objects to maintain symmetry about a selected line.

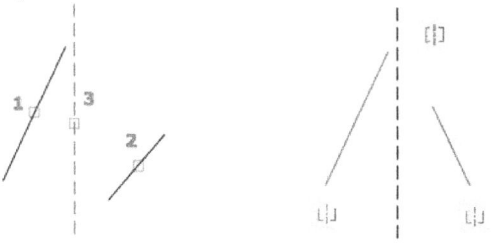

During Applying Symmetry

After Symmetry

5.1.12 Equal:

It constrains two lines or polyline segments to maintain equal lengths, or arcs and circles to maintain equal radius values. Use the 'Multiple' option to make two or more objects equal.

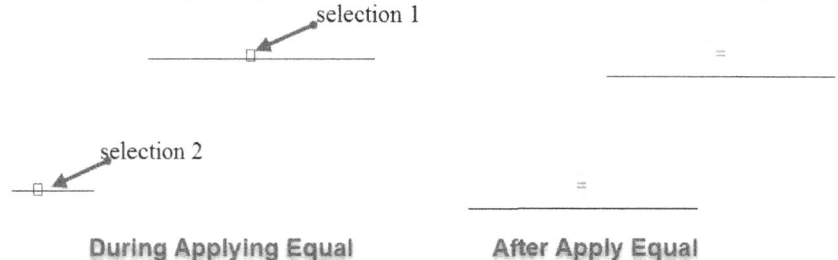

During Applying Equal

After Apply Equal

5.1.13 Auto Constrain:
If you want to apply geometric constrains automatically to the drawing then you will do that by Auto Constrain command. To understand it properly draws an object given below:

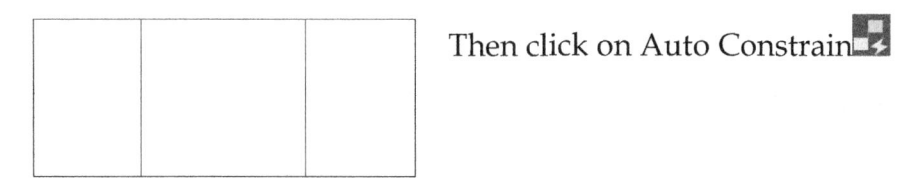

Then click on Auto Constrain

Autodesk AutoCAD 2021
Learn CAD With Ease.

After that select object and then you will see that the geometric constrains automatically applied to the drawing.

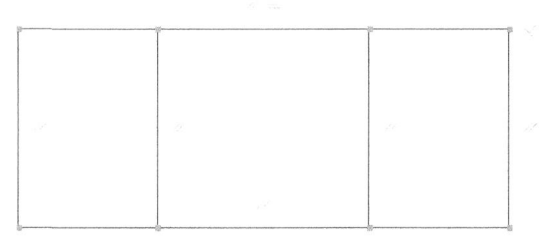

To set the order for applying geometric constraints to the drawing:

i. Click on Auto Constrain.
ii. Select object and then right click on it and select **Settings**, it will open **Constraint Settings** dialog box.
iii. In the **Constraint Settings** dialog box, select **Auto Constrain** tab, select a **Constraint Type** from given list and then click **Move Up** or Move Down. This changes the priority for that constraint when you apply geometric constraints automatically.

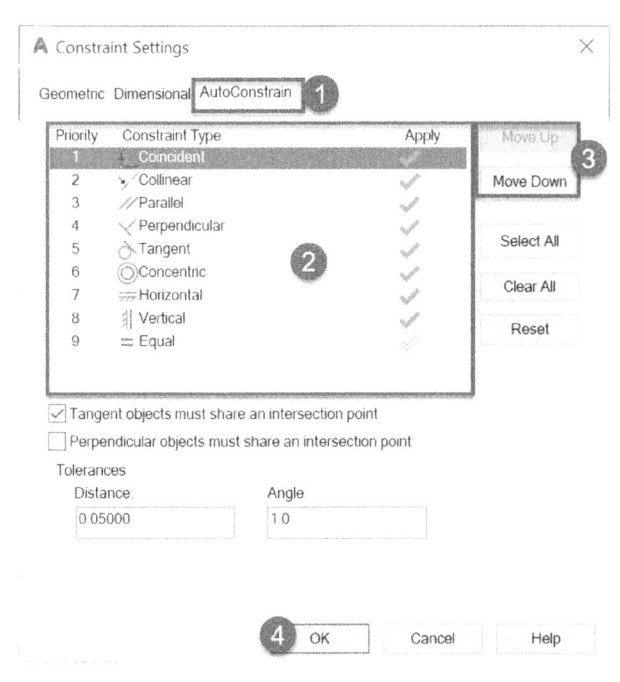

5.1.14 Show / Hide Geometric Constraints: It displays or hides geometric constraints for selected object.

5.1.15 Hide All: It hides all geometric constraints in the drawing.

5.1.16 Show all Geometric constraints: It displays all hidden geometric constraints in the drawing.

5.2 **Dimensional Constraints:** Dimensional constraints control the size and proportions of a design. They can constrain the following:

- Distances between objects, or between points on objects
- Angles between objects, or between points on objects
- Sizes of arcs and circles

If you change the value of a dimensional constraint, all the constraints on the object are evaluated, and the objects that are affected are updated automatically.
Parametric Tab → Dimensional.

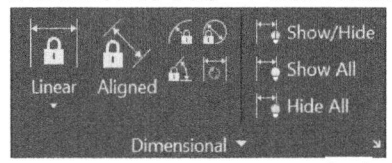

5.2.1 Linear Constraint: It constrains the horizontal or vertical distance between points. When a line or arc is selected, the horizontal or vertical distance between the endpoints of the object is constrained.

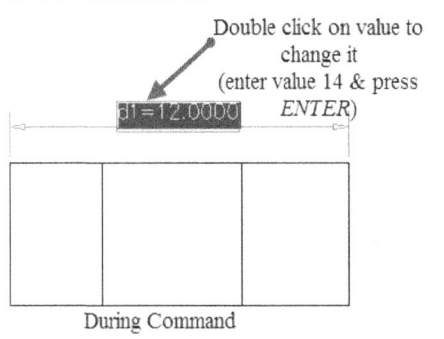

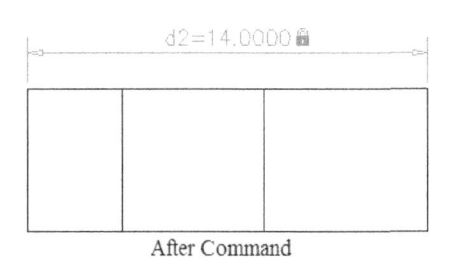

Double click on value to change it (enter value 14 & press ENTER)

d1=12.0000   d2=14.0000

During Command   After Command

5.2.2 Vertical Constraint ⬛: It constrains the vertical distance between points.

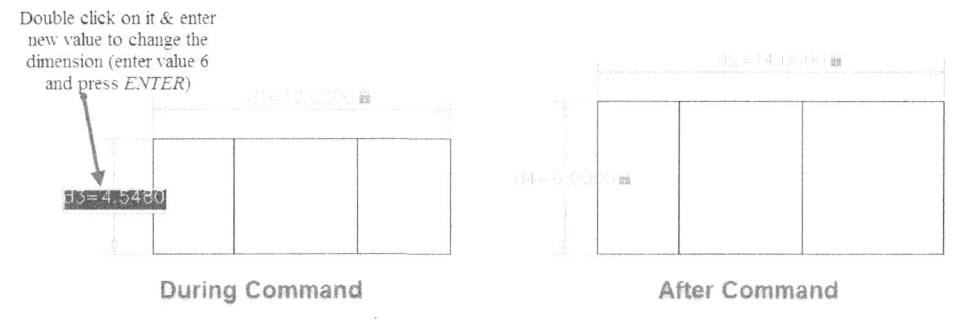

Double click on it & enter new value to change the dimension (enter value 6 and press *ENTER*)

During Command **After Command**

5.2.3 Aligned Constraint ⬛: It constrains the diagonal distance between two points.

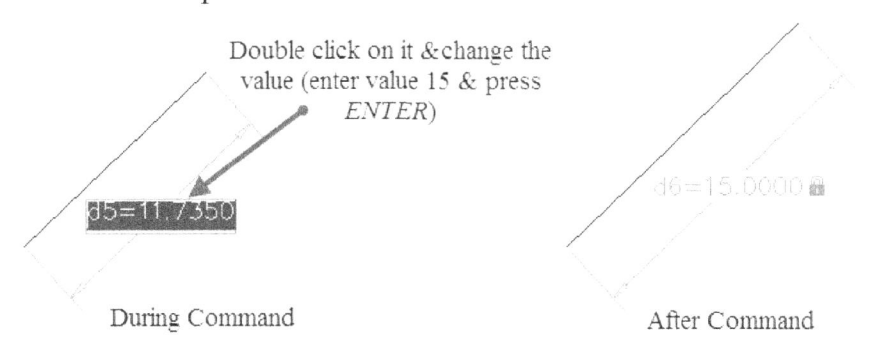

Double click on it & change the value (enter value 15 & press *ENTER*)

During Command After Command

5.2.4 Radius Constraint ⬛ : It constrains the radius of a circle or an arc.

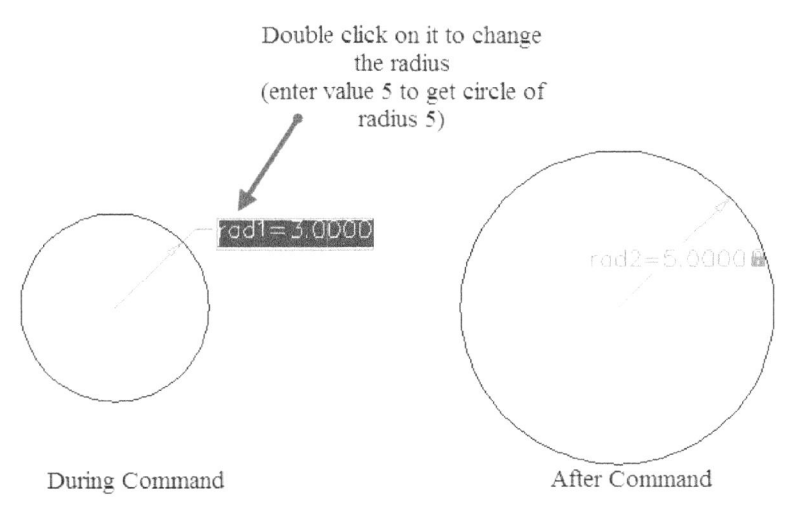

Double click on it to change the radius (enter value 5 to get circle of radius 5)

During Command After Command

Autodesk AutoCAD 2021
Learn CAD With Ease.

5.2.5 Diameter Constraint : It constrains the diameter of a circle or an arc.

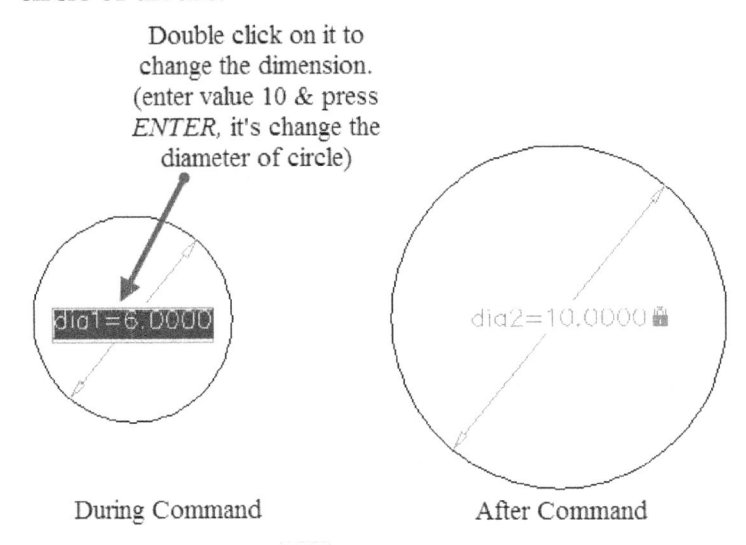

Double click on it to change the dimension. (enter value 10 & press ENTER, it's change the diameter of circle)

dia1=6.0000

dia2=10.0000

During Command   After Command

5.2.6 Angular Constraint : It constrains the angle between line or polyline segments, the angle swept out by an arc or a polyline arc segment, or the angle between three points on objects.

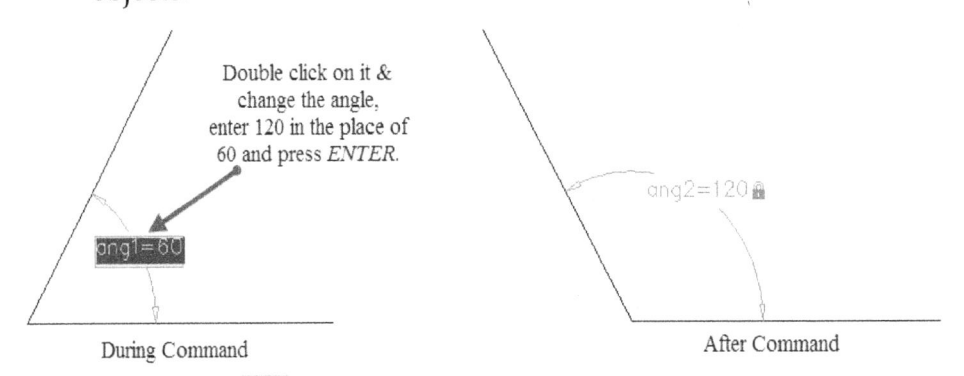

Double click on it & change the angle, enter 120 in the place of 60 and press ENTER.

ang1=60

ang2=120

During Command   After Command

5.2.7 Convert : It converts normal dimension in to dimensional constraints.

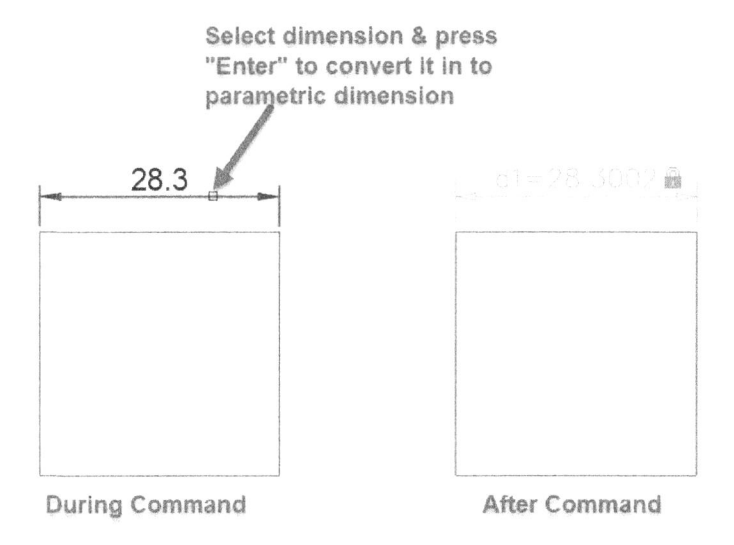

Autodesk AutoCAD 2021
Learn CAD With Ease.

Select dimension & press "Enter" to convert it in to parametric dimension

28.3

During Command   After Command

5.2.8 Show/ Hide: This command is used to show or hide dimensional constraints of a drawing.

5.2.9 Show All: This command is used to show all dimensional constraint applied on a drawing.

5.2.10 Hide All: This command is used to hide all dimensional constraints applied on a drawing.

5.3 Parameters Manager: You can modify dimensional constraints and user variables either directly or with the **Parameters Manager**.

Parametric Tab → Manage Panel → Parameters Manager.

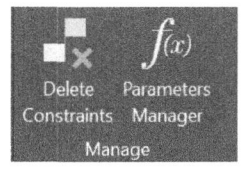

You can follow the given example to understand 'Parameters Manager' properly.

a. Create the diagram given below and assign dimensional parameters to it.

Autodesk AutoCAD 2021
Learn CAD With Ease.

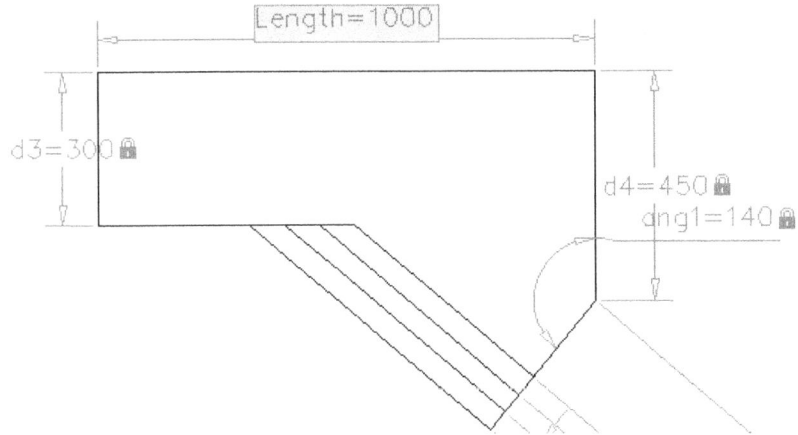

b. Double-click the dynamic constraint **d1**, and change the **d1** to **Length** as the new name. Press Enter or click outside the edit box to accept the change.

Another way to change the name of a dynamic constraint is to use the **Parameters Manager**.

c. On the Parametric tab, Manage panel, click **Parameters Manager**.

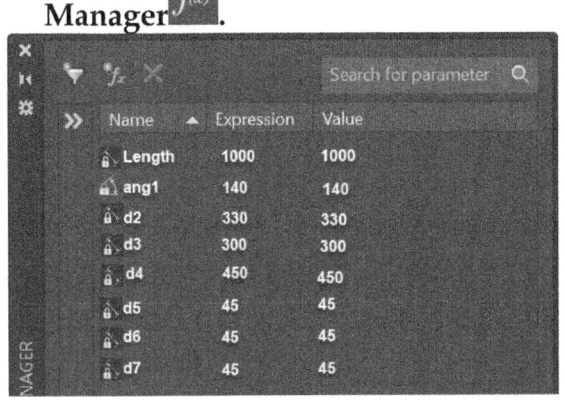

d. In the Name column, double-click **d2** and enter **Width**. Press Enter or click outside the edit box to accept the change.

Define User Variable:
Often, it is convenient to make a single change that affects multiple dynamic constraints. For example, you might want to experiment with several tread widths for the steps in the deck plan.

a. Double-click an empty row in the **Parameters Manager**.

Autodesk AutoCAD 2021
Learn CAD With Ease.

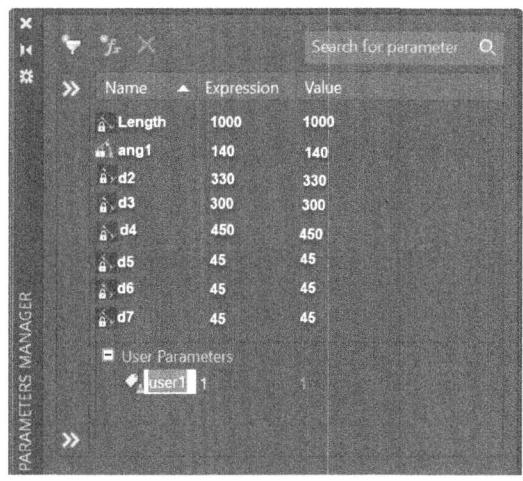

b. Change the name of the new user variable from user1 to **Tread**. Press Enter or click outside the Parameters Manager palette to accept the new name.

c. Change the value in the Expression column from 1 to 45. Press Enter or click outside the Parameters Manager to accept the new value.

d. In the Expression column of d5, d6, and d7, enter Tread.

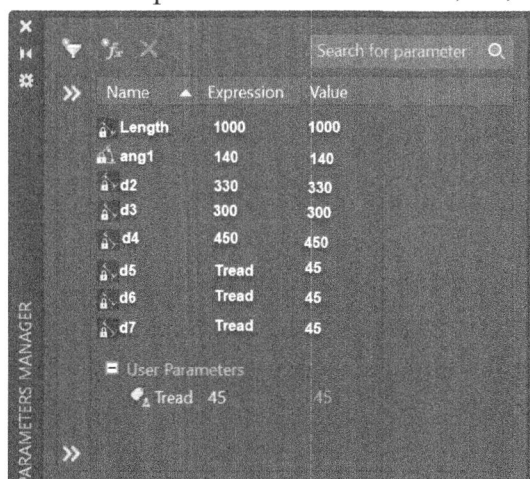

These changes associate the value of each of these distances with the user variable, Tread. Let's test your control over the tread widths.

e. In the Expression column of the user variable, **Tread**, change the value from 45 to 60. Then change it to 40. The changes are updated automatically in the deck plan.

Close the drawing without saving it.

298

By Madhumita Kshirsagar

Autodesk AutoCAD 2021
Learn CAD With Ease.

Create dimensional relationships between objects:

The Expression column in the Parameters Manager can contain constants, references to dynamic constraints, references to user variables, arithmetic operators, and functions. Consider the following example.

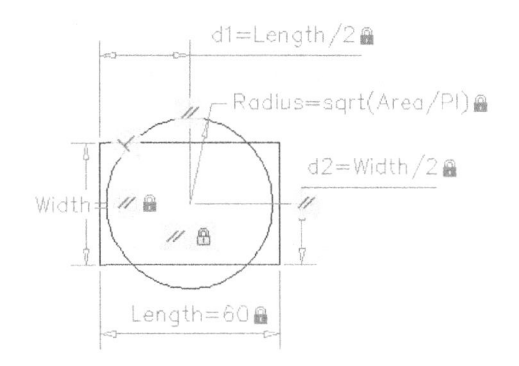

1. Draw a given diagram

This is a fully constrained drawing of a rectangle with a circle at its center. The circle always has the same area as the rectangle. Let's examine the dynamic constraints in detail.

1. If necessary, open the Parameters Manager fx.

Name	Expression	Value
⊟ Dimension...		
Length	60	60
Radius	sqrt(Area/PI)	28
Width	40	40
d1	Length/2	30
d2	Width/2	20
⊟ User Varia...		
Area	Length * Width	2400

2. In the Parameters Manager, click the **Length** row.
   As long as your cursor is in the **Parameters Manager**, the **Length** dynamic constraint remains highlighted in the drawing. **Length** is set to the constant 60.

3. Click the **Width** row and observe the highlighted dynamic constraint. To center the circle, the **d1** and **d2** dynamic constraints are defined as **Length/2** and **Width/2**. The user variable, **Area** is defined as the product of **Length** and **Width**, the area of the rectangle.

4. Click the **Radius** row.

The radius of the circle is defined with the expression containing the area of the rectangle, the square root function, and the constant, PI. This sets the radius of the circle to a value that constrains the area of the circle to be equal to the area of the rectangle.

Notice that you can store expressions in a dimensional constraint or in a user variable.

Experiment by changing the values for the length and width of the rectangle.

Notice that the Value column displays the current value of the expression in the Expression column. Are you curious what would happen if you set the length of the rectangle to 0 or -1?

Autodesk AutoCAD 2021
Learn CAD With Ease.

CHAPTER 6
PRINTING

In this chapter you will get knowledge of printing of drawings in an AutoCAD. There are many ways available in an AutoCAD to print the drawings.

After completing this chapter you are able to print drawings by:
❖ Direct print.
❖ Print by Layout.
❖ Sheet Set Manager.

6.1 Direct Print 🖨: When you have done the assignment and want to print it. To do this, bring up the plot dialog box by pressing (Ctrl + P) or click on **Plot** 🖨 available in **Quick Access Toolbar> Plot** 🖨 **or Application Menu> Print> Plot** 🖨. Set it up to print as shown below. Follow these steps for a successful plot (see diagram below):

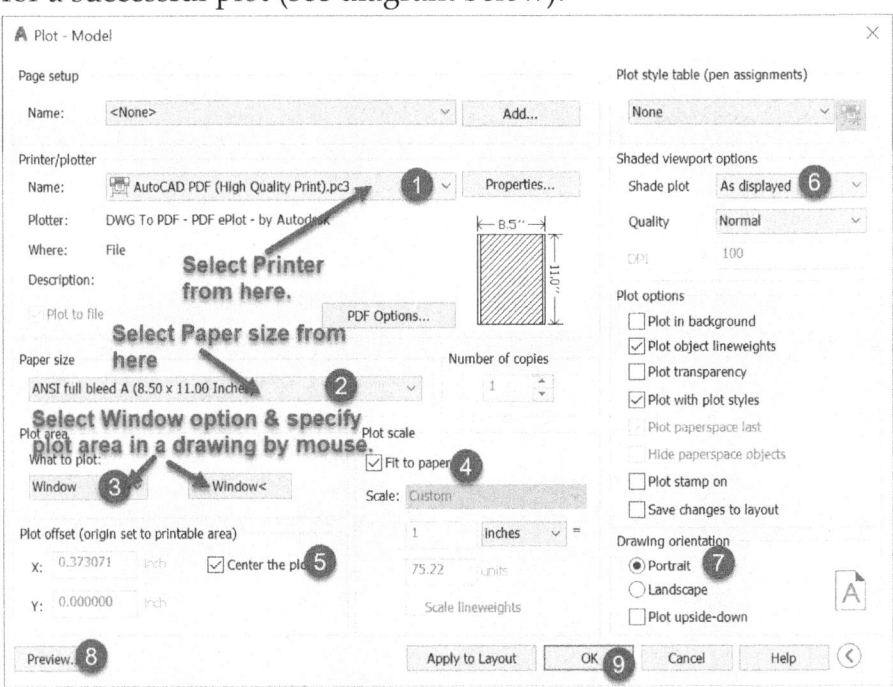

1. Select your printer - laser or inkjet will work fine.
2. Select the paper size – which you want.

3. For the "Plot Area", select "Extents" - that will plot everything you drew. If you want to print any specific drawing, select "Window" and select drawing to print.
4. Select the checkbox to "Center the Plot" on your sheet of paper (looks better).
5. Click on "Fit to Paper" to print drawing according to your paper size and you can also specify 'scale' on which you want printout.
6. Now Preview your drawing.
7. If you are sure that everything is ok (this is where good habits begin), press the OK button.

6.2 Print by Layout:

You can print your project using 'model space'. This topic will show you the preferred way of plotting your drawings. In AutoCAD there are two different workspaces: model space and Layout. For now think of model space where you make your drawings. Think of the **Layout Tabs** as where you print your drawing from, or layout the final drawing complete with dimensions, notes, title block, etc.

❖ Advantages of using Layout: There are many advantages of using layout.

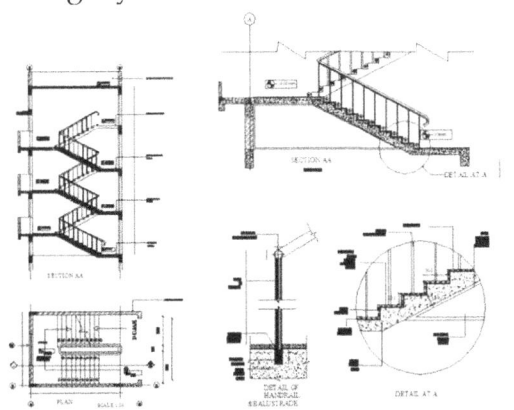

In a given diagram we have several drawings with different scales. To draw these types of drawings, we have two ways available in AutoCAD.

First one is, we were actually drawn them in different scales. If you have a detailed view, then you have to copy and scale that part of your drawing. When we need to change it, then we have to update them all manually.

Second way is using Layout for that purpose.

Using layout will give us several advantages below.

Autodesk AutoCAD 2021
Learn CAD With Ease.

1. We Always Draw in Full Scale:

It doesn't matter if you have 2, 4, or 10 different scales in your sheet later. We can always draw in full scale 1:1. Even for beginners can easily complete the drawing without having to think how they need to scale the drawing, creating different dimension styles, etc.

2. Show Different Area of One Model:

Even we only draw once with full scale, we can represent the model many times. We can represent the drawing with several viewports, showing different area of the model. Sometimes we simply need it because the model is too large for one sheet. And sometimes, we need it to show it in different scales for detailed drawings.

Because we only draw in one model, we only need to update the model space other viewports will automatically updated. We don't have to update each drawing separately.

3. Less Styles to Manage:

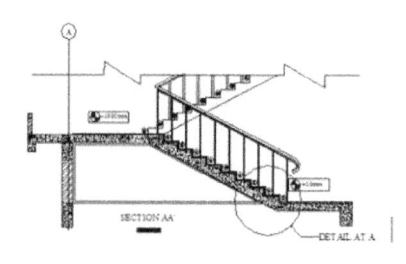

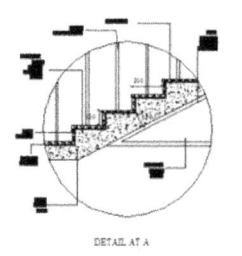

Let's see the image given at right. We have a stair section and create a detail from it. When we need to add dimension to both drawing, we have to create two dimension styles. They have different scales, so we need to create another dimension and control the dimension value by changing the scale factor. If you scale it 4x, then you need another dimension style with scale factor 1/4.

You can override the properties manually, but it will take more time. You have to switch between dimension styles and can bring unnecessary mistakes.

What if you have 3 or 4 different scales? What if in your model space you have more than one sheet with more different scales? You can do it by layout.

4. Easy to Control Drawing Scale:

Another good thing about layout is it's easy to control the drawing scale. As we discussed in no.1, we only need to draw in full scale. We can arrange them easily in layout.

It's not so easy to explain how to apply scale, drawing border, and placing title block in model space to a new user. Using viewport, it's easier to explain.

You can create a viewport, select it, and change the scale using viewport scale at the right bottom of your screen.

In the past, we have to use zoom scale. But today, it's very easy after AutoCAD has scale list feature.

ONE MODEL, MULTIPLE REPRESENTATIONS

If we work with model space, we treat it like drawing manually in a paper. When you need to represent a drawing several times, then you need to copy it to show each instance. Layout allows you to draw one model, and represent it several times. In no.2, we already discussed how we can show different areas with different scales. But there are more.

5. Different Drawing Orientation:

Each viewport can be configured to have different angle orientation. I don't explain much about it here, but you can do it with single drawing in model space too.

Autodesk AutoCAD 2021
Learn CAD With Ease.

For example you want to show a site plan with true north orientation. But you also want to show a building plan in the site plan with different orientation. It's quite easy to do it with layout.

6. Different Drawing Representation with Layer Properties per-Viewport:

In AutoCAD, we have 'layer properties per-viewport'. We can set the layer properties for each viewport independently. For example, you can turn on **hatch** layer for detailed drawing, but turn it off for larger scales. You can show detailed objects for some viewports, and hide it for the others by using **VP freeze** option in a layer for particular layout.

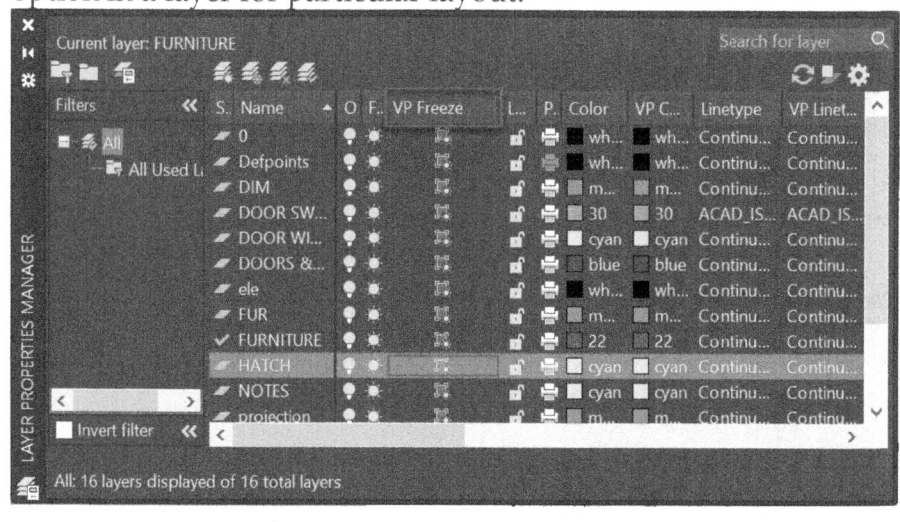

7. Get the Advantages of Annotation Scaling:

Another great feature that has been added to AutoCAD is **annotation scaling**. We can use it in model space, however, we can get the benefits mostly in layout.

Previously, we discussed how we need only to create one drawing and we can represent it in different scales. Annotation scale allows us to do it with annotation, ensuring our annotation readable in different scales. And because we only create one annotation for all scales, any changes will reflected to all of your viewports.

If annotation scaling doesn't suite your needs, you can annotate your drawings in layout. It's probably the most comfortable way for many users. Each of them has its own benefits. Either way, they are easier to manage than setting your sheets in model space.

8. Control Printing Preferences Easily:

Printing preferences are very easy to set when you use layout. If you are not familiar with setting up sheet in model space, remember that we draw in full scale. Then we add a border and title block to include the drawing. We need to calculate the scale in plot scale below.

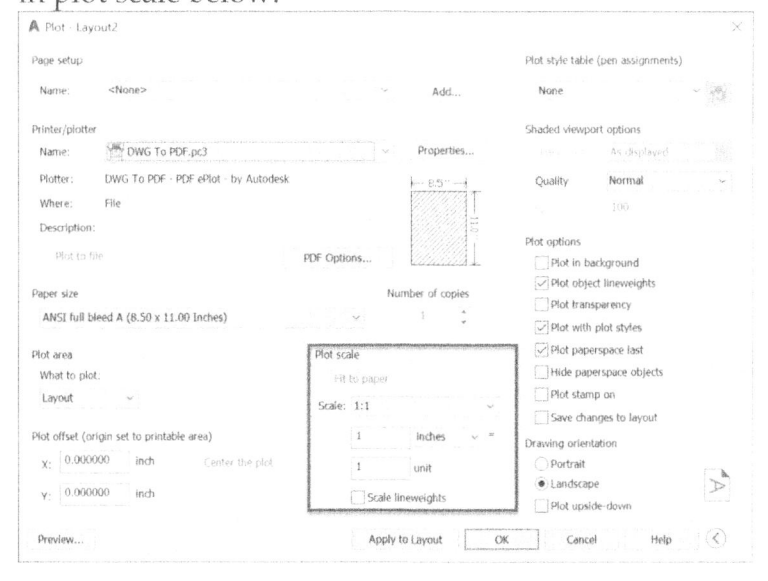

With layout you simply select the paper size, and always use 1:1 full scale. Plot margin will be shown in dashed lines. You can also use page setup to quickly apply your settings.

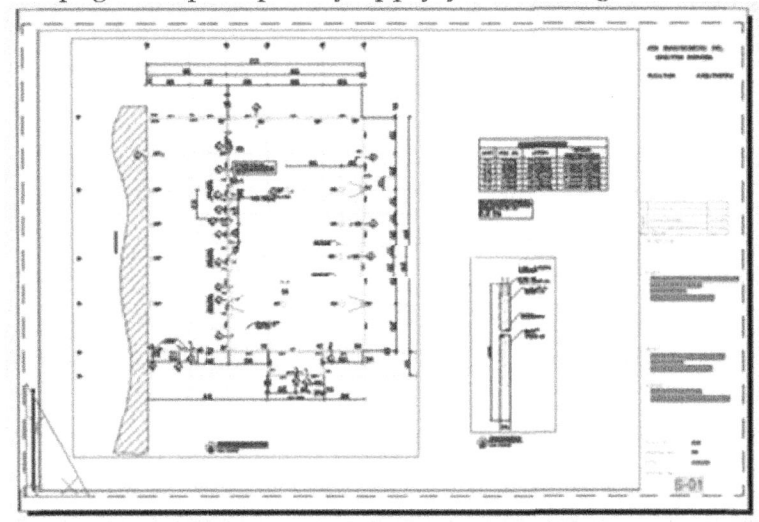

It is very easy to comprehend, even if you don't use AutoCAD intensively. If your company already has a template, it will be easier for you.

9. Sheet Set Manager Advantages:

Sheet set is a good tool to manage your drawings in a project. In short, we can manage the sheets so we can easily access them. After we have a drawing set, we can <u>eTransmit</u> and pack the whole project files as one zip file, ready to send along with dependent files. We can also plot them all at once with publish command.
You will get knowledge about sheet set manager later in this chapter.

10. Batch Plot:

You can plot many drawings at once with sheet set's publishing. However, if you don't use sheet set, you can also use publish manually and add layouts from many layouts.

Autodesk AutoCAD 2021
Learn CAD With Ease.

❖ **How to layout and scale a drawing in AutoCAD:**

Page Setup:
1. Open your AutoCAD drawing.
2. Select the 'Layout' tab (beside 'Model' tab in lower left corner of screen)
3. Then 'Right Click' on the Layout tab and select 'Rename' from the menu then type in the name of the sheet size that you want the drawing to be (ie. 11 x 17) and press [Enter].

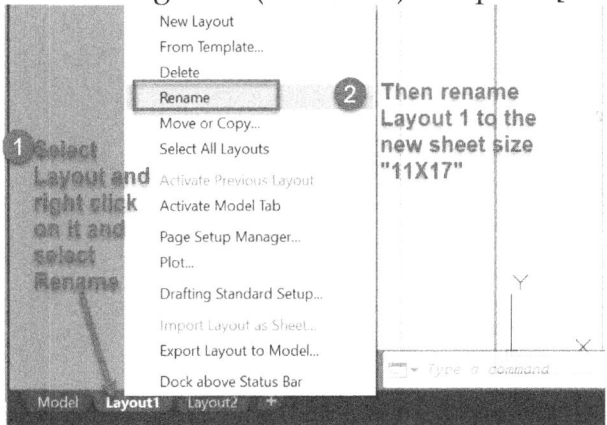

4. Then 'Right click' on the same layout tab and select 'Page Setup Manager' from the menu.
5. Select the new layout that you just renamed and click 'Modify'.

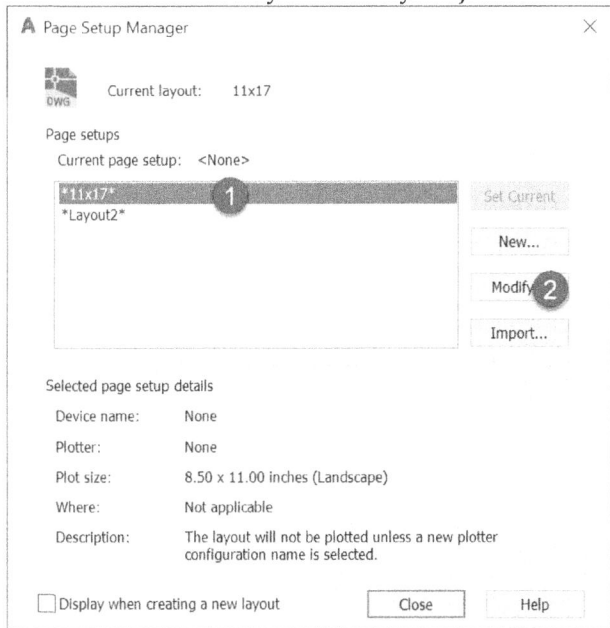

Autodesk AutoCAD 2021
Learn CAD With Ease.

6. In the page setup screen, select a printer/plotter from the drop down menu that can accommodate the sheet size drawing that you wish to set up.
*Note: a plotter is a large size printer that can print oversized sheets that smaller printers cannot.

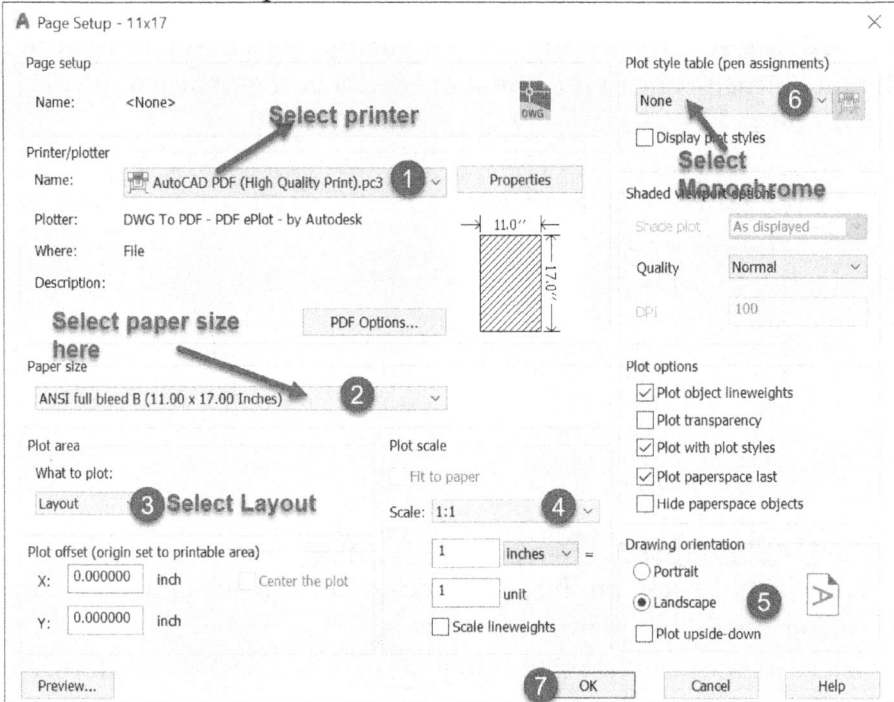

7. Select a paper size from the drop down menu that matches your desired final print size (ie. 11 x 17).
8. Select 'Layout' from the menu options for Plot Area.
9. Select '1:1' for a Plot Scale.
10. Select your drawing orientation 'Landscape' or 'Portrait'.
11. Select 'Monochrome' or 'Grayscale' from the pen assignment drop down menu.
12. Finally click 'Ok' then 'Close'.
13. Now you should see your real paper size. The dashed rectangle is the area where your printable area. Delete existing Viewport and place your title block here. You can insert existing title block if you already have one, or draw a new one by copy paste command. Remember, this is 1:1 scale. So if you want to have 3mm height text, use 3mm as it heights.

Autodesk AutoCAD 2021
Learn CAD With Ease.

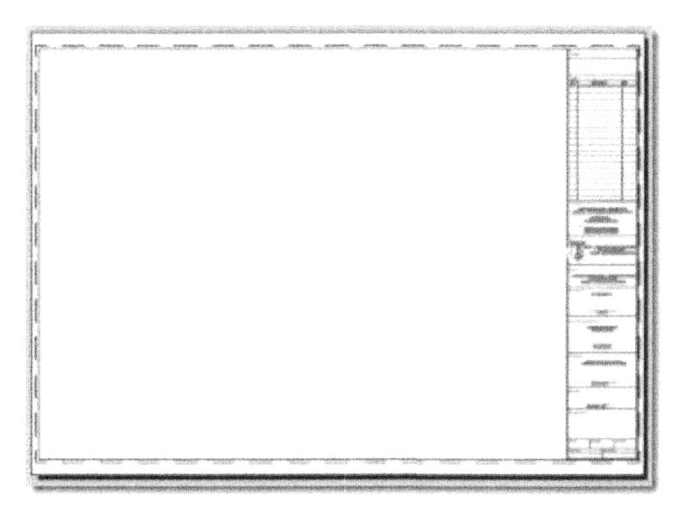

14. Place Viewports and Set the Scale
15. Now we are ready to place our viewport. You can place it by **+Vport or Mv** command.
    When you "**+Vport**" command, the AutoCAD asks for **"Tab index"**, type **1** and press **"Enter"**.

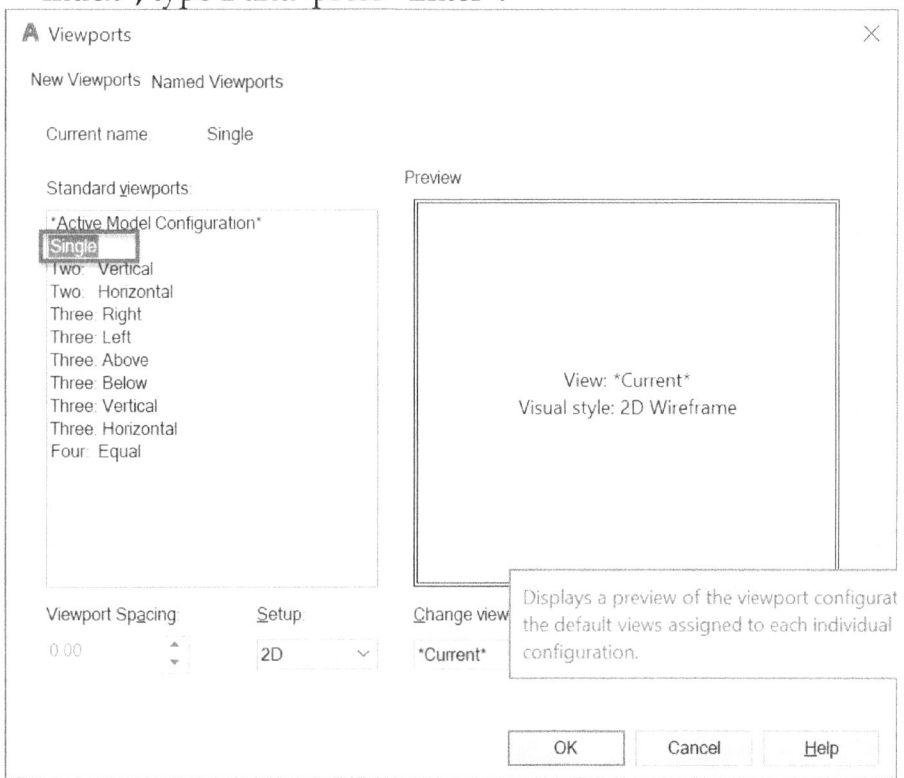

16. In the opened dialog box, select **single** standard viewport, and then click **OK**. Draw your viewport as you desired. You should see all drawings inside it. Or in the old way, I prefer to type MV then [enter] :)

    MV ←

    Specify corner of viewport or[ON/OFF/Fit/Shadeplot/Lock/NEw/NAmed/Object/Polygonal/Restore/LAyer/2/3/4] <Fit>: P ←

    Here, I enter P ← to create polygonal viewport, try other options yourself.

On: Makes a selected viewport active. An active viewport displays objects in model space. The MAXACTVP system variable controls the maximum number of viewports that can be active at one time. If your drawing contains more viewports than the number specified in MAXACTVP, you must turn one off to make another one active.

Off: Makes a selected viewport inactive. Objects in model space are not displayed in an inactive viewport.

Fit: Creates one viewport that fills the layout to the edges of the printable area. When the paper background and printable area are turned off, the viewport fills the display.

Shadeplot: Specifies how viewports in named (paper space) layouts are plotted.

As displayed: Specifies that a viewport is plotted the same way that it is displayed.

Wireframe: Specifies that a viewport is plotted with a wireframe style regardless of the current display.

Hidden: Specifies that a viewport is plotted with hidden lines removed regardless of the current display.

Object: Specifies a closed polyline, ellipse, spline, region, or circle to be converted into a layout viewport. If you select a polyline, it must be closed and contain at least three vertices. It can contain arc segments as well as line segments.

Polygonal: Creates an irregularly shaped viewport using specified points. The options available are similar to those in the PLINE command.

17. Next, set the scale for that select viewport.

Autodesk AutoCAD 2021
Learn CAD With Ease.

18. At the bottom right side of your screen locate the 'Viewport Scale' button (which only becomes visible when your Viewport is visible).
19. Click the 'Viewport Scale' button and select a scale from the menu that appears suitable for the page size that you have just setup.

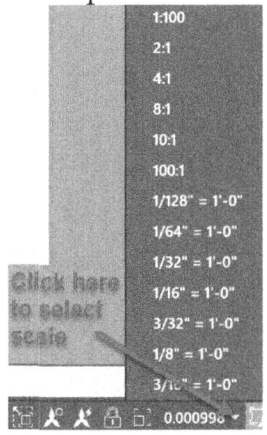

Note: if you simply require the drawing to 'fit' nicely on the page then selecting a suitable scale is just a matter of trial and error until you are satisfied with the way the drawing fits the page. Otherwise, you must know the specific scale requirement (ie. 1/8"=1'-0").

20. All the steps for 'Layout and Scaling' drawings are now complete. Your drawing is ready to print.
21. Just activate plot by hitting **Ctrl + P** or typing PLOT [enter]. Everything should be ready now, but check it first by seeing the preview and then press **OK.**

6.3 Sheet Set Manager: This is used to organize all sheets related to a project in a one place.

The Sheet Set Manager does all the organizational work for you so you can focus on the more important tasks at hand. You can use the **Sheet Set Manager** to quickly open files, add new sheets, and to print, archive and transmit any or all of your drawing files electronically. Imagine printing all of your sheets in a project with just two clicks!

Because all of the members of your design team will use the same sheet set when working on the project, you will only need to worry about a single file versus the many individual files that you've had to keep track of in the past.

312

By Madhumita Kshirsagar

Autodesk AutoCAD 2021
Learn CAD With Ease.

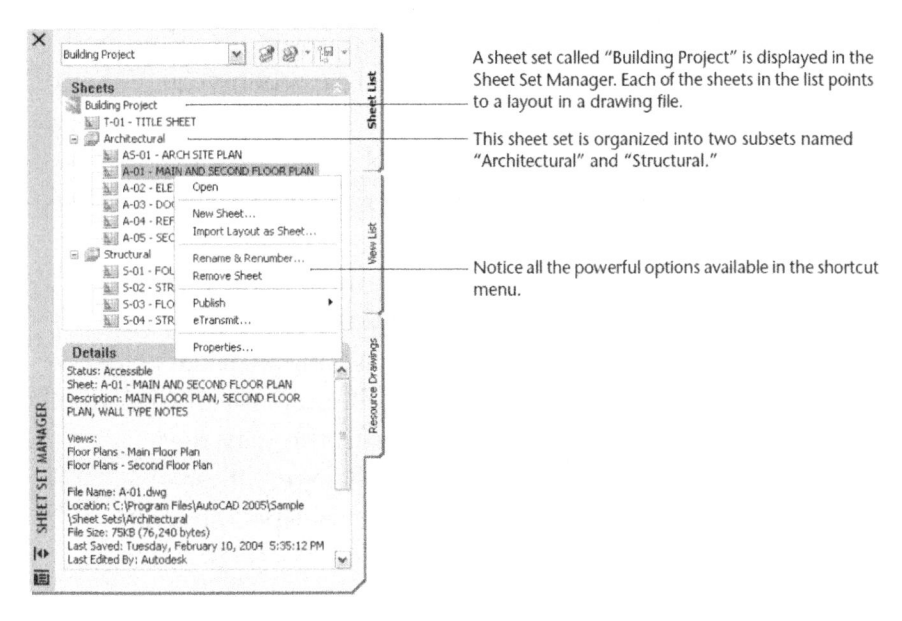

A sheet set called "Building Project" is displayed in the Sheet Set Manager. Each of the sheets in the list points to a layout in a drawing file.

This sheet set is organized into two subsets named "Architectural" and "Structural."

Notice all the powerful options available in the shortcut menu.

There is an assortment of tools available in AutoCAD 2013 that makes the Sheet Set Manager extremely powerful: one-click plotting, automated sheet indexes, more efficient eTransmit, archiving, DWF publishing.

How to Organize a Project Using the Sheet Set Manager:
With the **Sheet Set Manager**, you can create "links" to drawings called **sheets**. Sheets can be organized under logical headings called **subsets**, can display thumbnail images and descriptions, and can be used to open the drawings.

Command: New Sheet Set Manager
Alias   : SSM

View Tab → Palettes Panel → New Sheet Set Manager

Firstly create layouts of all drawings which you want to organize by sheet set manager.

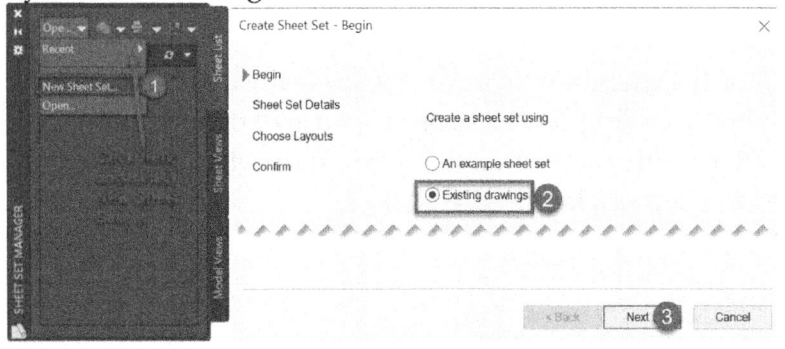

Autodesk AutoCAD 2021
Learn CAD With Ease.

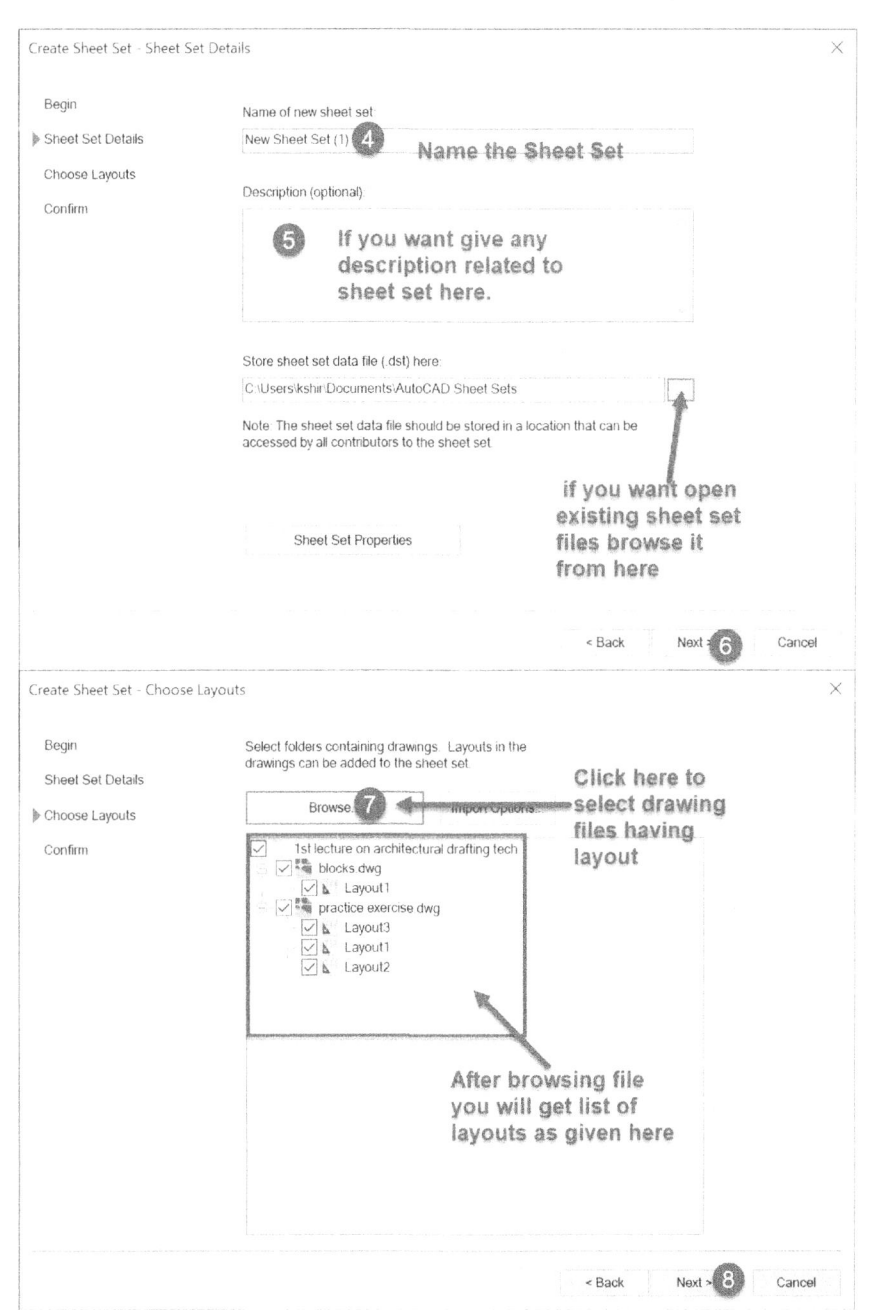

The **Sheet Set Manager** now lists the sheet names, each of which is a combination of an automatically assigned drawing number, the drawing file name, and the layout name. Remember, each sheet is simply a link to a layout in a drawing file.

314

By Madhumita Kshirsagar

Autodesk AutoCAD 2021
Learn CAD With Ease.

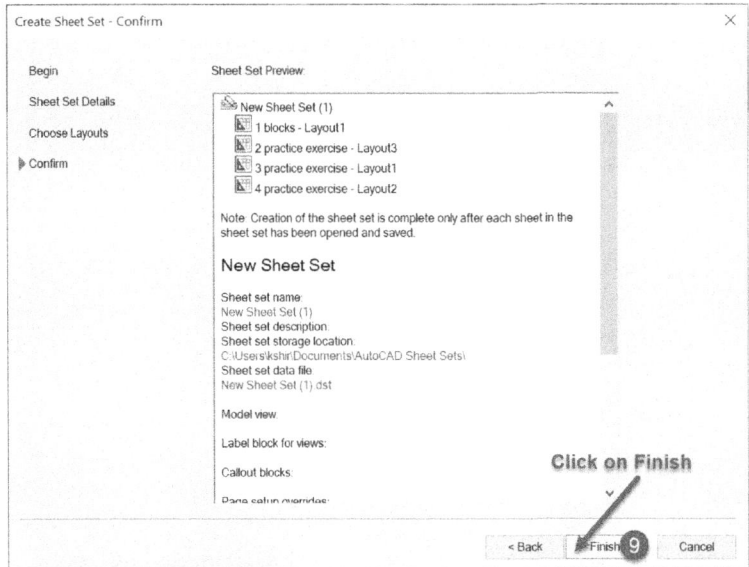

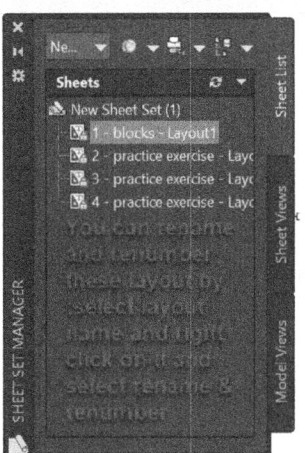

You can group your sheets logically using subsets. For project, I decided to use four subsets: Current Design, Details, Design Archive, and Alternative Design.

- ❖ To create subset, right-click the "New Sheet set 1" and then, click on **New Subset**.

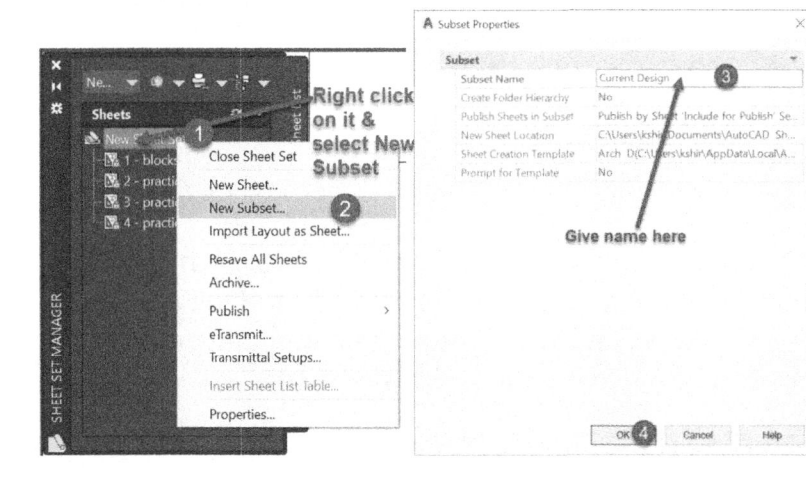

Autodesk AutoCAD 2021
Learn CAD With Ease.

❖ Enter the name of the subset, and repeat the process for each additional subset.

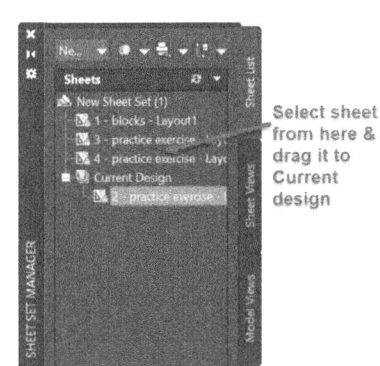

Next, drag each sheet into a subset. When you drag the first sheet into a subset, make sure you drag the sheet on top of the subset name, not above or below it.

Select sheet from here & drag it to Current design

How to Add a New Sheet to a Current Sheet Set:
If you create a new drawing, you can easily add it as a sheet to the current sheet set.
1. Right-click the sheet set node in the Sheet Set Manager.
2. Then, click **Import Layout as Sheet**.

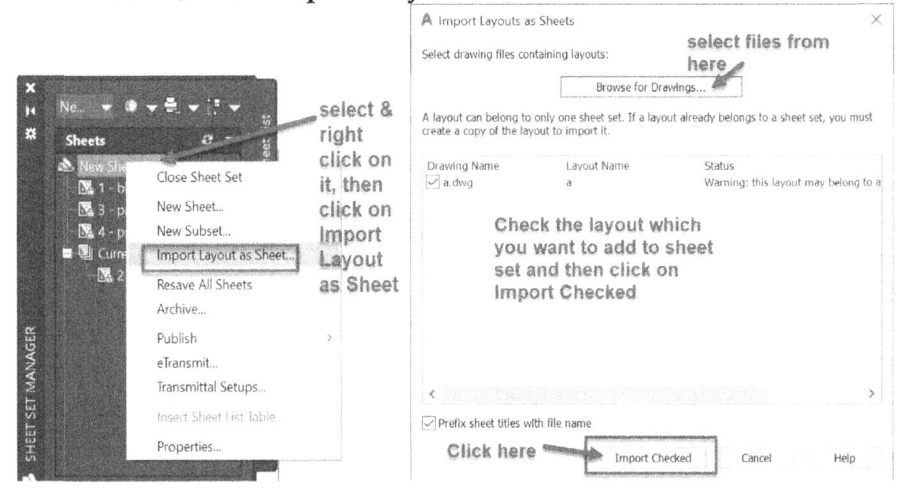

select & right click on it, then click on Import Layout as Sheet

select files from here

Check the layout which you want to add to sheet set and then click on Import Checked

Click here

Now double click on layout available in a sheet set to open it and then print it by Ctrl+ P command.

316

By Madhumita Kshirsagar

Autodesk AutoCAD 2021
Learn CAD With Ease.

SHORTCUT KEYS

Esc	
F1	Display Help
F2	Toggle text screen
F3	Toggle object snap mode
F4	Toggle 3DOsnap
F5	Toggle Isoplane
F6	Toggle Dynamic UCS
F7	Toggle grid mode
F8	Toggle ortho mode
F9	Toggle snap mode
F10	Toggle polar mode
F11	Toggle object snap tracking
F12	Toggle dynamic input mode

Keyboard key assignments:
- Q — QSAVE
- W — WBLOCK
- E — ERASE
- R — REDRAW
- T — MTEXT
- I — INSERT
- O — OFFSET
- P — PAN
- A — ARC
- S — STRETCH
- D — DIMSTYLE
- F — FILLET
- G — GROUP
- H — HATCH
- J — JOIN
- L — LINE
- Z — ZOOM
- X — EXPLODE
- C — CIRCLE
- V — VIEW
- B — BLOCK
- N — NEW
- M — MOVE
- Shift — TOGGLE ORTHO MODE

Q QSAVE / Saves the current drawing.

A ARC / Creates an arc.

Z ZOOM / Increases or decreases the magnification of the view in the current viewport.

W WBLOCK / Writes objects or a block to a new drawing file.

S STRETCH / Stretches objects crossed by a selection window or polygon.

X EXPLODE / Breaks a compound object into its component objects.

E ERASE / Removes objects from a drawing.

D DIMSTYLE / Creates and modifies dimension styles.

C CIRCLE / Creates a circle.

R REDRAW / Refreshes the display in the current viewport.

F FILLET / Rounds and fillets the edges of objects.

V VIEW / Saves and restores named views, camera views, layout views, and preset views.

T MTEXT / Creates a multiline text object.

G GROUP / Creates and manages saved sets of objects called groups.

B BLOCK / Creates a block definition from selected objects.

H HATCH / Fills an enclosed area or selected objects with a hatch pattern, solid fill, or gradient fill.

J JOIN / Joins similar objects to form a single, unbroken object.

M MOVE / Moves objects a specified distance in a specified direction.

I INSERT / Inserts a block or drawing into the current drawing.

O OFFSET / Creates concentric circles, parallel lines, and parallel curves.

L LINE / Creates straight line segments.

P PAN / Adds a parameter with grips to a dynamic block definition.

Toggle General Features

Ctrl+d	Toggle coordinate display
Ctrl+g	Toggle Grid
Ctrl+e	Cycle isometric planes
Ctrl+f	Toggle running object snaps
Ctrl+h	Toggle Pick Style
Ctrl+Shift+h	Toggle Hide pallets
Ctrl+i	Toggle Coords
Ctrl+Shift+i	Toggle Infer Constraints

Toggle Drawing Modes

F1	Display Help
F2	Toggle text screen

Manage Screen

Ctrl+0 (zero)	Clean Screen
Ctrl+1	Property Palette
Ctrl+2	Design Center Palette
Ctrl+3	Tool Palette
Ctrl+4	Sheet Set Palette
Ctrl+6	DBConnect Manager
Ctrl+7	Markup Set Manager Palette
Ctrl+8	Quick Calc
Ctrl+9	Command Line

Manage Workflow

Ctrl+c	Copy object

Manage Drawings

Ctrl+n	New Drawing
Ctrl+s	Save drawing
Ctrl+o	Open drawing
Ctrl+p	Plot dialog box
Ctrl+Tab	Switch to next
Ctrl+Shift+Tab	Switch to previous drawing
Ctrl+Page Up	Switch to previous tab in current drawing
Ctrl+Page Down	Switch to next tab in current drawing
Ctrl+q	Exit
Ctrl+a	Select all objects

Autodesk AutoCAD 2021
Learn CAD With Ease.

F3	Toggle object snap mode	Ctrl+x	Cut object
F4	Toggle 3DOsnap	Ctrl+v	Paste object
F5	Toggle Isoplane	Ctrl+Shift+c	Copy to clipboard with base point
F6	Toggle Dynamic UCS	Ctrl+Shift+v	Paste data as block
F7	Toggle grid mode	Ctrl+z	Undo last action
F8	Toggle ortho mode	Ctrl+y	Redo last action
F9	Toggle snap mode	Ctrl+[	Cancel current command (or ctrl+\)
F10	Toggle polar mode	ESC	Cancel current command
F11	Toggle object snap tracking		
F12	Toggle dynamic input mode		

A

A	ARC / Creates an arc.
AA	AREA / Calculates the area and perimeter of objects or of defined areas.
ADC	ADCENTER / Manages and inserts content such as blocks, xrefs, and hatch patterns.
AL	ALIGN / Aligns objects with other objects in 2D and 3D.
AP	APPLOAD / Load Application.
AR	ARRAY / Creates multiple copies of objects in a pattern.
ARR	ACTRECORD / Starts the Action Recorder.
ARM	ACTUSERMESSAGE / Inserts a user message into an action macro.
ARU	ACTUSERINPUT / Pauses for user input in an action macro.
ARS	ACTSTOP / Stops the Action Recorder and provides the option of saving the recorded actions to an action macro file.
ATI	ATTIPEDIT / Changes the textual content of an attribute within a block.
ATT	ATTDEF / Redefines a block and updates associated attributes.
ATE	ATTEDIT / Changes attribute information in a block.

B

B	BLOCK / Creates a block definition from selected objects.
BC	BCLOSE / Closes the Block Editor.
BE	BEDIT / Opens the block definition in the Block Editor.
BH	HATCH / Fills an enclosed area or selected objects with a hatch pattern, solid fill, or gradient fill.
BO	BOUNDARY / Creates a region or a polyline from an enclosed area.
BR	BREAK / Breaks the selected object between two points.
BS	BSAVE / Saves the current block definition.
BVS	BVSTATE / Creates, sets, or deletes a visibility state in a dynamic block.

C

C	CIRCLE / Creates a circle.
CAM	CAMERA / Sets a camera and target location to create and save a 3D perspective view of objects.
CBAR	CONSTRAINTBAR / A toolbar-like UI element that displays the available geometric constraints on an object.
CH	PROPERTIES / Controls properties of existing objects.
CHA	CHAMFER / Bevels the edges of objects.
CHK	CHECKSTANDARDS / Checks the current drawing for standards violations.
CLI	COMMANDLINE / Displays the Command Line window.
COL	COLOR / Sets the color for new objects.
CO	COPY / Copies objects a specified distance in a specified direction.
CT	CTABLESTYLE / Sets the name of the current table style.
CUBE	NAVVCUBE / Controls the visibility and display properties of the ViewCube tool.
CYL	CYLINDER / Creates a 3D solid cylinder.

D

D	DIMSTYLE / Creates and modifies dimension styles.
DAN	DIMANGULAR / Creates an angular dimension.
DAR	DIMARC / Creates an arc length dimension.
DBA	DIMBASELINE / Creates a linear, angular, or ordinate dimension from the baseline of the previous or selected dimension.
DBC	DBCONNECT / Provides an interface to external database tables.
DCE	DIMCENTER / Creates the center mark or the centerlines of circles and arcs.
DCO	DIMCONTINUE / Creates a dimension that starts from an extension line of a previously created dimension.
DI	DIST / Measures the distance and angle between two points.
DIV	DIVIDE / Creates evenly spaced point objects or blocks along the length or perimeter of an object.
DJL	DIMJOGLINE / Adds or removes a jog line on a linear or aligned dimension.
DJO	DIMJOGGED / Creates jogged dimensions for circles and arcs.
DL	DATALINK / The Data Link dialog box is displayed.
DLU	DATALINKUPDATE / Updates data to or from an established external data link.
DO	DONUT / Creates a filled circle or a wide ring.
DOR	DIMORDINATE / Creates ordinate dimensions.
DRM	DRAWINGRECOVERY / Displays a list of drawing files that can be recovered after a program or system failure.
DS	DSETTINGS / Sets grid and snap, polar and object snap tracking, object snap modes, Dynamic Input, and Quick Properties.
DT	TEXT / Creates a single-line text object.
DV	DVIEW / Defines parallel projection or perspective views by using a camera and target.
DX	DATAEXTRACTION / Extracts drawing data and merges data from an external source to a data extraction table or external file.

318

By Madhumita Kshirsagar

Autodesk AutoCAD 2021
Learn CAD With Ease.

DCON	DIMCONSTRAINT / Applies dimensional constraints to selected objects or points on objects.		DOV	DIMOVERRIDE / Controls overrides of system variables used in selected dimensions.
DDA	DIMDISASSOCIATE / Removes associativity from selected dimensions.		DR	DRAWORDER / Changes the draw order of images and other objects.
DDI	DIMDIAMETER / Creates a diameter dimension for a circle or an arc.		DRA	DIMRADIUS / Creates a radius dimension for a circle or an arc.
DED	DIMEDIT / Edits dimension text and extension lines.		DRE	DIMREASSOCIATE / Associates or re-associates selected dimensions to objects or points on objects.

E–F

E	ERASE / Removes objects from a drawing.
ED	DDEDIT / Edits single-line text, dimension text, attribute definitions, and feature control frames.
EL	ELLIPSE / Creates an ellipse or an elliptical arc.
EPDF	EXPORTPDF / Exports drawing to PDF.
ER	EXTERNALREFERENCES / Opens the External References palette.
EX	EXTEND / Extends objects to meet the edges of other objects.
EXIT	QUIT / Exits the program.
EXP	EXPORT / Saves the objects in a drawing to a different file format.
EXT	EXTRUDE / Extends the dimensions of a 2D object or 3D face into 3D space.
F	FILLET / Rounds and fillets the edges of objects.
FI	FILTER / Creates a list of requirements that an object must meet to be included in a selection set.
FS	FSMODE / Creates a selection set of all objects that touch the selected object.
FSHOT	FLATSHOT / Creates a 2D representation of all 3D objects based on the current view.

G–H

G	GROUP / Creates and manages saved sets of objects called groups.
GCON	GEOCONSTRAINT / Applies or persists geometric relationships between objects or points on objects.
GD	GRADIENT / Fills an enclosed area or selected objects with a gradient fill.
GEO	GEOGRAPHICLOCATION / Specifies the geographic location information for a drawing file.
H	HATCH / Fills an enclosed area or selected objects with a hatch pattern, solid fill, or gradient fill.
HE	HATCHEDIT / Modifies an existing hatch or fill.
HI	HIDE / Regenerates a 3D wireframe model with hidden lines suppressed.

I–K

I	INSERT / Inserts a block or drawing into the current drawing.
IAD	IMAGEADJUST / Controls the image display of the brightness, contrast, and fade values of images.
IAT	IMAGEATTACH / Inserts a reference to an image file.
ICL	IMAGECLIP / Crops the display of a selected image to a specified boundary.
ID	ID / Displays the UCS coordinate values of a specified location.
IM	IMAGE / Displays the External References palette.
IMP	IMPORT / Imports files of different formats into the current drawing.
IN	INTERSECT / Creates a 3D solid, surface, or 2D region from overlapping solids, surfaces, or regions.
INF	INTERFERE / Creates a temporary 3D solid from the interferences between two sets of selected 3D solids.
IO	INSERTOBJ / Inserts a linked or embedded object.
J	JOIN / Joins similar objects to form a single, unbroken object.
JOG	DIMJOGGED / Creates jogged dimensions for circles and arcs.

L–M

L	LINE / Creates straight line segments.
LA	LAYER / Manages layers and layer properties.
LAS	LAYERSTATE / Saves, restores, and manages named layer states.
LE	QLEADER / Creates a leader and leader annotation.
LEN	LENGTHEN / Changes the length of objects and the included angle of arcs.
LESS	MESHSMOOTHLESS / Decreases the level of smoothness for mesh objects by one level.
LI	LIST / Displays property data for selected objects.
LO	LAYOUT / Creates and modifies drawing layout tabs.
LT	LINETYPE / Loads, sets, and modifies linetypes.
LTS	LTSCALE / Changes the scale factor of linetypes for all objects in a drawing.
MAT	MATERIALS / Shows or hides the Materials window.
ME	MEASURE / Creates point objects or blocks at measured intervals along the length or perimeter of an object.
MEA	MEASUREGEOM / Measures the distance, radius, angle, area, and volume of selected objects or sequence of points.
MI	MIRROR / Creates a mirrored copy of selected objects.
ML	MLINE / Creates multiple parallel lines.
MLA	MLEADERALIGN / Aligns and spaces selected multileader objects.
MLC	MLEADERCOLLECT / Organizes selected multileaders that contain blocks into rows or columns, and displays the result with a single leader.
MLD	MLEADER / Creates a multileader object.
MLE	MLEADEREDIT / Adds leader lines to, or removes leader lines from, a multileader object.
MSM	MARKUP / Opens the Markup Set Manager.
MT	MTEXT / Creates a multiline text object.
MV	MVIEW / Creates and controls layout viewports.

N–O

NORTH	GEOGRAPHICLOCATION / Specifies the geographic location information for a drawing file.
NSHOT	NEWSHOT / Creates a named view with motion that is played back when viewed with ShowMotion.
NVIEW	NEWVIEW / Creates a named view with no motion.
O	OFFSET / Creates concentric circles, parallel lines, and parallel curves.
OP	OPTIONS / Customizes the program settings.

Autodesk AutoCAD 2021
Learn CAD With Ease.

LW	LWEIGHT / Sets the current lineweight, lineweight display options, and lineweight units.	MLS	MLEADERSTYLE / Creates and modifies multileader styles.	ORBIT	3DORBIT / Rotates the view in 3D space, but constrained to horizontal and vertical orbit only.
M	MOVE / Moves objects a specified distance in a specified direction.	MO	PROPERTIES / Controls properties of existing objects.	OS	OSNAP / Sets running object snap modes.
MA	MATCHPROP / Applies the properties of a selected object to other objects.	MORE	MESHSMOOTHMORE / Increases the level of smoothness for mesh objects by one level.		
		MS	MSPACE / Switches from paper space to a model space viewport.		

P

P	PAN / Adds a parameter with grips to a dynamic block definition.
PA	PASTESPEC / Pastes objects from the Clipboard into the current drawing and controls the format of the data.
PAR	PARAMETERS / Controls the associative parameters used in the drawing.
PARAM	BPARAMETER / Adds a parameter with grips to a dynamic block definition.
PATCH	SURFPATCH / Creates a new surface by fitting a cap over a surface edge that forms a closed loop.
PC	POINTCLOUD / Provides options to create and attach point cloud files.
PCATTACH	POINTCLOUDATTACH / Inserts an indexed point cloud file into the current drawing.
PCINDEX	POINTCLOUDINDEX / Creates an indexed point cloud (PCG or PCD) file from a scan file.
PE	PEDIT / Edits polylines and 3D polygon meshes.
PL	PLINE / Creates a 2D polyline.
PO	POINT / Creates a point object.
POFF	HIDEPALETTES / Hides currently displayed palettes (including the command line).

POL	POLYGON / Creates an equilateral closed polyline.
PON	SHOWPALETTES / Restores the display of hidden palettes.
PR	PROPERTIES / Displays Properties palette.
PRE	PREVIEW / Displays the drawing as it will be plotted.
PRINT	PLOT / Plots a drawing to a plotter, printer, or file.
PS	PSPACE / Switches from a model space viewport to paper space.
PSOLID	POLYSOLID / Creates a 3D wall-like polysolid.
PU	PURGE / Removes unused items, such as block definitions and layers, from the drawing.
PYR	PYRAMID / Creates a 3D solid pyramid.

Q

QC	QUICKCALC / Opens the QuickCalc calculator.
QCUI	QUICKCUI / Displays the Customize User Interface Editor in a collapsed state.
QP	QUICKPROPERTIES / Displays open drawings and layouts in a drawing to preview images.
QSAVE	QSAVE / Saves the current drawing.
QVD	QVDRAWING / Displays open drawings and layouts in a drawing using preview images.
QVDC	QVDRAWINGCLOSE / Closes preview images of open drawings and layouts in a drawing.
QVL	QVLAYOUT / Displays preview images of model space and layouts in a drawing.
QVLC	QVLAYOUTCLOSE / Closes preview images of model space and layouts in the current drawing.

R

R	REDRAW / Refreshes the display in the current viewport.
RA	REDRAWALL / Refreshes the display in all viewports.
RC	RENDERCROP / Renders a specified rectangular area, called a crop window, within a viewport.
RE	REGEN / Regenerates the entire drawing from the current viewport.
REA	REGENALL / Regenerates the drawing and refreshes all viewports.
REC	RECTANG / Creates a rectangular polyline.
REG	REGION / Converts an object that encloses an area into a region object.
REN	RENAME / Changes the names assigned to items such as layers and dimension styles.
REV	REVOLVE / Creates a 3D solid or surface by sweeping a 2D object around an axis.
RO	ROTATE / Rotates objects around a base point.

RR	RENDER / Creates a photorealistic or realistically shaded image of a 3D solid or surface model.
RW	RENDERWIN / Displays the Render window without starting a rendering operation.

S

S	STRETCH / Stretches objects crossed by a selection window or polygon.
SC	SCALE / Enlarges or reduces selected objects, keeping the proportions of the object the same after scaling.
SCR	SCRIPT / Executes a sequence of commands from a script file.
SEC	SECTION / Uses the intersection of a plane and solids, surfaces, or mesh to create a region.
SET	SETVAR / Lists or changes the values of system variables.
SHA	SHADEMODE / Starts the VSCURRENT command.

SP	SPELL / Checks spelling in a drawing.
SPE	SPLINEDIT / Edits a spline or spline-fit polyline.
SPL	SPLINE / Creates a smooth curve that passes through or near specified points.
SPLANE	SECTIONPLANE / Creates a section object that acts as a cutting plane through 3D objects.
SPLAY	SEQUENCEPLAY / Plays named views in one category.
SPLIT	MESHSPLIT / Splits a mesh face into two faces.
SPE	SPLINEDIT / Edits a spline or spline-fit polyline.
SSM	SHEETSET / Opens the Sheet Set Manager.
ST	STYLE / Creates, modifies, or specifies text styles.
STA	STANDARDS / Manages the association of standards files with drawings.
SU	SUBTRACT / Combines selected 3D solids, surfaces, or 2D regions by subtraction.

320

By Madhumita Kshirsagar

Autodesk AutoCAD 2021
Learn CAD With Ease.

RP	**RENDERPRESETS** / Specifies render presets, reusable rendering parameters, for rendering an image.	SL	**SLICE** / Creates new 3D solids and surfaces by slicing, or dividing, existing objects.	
RPR	**RPREF** / Displays or hides the Advanced Render Settings palette for access to advanced rendering settings.	SN	**SNAP** / Restricts cursor movement to specified intervals.	
		SO	**SOLID** / Creates solid-filled triangles and quadrilaterals.	

T   U–W   X–Z

T	**MTEXT** / Creates a multiline text object.	UC	**UCSMAN** / Manages defined user coordinate systems.	X	**EXPLODE** / Breaks a compound object into its component objects.
TA	**TEXTALIGN** / Aligns multiple text objects vertically, horizontally, or obliquely.	UN	**UNITS** / Controls coordinate and angle display formats and precision.	XA	**XATTACH** / Inserts a DWG file as an external reference (xref).
TB	**TABLE** / Creates an empty table object.	UNHIDE / UNISOLATE	**UNISOLATEOBJECTS** / Displays objects previously hidden with the ISOLATEOBJECTS or HIDEOBJECTS command.	XB	**XBIND** / Binds one or more definitions of named objects in an xref to the current drawing.
TEDIT	**TEXTEDIT** / Edits a dimensional constraint, dimension, or text object.			XC	**XCLIP** / Crops the display of a selected external reference or block reference to a specified boundary.
TH	**THICKNESS** / Sets the default 3D thickness property when creating 2D geometric objects.	UNI	**UNION** / Unions two solid or two region objects.	XL	**XLINE** / Creates a line of infinite length.
TI	**TILEMODE** / Controls whether paper space can be accessed.	V	**VIEW** / Saves and restores named views, camera views, layout views, and preset views.	XR	**XREF** / Starts the EXTERNALREFERENCES command.
TO	**TOOLBAR** / Displays, hides, and customizes toolbars.	VGO	**VIEWGO** / Restores a named view.	Z	**ZOOM** / Increases or decreases the magnification of the view in the current viewport.
TOL	**TOLERANCE** / Creates geometric tolerances contained in a feature control frame.	VP	**DDVPOINT** / Sets the 3D viewing direction.	ZEBRA	**ANALYSISZEBRA** / Projects stripes onto a 3D model to analyze surface continuity.
TOR	**TORUS** / Creates a donut-shaped 3D solid.	VPLAY	**VIEWPLAY** / Plays the animation associated to a named view.	ZIP	**ETRANSMIT** / Creates a Self-Extracting or Zipped Transmittal Package.
TP	**TOOLPALETTES** / Opens the Tool Palettes window.	VS	**VSCURRENT** / Sets the visual style in the current viewport.		
TR	**TRIM** / Trims objects to meet the edges of other objects.	VSM	**VISUALSTYLES** / Creates and modifies visual styles and applies a visual style to a viewport.		
TS	**TABLESTYLE** / Creates, modifies, or specifies table styles.	W	**WBLOCK** / Writes objects or a block to a new drawing file.		
		WE	**WEDGE** / Creates a 3D solid wedge.		
		WHEEL	**NAVSWHEEL** / Displays a wheel that contains a collection of view navigation tools.		

Autodesk AutoCAD 2021
Learn CAD With Ease.

Shortcut keys on keyboard:

F1 Help	F2 Text Screen	F3 Object Snap	F5 Isoplane	F7 Grid	F8 Ortho	F9 Snap	F10 Polar	F11 Object Snap Tracking	F12 Dynamic Input	N NEW
Q QSAVE	W WBLOCK	E ERASE	R REDRAW	T MTEXT	I INSERT	O OFFSET	P PAN	A ARC	S STRETCH	D DIMSTYLE
F FILLET	G GROUP	H HATCH	J JOIN	L LINE	Z ZOOM	X EXPLODE	C CIRCLE	V VIEW	B BLOCK	M MOVE

F1 Help	F2 Text Screen	F3 Object Snap	F5 Isoplane	F7 Grid	F8 Ortho	F9 Snap	F10 Polar	F11 Object Snap Tracking	F12 Dynamic Input	N NEW
Q QSAVE	W WBLOCK	E ERASE	R REDRAW	T MTEXT	I INSERT	O OFFSET	P PAN	A ARC	S STRETCH	D DIMSTYLE
F FILLET	G GROUP	H HATCH	J JOIN	L LINE	Z ZOOM	X EXPLODE	C CIRCLE	V VIEW	B BLOCK	M MOVE

F1 Help	F2 Text Screen	F3 Object Snap	F5 Isoplane	F7 Grid	F8 Ortho	F9 Snap	F10 Polar	F11 Object Snap Tracking	F12 Dynamic Input	N NEW
Q QSAVE	W WBLOCK	E ERASE	R REDRAW	T MTEXT	I INSERT	O OFFSET	P PAN	A ARC	S STRETCH	D DIMSTYLE
F FILLET	G GROUP	H HATCH	J JOIN	L LINE	Z ZOOM	X EXPLODE	C CIRCLE	V VIEW	B BLOCK	M MOVE

F1 Help	F2 Text Screen	F3 Object Snap	F5 Isoplane	F7 Grid	F8 Ortho	F9 Snap	F10 Polar	F11 Object Snap Tracking	F12 Dynamic Input	N NEW

By Madhumita Kshirsagar

Autodesk AutoCAD 2021
Learn CAD With Ease.

Made in the USA
Coppell, TX
08 December 2021